FEMALE SEXUALITY

FEMALE SEXUALITY

The Early Psychoanalytic Controversies

Edited by

Russell Grigg, Dominique Hecq,
and Craig Smith

Routledge
Taylor & Francis Group

LONDON AND NEW YORK

First published 1999 by Rebus Press

This edition published in 2015 by
Karnac Books Ltd

Published 2018 by Routledge
2 Park Square, Milton Park, Abingdon, Oxon OX14 4RN
711 Third Avenue, New York, NY 10017, USA

Routledge is an imprint of the Taylor & Francis Group, an informa business

British Library Cataloguing in Publication Data
A C.I.P. for this book is available from the British Library

ISBN: 9781782200222 (pbk)

Contents

Preface

The papers included in this collection were originally published in *The International Journal of Psycho-Analysis*, with two exceptions. Karl Abraham's 'Origins and Growth of Object-Love', central to the debate, appeared in his *Selected Writings* and Helene Deutsch's 'On Female Homosexuality' appeared in the first volume of the new American journal, *The Psychoanalytic Quarterly*. They cover a period from June 1917, when Johan van Ophuijsen presented his paper on the masculinity complex in women to the Dutch Psycho-Analytical Society, to April 1935, when Ernest Jones read a paper on early female sexuality to the Vienna Psycho-Analytical Society.

Though these papers are often referred to in discussions of female sexuality, and though some individual papers have been reproduced elsewhere, they have never before appeared together as a collection. Anyone who has read these papers will be aware of their importance to the topic of female sexuality. But it is not the theme alone that unifies the collection; there are two further considerations of equal importance: the dialogue and debate that take place between the papers, from first to last; and the considerable impact they had on the development of certain of Freud's key theses. The papers have a clear historical interest, then, but rereading them today will also show their continuing relevance to debates within and outside psychoanalysis on female sexuality.

We have corrected some minor typographical, grammatical and spelling errors in the original articles. Where subsequent and more readily accessible versions of important works are available, we have updated the references. This includes all references to Freud's work, which have been altered to volume and page number of *The Standard Edition of the Complete Psychological Works of Sigmund Freud*, 24 vols. (London: Hogarth Press and the Institute of Psycho-Analysis, 1953-1974).

The articles have been placed in chronological order according to date of publication. The one exception to this is Van Ophuijsen's paper, which opens the collection. This is because it was presented and subsequently debated in the literature, quite some time before appearing in print.

Acknowledgments

We should like to thank the International Journal of Psycho-analysis for permission to publish the following:

Karl Abraham. "Manifestations of the female castration complex." 3 (1920) pp.1-29.
Marie Bonaparte. "Passivity masochism and femininity." 16 (1935) pp.325-33.
Helene Deutsch. "The psychology of women in relation to the function of reproduction." 6 (1925) pp. 405-418.
Helene Deutsch. "The significance of masochism in the mental life of women." 11 (1930) pp.48-60.
Otto Fenichel. "The pregenital antecedents of the oedipus complex." 12 (1931) pp. 141-66.
Karen Horney. "The flight from womanhood: the masculinity-complex in women, as viewed my men and by women." 7 (1926) pp.324-39.
Karen Horney. "The denial of the vagina: a contribution to the problem of the genital anxieties specific to women." 14 (1933) pp. 57-70.
Karen Horney. "The dread of women: observations on a specific difference in the dread felt by men and by women respectively for the opposite sex." 13 (1932) pp. 348-60.
Ernest Jones. "The early development of female sexuality." 8 (1927) pp.459-472.
Ernest Jones. " Early female sexuality." 16 (1935) pp. 263-73.
Melanie Klein. "Early stages of the Oedipus conflict." 9 (1928) pp. 167-80.
Jeanne Lampl de Groot. "The evolution of the Oedipus complex in women." Int. J. Psycho-Anal. 9 (1928) pp. 332-45.
Muller, Josine. "A contribution to the problem of libidinal development of the genital phase in girls." 13 (1932) pp. 361-68
Muller Braunschweig, Carl. "The genesis of the feminine super-ego." 7 (1926). pp. 359-62.
J.H.W. Ophuijsen. "Contributions to the masculinity complex in women." 5 (1924) pp. 39-49.
Joan Riviere. "Womanliness as masquerade." 9 (1929) pp. 303-13.
Stärke, August. "The castration complex." 2 (1921) pp.179-201

Our thanks are due to the Psychoanalytic Quarterly, for permission to publish

Helene Deutsch, "On Female Homosexuality." Vol. 1 (1932) pp. 484-510.

We should also like to thank the Australian Research Council and Deakin University for their financial support of this project.

Abbreviations

SE   *Standard Edition of the Complete Psychological Works of Sigmund Freud.* 24 Vols. Translated and edited by James Strachey in collaboration with Anna Freud, assisted by Alix Strachey and Alan Tyson. London: The Hogarth Press and the Institute of Psycho-Analysis; New York: Norton, 1953-1974.

Notes on the Editors

Russell Grigg is lectures in philosophy and co-ordinator of psychoanalytic studies at Deakin University. He is a psychoanalyst in private practice. Dr. Grigg has a PhD in psychoanalysis and has published extensively on psychoanalysis. He is also known for his translations of the seminars of Jacques Lacan.

Dominique Hecq-Murphy is a research fellow in psychoanalytic studies at Deakin University. Dr. Hecq-Murphy has a PhD in literature and a background in French and German, with qualifications in translating. She has published in the field of literary studies and has had her own stories and poetry published.

Craig Smith is a PhD candidate in psychoanalytic studies at Deakin University. He has degrees in political science from the University of Melbourne and Victoria University of Wellington.

Biographical Notes

Karl Abraham (1877 - 1925)

As a member of Freud's inner circle, the 'Committee', Karl Abraham played a prominent role in the development of psychoanalysis. Trained as a psychiatrist, Abraham first met Freud in 1907 and soon became a close personal friend. Abraham established the first psychoanalytic practice in Berlin and, in 1910, founded the Berlin Psychoanalytic Society. He quickly established a successful practice and was highly sought after as a training analyst. Among the analysts he trained were Melanie Klein, Helene Deutsch, Edward Glover, James Glover and Sándor Rado. His untimely death in 1925 prompted Freud to state that 'Abraham's death is perhaps the greatest loss that could strike us, and it has struck us'. During his relatively short lifetime Abraham produced a number of important writings on psychoanalytic theory and practice. These have been published in *The Selected Papers of Karl Abraham*.

Marie Bonaparte (1882 - 1962)

Marie Bonaparte went to Vienna for an analysis with Freud in 1925. She subsequently came to play a central role in institutionalising and expanding psychoanalysis in France, using her considerable wealth to support both the Psychoanalytic Society of Paris and the International Psychoanalytical Association. In 1938 after Nazi Germany's annexation of Austria, Bonaparte played a leading role in securing Freud's passage out of Austria to Britain. She wrote widely on psychoanalysis and female sexuality, especially in relation to female anatomy. Her *Female Sexuality* (1951) provides her most complete treatment of this theme.

Ruth Mack Brunswick (1897 - 1946)

An American, Ruth Mack Brunswick went to Vienna in 1922 for an analysis with Freud. At that time she was married to a cardiologist named Hermann Blumgart from whom she separated while in Vienna. Though she is mainly known as one of Freud's patients and pupils, she began practicing as a psychoanalyst in 1925. In 1926 Freud referred to her his patient Sergei Pankejeff, better known as the 'Wolf Man'. In the words of Freud to his son Ernst, 'Ruth almost belongs to the family,' and in March 1927 Freud acted as witness when she married the composer Mark Brunswick. On Monday 14 September 1936, she filmed the Freuds' golden wedding celebrations.

Helene Deutsch (1884 - 1982)

Helene Deutsch spent her childhood in what is now Poland. In 1907 Deutsch enrolled at the University of Vienna to train as a doctor and went on to specialize in psychiatry. By 1918 she had joined the Vienna Psychoanalytic Society and shortly afterwards began an analysis with Freud. She rapidly came to prominence in the Society and in 1924 was appointed head of the Society's newly established Training Institute. In 1935 Deutsch migrated to the United States to take up a position in Boston, where she remained, teaching, writing and analysing until her death in 1982. Her later views on female sexuality are to be found in her two volume work, *The Psychology of Women*.

Otto Fenichel (1898 - 1946)

Otto Fenichel was one of the younger members of the Berlin group. Analyzed by the Hungarian analyst Sandor Rado, Fenichel went on to establish himself as a highly regarded teacher and practitioner of psychoanalysis. His pedagogic reputation led to a number of positions in the 1930s, culminating in a training position in Los Angeles in 1938. Shortly before his premature death at the age of 48, Fenichel published what has been described as a 'classic textbook' of psychoanalysis, *The Psychoanalytic Theory of Neurosis*.

Karen Horney (1885 - 1952)

Karen Horney trained as a doctor at the University of Berlin and went on to train in psychiatry and psychoanalysis. She was in analysis with Karl Abraham and then Hans Sachs. In response to the rise of Nazism in 1932 Horney migrated to the United States, first to Chicago under the sponsorship of Franz Alexander, then to New York. In 1941 the New York Psychoanalytic Institute withdrew her name as a training analyst and instructor. Horney resigned and was active in founding an alternative group, the American Association for the Advancement of Psychoanalysis. In the United States her work came increasingly to emphasise cultural factors in the determination of psychopathology. This is particularly evident in two of her late, popular works, *The Neurotic Personality of Our Time* and *Neurosis and Human Growth*.

Ernest Jones (1879 - 1958)

Freud's biographer, Ernest Jones was a relentless campaigner for psychoanalysis. He was a major figure in the founding and subsequent running of the British Psycho-Analytical Society and the American Psychoanalytic Association and would later become president of the International Psychoanalytical Association for an unequalled term of seventeen years. Jones was a prolific writer and noted polemicist in psychoanalytic matters. He originally trained as a doctor and specialized in psychiatry before coming into Freud's circle around the same time as Karl Abraham. It was at his suggestion that Freud established the secret inner group known as the 'Committee', made up of the 'best and most trustworthy' of Freud's followers; and it was Jones that Freud described as 'a fanatic who smiles at my faint-heartedness'. On the other hand, Jones's writings on female sexuality represent a major break with Freud's position, rejecting what he was the first to term Freud's 'phallocentrism'. Jones's papers have been published in his *Papers on Psycho-Analysis* and *Essays in Applied Psycho-Analysis*.

Melanie Klein (1882 - 1960)

Klein has been one of the most influential, albeit controversial, figures in the history of psychoanalysis. The paper included here is from her early period, presented shortly after she had settled in London. Klein was born in Vienna, but moved to Hungary in 1909 and entered analysis with Sándor Ferenczi. After the counter-revolution in Budapest in 1919 she moved again, this time to Berlin, where she undertook a further analysis with Karl Abraham. Around this time Klein began developing the play technique in order to facilitate analysis with very young children. Klein also introduced new concepts and a new emphasis in orientation for psychoanalysts, especially in regard to the emergence of psychical processes in infancy. Her numerous publications have appeared in a four-volume edition, *The Writings of Melanie Klein*.

Jeanne Lampl de Groot (1894 -1987)

Jeanne de Groot was a Dutch doctor who went to Vienna in 1921 to have an analysis with Freud. In 1925 she married Hans Lampl and moved to Berlin where she began working at the Berlin Psychoanalytic Clinic. It was on Freud's advice that at the end of August 1933 Jeanne Lampl de Groot and family (now including two daughters) moved back to Vienna. Following the annexation of Austria in 1938, they moved again, this time to Jeanne Lampl de Groot's native Holland, where they continued their psychoanalytic work.

Josine Müller (1884 - 1930)

Josine Müller, née Ebsen, studied medicine in Freiburg and Munich. In 1911 she settled in Berlin where she undertook studies in biochemistry and completed her own research in physiological chemistry. From 1912 to 1915 she was an intern at the Women and Children's Hospital, specializing in infectious diseases. She then moved to the Dr Fränkel-Olivens Sanatorium to complete her training in the area of neurological psychiatry. Her interest in psychoanalysis developed when she moved to Berlin, where she set up her own medical practice in 1916. Her work as a doctor is said to have become increasingly influenced by her interest in psychoanalysis, and more particularly in the area of early female sexuality and psychosexual development. She is probably best known for her articles on this topic. Josine Müller underwent an analysis with Abraham in 1912-1913 and with Hans Sachs between 1923 and 1926.

Carl Müller-Braunschweig (1881 - 1958)

Carl Müller-Braunschweig first studied philosophy and, after completing a doctoral dissertation, published several papers on Kantian ethics. He gave up a career as a philosophy lecturer to pursue his work in psychoanalysis, although his interest in Kant never abated. For example in 1953-1954 he lectured on 'Freud and Kant: Psychoanalysis and a Philosophy of Morals'. Müller-Braunschweig underwent analyses with both Karl Abraham and Hans Sachs and from the 1920s onward became a key figure in the Berlin Psychoanalytic Society. Controversy surrounds the role Müller-Braunschweig played in accommodating the Nazi authorities' demand for the 'aryanization' of psychoanalytic societies during the 1930s. After the war Müller-Braunschweig helped re-establish the Berlin

Psychoanalytic Society which was readmitted to the International Psychoanalytical Association in 1951.

Johan H. W. van Ophuijsen (1882 - 1950)

Another member of the Dutch group, van Ophuijsen was born in Sumatra (formerly the Dutch East Indies) and continued his schooling in the Netherlands from the age of thirteen. He went on to study medicine, neurology and psychiatry, with a particular interest in psychoses. In 1917 he co-founded the Dutch Psychoanalytic Society along with August Stärcke and others, as well as organising the international congress of psychoanalysts there in 1920, the first to be held after the First World War. In 1935 he emigrated to the United States where he worked on the psychiatric staff of a number of psychiatric institutions. Van Ophuijsen never lost his interest in neuro-biology and psychoanalysis, and when he died in 1950 he left behind plans for a research program to study the somatic causes of the drives and their pathology.

Joan Riviere (1883 - 1962)

Joan Riviere was analyed first by Ernest Jones in 1915, and then by Freud in 1922. In 1919, at Jones' invitation, she became one of the founding members of the British Psychoanalytical Society. Born Joan Verrall, Riviere came from a family with scholarly connections to Cambridge—a fact which led James Strachey to remark that they had both come out of the same middle-class, cultured, late Victorian box. After a brief career as a professional dressmaker, Riviere immersed herself in the study and practice of psychoanalysis. Aside from her papers, perhaps her greatest contribution lies in her outstanding translations of Freud's works (in conjunction with James and Alix Strachey), as well as translations from the *Zeitschrift* and *Imago* journals which were published under her editorial guidance in the *International Journal of Psycho-Analysis*. Her collected papers have been published as *The Inner World and Joan Riviere*.

August Stärcke (1880 - 1954)

August Stärcke was one of the founding members of the Dutch Psychoanalytic Society. He completed his early training as a doctor specializing in psychiatry and unlike the other contributors listed here,

Stärcke always saw himself primarily as a psychiatrist rather than as a psychoanalyst. Stärcke produced numerous papers on issues ranging from psychoanalysis to neurology and psychiatry, with his last paper, an intriguingly titled 'There Will Never Be Peace in Nomenclature', intended for publication in an entomological journal.

Introduction

> Throughout history people have
> knocked their heads against the
> riddle of the nature of femininity[1]

Throughout his work Freud repeatedly declared his ignorance of female sexuality. At first inclined to regard this ignorance as being due to social factors, he increasingly came to view it as arising from the psychology of women and the nature of femininity itself. Early on, in 1905, he ascribed the 'impenetrable obscurity' surrounding female sexuality partly to the 'stunting effect of civilised conditions' and partly to the 'conventional secretiveness and insincerity' of women.[2] Some three years later in 1908 he made a similar, though less specific, comment, where this obscurity is said to be due to 'unfavourable circumstances both of an external and internal nature'.[3]

However, much later, when the explanation given for why the sexual life of women is '"a dark continent" for psychology' is that the 'nature of femininity' is itself a riddle, Freud adopts a new caution regarding the applicability of the Oedipal model to the little girl.[4] In point of fact, what Freud says appears contradictory: even as he refers to the primacy of the phallus for both sexes, he warns that 'we can describe this state of things only as it affects the male child; the corresponding processes in the little girl are not known to us'.[5] This last remark is a very surprising one indeed, since, as James Strachey notes, Freud had over many years spoken of a complete parallel in the psychosexual development of the sexes—and now it appears that the basis for this view was that he had simply extrapolated from the case of the little boy to that of the girl, changing the positions accordingly. The remark is even more surprising on another count. Almost none of Freud's initial discoveries can be dissociated from his early work with women patients—recall the women of *Studies on Hysteria*, the case history of Dora. Indeed, doesn't Freud owe his discovery of the unconscious and the technique of psychoanalysis to his encounter with hysteria, to which the question of female sexuality and desire, even female identity, is the key? Moreover, James Strachey's claim that Freud did not direct his attention to feminine psychology for fifteen years after Dora is somewhat misleading.[6] While it is true that all Freud's case studies of this period are of males, such a claim has to consider as inconsequential the numerous texts in which Freud deals with women or issues relevant to female sexuality. It means neglecting the women patients discussed in the 1907 article on compulsive actions and in the *Introductory Lectures on Psycho-Analysis* of 1916-1917, just as it means ignoring the discussion of issues relevant to female sexuality in his article on hysterical fantasies (1908) and hysterical attacks (1909), as well as the 1917 piece on the transformation of drives and the article on the taboo of virginity of the following year. In all these places, and others as well, Freud is repeatedly touching on related issues, and, moreover, beginning to articulate claims that will subsequently make their way into his later writings and that are at the heart of the controversy on female sexuality.

For it is obvious that in the 1920s Freud's thinking on this issue takes a new turn. Something changes fundamentally, as is indicated both by his abandonment of the earlier symmetry of the Oedipus complex and by his accompanying insistence upon the centrality of the phallic phase for both sexes—a fundamental reorientation that marks everything that Freud henceforth writes on the subject of female sexuality. One of many consequences of this is a development that occurs in 1931 when, gradually, Freud comes to the realisation of something that he had been unable to see before: that behind the woman's entire sexual development lies the little girl's attachment to the 'pre-oedipal' mother. He henceforth appropriately praises the work of women analysts and explains his ignorance as a problem of counter-transference. That is to say, while it is true that Freud never relinquishes his belief in the importance of penis envy for female sexuality; in *Analysis Terminable and Interminable* he describes the 'suspicion that one has been "preaching to the winds"' . . . when one is trying to persuade a woman to abandon her wish for a penis',[7] in his late work he nevertheless also stresses the significance for female sexuality of an intense and enduring attachment to the pre-oedipal mother—an attachment that marks all subsequent love objects, including, most importantly, the attachment to the Oedipal father.

Yet despite all the positive statements and claims, nothing characterises Freud's position with respect to female sexuality better than his question: *Was will das Weib?*, What does a woman want? For classical psychoanalysis female sexuality has remained the great riddle. And Freud seeks comfort in the observation that it has always been the same 'throughout history'.

There is however another way of viewing what Freud is doing, indicated by the remark that 'psychoanalysis does not try to describe what a woman is, but sets about inquiring how she comes into being'.[8] For, however many issues there are that arise in the course of the discussions of female sexuality, what remains fundamentally at stake in the debate, when all is said and done, is the issue of castration. It is the key to the little girl's negotiating the Oedipus complex and thus to many further aspects of the nature and development of femininity and, in turn, it has important repercussions for clinical issues. Two crucial texts on the question of femininity, both revolving around the castration complex in girls, appear in the early thirties, 'Female Sexuality' and the lecture on 'Femininity' in *New Introductory Lectures*, whose material is briefly re-visited five years later in 'Analysis Terminable and Interminable' and also in Chapter 7 of the posthumous *Outline of Psychoanalysis*.

While some of the papers included in this collection predate Freud's papers, 'The Infantile Genital Organisation' (1923) and 'The Dissolution of the Oedipus Complex' (1924), the controversy was really triggered by these two important contributions. As a consequence of their publication the debate takes on a life of its own in the late 1920s.

It is a dispute that soon takes on the proportions of a controversy involving psychoanalytic circles from Vienna to London, via Berlin, The Hague and Paris. The controversy is usually referred to as the 'Freud-Jones debate'. However, at least one recent re-examination of the terms of the disagreement rejects this.[9] And indeed, when one reads the articles collected here it becomes obvious that the real dispute, though it remains unacknowledged throughout, is between Freud and Abraham, with one of Abraham's clinical papers being central to the controversy.[10] Object-love: here is the concept that would enable a re-thinking of female psychosexual development and eventually a theorizing of the articulation between the Oedipus complex and the castration complex in the little girl. It gradually becomes clear over the course of the debate that there are really two camps: those who, like Helene Deutsch, Jeanne Lampl De Groot, Ruth Mack Brunswick and Marie Bonaparte, support Freud, and those who oppose him. Amongst the latter are Ernest Jones and two of Abraham's students: Karen Horney and Melanie Klein.

What also becomes clear when reading these essays is that some allegedly marginal figures in the controversy actually play a major role, and not only in relation to the controversy itself, but also in relation to the course and development of Freud's subsequent research into female sexuality—the contribution by Karl Abraham (who died too early: one year after the publication of his important paper) is a case in point. It should also be mentioned that some lesser figures in the history of psychoanalysis such as Johan van Ophuijsen and Jeanne Lampl de Groot here make crucial contributions.

In a letter of September 1930 to Viereck, Freud writes that he is working on a version of femininity that will be 'as distant from the poetical as from the pseudo-science of Hirschfeld'.[11] Ironically, it is with a poetic riddle that Freud introduces his 1932 lecture 'Femininity', which is a recapitulation of more than a decade of work on the topic. A poetic riddle, because Freud quotes from a poem which looks incongruous in the context of his lecture, but also because, like an extended metaphor, it conjures up a series of further questions. It is a riddle about a riddle which covers woman—and not only by virtue of the potential pun about maidenheads in English:

> Heads in hieroglyphic bonnets,
> Heads in turbans and black birettas,
> Heads in wigs and thousand other
> Wretched, sweating heads of humans.

The quotation is from Heinrich Heine's poem *Nordsee*, from a section entitled *'Fragen'* where a youth asks the sea: 'Tell me, what signifies man? From whence doth he come? And where doth he go?'[12] The sea, like woman and the unconscious—all three have often been related in the poetic imagination—holds back the answer. A murmur, though, can be heard— another riddle, as it were. For the informed reader, then, Freud's lecture on the problem of the nature of femininity opens with some kind of ironic reversal: 'And a fool is awaiting the answer' is the last line in Heine's poem.

The problem is compounded in part by the female Oedipus complex, and Freud is led to reconsider not the outcome, but the outset, of the Oedipus complex in the little girl, thus shifting the emphasis onto the 'pre-Oedipus period' and all the reconsiderations that this entails:

> For a long time the girl's Oedipus complex concealed her pre-Oedipus attachment to her mother from our view, though it is nevertheless so important and leaves such lasting fixations behind it. For girls the Oedipus situation is the outcome of a long and difficult development; it is a kind of preliminary solution, a position of rest which is not soon abandoned, especially as the beginning of the latency period is not far distant. And we are now struck by a difference between the two sexes, *which is probably momentous*, in regard to the relation of the Oedipus to the castration complex.[13]

Freud first mentions the Oedipus complex, though not under this name, in a private letter to his friend Wilhelm Fliess with a reference to both *Oedipus Rex* and *Hamlet*, a dual reference that re-emerges in *The Interpretation of Dreams*. And although the Oedipus complex also underlies the drift of *The Three Essays on the Theory of Sexuality* and 'The Sexual Theories of Children', where the theory of penis envy is first hinted at,[14] it is only first named in a piece of 1910 entitled 'A Special Type of Choice of Object Made by Men'.[15] By then, it has become the cornerstone of psycho-analysis and will remain so. It will also determine the development of his thought on the whole issue of sexual difference. Of course, the 1920s debate, which centres on the issue of castration, will greatly contribute to this, for what should be stressed here is that the full significance of the Oedipus complex only appears with the castration complex and the role this plays in the distinction between the sexes. Thus the original formulation of the Oedipus Complex as the desire for the parent of the opposite sex, coupled with the hatred for the parent of the same sex, is insufficient by itself to account for the difference between the sexes; moreover, as the case of Dora demonstrates only too well, this original formulation is also an impediment to the advance of Freud's clinical work.

As Freud subsequently indicated, the accent in the *Three Essays* had originally been 'on a portrayal of the fundamental difference between the sexual life of children and of adults', while his later work emphasized 'the *pregenital organizations* of the libido'.[16] This shift in emphasis is crucial because it throws into relief the castration complex. The problem from here onwards is to articulate the link between this castration complex and the Oedipus complex—an articulation which Freud only achieves in the mid-nineteen twenties. This in turn highlights the difference between the sexes, or rather, the fact that the difference between the sexes is inseparable from the question of castration.

In 'Some Psychical Consequences of the Anatomical Distinction Between the Sexes' Freud compares male and female infantile sexuality and suggests that penis envy develops into a desire for a child as a substitute penis for little girls, '*and with that purpose in view* she takes her father as a love-object. Her mother becomes the object of her jealousy. The girl has turned into a little woman.'[17] This is when the castration complex really becomes central to the theory of sexuality, and also when identification becomes central to the whole notion of sexual difference, for identification is increasingly suggested as the process by which the crisis is resolved.[18] Boys experience a castration complex which shatters the Oedipus complex, and their sublimated desires subsequently form the core of the super-ego. Girls are spared this stage, it would seem, from which Freud infers that their super-ego is weaker. More relevant to an understanding of the nature of femininity, however, is what Freud makes clear in 'The Dissolution of the Oedipus Complex,' namely, that the little girl can respond in three ways to castration, and thus that the Oedipus complex has three possible outcomes for women: the masculinity complex, hysteria, or a normality—which, by the way, still needs defining in 1932.[19]

> In little girls the Oedipus complex raises one problem more than in boys. In both cases the mother is the original object; and there

is no cause for surprise that boys retain that object in the Oedipus complex. But how does it happen that girls abandon it and instead take their father as an object?[20]

Both the 1931 paper on 'Female Sexuality', and the 1932 lecture on 'Femininity' are further explorations of this topic, but rather than focusing on the *outcome* of the Oedipus complex as did Freud's writings from 1923 to 1925 (witness the preceding quotation, which was written in 1925), they focus on the *entry* into the Oedipus complex and thus emphasize the pre-oedipal relationship of the little girl to her mother: 'With the small girl it is different. Her first object, too, was her mother. How does she find her way to her father? How, when and why did she detach herself from her mother?'[21] This question leads to others: 'What does the little girl require of her mother? What is the nature of her sexual aims during the time of exclusive attachment to her mother?'[22] Although the question remains to establish how it is that the little girl changes love objects, Freud now traces the different stages involved in this change, focusing on the reasons for the first attachment to the mother rather than working out why she should secure a secondary attachment to the father. He now suggests that the little girl progresses directly from an attachment to her mother to one onto the father: consequently her Oedipus complex is a later development and one that is often not surmounted. This means that the consequences for the Oedipus complex, the phallic phase, castration and the way they are linked are different for each of the sexes—Freud's comments about the super-ego, mentioned above, being very much to the point. But as he implies in 1932, this further shift in emphasis is one of the main consequences of the 1920s controversy within the larger field of psychoanalysis.

Thus, for Freud, the castration complex is the secret of the distinction between the sexes. Although he postulates an innate bisexuality, he does not assume an innate masculinity or femininity. Moreover, there is only one libido: the male one. The papers we have included in this collection are testimony to the objections that are bound to arise with a theory of castration which eschews anatomical dispositions, innate propensities, as well as issues of identification and of a possible psychology of sexual difference, not to mention the significance of hereditary and environmental factors. These objections revolve around three axes: the nature of female sexuality; the presupposition that femininity is defined by a libido which is male and primarily phallic; and the mother-child relationship.

Notwithstanding the disagreements, all participants in the controversy concur on one point: penis envy. This means that the theory of femininity, and indeed the whole development of female sexuality, has to take into account, that is either explain or explain away, the fact of the little girl's disappointment at not having a penis, or at having lost it—this being the primary evidence for the postulation of an early phallic phase. Questions of a general nature arise. For instance, is sexuality predicated upon anatomical destiny? Or is it rather determined by culture? Is the little girl a castrated little boy? Is the feminine drive masochistic, as opposed to the male drive which is sadistic, or should it be seen as passive, as opposed to active? Are these categories relevant at all? Does the development of the Oedipus complex in the little girl mirror that of the little boy? Is it ever dissolved? All these questions are addressed in the debate. But the debate raises further, more fundamental issues as well. Is it so clear what castration means here? Does it mean losing the object itself or losing what the object symbolizes? That is, is the fundamental fear the fear of castration or the fear of losing the object's love? The question now in need of an answer is—what specifies the privileged character of the phallus? Freud keeps quiet while his students argue with each other. There is something missing in his theory. It is, however, already quite clear to some that an understanding of castration should not be narrowed down to the loss of the penis: castration is, as August Stärcke suggests in a response to van Ophuijsen's paper on the masculinity complex as early as 1920, a symbolic concept.[23] But if this is so, it seems that Freud's theory of the castration complex no longer explains the question of sexual difference: if castration is but one in a series of separations common to both sexes, and if Jones is right in reducing it to *aphanisis*, it cannot be the arbiter of sexual difference. A new direction needs to be taken, a new focus found, a new question asked.

What really focuses the controversy is the most perplexing question of all: how does the little girl manage to relinquish her love for her mother and turn to her father? This question of the substitution of objects is precisely one of the key questions Abraham tackles in the article mentioned above.[24] The most relevant passage is in fact the table surveying the various stages of sexual organization and object-love traversed in the course of sexual development:

Stages of Libidinal Organization.	Stages of Object-love.	
VI. Final Genital Stage	Object-love	(Post-ambivalent)
V. Earlier Genital Stage (phallic)	Object-love with exclusion of genitals	
IV. Later Anal-sadistic Stage	Partial love	(Ambivalent)
III. Earlier Anal-sadistic Stage	Partial love with incorporation	
II. Later Oral Stage (cannibalistic)	Narcissism (total incorporation of object)	
I. Earlier Oral Stage (sucking)	Auto-erotism (wthout object)	(Pre-ambivalent)

Note that all the participants in the controversy discuss this passage—all, that is, with the single exception of Freud. In this clinical paper where Abraham investigates the castration complex in two women ('X' and 'Y') with symptoms of melancholia he not only traces the genesis of penis envy to a fixation at the oral stage, but also suggests, by drawing parallels with symptoms observed in men, and by teasing out some general conclusions, that both sexes fear castration—hence making a literal understanding of penis envy somewhat redundant. In fact, Abraham's understanding of penis envy links up perfectly with Stärcke's premise that weaning is the primary loss. So Freud remains silent while others (Fenichel, Horney, Klein, Jones, and even Deutsch) adopt some of Abraham's terms or ideas (the identification with the father as cannibalistic incorporation of the phallus; object love; oral sadism as the cause of penis envy) and grapple with them, reject, or develop them—perhaps most striking in this respect is Fenichel in 'The Pregenital Antecedents of the Oedipus Complex'.[25] Worth considering here too are Abraham's discussions of partial love as preliminary to object-love on the one hand and of identification on the other, which seem to anticipate Freud's differentiation between primary and secondary identifications.

It is now obvious why the emphasis of the debate shifts to the much neglected issue of the little girl's relationship with her mother, and hence to the nature of female sexuality, and away from the construction of sexual difference. Obvious too is the reason why arguments become more intense with Freud's insistence on the phallic phase in his work on 'The Dissolution of the Oedipus Complex'. But it is as though the controversy is now taking place on two levels. It is as though Freud is now alone. For both Freud's opponents and his defenders look for answers in biology or anatomy even though they take object-relations as the focus of their discussions.

In point of fact Freud reacted by accusing his opponents of looking for answers outside the psychoanalytic field of inquiry, disapproving of what might be called this return of biology.

> I object to all of you [Müller-Braunschweig, Horney, Jones, Rado, etc.] to the extent that you do not distinguish more clearly and cleanly between what is psychic and what is biological, that you try to establish a neat parallelism between the two and that you, motivated by such intent, unthinkingly construe psychic facts which are unprovable and that you, in the process of so doing, must declare as reactive or regressive much that without doing so is primary. . . . In addition, I would only like to emphasize that we must keep psychoanalysis separate from biology just as we have kept it separate from anatomy and physiology.[26]

And yet, here there is also a turning point in Freud's work: emphasis is placed increasingly upon the mother-child dyad. It is, moreover, at this point that Freud reformulates the question of the substitution of objects in oedipal terms: 'how' rather than 'why' the little girl changes love objects.[27]

By 1925, it is with great reluctance that the little girl enters the Oedipus Complex; it is because of her penis envy that she turns to her father who now outshines the mother; the lack of symmetry between the sexes is now established. In the contributions that follow the issue takes a subtle but momentous turn. It moves away from the issue of the distinction between the sexes to a discussion of what defines masculinity and femininity, each considered in isolation from the other; a diacritical approach gives way to an essentialism rooted in biology. It would seem that penis envy, far from characterizing femininity, is now nothing other than the castration complex as the over-determined symptom in girls.

Some argue that the controversy reaches its peak in 1935, when Jones, invited to Vienna to shed some light on the growing disagreements between British and Viennese analysts, offers a talk on female sexuality.[28] But perhaps it is more accurate to see the controversy sealed, if not encapsulated, in Freud's 1931 and 1932 essays on the topic. In any case, a split between London and Vienna is more than obvious in 1935. And by then, the political climate in Europe cannot be said to be conducive to either research or reconciliation. Jones's visit to Vienna in 1935 to read a paper, as he says, on the disagreements between London and Vienna was intended as the first in a series of exchanges between the two most important centres of psychoanalysis. Owing to the deteriorating situation in Europe it was the only one, and so it became the last major contribution to the debate to be made during Freud's lifetime.

In addition to the allure of the freshness and topicality of the single most important debate to take place inside psychoanalysis during Freud's lifetime, indeed up to the time when Jacques Lacan revives it, there are the passionate responses contributed by analysts from all parts of Europe at the time. The papers collected here are significant for two reasons: not only do they throw light on the early controversy surrounding female sexuality, they also compel the reader to re-read Freud's work in a different light, the light that brings back into full view the ideas or concepts belonging to those whose names are missing from Freud's 'Female Sexuality' and 'Femininity'. It is indeed puzzling to see the partial way in which Freud acknowledges his debt: in both papers he mentions certain names, ignores others altogether, gets papers by the same person confused, alludes to other contributors without mentioning them by name, making sure, perhaps, that he appears as the true and only father of this new science called psychoanalysis. In 1931 he acknowledges the work of those whom, except for Deutsch, of course, we might now see as his opponents: Abraham, Lampl de Groot, Fenichel, Klein, Horney and Jones. But he omits to mention those who made the most valuable contributions in conceptual terms (except for Abraham, but he is no longer alive): van Ophuijsen, Stärcke, Mack Brunswick and Riviere. In 1932, only three contributors are named; all are women, which is perhaps explicable by the fact that the lecture partly aims at dissipating suggestions of misogyny. But how should we understand the omissions and confusions? Is Freud, in the name of psychoanalysis, taking as his own the product of research prompted by his own findings? It is only in the light of the papers presented here in this collection that it is possible to uncover the answer to such questions.

Given that it all happened more than three-quarters of a century ago, our position is necessarily at a distance from the cross-firing of arguments within the early controversy about femininity. But it is important to maintain this distance, for our concern is to suggest why the argument around the issue of castration was needed, and hence to show how legitimate the controversy was. Ultimately, our concern is to foreground the terms of the controversy in order to present Freud's conceptual framework from within the perspective of the exchanges that made it possible, as well as to suggest new points of view, if not new starting points, in the current re-examination of female sexuality. This is why we have adopted a chronological ordering of what we consider as the significant material produced by the main contributors to the controversy—all except for Freud, but it goes without saying that, given the intellectual interaction that occurred from around 1920 up to the mid-thirties, his own contributions should be read alongside this collection.

While Freud insisted on the distinction between psychoanalysis and biology, he also insisted on the reciprocal influence of psychical and biological events in the course of adaptation to sexual stages. Thus even though Freud exhorted his followers to keep psychoanalysis separate from biology, the fundamental question about sexual difference that children ask, is also the one adults reformulate on the couch, dealing with the very nature of sexuality: are there indeed psychical consequences to the anatomical difference between the sexes?[29]

Apart from the question of femininity, there remains one riddle though. What was it that caused Freud's blindness in the area of femininity, and more particularly his delay in recognizing the crucial mother-daughter dyad? Was this inadequacy dictated by Freud's own masculinity and status as father, as, ultimately, he and others suggest, or by the phallocentric and patrocentric nature of psychoanalysis as he conceived it,[30] by his self-diagnosed hysteria,[31] by his hysterical phobia as diagnosed by Didier Anzieu?[32] Perhaps some or even all of these features played a role;

but in our view more fundamental is the fact that Freud's approach to research has an affinity with the analytical process itself, with its 'working-through', resistance, and return of the repressed. And it is one of the great strengths of this collection that it shows how this approach permeates the community of psychoanalysts of his day. It is perhaps in the inseparability of this analytic process itself from the discoveries made in its name that one can find what is specific to the method of psychoanalysis.

Russell Grigg
Dominique Hecq
Craig Smith

Notes

[1] Sigmund Freud, 'Femininity', in *New Introductory Lectures on Psycho-Analysis* (1933a), SE 22:113.

[2] *Three Essays on the Theory of Sexuality* (1905d), SE 7:151.

[3] 'On the Sexual Theories of Children' (1908c), SE 9:211.

[4] 'Femininity', SE 22:113.

[5] 'The Infantile Genital Organization' (1923e), SE 19:142. In addition to this paper, see 'The Dissolution of the Oedipus Complex' (1924d) and 'Some Psychical Consequences of the Anatomical Distinction Between the Sexes' (1925j).

[6] Editor's note to 'Psychical Consequences', SE 19:245.

[7] SE 22:252.

[8] *New Introductory Lectures*, SE 22:149.

[9] See for instance Juliet Mitchell and Jacqueline Rose, *Feminine Sexuality: Jacques Lacan and the Ecole Freudienne* (Macmillan: London, 1982), pp. 8 and 15-16 in particular, where Juliet Mitchell briefly explains why 'Karl Abraham's work is crucial'. For a more radical revision of the dynamics of the debate, see Marie-Christine Hamon, *Pourquoi les femmes aiment-elles les hommes?* (Seuil: Paris, 1992).

[10] See Karl Abraham, 'Origins and Growth of Object-Love', Part II of 'Development of the Libido' (1924). Reprinted below.

[11] Freud-Viereck 21.9.1930, *The Diary of Sigmund Freud 1929-1939: A Record of the Final Decade* (London: The Hogarth Press,1992), 283.

[12] *The Complete Poems of Heine*, trans. Edgar Alfred Bowring (G. Bell and Sons, 1916), 260.

[13] 'Femininity', SE 19:129 (emphasis added).

[14] 'On the Sexual Theories of Children' (1908c), SE 9:205-26, links the alleged universal possession of a penis in children (p. 215) with the proposed theory of the little girl's disappointment at not having it (p. 218).

[15] SE 11:165-75.

[16] 'The Infantile Genital Organization' (1923e), SE 19:141.

[17] 'Psychical Consequences', 256. Worth noting is that the question underlying this statement is, 'Why does the little girl change love objects?'

[18] Identification, though a key concept, is an elusive one. There is, obviously, a conceptual difficulty in dealing with the preoedipal mother. This probably makes sense, since whether a construct or a fact, motherhood is part of the whole phallic economy. Here lies and follows the conceptual difficulty in dealing with the preoedipal, rather than oedipal, mother. (Contrast with Freud's essay on Leonardo da Vinci.)

[19] A point somewhat refined in 1933, though Freud admits then: 'We have learned a fair amount, though not everything, about all three.' ('Femininity', 129)

[20] 'Psychical Consequences', SE 19:251.

[21] 'Female Sexuality', SE 21:225.

[22] 'Female Sexuality', SE 21:235.

[23] August Stärcke, 'The Castration complex', below.

[24] Karl Abraham, 'Origins and Growth of Object-Love', below.

[25] See below.

[26] 'Letter to Carl Müller-Braunschweig' (1935), published as 'Freud and female sexuality: a previously unpublished letter', *Psychiatry*, 34(1971):328-9.

[27] See the passage quoted above from 'Psychical Consequences', SE 19:251.

[28] Juliet Mitchell, *Female Sexuality*, 20.

[29] William I. Grossman, 'Discussion of "Freud and Female Sexuality"', *International Journal of Psycho-Analysis*, 57(1976):301.

[30] Juliet Mitchell, *Feminine Sexuality*, 23.

[31] See letters to Fliess of 14.9.1897, 30.9.1897 and 3.10.1897, in *Letters to Fliess*, 261, 270 and 325.

[32] Didier Anzieu, *Le Corps de l'oeuvre* (Gallimard: Paris, 1981), 61.

1

Contributions to the Masculinity Complex in Women

J. H. W. Van Ophuijsen (1917)

International Journal of Psycho-Analysis 5(1924):39-49

Undoubtedly, 'Contributions to the Masculinity Complex in Women,' is an underrated paper. This may be due to its not being published in English until 1924, well after Freud introduced the term 'masculinity complex' into his own writings. However, Van Ophuijsen's paper was originally presented to the Dutch Psycho-Analytical Society much earlier, on 23rd June 1917. It was published in German the same year and in Dutch the following year.

The term 'masculinity complex' is in fact van Ophuijsen's invention and Freud acknowledges his debt in his 1919 paper, 'A Child is Being Beaten'. It is also in the present paper that various manifestations and possible consequences of penis envy are first clearly expressed, just as the libidinal investment in the 'virile' erogenous zone is linked to the attachment to the mother. This last point is particularly important, and Freud will later appeal to it in explaining the phallicism of the little girl.

The material van Ophuijsen draws on derives from five case studies of obsessional women. One of the cases, who is here simply referred to as H., is subsequently discussed by Jeanne Lampl de Groot in her 1928 paper, 'Evolution of the Oedipus Complex in Women', a discussion Freud alludes to in his 'Female Sexuality' of 1931. The analysand was referred to Lampl de Groot because of difficulties encountered in the transference to a male analyst. It is also worth noting that van Ophuijsen takes her to be an obsessional, while Lampl de Groot diagnoses hysteria.

Van Ophuijsen's starting point concerns one aspect of the theory of penis envy; namely, that it derives from the sense a woman has of having been injured in infancy through no fault of her own and hence she will blame her mother for having brought her into this world as a woman instead of a man. This matches some character types encountered in analysis, van Ophuijsen conjectures. He also points out that this turning against the mother is, as with the castration complex, founded on a belief in the possibility of possessing the penis. The difference between the castration and masculinity complexes is that the sense of guilt attached to the former is absent from the masculinity complex, in which, on the other hand, what predominate are the sense of having been wronged and accompanying bitterness and reproaches. Moreover, the term is intended to connote the presence of a form of rivalry with men rather than the presence of any overt masculine characteristics.

Finally, one should note the connection between the masculinity complex and the urethral erotism which van Ophuijsen explains in terms of a regression to the auto-erotic stage later tackled by other analysts such as Karen Horney.

* * *

In his essay on 'Some Character-Types Met with in Psycho-Analytic Work', Freud writes:

> As we learn from psycho-analytic work, women regard them-selves as having been damaged in infancy, as having been unde-servedly cut short of something and unfairly treated; and the embitterment of so many daughters against their mother derives, ultimately, from the reproach against her of having brought them into the world as women instead of as men.[1]

These lines came to my notice at the very moment when my attention had been directed in a small sequence of cases to a particular form of reac-tion to the complex referred to, and when I believed that in one case I also had determined some of the conditions of its origin. In the following paper I will give an account of my conclusions.

The type of reaction with which we are concerned is, in common with the castration complex in women, founded on a belief in the possibility of possessing a male genital organ. The chief difference between the two lies in the fact that a consciousness of guilt belongs to the castration complex. The loss, the damage, or the faulty development of the genital organ is supposed to be the result of wrong-doing, often punishment for a sexual lapse. The feeling of guilt is absent in the cases of which I shall speak here—not always, of course, completely, but the feeling of having been ill-treated and the consequent reaction of bitterness is in all very strongly developed. In view of this second group of cases, in which the protest (which seeks to make up for the want) is predominant, I propose to intro-duce the term 'masculinity complex'.

The origin of the masculinity complex is, of course, to be traced to the sight of a male organ, belonging either to the father or the brother, or some other man; and in the history of most women patients, and without excep-tion in those with a strongly-marked masculinity complex, there is found the memory of such an observation and of the comparison of the patient's own body with that of a man. In one of the cases I have analysed, the patient, D., tells me quite clearly that the wish to be a boy developed from the desire to be able to urinate like a boy, after she once saw a boy perform this act. This incident has determined till to-day the manner of her sexual satisfaction through masturbation. Another patient, H., was able to observe her father and uncle, who were not ashamed to urinate before her.

Yet the question arises, by what instincts the phantasy of masculinity is nourished, and how it is that the phantasy, in spite of later experience and information, not only continues to exist but even causes women frequently to behave as though they possessed male genitals. A patient, P., tells me that for some time past in urinating she has given up a sitting for a standing position, nominally because her hip-joints have become too stiff. She also sits down as though she had to guard against crushing her genitals, as if they were male organs.

Recollection of the masculinity complex does not always exist in consciousness, at any rate in the primitive form of a belief in the possession of a male genital. Often the recollection only becomes conscious during discussion of the so-called masculine attitude. But in every case it requires close study to establish that the complex is still effective in its original form in spite of repression or experience.

The small sequence of cases which first turned my attention to the complex consists of five patients, who were suffering from psychasthenia with obsessions, otherwise called obsessional neurosis. I have been able to observe four of them for quite a long period; the fifth, however, gave up the analysis very soon. But this fifth patient came to me for treatment just after I had learnt to take sufficient notice of the phantasy of being a man. All the facts of her case pointed to her as the type sketched by Freud in the lines quoted above; and I think, therefore, it will be agreed that there can be no misunderstanding about this statement of hers: 'Often when I am restless and don't know what to do with myself I have a feeling that I would like to ask my mother to give me something that she cannot give me.' The behaviour of one of the four other patients had for a long time inclined me to think that in her case also the problem was the influence of her unconscious wish to be a man. For instance, her obsessional movements in lying or sitting down are of such a kind as to give one the impression that she has to make the same overtures to the sofa or chair that a cock makes to his hens. Only a short time ago she said to me, 'I feel as though I coquetted with the sofa.' It might perhaps be not without significance that three of the five patients informed me of their own accord that they possessed 'Hottentot nymphae'; this fact, which they had already noticed very early in their lives, led them to the conviction that they were different from other women. I did not find to any great extent in any of these cases what is called a masculine disposition; nor indeed a masculine appearance and expression, a contempt for men, or a predilection for masculine activities. I would rather define the attitude present as one of rivalry with men in the intellectual and artistic spheres. A pronounced homosexual component makes no difference to this, as the resulting rivalry in sexual matters expresses itself only in symptoms and symptomatic acts.

Returning to the question put above, we may state that we have already learnt from experience, when the recollection of an observation or of an event is being retained and used as the starting-point for a new phantasy-system (screen-memory), that we then have to do with the return of a repressed wish under fresh distortion. We are tempted to surmise such a return from the unconscious when a girl reacts to the experience of seeing or observing a male genital organ with the violent, embittered thought, 'Why haven't I anything like that?' or 'I ought to have had one too'; or on the other hand with anxiety and a consciousness of guilt, 'I might have had one too—what a pity that I injured myself to such an extent'; or with the expectation, 'It won't be long before I grow one too'; or even with the reassurance, 'Yet I do possess one!' These are only examples of such a reaction; there are still a number of another kind, and the form of the bodily symptoms almost always present changes with these reactions. For instance in place of the genital so passionately desired, there is usually felt to be a 'wound', which is either painful or irritating, according to the manner in which the patient regards the lack of the organ.

Now what are the repressed impulses which, after the trauma of seeing a male organ, can find an outlet in the newly appearing idea of having such an organ? We may assume that these bear a certain relation or likeness to the content of the masculinity idea. In an allusive way the patients speak of this themselves, by making vague contrasts—and this often happens—between their masculine traits and their feminine inclinations, also quite well-known to them. Even when they do not mention the thing they seek, the meaning of their expressions is quite clear to the analyst. That is to say, they usually express a wish to take possession of a person, instead of devoting and subjecting themselves to him; or they have the feeling that they wish to penetrate someone else, instead of themselves being penetrated; or they remark that a state of tension would disappear if they could but give out something instead of taking something in. Such expressions are of course used then in a hyperbolical sense; but not seldom associations of this kind afford evidence that they should be taken to a certain extent literally—in fact, it is one of the several ways in which one can discover the masculinity complex in analysis.

At the central point of the childhood-reminiscences of one of my patients, whom I shall call H., and of whose analysis I shall give the most detailed account, there stands the following dream; it dates from about her fourth year when she still slept in her parents' bedroom. She dreamed—it may perhaps be a mere phantasy—that she lay in bed and her mother stood near her. She had a surprisingly pleasant bodily sensation and her mother told her it was quite all right, there was no harm in it. Whereupon she experienced a kind of orgasm and awoke. To her astonishment and horror she found that she had soiled the bed. She called her mother, who came to her assistance without being angry. Since that time the patient has always remained shy, has had anxiety during the night, has suffered to an increasing extent from sleeplessness, and so has gradually developed a neurosis; this neurosis grew very much worse at the age of thirteen, when she lost her mother, and again at nineteen, when she lost her brother; its chief symptom is shyness with men. We may suppose that the sensations which the patient had in her dream were derived from her filled bladder, and that the emptying of it corresponds to the orgasm of the dream. Her feeling of shame and astonishment on waking prove to us that the girl must already have learnt to control the bladder-function. As a contrast there is in the dream a return to an earlier period before she had learned this control, associated with the idea of the methods of teaching her cleanliness: the mother near the bed, who tells her to let it happen, is obviously the mother who makes her use the chamber. Urinating into a chamber has had considerable significance to her; her father also helped her with this function later, and imitated the noise to her in order to make her urinate. And in addition she had in her early youth heard the sound of her father urinating in the next room.

The patient is very gifted musically and composed music even as a child. It often happened that while she sat on the closet she let a stream of water run from a tap in order to catch a melody from the noise. When she plays at a concert she often feels as though through her playing she were to put an end to the tension which she feels in the public or in an individual listener—sometimes the public is replaced by the composer. If she succeeds in feeling in this way, she plays well. From her associations there appeared an analogy in this with the childhood-situation in which by urinating she produced the noise which her father had either produced for her with his mouth or by urinating in another room; she transfers this detail, therefore, of her father-complex to the composer: The tension either actually felt or unconsciously existing in herself is projected into the audience or again into the composer. In addition her father has always encouraged her musical ambitions, with the result that the patient has identified herself with him in the musical sphere and has regarded herself as the instrument of his will. One very primitive expression of this identification is the idea of being her father's genital organ.[2] One has only to remember her attitude at concerts, which I have just mentioned; she is to be the organ which provides relief for the tension she feels in the audience. The association of music with urination led to this phantasy. Moreover, she has already inferred a connection between the symptom of congestion (due to the pressure from constipation) and the reddened glans penis she had seen in her brother's genitals, and had interpreted her convulsions of weeping as ejaculations. The sobbing and sighing which accompanies such a convulsion reminded her of what she used to hear in her parents' bedroom.

In this connection the following fact is also of importance. The patient was awaiting her last examination at the Conservatoire and had considerable anxiety about it. A vision, as she calls it, came to her rescue in her need: Someone standing near her bed speaks to her during the night about her attitude to music and to her examination; she is to forget herself and to surrender herself entirely to the intentions of the composer, and give herself free rein. After the vision she fell into a state of exaltation, slept no more, but played very well at her examination. The agreement of this vision with the dream in childhood must of course occur to everyone; the identification with her father to which I have alluded above was also in operation in this experience.

It is natural to conclude that *hearing* has played a large part in the development of this interest in little H. We have already mentioned the fact that she listened when anyone passed water in the room, or in the next room. The patient suffered quite early from sleeplessness. At night she always felt obliged to listen, either to the music that was going on in the house, or lest burglars were in the room, or to hear what her parents were saying on the other side of the wall against which her own bed stood. This habit of listening had begun when she ceased to sleep in her parents' room. I cannot prove that she had observed, or tried to observe, parental coitus on one or more occasions, but from what has been said above it is obvious that she had been greatly interested in what went on in her parents' bedroom or bed. The reason for her sleeplessness was the tension produced by sexual curiosity.

The patient herself suggested that the childhood-dream might be due to her having witnessed parental coitus and that she probably identified herself with her father. It is a fact that many associations pointed to a possibility of this sort, but no recollection of it has come into consciousness. We know that children sometimes imagine that the man passes urine into the woman; it would be in agreement with this idea if we looked upon this dream as a homosexual coitus dream. Of course the material used to represent the fulfilment of the desire to perform coitus with the mother (or rather, to do with her what the patient thought her father did) is taken from an earlier period.

A whole series of recollections bear witness to infantile intimacy with the mother, and particularly to occasions when they went to the closet together and her mother passed urine as well as she herself. We may assume that the child's wish to see what her mother looked like and how she did this was a preliminary phase of the later curiosity. Sometimes, too, little H. had difficulty in defecation; she suffered from constipation, and she clearly remembered that when she strained very hard her mother told her not to do so. When straining in this way she had a curious sensation in her head, a kind of giddiness, which recurred later accompanying her shyness. Here, the infantile situation in the closet has been transferred to later situations when she has been overcome by shyness. By means of displacement from below upwards, into which I do not wish to enter here, the mouth has become an anus and that which proceeds from the mouth, namely speech, is faeces and flatus. For instance, in talking to anyone, she is compelled to notice whether any odour proceeds from that particular person's mouth. In the same way there has been a transference of details connected with the bladder-function, and to this is to be traced the struggle with fits of crying which is another of the symptoms connected with shyness.

Quite suddenly these intimate relations with her mother were stopped; she was no longer allowed to go to the closet with her, and so on. Suddenly, too, her relations with her father in these matters were forcibly interrupted. She was already suffering from sleeplessness, probably at the beginning of her fifth year, and she had formed a habit of calling her parents, whereupon she was helped on to the chamber. One night she called more than once and her father came in angrily and gave the unsuspecting child a box on the ear. She was much embittered by this and vowed to herself that she would never call out again. In order to attract her parents' attention, or possibly to disturb them, she then bethought her of the plan of shaking her bed.

It is quite likely that being suddenly forced to give up her infantile pleasure for which no substitute was provided may have had a traumatic effect and have produced an embittered frame of mind, which might have been avoided if the parents had gone about her training in a less abrupt manner. We find something similar if we leave this period of the patient's life and observe her in the following period when she was in the infants' school and the first class of a preparatory school. She was compelled to go to school, and once more, at least so she thinks, the order was given quite unexpectedly. On one fateful day she was restless and lay down on a table and rolled about on it, without any definite idea of what she wanted. Whereupon she was suddenly told: 'Now you will have to go to school.' She has always felt this conduct on the part of her mother as a great injustice and it left its traces of resentment and anxiety—anxiety due to an uncertainty of what unpleasant thing might happen next because of something she quite innocently did or said. It was as if something had been taken from her, which she herself could not put into any definite words.

But from that day on she inwardly resisted the rules made by those who brought her up, even though she seemed to submit and obey them. Her mental picture of the infants' school is linked up with the recollection of several forbidden things, two of which I will mention. Her mother forbade her to go to the closet at school, but she once did so all the same, out of curiosity. Moreover, she has never quite lost her curiosity in relation to the functions of the bladder and bowel or her interest in excrement, which is in agreement with what has been said above. Secondly, when sitting on the form she played with her genitals and then, afraid lest the smell on her hand should be detected, she licked her fingers till no smell could be noticed. It is a remarkable thing that the patient cannot say whether she had masturbated before that as well. Analysis has not been able to decide this point either. But it is quite possible that the childhood-dream indicates the beginning, the first perception, of clitoris sensations. For the feeling of gratification was, as the patient expressly said, hitherto unknown to her, and after this experience she felt different from what she was before, as though she possessed something special, a kind of secret, which from that time on made her different from other people. In general, a connection between the function of the bladder and that of the clitoris is established very early; probably this is partly due to the anatomical condition. Freud in one of his writings emphasizes the connection between strongly developed urethral erotism and ambition. Certainly my patient was ambitious in every direction; her ambition was fostered, moreover, by her father's expectations based on her musical talent, and it culminated in a phantasy which I do not wish to go into in detail here: The so-called 'hospital phantasy' in which she figured to some extent as a healer but treated people with extraordinarily cruel remedies. In the same way her ambition was fed by rivalry with a sister a year older than herself but less talented. She succeeded too in apparently excelling her in almost every respect, but on the other hand there were various relations, especially that with her father, in which she was inhibited, constrained and shy. In later years impulses of rivalry caused her to attach herself rather to her brother, who was some years her junior—at first as his school-fellow, and afterwards, when their mother died, with a mother's devotion.

She often heard it said that, before she was born, her parents wanted a boy and that they were somewhat disappointed when another girl was born. She noticed too how proud they were of their son. Here again was an injustice which she never forgot. She could not say whether at that time the thought already occurred to her—at any rate it was a familiar thought—that she too might have been a boy if only she had been born rather later. She regarded herself as having been born too soon. The same bitterness was displayed in her analysis in a striking way when, for certain reasons, I fixed a time for the treatment to end—I too, then, was making her go before she was ready. I think that the idea of being born too early is somehow connected with the experience, several times undergone by the patient, that something was ordered or forbidden, some renunciation imposed upon her or the fulfilment of a duty required of her, before she had enjoyed the infantile modes of gratification long enough. Here of course there may also be the wish to retain a form of gratification as long as possible, an attitude originating in strongly developed anal erotism.

The patient observed the male genital principally in her brother, but also in her father and an uncle, with whom many years later she fell in love; this unfortunate love-affair was the direct cause of her illness growing worse and of treatment being undertaken. In those early days she made comparisons of the male organ with her own genitals, and once more I found in her case too the familiar expectation that an organ would grow out from within. This expectation was supported by the Hottentot nymphae, which she noticed very early and construed as something peculiar to herself. Her conviction that she was an exception found plenty of evidence in this respect.

The expectation I have just mentioned, that a penis would grow out from within, was also for a time transferred to the intestines. I have several times had the opportunity of observing a similar process in girls who had witnessed coitus in dogs. Phantasies occur too of an auto-erotic coitus in which the rectum stands for the vagina and the faeces for the penis. The discovery of phantasies of this sort has led me to wonder whether the vaginal sensations which should develop later are not derivable from anal feelings. It is not surprising that the patient developed strong homosexual tendencies, for in the first place her intimate relations with her mother and later the identification with her father were a most favourable soil for such tendencies. But, of course, here too gratification was denied her, or else the tendencies always became inhibited by strong negative feelings. Only when her incestuous love for her uncle, at the beginning of her illness, threatened to overwhelm her did she take refuge in a homosexual relation which in a short time resulted in an acute confusional condition.

If we sum up what we know of this patient we may say briefly that here is a case where the idea of being a male, an idea based on identification with the father or the brother, is the central feature of the picture. The idea of masculinity, so closely bound up with clitoris erotism, finds congenial soil in the repression of the strongly developed bladder and urethral erotism. Owing to the failure to effect a permanent and satisfactory transference to homosexual and heterosexual objects there is regression to the auto-erotic stage of libido-development, principally to that of urethral erotism.

In the other patient, too, the connection between the masculinity complex and urethral erotism is perfectly plain.

The patient D., of whom I have already said that the masculinity complex manifested itself in her in the desire to urinate like a man, either tries to lengthen the urethra, for instance by passing her urine through a tube, or she passes it into vessels not intended for that purpose. Tricks of this sort, occasioned by an already existing sexual tension, then invariably lead to masturbation. This patient has marked homosexual tendencies, which are displayed far more strongly than her heterosexual desires. The latter are confined to innumerable fleeting experiences of being in love—underneath there is a firm fixation to a childish love-relation which continues to exercise a powerful inhibitory influence. Her psychasthenic symptoms are those of obsessive doubt and speculating. These probably originate in a strongly developed childish curiosity, which in this particular case culminated in the question: 'How do men do it?' i.e. how does he (the father) perform the act of defecation? The patient is the only daughter of an elderly couple; her father died when she was about sixteen. At one time she had turned from him and had thoughts of hatred and death wishes against him; after his death she reproached herself for feeling it to be a deliverance rather than a loss, and was troubled with doubts whether her thoughts could have caused him to die. Later she also developed negative feelings towards her mother, and asked herself whether she were to blame for her mother's illness, a kind of arthritis deformans. We understand the meaning of such wishes, especially when we know further that the patient had to help her mother in everything because the latter could hardly move at all. The attachment to the incestuous homosexual object was thus not threatened by prohibitions from without, and this gave ample scope for a large amount of infantile libido to come into action. The patient never sucked, either at the breast or from a bottle; she always drank her milk from a cup or a spoon. She herself now uses this fact as a pretext for regarding herself as an exception.

I mentioned a third patient, P., as an example of a woman who behaves as though she were a man, or at least as though she had a male genital. In this case I have not been able to prove the connection with urethral erotism so clearly as in the other. But this is not very surprising, for the patient in question is somewhat older. In any case I could not prove that there was any other form of infantile auto-erotic sexual activity corresponding to the extreme development of the masculinity complex, and there was not much difficulty in discovering the connection with the earlier masturbation which was generally accompanied by homosexual phantasies of an incestuous sadistic-masochistic type. In this case, however, the masculinity complex had long been conscious. As a child the patient used

to enjoy making bread or dough into figures shaped like a phallus and recognized them as such. As late as her tenth or twelfth year she used to play
a kind of shadow-game with her sisters, and used to like to make her own
shadow project in the region of the genitals. Her principal symptoms represented the fulfilment of the wish to have a male organ, and were accompanied by a feeling of envy of men for their possession of it, and by an attitude to women which must be regarded as an over-compensation for her
embitterment against her mother for withholding it from her.

I feel as if I had not really succeeded in making it clear how strong an
impression I have received in my analytic work of the intimate connection
between the masculinity complex, infantile masturbation of the clitoris
and urethral erotism. I have said to myself that the observations which I
happened to make all at one time might be merely accidental findings.
Nevertheless I decided to publish them, because I am convinced that publication of the result of any careful observations may be of some value.

Notes

1 Sigmund Freud (1916*d*), SE 14:315.
2 This phantasy connects with infantile birth-theories.

The Castration Complex

August Stärcke (1920)

International Journal of Psycho-Analysis 2(1921):179-201. Translation by
Douglas Bryan.

*First read at the Sixth International Psycho-Analytical Congress in September
1920 at The Hague and published in English one year later, Stärcke's paper is in
part a response to van Ophuijsen's views on the masculinity complex. He denies
that in the masculinity complex of women, feelings of guilt are absent; it is just
that they are projected onto others and expressed as embitterment and feelings of
injustice. In thus questioning the rationale for van Ophuijsen's distinction
between masculinity complex and castration complex, Stärcke anticipates later
developments proposed by Joan Riviere.*

*Stärcke is concerned by the same problem that led to van Ophuijsen's posi-
tion: the universality, in both men and women, of the castration complex. It is a
problem because of the assumption that the fear of castration must be based on a
concrete experience. In the case of the boy this experience is clearly the threat of
the loss of the penis; but there can be no corresponding threat for the girl. His logic
leads him to focus on the situation of the child at the breast and the event of weaning, since this alone can account for the universality of the complex. The paper
focuses on exploring the reasons why this loss is displaced from the mouth onto
the genitals.*

*Stärcke is the first to see weaning as the prototype of castration. Placing the
origins of castration in the experience of the breast has the advantage for Stärcke
that all the consequences of castration can be traced back to the concrete experiences of childhood. It of course also effaces the distinction between the sexes.*

*Stärcke's line of thought is subsequently taken up by other participants in the
controversy, such as Helene Deutsch.*

* * *

I

In psychoanalytical literature the term 'castration complex' implies a network of unconscious thoughts and strivings, in the centre of which is the
idea of having been deprived, or the expectation of becoming deprived, of
the external (male) genitals. This complex is a general one, probably universal, but the intensity of its effects varies.

Van Ophuijsen[1] would reserve the term castration complex for those cases in which the feeling that the genitals are damaged or imperfectly developed is associated with the feeling that this signifies a punishment for a sexual offence; and he comprises the whole group of ideas under the term 'masculinity complex' of women, of which the castration complex might be one manifestation.

In the following remarks I do not adopt this definition; my reason for this will be clear at the conclusion. I also consider as effects of the castration complex those cases in which the feeling of guilt is not perceived as such, but is projected on to the surroundings and contributes towards the intensification of the feeling of hate against them, and is expressed by a marked feeling of having been unjustly treated, together with that of embitterment. I adopt this view because it is necessary for my purpose to lay stress more on the agreements than on the differences between these groups of ideas. It is clear that the strivings which constitute this broader (original) idea of the castration complex are only one part of an ambivalent attitude; the other part of this attitude I also include in this discussion. Viewed in this way the castration wishes and fears can be classified under the following four types.

1   I am castrated (sexually deprived, slighted), I shall be castrated.
2   I will (wish to) receive a penis.
3   Another person is castrated, has to (will) be castrated.
4   Another person will receive a penis (has a penis).

The first three types are manifest as wishes, strivings or fears. The fourth type is principally expressed in the infantile theory of the 'woman with a penis'[2]

II

The castration complex is usually traced to a 'threat of castration' on the part of one or other of the child's parents, in which cutting off the penis is threatened as a punishment for some offence, generally masturbation. We find the best description of this threat in Freud's 'Analysis of a Phobia in a Five-Year-Old Boy'.

> When he was three and a half his mother found him with his hand on his penis. She threatened him in these words: 'If you do that, I shall send for Dr. A. to cut off your widdler. And then what will you widdle with?'
> Hans: 'With my bottom'.
> He made this reply without having any sense of guilt as yet.

But this was the occasion of his acquiring the 'castration complex', the presence of which we are so often obliged to infer in analysing neurotics, though they one and all struggle violently against recognizing it.[3]

It occasionally happens that an event like that related by Freud is not consciously remembered in spite of the obvious existence of a 'castration complex' and despite all analysis. I do not believe that the resistance is wholly responsible for this, but that in such cases the threat had been expressed in some other form, such as, 'If you do that you will go mad', 'Through that you may become very ill', 'If you do that you will be severely punished', or as a simple prohibition. The question then remains why a threat of this kind is transformed into anxious expectation or fear of actual loss of the penis; for this undoubtedly occurs as shown in cases where the wording of the original threat is remembered and did not take the form of castration.

Some girls have the idea that, as a punishment, they have been deprived of a penis which they formerly possessed. In these cases there certainly had not been a direct threat of castration. We are here confronted with a problem, and I bring forward the four following considerations towards its solution.

A   In consequence of the talion expectation *any* threat will tend to be realised in the child's phantasy at the spot in connection with which he feels a sense of sin. And, as the threat is probably always uttered on account of genital manipulations, the expectation of punishment is localised to the genitals and hands.

B   It has to be borne in mind that the genitals have a certain measure of guilt attached to them very early, which is derived from the struggle regarding cleanliness; this being the first conflict between the child and its nurse. The transgression of the orders regarding cleanliness loads the genital region with a primal guilt which remains fixed for life, and all future expectations of punishment are in the first instance attracted to this region.

C   The third factor does not apply to all cases, though I have come across some in which it has contributed to the metamorphosis of the atypical form of the castration threat into the typical one. In these cases a balanitis or a leucorrhoea has localised the anxiety of punishment.

D   The fourth reflection deals with an actual situation that occurs to every child. The present paper is devoted to consideration of it.

III

We have to remember that the castration complex has also a positive side, the content of which is that a penis is imagined in a part of the body where it does not exist. We have therefore to look for an infantile situation of universal occurrence in which a penis-like part of the body is taken from another person, given to the child as his own (a situation with which are associated pleasurable sensations), and then taken away from the child causing 'pain' (*Unlust*). This situation can be none other than that of the child at the breast.

Before proceeding further I should like to mention some facts from the analysis of dreams which have given me the idea that the content of the castration thoughts is the withdrawal of the nipple.

Discretion compels me to mention only the following details from the first dream. The dreamer was a woman. *Primo*: All kinds of wishes from the castration complex; complaints at not having received a penis, instead of it only a 'niggardly female organ', a 'cypher', a 'button-hole without a button'; scorn at the defective penis function in other people, or castration wishes directed on to me and on to the male members of the family. *Secundo*: Excremental-oral-erotic pictures; especially wishes to drink or to be allowed to drink urine. *Tertio*: Drinking from a woman's breast, whereby blood forms the transition between milk and urine. The symbolic equation would read: Urine = menstruation urine = blood = blood of the pelican with which it feeds its young = milk. The dreamer has an aversion to imitation jewellery; this, like her repugnance to the female breast, means that it is repugnant to her to possess nipples because they are false, that is to say, because they cannot become a proper penis,⁴ any more than the clitoris. There is also a second meaning: the female breast has disappointed her, it has not brought the proper gratification; this she therefore seeks in women, but is always again disappointed.

The dreamer often had preconscious phantasies of sucking at a penis; and many of her symptoms were based on the oral impregnation theory. Freud has several times pointed out that the perversion of sucking at the penis has a very innocent and infantile prototype—the sucking at the breast. There exists behind the preconscious phantasy of sucking at the penis the unconscious one of sucking at the mother's breast, an unchanged infantile reminiscence, the pleasurable sensation of which demands endless repetition.

As far as I know it has not been pointed out how these conditions throw light on the castration complex. In our dreamer the same dream symbols represent both urine drinking and drinking from the breast. The unconscious picture of the nipple corresponds to the preconscious picture of the penis. The anamnesis gave sufficient proof of an oral-erotic-mammary ambivalent attitude behind the dream.

A symbolic representation of castration occurred in a second dream. This symbolic castration was carried out upon a Mrs. X. who was a cover-figure for the dreamer's mother. The castration was a revenge for lack of motherliness. The punishment is consummated 'on the member, on the member with which you have most sinned'. The castration (in the dream another symbolic act, representing the removal of the breasts) was a talion punishment for her being deprived of her mother's breasts through weaning.

I can give fuller details of a third dream because I was the dreamer.

Introduction: In May 1917 my beloved brother died. The dream occurred at a period when the pain of his loss had been softened by time, and had left a feeling of longing and yearning. During the day previous to the dream these latter feelings had prevailed without my having consciously thought much about him.

Dream: I was somewhere by the sea. A pair of storks were flying about and then flew off to the left; a smaller one was flying after them. I had a feeling of intense joy because a beautiful opportunity to observe birds of passage here presented itself. This joy increased when the small bird after flying backwards and forwards several times settled near me. I then saw it was an avocet (recurvirostra avocetta, Dutch = kluit); it was beautifully coloured though somewhat more pink than is usually the case. It came at my call and took food from my hand or my mouth. Then I held it under my left arm and took it with me, feeling exceedingly happy with the magnificent bird. Then I was at the entrance of a cheese store, and to my great disappointment became aware that the bird had disappeared, and that in its place I held a walking stick. On a board were two small cheeses, one red, the other yellow.

Partial Interpretation: I may say at once that the *two storks by the sea* represented my parents. The sea formed their two beds pushed close together. The *small bird* stood for my dead brother; also my mother's breast, and the penis. I cannot express the beauty of the bird in the dream; however, the *avocet* really is a very beautiful bird. One of its peculiarities is that its beak is curved upwards; it is also long-legged, as my brother and I had been jokingly called. Its colour is white and black. I first had my attention drawn to this beautiful bird many years ago through an essay entitled 'A Week in a Bird *Paradise*'. In the same periodical there was another essay by Frederik van *Eeden* on the stonechat, also a black and white bird. The 'bird with a decoy-tail' van Eeden has named it. I next thought of Boutens' fine poem on a swan from 'Carmina' (carmine = pink). (The swan is also a bird of passage seen by the sea.) I had recently read this poem with deep emotion, and it brought to mind my brother. During the whole day previous to the dream there had been running in my head Lohengrin's Parting Song, in which this stanza occurs:

Then blissfully, by the Grail accompanied,
Returned the brother whom you thought dead.

This bliss (cf. also the Bird's Paradise) occurred also in the dream, namely, the solemn rapture when I was again united with the beautiful bird. I am obviously jealous of this blissfulness, because I have transferred it to myself in the dream. This delightful frame of mind recalls another scene from a work by van Eeden (Eden = Paradise) in which he describes the feelings of 'Little John' who, after weary wandering, sees at last the infinite sea across the dunes. John was also my brother's name.

Birds of passage are birds which come back in the spring, they are only absent *for a while*. A similar idea of life is associated with the name van Eeden, namely, Paul van Eeden's motto, 'It is just for a moment', and his book *Paul's Awakening*, which is the author's expression of his profound grief over his son's death. 'Death and Transfiguration' it might also have been called, like a part of one of the Wagnerian musical dramas.[5] My brother was friendly with Paul van Eeden. Then I think of a poem written by my brother shortly before his death, entitled, 'Hirépolis'. 'Hirépolis' is a word he had dreamed, and was meant to signify the 'Egyptian sand-martin' (*Uferschwalbe*, literally, beach swallow). This word, 'Hirépolis', is a condensation of 'Hirundo' (swallow—again a bird of passage) and 'polis' (the last syllables of the name of Egyptian towns). It is an acrostic about a phthisical girl with kindly eyes; the initial letters form the word Hirépolis. The acrostic, literally translated, is as follows:

Halfway descended
Into the depth of death
Reachest thou with kind eyes
E'er the last light fades away.
Pleadest thou with me to come
O'er the feast to which He invites thee.
Last swallows of the eyes
In the Nile Valley of death.
So to die is not to my liking.

The idea of death is here thought of ambivalently; that is to say, as enticement to return to the womb of Mother Earth; the Nile Valley of death is mentioned, the Nile Valley where the first known history of mankind was enacted. The idea of death is also elaborated into the idea of re-birth (birds of passage, swallows). The idea of the *return of something lost* is well represented in the associations (Paul's awakening, birds of passage, the return of the lost brother as Lohengrin).

The *walking stick* I borrow from another Wagnerian drama. It is Tannhäuser's magic wand which bursts into leaf. Paul is also my little son's first name. I had previously thought that the motive of the Lohengrin Saga was a castration idea: the losing the penis through guilt, with a pre-lude in which the 'brother' is innocently lost. At that time the thought crossed my mind that this might mean the loss of the mother's nipple which returns as a penis (Lohengrin—Swan—Husband), the magic of which, nevertheless, would be broken if origin and name is investigated, that is to say, when it is established that the lost brother is really himself; so that the incest prohibition falls on him and he is recalled. In other words, love disappears when it becomes conscious as repetition.

The *cheese store* at once reminded me on waking of butter making and dairy work. At its entrance I lost the beautiful bird, and in its place I had a walking stick. This is another elaboration of the Lohengrin *motif*: engram complexes from the suckling period form its original melody: faint mem-ories of the joy of sucking at the mother's breast: the beautiful bird, some-what more pink than the real avocet, that fed out of my mouth or my hand. If 'or' is replaced by 'and' one arrives at the situation of the sucking child who touches the breast with mouth *and* little hands. The beautiful bird is not only my brother, but also my mother's breast. The entrance to the cheese store represents a *booking office*, this leads to distribution; it is a place where something is served out.

The feeling of disappointment over the loss of the beautiful bird at the entrance to the cheese store is the reproduction of that first disappoint-ment where the nipple turns out to be only a temporary possession of the ego, and disappears, leaving only the genitals and the thumb as a solace. Moreover, the Dutch name for the dream-bird 'Kluit' (avocet) recalls a sim-ilar word that means testicle.

Why is the mother's breast represented as a cheese store? 'Adipocire' came as an association to *the two cheeses* on the board: they could represent the two round breasts. But why a cheese store and not a dairy? Then sud-denly there came to mind something my mother had often told me: the milk in her breasts had clotted and become cheese, according to the doc-tor's statement, and he had warded off a commencing mastitis by mas-sage. The clotting ('klonteren', Dutch) again recalls the name of the bird. 'Kluit' (Klumpen) is also a name for butter.

Black and white are the real colours of avocets. The associations to these colours are: the white breast and the dark areola, the ambivalence, white love and black hate. White and black are also the two colours of death. Death recalls Paul's awakening, and that other black and white bird the stone-chat, which Paul's father (F. van Eeden) has praised and described as the 'bird with the decoy-tail'. I find that associations to one dream element constantly lead me to a train of thought that had already occurred with another dream element, which expresses the tendency to do away with a separation, a tendency which had persisted during the work of interpretation in the morning. It also implies a resistance against ideas connected with my own and another's death, the same trend of thought that was suppressed after 'Adipocire', and also against another series of ideas not entirely separate from it, which deals with the theme of jealous impulses. My brother was a more gifted writer than myself. I had an extremely high opinion of his accomplishments in this respect, and when he gained that appreciation to which he was entitled I was as glad as though it had happened to me. At the same time I certainly do not reject self-esteem as a means to happiness, and when a benevolent colleague termed my small contributions to scientific work indigestible explosive bodies I could only partly agree with this, although I considered the criticism a just one. The repeated experience, that an idea to which I had in vain called attention in my contributions was later taken up and advanced by a colleague who had read it, could annoy me, and I was unable to suppress entirely this annoyance by a calm conviction acquired later that everybody has that experience, and that ideas generally spring up in many places simultaneously when the time is ripe for them. The fact that the associations so obstinately compare the two white-and-black birds with each other, and also thrust forward the works of F. v. Eeden (Paul v. Eeden's father), signifies that the other black-on-white 'creations of the mind' which 'Paul's' father (i.e. myself), has written, are also very beautiful; my avocet is as beautiful a bird as his Egyptian sand-martin. When writing there also occurs to me another work of v. E., called 'The Brothers', which shows still further connections with the dream thoughts. Associations of rivalry lead to an amusing childhood scene similar to those depicted by van Looy in his 'Jaapje', and which appears to justify my claims.

One of my brother's writings particularly occurs to me; he published it under a pseudonym which contained the names of two black-and-white birds (black and white—death colours).

I carry the beautiful bird *under my left arm*. This reminds me of Anne Boleyn who, according to tradition, had a supernumerary breast in this part of the body. Further associations lead to all kinds of memories from the nursery relating to right and left symbolism. From these associations another arises which refers to incestuous object erotism. The beautiful bird with the upturned beak is the penis. The cheese store is the 'mamma', this word means both breast and mother. At the entrance to the cheese store the bird is changed into a walking stick. Finally, the cheese store is my spare room where I concealed my hoarded cheese during the war.

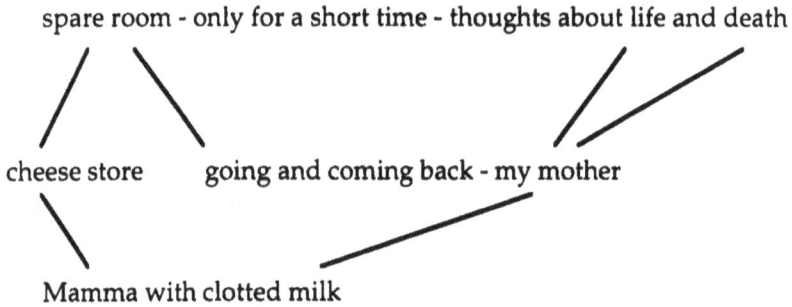

spare room - only for a short time - thoughts about life and death

cheese store   going and coming back - my mother

Mamma with clotted milk

For reasons that can be understood and in order not to distract the attention too much, I refrain from amplifying a number of trains of thought; the details that are important for this subject are sufficiently represented in what I have said to admit of conclusions. The dream portrays a part of my work of sorrow. It concerns the undoing of losses felt to be castration; at the same time the castration is carried through by the wish-capacity of the secondary meanings of its symbols which express the removal of rivals and the representation of incest.

I shall now restrict myself to the consideration of the oral-erotic significance of the castration complex.

The dream puts me back in the suckling period, that paradise where feelings exist and thoughts are scarcely known. The dream reflects the joy at possession of the source of life and the disappointment when my mother's mastitis made suckling difficult or impossible.

A second scene can be reconstructed; namely, my witnessing the way in which my little brother (two-and-a-quarter years younger than myself) was suckled by my mother. This situation must have made a very great impression upon me, seeing that all its elements, my mother, her nipple, my little brother and myself, have become condensed into a unity, the elements of which can represent each other symbolically. (The beautiful bird symbolises all the elements that are lacking in me). In this powerful sensation the older feelings of disappointment are fused with that of jealousy when the newcomer receives what has been taken from me. At the same time I identify myself with him, and thus, through him, enjoy my lost happiness. When I lose my brother the dream phantasy seizes upon the same means of consolation which had healed my first great loss (viz. that of the nipple).

If I arrange the memories and wishes that form the content of this dream according to the three levels, conscious, preconscious, and unconscious, I find as conscious wishes my yearning for the sea and dunes where we spent our holidays when children, and the observation of birds of passage, etc. As preconscious I find trends of feelings of love and hate, life and death, death and sexuality, erotic wishes from all possible stages, envy and jealousy, and longing for justification, i.e. various expressions of the castration complex. Finally, as unconscious, incest phantasies, and the castration complex in its double meaning—namely, that of the penis which is lost through the incest phantasies (at the entrance of the cheese store), and that of the mother's nipple which was taken from me. The latter is the older meaning and must be considered the primary one.

The connection between incest phantasies and the castration complex appears in this connection:

My penis disappears into my mother,

that is to say, my nipple (my mother's nipple in my mouth) is again lost in the 'mamma'.

IV

In order better to understand the importance of these connections it will be necessary to turn our attention to the nature of memory.

The engram depository consists of a number of associated engram complexes, each one of which is derived from a whole situation of being stimulated and forms its residue. Let us take as an example the situation of the child at the breast. In this situation occur feelings of pleasure, feelings of position and movement of the lips and tongue, the feelings awakened by the simultaneous touching movements of the little hands, etc., and these feelings later become separated in other combinations. The sum of these pleasure-traces forms an important part of the positive personality of the child at the breast, namely, its *sucking erotism*, which later, in so far as it does not become active as such, will be distributed over its positive narcissism and the object-erotic mother erotism.

The ego-impulse and the libido during sucking are active and are gratified in one and the same act, although theoretically they can be differentiated in the same way as the energy of two horses that are together drawing a wagon.

The ego here coincides with the libidinous personality, that is to say, there is no doubt that the nipple in the mouth of the sucking child leaves behind engrams which by their later ecphoria give rise to something psychical, which, translated into the language of later life, would be something like: *the memory of having possessed a nipple-like organ*, and, moreover, a perfect one.

The question arises: How is it that the castration complex does not complain about the absence of the nipple in the child or man, but rather the absence of the penis in the woman; and why is this deficiency referred to the genitals and not to the mouth?

I do not venture to assert that the answer to these questions will be entirely satisfactory. However, we need not be discouraged if we are convinced that our hypothesis is a useful one; and that the apparent contradictions have to be attributed to the complexity of the subject.

In the first place the child will undoubtedly observe that people's mouths are almost all alike, and that their genitals vary. Any envy, from whatever source it may come, will be most easily directed towards the genitals.

A further cause of this envy may be the fact that girls can only feebly direct their stream of urine; but I do not consider this the main cause. It is the feeling of the loss of the nipple in the mouth zone that is displaced to the genital region in virtue of the difference of the genitals; perhaps also it is directed by a common third reason of a genital feeling during sucking, analogous to that during kissing.[6]

Secondly it is doubtful whether feelings of loss do not actually continue to exist in the mouth. Hunger and appetite not only stand for intestinal sensations, but also for mouth sensations in the sense of the perception of the difference between the real actuality of the gratification of the mouth libido, and the infantile situation, the repetition of which is desired.[7]

In these mouth sensations we have to look for that part of the quantity of libido set free by the withdrawal of the nipple, which remains after the displacement of its other part to the genitals as a contribution of oral-papillary erotism to the Oedipus complex, and, in another combination of positive and negative factors, to the castration complex. Real compensation and gratification is easily obtained for this feeling and its correlated impulses.

Mankind is divided into two large groups according to the nature of these compensations. The first group forms an association rather with the colour and form of the missing organ, and finds its consolation and gratification in *smoking*. The second group forms an association rather with the sensation of taste of the mother's milk and demands its repetition, which it obtains by *eating sweet things*.

The *sucking movement* which these two conditions repeat in their oral gratification becomes, finally, the almost exclusive gratification in tobacco chewers. That the nicotine only plays a secondary part is shown by the use of chewing gum.[8] Sweet eaters are not as a rule smokers. It cannot be chance that smokers are mostly found amongst the sex that has the least cause to displace its feeling of loss of an organ on to the genitals.

The mouth is supplied with a number of *accessories* the manifest object of which is to replace the parts that have been lost. The common derivation of the feeling of loss in the mouth and in the genitals from the withdrawal of the mother's nipple also explains an obscure symbolic association, namely, that of tooth-drawing and masturbation. The tooth extracting ecphoriates the old complex of sensations associated with the withdrawal of the nipple from the mouth. The same complex is also ecphoriated in masturbation. The castration occurs as a direct consequence of masturbation, really as a part of it.

To sum up: The feeling of the loss of an organ from the mouth in part remains, and finds real local gratification; sufficient motives exist for its partial displacement downwards.

The second of the two questions which stood in the way of our hypothesis is thereby settled. The first remains to be answered. How is it that there does not exist in men a counterpart of the castration complex that has for its content the loss of well-developed breasts or feelings of neglect on this basis? The answer is that this difference does not exist at an earlier age, and it is only at that time that the experiences have such after-effects.

If we adopt von Uexküll's[9] idea and separate 'outer world' from 'environment', we can say that the child, and particularly the infant at the breast, has quite a different *outer world* from the adult, although the *environment* of the child and adults is the same.

Thereby I consider the objections raised are settled, and we can pass on to formulate our ideas regarding the influence which the sucking erotism must have had upon the formation of the castration complex.

I am firmly convinced that the wish phantasies of the unconscious are ultimately repetitions of real situations; these phantasies only appear peculiar and unconnected with reality through the difference between infantile and adult thought. Thus in a previous article I have specially singled out defecation in the infant as that situation from which the later delusion of persecution is derived: the original persecutor is found in the *imago* (counter-world) of the engram complex, from which scybalum and nurse are later formed as separated thought contents.[10]

In a similar manner I now particularly single out as the primitive castration the withdrawal of the mother's nipple from the infant who is not fully satisfied. The fact that this may happen at each nursing and is a constant fact at the weaning accounts for the universal occurrence of the castration complex.

V

I consider this fragment of infantile sexual theory just discussed sufficiently important to add a few more remarks to it. The mammary and papillary erotism, according to its character, belongs to Freud's earliest pre-genital organisation stage of sexuality. It forms the object-erotic supplement of the mouth erotism and the commencing hand and smell erotism. Its relation to the castration complex is so important that it must be looked upon as its real root, and compared with it other sources recede into the background.

Freud three years ago in his work, 'On Transformations of Instinct as Exemplified in Anal Erotism',[11] referred to defecation (and micturition) as an extra-genital origin of the castration complex.[12] On page 130 he writes: 'Defecation affords the first occasion on which the child must decide between a narcissistic and an object-loving attitude.' On page 133:

> Another part of the nexus of relations can be observed more clearly in the male. It arises when the boy's sexual researches lead him to the discovery of the absence of a penis in women. He concludes that the penis must be a detachable part of the body, something analogous to faeces, the first piece of bodily substance the child has to part with. Thus the old anal defiance enters into the composition of the castration complex.

We now obtain a further contribution to this theme. The mother's nipple in the infant's mouth is certainly not less a part of its own body than its motion or its urine. The nipple, however, has rather to be compared with the penis, and it also resembles it in its relation to fluid. Besides the nipple, other parts of the body which were lost early have to be taken into consideration—the stump of the umbilical cord, the motions, urine, and clothes. It may be postulated that their removal cooperates in the genesis of the castration complex. However, the nipple takes the leading part. The nipple has also to have a place assigned it in any other relations of the transposition of instincts.

VI

It is seen from the above considerations that the difference between breast and bottle feeding must also be of great significance in the development of the mind, irrespective of the chemical composition of the food. It is perhaps curious that psychologists have paid little attention to this subject; a good example of a negative delusion.

In the case of a child of seven who had a transitory compulsion to soil I found the primary motive for this in an abnormal process of weaning. The child had not been getting sufficient milk for some time, and so had to endure the trauma of the feeding-bottle; at first it thrived better until it reacted to a second feeding-bottle with violent opposition. The compulsion to wet appeared later, and subsequent to an occurrence that was repeated for a time almost every night. When the child's mother went to bed she was accustomed to take him up in order to let him pass water; he usually had such an erection that the stream would miss the chamber-pot. His mother did not like to see an erection in so small a child, and showed her displeasure by giving the refractory member a gentle tap. The child obtained the repetition of this erection complex in its compulsion to soil and especially to wet. I consider this process is an expression of the castration complex.[13] However, the castration complex was not acquired on this occasion, but much earlier, i.e. at the transition from the first feeding-bottle which he accepted, to the second which was refused for unknown reasons (different smell?) and to which he reacted with anger and vomiting.

Every loss re-ecphoriates all earlier losses back to the very first—namely, the disintegration of sucking erotism and of excremental desires. The most important contribution to the clinical phenomena of grief and melancholy (or mania) comes from the castration complex. When with an expression of contrition the melancholic admits that she will not eat 'because she has eaten human beings, although she has not eaten them', this is a partly correct reminiscence from the period at the breast, when she actually fed off her mother. If the censorship regresses to a lower level in melancholia and allows the ecphoria of the engram complexes of this period to pass without sufficient distortion, or if the over-charge of the remaining symbols in grief—also without regression—renders the work of censorship difficult, then these ecphoriae are unable to find suitable words for their proper expression. Their cultural splitting up goes only a certain distance, and their end-products, foetal position of the body or attitudes approximating to this, early infantile methods of feeding, new editions of already surmounted attitudes of conflict, partly prevail, and partly also encounter and mingle with inhibitions that have not regressed so far, or are finally repulsed; but all this happens at the expense of psychic work which consumes all the individual's energy. In this the oral-erotism certainly plays the important role which Abraham (*l.c.*) has ascribed to it. Mankind has its cannibalistic stage not only phylogenetically; it is also repeated in the individual life of every human being who was fed at the mother's breast or the bottle.

In future all these things will have to be taken into consideration; the duration of the sucking, the abundance or the scarcity of the milk, the kind of feeding bottle, even the width of its opening, all these are of importance and will find their place in the history of the mental illness. At this tender age the most trifling differences can have just as important a result on the mind as a microscopic amniotic thread, which cuts off a few cells from the germ, can have on the body.

VII

The infantile theory, the 'woman with a penis', originates very simply from the situation of the infant at the breast. It is quite natural that the child whose first association with a woman is directly dependent upon her penis-like organ, the nipple, should retain a memory of this. It is the certainty and force of this memory that mainly support the belief in a penis in the woman. When the child learns later that a girl has not this organ, this knowledge is the first result of investigation which confuses the child and places before it the choice of disregarding either the memory, the observation, or the information. If the child is told the real facts, then on the basis of its experience it in all probability considers it a lie, and thus feels justified in accepting later explanations with suspicion. Another way to solve the problem is doubt; the mother's sex is doubted. With regard to girls the information is accepted, but a special position is assigned to the mother; she has, so to speak, no sex, only *she* remains 'the woman with a penis'.

VIII

Another important source of the mother-complex, therefore object-erotism, arises from the situation at the breast. If we ask how it is that such an important sphere of auto-erotism as the oral zone, which is at the same time one of the earliest discovered, occurs relatively infrequently in the history of patients, we may conclude that this probably results from the fact that its auto-erotic significance has become hidden through the object-erotic significance contained in the mother-complex. Every expression of object-erotic mother-erotism can at the same time contain auto-erotic sucking-erotism. The 'mamma' can signify the mother as well as the breast.

IX

From somewhat scanty material, but on the basis of well-substantiated facts, I believe I can also find some connection in the situation at the breast with the origin of a very obscure perversion, namely, sadism. If I adhere to my belief that every erotic phantasy is based on a real experience, then it is evident that the basis for cruelty is to be found in the beast of prey which mangles its victim and thus creates fixed paths between gratification through taking nourishment, and the expressions of the victim's pain, humiliation, and seizure. But what may be an explanation in the case of beasts of prey does not apply to human beings, and therefore we have to fall back upon our tendency of making heredity accountable for all that we do not know, of putting all guilt that we do not wish to bear on our parent's shoulders, and of calling archaic what we do not wish to call infantile.

Our working hypothesis, that a real basis is to be found in ontogenesis, helps us over this difficulty. We find the situation of the beast of prey in possession of its living victim roughly produced in the infant at the breast. If the mother during suckling has cracked nipples or pain due to other causes, then we have a real situation in which the child perceives expressions of pain in a person of whom he takes possession, and at the same time experiences most intense gratification. This genesis was actually confirmed in one case.

Several varieties of sadism can be brought into line with this mode of origin. The above situation fits very well the algolagnic form. If kissing originates from the erotic part of sucking, then sadistic pleasure in biting can arise from the same source. With regard to the compulsion to wet or besmear somebody, the amusement of many infants to slobber on the mother is to be considered in conjunction with the excremental factors.

Finally there is pleasure in striking. A more careful consideration of the sucking erotism shows that it can be divided into two large complexes, namely, that of the nipple in which the mouth zone of the infant finds gratification, and that of the mamma in connection with which the little hand of the infant forms the reciprocal zone. This latter complex, mamma-little hand, we again find in flagellation mania, which primarily finds its object in the nates, i.e. the new edition of those other hemispheres, the mammae. Also beyond the true sadism there is a certain affinity between hand and buttocks. The application to this region seems a matter of course in every thrashing. Without underestimating the influence of the neighbouring anal zone I prefer to see in this affinity a reflection of the infant's love and pleasure-touching of its first and greatest source of life by means of its little hands.

I consider it an advantage that my hypothesis is capable of objective control, for cracked nipples are often well-remembered by mothers. The decision rests on the facts.

X

I might briefly allude to the possibility that in the repeated alternation between becoming one's own and not one's own, which occurs during lactation, there lies a prototype for the child and a path for the later psychic process of projection, just as it must also give rise to a displacement of narcissistic quantities in the mother.

To recapitulate: Besides the removal of excrement it is in the situation of being suckled that there lies a real basis for the wishes, strivings and dispositions that are comprised under the term castration complex. There is also the possibility that on the same basis is founded the infantile theory of the 'woman with a penis', many symptoms of neurosis, details of incestuous object-erotism, particular forms of sadism, and that also the situation of being suckled plays a part in the origin of the mechanism of projection.

If I now ask whether the psychoanalytic therapy gains anything from all this, I am bound to confess that the discovery of less objectionable motives behind the sadistic-anal-erotic organisation, which succumb so much to repression, is fraught with the risk of not sufficiently removing these repressions. And since the therapy aims at the removal of repressions it will be more interested in the later elaboration of the papillary-oral-erotic quantities which succumb to repression after having experienced 'displacement downwards'. Nor is there any sense in creating a problem where it is not thrust upon us.

Because I maintain that the importance of the oral-erotic interpretation is not to be under-estimated I do not consider the analysis should end there; although the deepest meaning of many symptoms is to be found in oral-erotism and this meaning lies farthest back in the ontogenesis, still these factors need not be the most deeply repressed ones.

The experience we had in the Dutch Society shows that in the normal human being who is perhaps a smoker or sweet-eater the oral-erotic interpretation finds sufficient resistances.

XI

The analysis of a few dreams was the starting-point of my views. These views have increased in ever-widening circles from this central point, like rings from a stone that is thrown into water. A final ring has yet to be described.

Von Uexküll's useful views have led me to this final idea, and particularly where he throws light on the influence of the 'structural plan' on the outer and inner world of animals.

But even the statement that the varying individuals of a species are more or less adapted to their surroundings is a pure invention. Every varying individual is different in correspondence with his altered structural plan, but at the same time is perfectly suited to his environment. The structural plan creates the outer world of the animal automatically and within broad limits. . . .

It is not difficult to observe any given animal in its surroundings, but this does not solve the problem. The experimenter must endeavour to settle what part of these surroundings act upon the animal, and in what form. Our anthropocentric mode of consideration has more and more to recede, and that of the animal alone becomes the deciding factor. Thus everything disappears which we consider self-evident: the whole of nature, the earth, the heavens, the stars, indeed all objects that surround us, and there remain as world factors only those influences which, corresponding to its structural plan, exercise an influence on the animal. Their number and their homogeneity is determined by structural plan. If this connection of the structural plan with the external factors is carefully investigated, then a new world, totally different from our own, is created around every animal, its outer world.[14] The effects produced by factors of the outer world on the nervous system have to be considered objectively just like the factors themselves. These effects are sifted and regulated by the structural plan; and together form the inner world of the animal'[15]

Von Uexküll considers the distinction between inner and external world as self-evident, but this is only permissible if the ego of the animal is represented as sharply limited from the beginning. The distinction between external and inner world is not at all self-evident if, as the author demands, one takes the standpoint of the animal; this distinction has rather an anthropocentric character. It is probable that in living beings this distinction is only gradually acquired,[16] and that in the beginning a period exists in which no distinction is made between ego and external world.

I have already indicated that it is the processes of sucking, defecation and micturition (perhaps also undressing in human beings) which are the chief factors in bringing about this separation. On account of this the stage of primitive narcissism gives way to a life of pleasure divided into two parts—namely, narcissism and object-erotism; these two then carry out their evolution separately, although with reciprocal effects. The separation occurs gradually, and does not take place in the different erotogenic zones simultaneously.

Since the separation does not exist during the phase of primitive narcissism,[17] one cannot speak of an external and inner world; all that can be said is that engram complexes are imprinted, and that their ecphoria at the same time represents that which latter will be distinguished as ego and external world.

The infant at the breast at first does nothing else than suck, urinate and defecate; suck, urinate and defecate. But it undoubtedly has—that is to say, according to its structural plan—sensations other than we should have in the same situation. When we drink out of a glass, the glass remains a glass, that is, a part of the external world, and our ego remains the same ego. But when the infant sucks, the nipple or dummy belongs to it and remains belonging to it, although it is clear to us that this is not so.

The impressions of the sense organs teach the infant to separate the engram complexes of this primitive ego into one part which answers to the wish for repetition, and into another part which is withdrawn from the tendency to repetition (Freud). The withdrawal of the nipple, defecation, and micturition, especially supply material for these observations. Nipple, faeces, urine are the bridges from the ego to the comprehension of the external world.

Our primitive and auto-erotic ego is by preference a pleasure ego; the formation of the concept of the external world is associated with pain factors (*Unlustmomente*); and so from the very beginning the external world constitutes an enemy,[18] until the sense organs of distance, eye, ear, and nose, secondarily add pleasure which is withdrawn from the primitive ego's investment with pleasure. Thus our final pleasure-ego is a remnant—a remnant which owes its origin to the fact that something is removed from us of which the sense organs have taken possession, and which they have stamped with their seal and offer us as external world.

In all views of life one finds again the wish to undo the separation between ego and external world. One speaks of the necessary synthesis of macro- and micro-cosmos, of life in harmony with the infinite, of the feeling of being one with nature, and calls this the condition and essence of happiness.

This happiness that all mean to strive after, for which everyone yearns, is bound up with the primitive narcissism and auto-erotism. Sucking, defecation and micturition are the kernels of this concept; but the nipple is the leader in this triumvirate, and thus it happens that the mamma as mother becomes the central concept of the external world, for whom the desire for reunion strives, while the nipple in the form of its later double, the penis, is perceived as the centre of one's own personality, and an injury to it is felt as a severe injury to the ego itself.

It is this separation in the primitive ego, the formation of the external world, which, properly speaking, is the primitive castration; and when I spoke of the withdrawal of the nipple as castration it is only another way of expressing the same thought.

Notes

[1] 'Contributions to the Masculinity Complex in Women', above.

[2] That a woman has no penis though originally she possessed one occurs as an intermediate idea, which belongs to the third type. It is to be noted that the reverse theory occurs. I recall an anecdote related to me by Prof. Wertheim Salomonson fifteen years ago in the course of a conversation on the sexual factor in the neuroses: Little Elly was seated at table with the adults. Suddenly to her parents' horror she remarked, 'Hermann (her little brother) has a little lump on his legs'. 'But it will go away', she added to their—and her own—relief. Whether this is only an anecdote or a fact, at any rate it proves the occurrence of this phantasy in the human mind. I should like to think it probable that such 'compensatory' theories actually occur, but they cannot be distinguished in the large complex of the castration wishes.

[3] Sigmund Freud (1909*b*), SE 10:7-8.

[4] Also not a proper breast nipple; she wanted a breast nipple *in the mouth*.

[5] Footnote on reading the proof: This mistake has arisen through confusion with 'Isoldes Liebestod' which has a similar meaning.

[6] After being at the breast the infant generally empties its bladder: there are therefore connections.

[7] See Karl Abraham (1916), 'The First Pregenital Stage of the Libido' *Selected Papers of Karl Abraham* (London: Hogarth Press, 1927), 248-79.

[8] Of course these habits are only mentioned here with reference to their oral-erotic derivation: their analysis is not yet exhausted, and even the oral-erotic part has other *Imagines* than the nipple.

[9] J. von Uexküll, *Umwelt und Innenwelt der Tiere*, Berlin, 1909; J. von Uexküll, *Biologische Weltanschauung*, Munich, 1913.

For example, it is not the form of the chair, the cart, the horse, that the word expresses, but what it performs for us.

The meaning of the object for our existence is in what it performs for us. It is this that the coach-builder has in his mind, the architect who designs the plan of the house, the butcher who kills the ox, the author who writes the book, and the watch-maker who makes the watch. Everything that surrounds us in the town has only sense and meaning through its relation to us human beings'. . . .

Thus it appears that in the midst of the daily increasing multitude of human productions thousands of people live who treat these things as the only reality.

And yet we need only take a dog with us on our walk through the town in order to be taught differently. The dog hurries past the tailor's shop. The clothes have a meaning for him only after his master has worn them and bestowed on them the odour of his body; then they become important attributes in the dog's life. Our clocks and books do not represent particular objects to the dog. The unimportant confusion of colours and forms leaves it quite indifferent. Only the butcher's shop absorbs its whole interest. The smell of the raw flesh and cooked sausages stimulates its appetite, while the odour of putrefying fish produces the desire to roll itself in it.

The kerbstone, which we carelessly pass by, is quite as important to the dog as the butcher's shop, because every dog leaves behind on it its redolent visiting card. The dog runs up the stairs as it would run up any hill. The balustrade has no meaning to it. It uses only the upholstered chairs. It rests best in the place where the shadows of the trees do not disturb it. The flower bed only attracts its attention when a little mouse appears.

Nobody would willingly assert that the dog had passed through the town in a manner similar to ourselves.

(*Biologische Weltanschauung*, 79–80).

[10] 'The Reversal of the Libido-Sign in Delusions of Persecution', *International Journal of Psycho-Analysis* 1(1920):231-4.

[11] Sigmund Freud (1917*c*), SE 17:125-33.

[12] These factors are also represented in my material, although I have not called special attention to them.

[13] That is to say: the disturbance which is occasioned in the genital development of its Oedipus complex through the prohibition from outside, furnishes libido quantities to the castration complex, which represents another arm of the mother-complex. His compulsive habit of upsetting things filled with liquids is a surrogate for the forbidden Oedipus-erection. The accent is transmitted from the erection to the spilling of liquids which accompanied it.

[14] Later renamed by v. Uexküll, 'Merkwelt'.

[15] *Umwelt und Innenwelt der Tiere*, 5-6.

[16] See Sandor Ferenczi (1909), 'Introjection and Transference', *First Contributions to Psycho-Analysis* (London: Hogarth Press, 1952), 35-93; (1912), 'On the Definition of Introjection', *Final Contributions to the Problems and Methods of Psycho-Analysis* (London: Hogarth, 1955).

[17] That is to say, if one puts oneself on the standpoint of the individual under consideration.

[18] That is to say, ambivalency. Really it would be more correct to say the hostile thing is the external world. It is therefore so easy to draw back object-erotic quantities to a painful organ. The painful organ belongs as well to the external world through its pain, as it belongs to the ego through its remaining qualities. This may also contribute to the explanation of masochism. The primitive ego finds itself again in the pain-pleasure.

3

Manifestations of the Female Castration Complex

Karl Abraham (1922)

International Journal of Psycho-Analysis 3(1922): 1-29

Abraham's 'Manifestations of the Female Castration Complex' is an amplified version of a paper read at the Sixth International Psychoanalytical Congress in 1920 at The Hague. It was published in English two years later.

Drawing on a number of clinical examples, Abraham rigorously explores some of the manifestations of the female castration complex. The paper starts with the observation that many women want to be a man and dislike being a woman. Abraham cites the 'poverty in their external genitalia' as the basis for this envy and later psychopathology. He then draws on Freud and sets the evolution of woman in developmental stages, discussing both its normative aim and some of its deviations. For Abraham, the girl mistakes her primary 'defect', which is that in comparison with the boy she lacks a penis, as secondary: she had a penis, but it was taken away. This idea that she has been robbed combines with the associated idea of female genitalia as a wound to explain the hostility or wish for revenge sometimes expressed by women towards men.

Abraham describes the normal attitude for the woman as one of reconciliation with her sexual role—desiring passive gratification and longing for a child. It is important to note, however, that this normal outcome is rarely achieved. The trauma of castration is apt to be reactivated at key points in sexual development, such as menstruation, defloration and childbirth, whether in the actual experience or in fantasies about them. Traces of the castration complex, he argues, are universal and differ only in their severity and specificity.

Woman's primary idea of the wound has three possible outcomes: normality, homosexuality and neurosis. The two deviations are elaborated upon: their homosexuality is either lived out (women who adopt a masculine role in relationships with other women), or sublimated (those who take up masculine interests of an intellectual and professional order); neurotic transformations are either of the wish-fulfilment type (this entails repression of the desire to be male, which Abraham links to van Ophuijsen's masculinity complex) or of the revenge type.

He concludes with a warning against the tendency to overestimate a single determinant in psychopathology, given that all psychical ideas are fundamentally overdetermined.

* * *

The psychological phenomena which we ascribe to the so-called castration complex of the female sex are so numerous and multiform that even a detailed description cannot do full justice to them. These questions are made still more complicated by their relations to biological and physiological processes. The following investigation, therefore, does not pretend to present the problem of the female castration complex in all its aspects, but is limited to the purely psychological consideration of material gathered from a wide field of clinical observation.

I

Many women suffer temporarily or permanently, in childhood or in adult age, from the fact that they have been born female. Psychoanalysis further shows that a great number of women have repressed the wish to be male; we come across this wish in all products of the unconscious, especially in dreams and neurotic symptoms. The extraordinary frequency of these observations suggests that this wish is one common to and occurring in all women. If we incline to this view then we place ourselves under the obligation of examining both thoroughly and without prejudice the facts to which we attribute such a general significance.

Many women are often quite conscious of the fact that certain phenomena of their mental life arise from an intense dislike of being a woman; but, on the other hand, many of them are quite in the dark as regards the motives of such an aversion. Certain arguments are again and again brought forward to explain this attitude: for instance, it is said that girls even in childhood are at a disadvantage to boys because boys are allowed greater freedom; or, in later life, men are permitted to choose their profession and can extend their sphere of activity in many directions, and especially that they are subjected to far fewer restrictions in their sexual life. Psychoanalysis, however, shows that conscious arguments of this sort are of limited value, and are the result of rationalisation—a process which veils the motives lying deeper. Direct observation of young girls shows unequivocally that at a certain stage of their development they feel at a disadvantage as regards the male sex by their poverty in external genitals. The results of the psychoanalysis of adults fully agree with this observation. We find that a large proportion of women have not overcome this disadvantage; or, expressed psychoanalytically, they have not successfully repressed and sublimated it. Ideas belonging to it often impinge with great force, arising in their strong charge of libido, against the barriers which oppose their entry into consciousness. This struggle of repressed material with the censorship can be demonstrated in a great variety of neurotic symptoms, dreams, etc.

The observation that the non-possession of a male organ produces such a serious and lasting effect in the woman's mental life would justify us in denoting all the mental derivatives relating to it by the collective name 'genital complex'. We prefer, however, to make use of an expression taken from the psychology of male neurotics, and to speak of the 'castration complex' also in the female sex; we have good reasons for this.

The child's high estimation of its own body is closely connected with its narcissism. A girl has primarily no feeling of inferiority in regard to her own body, and does not recognise that it exhibits a defect in comparison with a boy's. A girl, incapable of recognising a *primary* defect in her body, forms then the following idea, as we have often observed: 'I had a penis once as boys have, but it has been taken away from me'. She therefore endeavours to represent the painfully perceived defect as a secondary loss, one resulting from castration.

This idea is closely associated with another which we shall later treat of in detail. The female genital is looked upon as a *wound*, and as such it represents an effect of castration.

We also come across phantasies and neurotic symptoms, and occasionally impulses and actions, which indicate a hostile tendency towards the male sex. In many women the idea that they have been damaged gives rise to the wish to revenge themselves on the privileged man. The aim of such an impulse is to castrate the man.

We find therefore in the female sex not only the tendency to represent a painfully perceived and primary defect as a secondary idea of 'having been robbed', but also active and passive phantasies of mutilation alongside each other, just as in the male castration complex. These facts then justify us in using the same designation in both sexes.

II

As was mentioned above, a girl's discovery of the male genitals acts as an injury to her narcissism. In the narcissistic period of development a child carefully watches over its possessions, and regards those of others with jealousy. It wants to keep what it has and to get what it sees. If anyone has an advantage over it then two reactions occur which are closely associated with each other; a hostile feeling against the other person is associated with the impulse to rob that other of what he possesses. The union of these two reactions constitutes *envy*, which represents a typical expression of the sadistic-anal developmental phase of the libido.[1]

A child's avaricious-hostile reaction to any additional possession it has noticed in another person may often be lessened in a simple manner: one tells the child that it will eventually receive what it longs for. There are many ways in which such pacifying promises may be made to a little girl with respect to her own body. Her doubts may be relieved by telling her that she will grow as big as her mother, that she will have long hair like her sister, etc., and she will be satisfied with these assurances; but the subsequent growth of a male organ one cannot promise her. However in this latter case the little girl herself makes use of the method that has often been successful; for a long time she seems to cling to the hope of this expectation being fulfilled as to something that is obvious, as though the idea of a life-long defect were quite incomprehensible to her.

The following observation of a little girl, two years old, is particularly instructive in this respect. The little one saw her parents taking coffee at table. A box of cigars stood on a low cabinet near by. The child opened the box, took out a cigar and brought it to her father. She went back and brought one for her mother. Then she took a third cigar and held it out against the lower part of her body. Her mother put the three cigars back in the box. The child waited a little while and then played the same game over again.

The repetition of this game excluded its being due to chance. Its meaning is clear; the little one grants her mother a male organ like her father's. She represents the possession of the organ not as a privilege of men but of adults in general, and then she can expect to get one herself in the future. A cigar is not only a suitable symbol for the child's wish on account of its form. The child of course has long noticed that only her father smokes cigars and not her mother. The tendency to put man and woman on an equality is palpably expressed in presenting a cigar to her mother as well.

We are well acquainted with the attempts of little girls to adopt the male position in urination. Their narcissism cannot endure their not being able to do what another can, and therefore they endeavour to arouse the impression that their physical form does not prevent them from doing the same as boys do.

When a child sees its brother or sister receive something to eat or play with which it does not possess itself it looks to those persons who are the givers, and these in the first instance are the parents. It does not like to be less well off than its rivals. A girl, who compares her body with her brother's, often in phantasy expects that her father will 'make her a present' of that part of the body she painfully misses; for the child's narcissistic confidence still leads her to believe that she could not possibly be permanently defective, and creative 'omnipotence' is readily ascribed to the father who can bestow on the child everything it desires.

But all these dreams crumble after a time. The pleasure principle ceases to dominate psychical processes unconditionally, adaptation to reality commences and with it the criticism of one's own wishes. The girl has now in the course of her psychosexual development to carry out an adaptation which is not demanded of boys in a similar manner; she has to reconcile herself to the fact of her physical 'defect', and to her female sexual role. The undisturbed enjoyment of early genital sensations will be a considerable aid in facilitating the renunciation of masculinity, for by this means the female genitals will regain their narcissistic value.

In reality, however, the process is considerably more complicated. Freud has drawn our attention to the close association of certain ideas in the child, namely, that the idea of a proof of love is inseparable from that of a *gift*. The first proof of love, which creates a lasting impression on the child and is repeated many times, is feeding from the mother. This act brings food to the child and therefore increases its material property, and at the same time acts as an agreeable stimulus to its erotogenic zones. It is interesting that in certain districts of Germany (according to my colleague Herr Koerber) the suckling of a child is denoted 'Schenken' (to give, to pour). The child within certain limits repays the mother's 'gift' by a 'gift' in return—it regulates its bodily evacuations according to her wishes. The motions at an early age are the child's material gift par excellence in return for all the proofs of love it receives.

Psychoanalysis, however, has shown that the child in this early psychosexual period of development considers its faeces as a part of its own body. The process of identification further establishes a close relation between the ideas 'motion' and 'penis'. The boy's anxiety regarding the loss of the penis is based on this equating of the two ideas; the penis may be detached from the body in the same way as the motion is. In girls, however, the phantasy occurs of obtaining a penis by way of defecation—to make one herself—or to receive it as a gift: the father as beatus possidens is usually the giver. The psychical process is thus dominated by the equation: motion=gift=penis.

The little girl's narcissism undergoes a severe test of endurance in the subsequent period. The hope that a penis will grow is just as little fulfilled as the phantasies of obtaining one by herself or as a gift. Thus disappointed the child is likely to direct an intense and lasting hostility towards those from whom she has in vain expected the gift. Nevertheless, the phantasy of the child normally finds a way out of this situation. Freud has shown that besides 'motion' and 'penis' signifying 'gift' there is still a third idea which is identified with both of them, namely, the idea of 'child'. The infantile theories of procreation and birth adequately explain this connection.

The little girl now cherishes the hope of getting a child from her father—as a substitute for the penis not granted her, again as a 'gift'. The wish for a child can be fulfilled, although in the future and with the help of a later love object. The wish therefore signifies an approximation to reality. The child by raising the father to the love object now enters into that stage of libido development which is characterised by the domination of the female Oedipus complex. At the same time maternal impulses develop through identification with the mother. The hoped-for possession of a child is therefore destined to compensate the woman for her physical defect.

We regard it as normal for the libido of a woman to be narcissistically bound to a greater extent than in a man, but it is not to be inferred from this that it does not experience far-reaching alterations right up to adult age.

The girl's original so-called 'penis envy' is at first replaced by envy of the mother's possession of children in virtue of the identification of her own ego with the mother. These hostile impulses need sublimation just as the libidinal tendencies directed towards the father. A latency period now sets in, as with boys, and when the age of puberty is reached the wishes which were directed to the first love object are re-awakened. The wish for the gift (child) has now to be detached from the idea of the father, and the libido thus freed has to find a new object. If this process of development is gone through in a favourable manner, the female libido is from now on attached to the idea of expectancy in connection with the man. Its expression is regulated by certain inhibitions (feelings of shame). The normal adult woman becomes reconciled to her own sexual role and to that of the man, and in particular to the facts of male and female genitality; she desires passive gratification and longs for a child. The castration complex then gives rise to no disturbing effects.

Daily observation, however, shows us how frequently this normal end-aim of development is not attained. This fact should not astonish us, for a woman's life gives cause enough to render the overcoming of the castration complex difficult. We refer to those factors which keep bringing back to memory the 'castration' of the woman. The primary idea of the 'wound' is re-animated by the impression created by the first and each succeeding *menstruation*, and then once again by *defloration*; for both processes are connected with loss of blood and thus resemble an injury. A girl need never have experienced either of these events; the very idea of being subjected to them in the future has the same effect on the growing-up girl. We can readily understand from the standpoint of the infantile sexual theories that delivery (or child-birth) is conceived of in a similar manner in the phantasies of young girls; we need only call to mind, for example, the 'Caesarean section theory' which conceives of delivery as a bloody operation.

In these circumstances we must be prepared to find in every female person some traces of the castration complex. The individual differences are only a matter of degree. In normal women we perhaps occasionally come across dreams with male tendencies in them. From these very slight expressions of the castration complex transitions lead to severe and complicated phenomena of a pronounced pathological kind, and it is with these latter that this investigation is principally concerned. In this respect also, therefore, we find a similar state of affairs to that obtaining in the male sex.

III

In his essay on 'The Taboo of Virginity' Freud contrasts the normal outcome of the castration complex, which is in accord with the prevailing demand of civilisation, with the 'archaic' type. With many primitive peoples custom forbids a man to deflorate his wife; the defloration has to be carried out by a priest as a sacramental act, or must occur in some other way outside wedlock. Freud shows in his convincing analysis that this peculiar precept has arisen from the psychological risk of an ambivalent reaction on the part of the woman towards the man who has deflorated her. Living with the woman whom he has deflorated might therefore be dangerous for a man.

Psychoanalytical experience shows that an inhibition of the psychosexual development is manifested in phenomena which are closely related to the conduct of primitive peoples. It is by no means rare for us to come across women in our civilisation of to-day who react to defloration in a way which is at all events closely related to that 'archaic' form. I know several cases in which women after defloration produced an outburst of affect and hit or throttled their husband. One of my patients went to sleep with her husband after the first intercourse, then woke up, seized him violently and only gradually came to her senses. There is no mistaking the significance of such conduct: the woman revenges herself for the injury to her physical integrity. Psychoanalysis, however, enables us to recognise a historical layer in the motivation of such an impulse of revenge. The retaliation is connected with the recent defloration; this experience undoubtedly serves as a convincing proof of male activity, and puts an end to all attempts to obliterate the functional difference between male and female sexuality. Nevertheless every profound analysis reveals the close connection of the phantasies of revenge with all the earlier events—phantasized or real—which have been equivalent to castration. The retaliation is found to refer ultimately to the injustice suffered at the hands of the father. The unconscious of the adult daughter takes a late revenge for the father's omission to bestow upon her a penis, either to begin with or subsequently; she takes it, however, not on the father in person, but on the man who in consequence of her transference of libido has assumed the father's part. The only adequate revenge for the suffered injustice—the castration—is castration. This can, it is true, be replaced symbolically by aggressive measures; among these strangling is a typical substitutive action.

The contrast of such cases with the normal issue is evident. The normal attitude of love towards the other sex is in both man and woman indissolubly bound up with the conscious or unconscious desire for genital gratification in conjunction with the love object. On the other hand, in the cases just described we find a sadistic-hostile attitude with the aim of possession arising from anal motives, in place of an attitude of love with a genital aim. The tendency to take away by force is evident from numerous accompanying psychical conditions. This phantasy of robbery exists in close connection with the idea of transferring the robbed penis to oneself. We shall return to this later.

The woman's wishes for masculinity, as already mentioned, only occasionally succeed in breaking through in this 'archaic' sense. On the other hand, there is a considerable number of women who are unable to carry out full psychical adaptation to the female sexual role. A third possibility remains to these women, namely, the way to homosexuality in virtue of the bisexual disposition common to humanity; they tend to adopt the male role in erotic relations with other women. They love to exhibit their masculinity in dress, in the way of doing their hair, and in their general behaviour. Other cases approximate to these in which the homosexuality does not break through to consciousness; the repressed wish to be male is here found in a sublimated form, i.e. masculine interests of an intellectual and professional character and other kinds are preferred and accentuated. Femininity, however, is not consciously denied; they usually proclaim that these interests are just as much feminine as masculine ones. They consider it irrelevant to say that the performances of a human being, especially in the intellectual sphere, belong to the one or the other sex. This type of woman is well represented in the woman's movement of to-day.

I have not thus briefly described these groups because I lightly value their practical significance. The phenomena of both types are well known, however, and have been sufficiently treated in psychoanalytical literature, so that I can rapidly pass on to the consideration of the *neurotic transformations* of the castration complex. There are many of them and they must be described exactly, some of them for the first time, and rendered intelligible from psychoanalytical points of view.

IV

The neurotic transformations originating in the female castration complex may be divided into two groups. The phenomena of one group rest on a strong, emotionally-toned, but not conscious desire to adopt the male role, i.e. on the phantasy of possessing a male organ. In the phenomena of the other group is expressed the unconscious refusal of the female role, and also the repressed desire for revenge on the privileged man. There is no sharp line of demarcation between these two groups. The phenomena of one group do not exclude those of the other in the same individual; they supplement each other. The preponderance of this or that attitude can nevertheless often be clearly recognised. One may then speak of the preponderating reaction of a *wish-fulfilment type* or a *revenge type*.

We have already learned that besides the normal outcome of the female castration complex there are two abnormal forms of conscious reaction, namely, the homosexual type and the archaic (revenge) type. We have only to recall the general relation between perversion and neurosis with which we are familiar from Freud's investigations in order to be able to estimate the two neurotic types above described in respect to their psychogenesis. They are the 'negative' of the homosexual and sadistic types; they contain the same motives and tendencies, but in repressed form.

The psychical phenomena which arise from the unconscious wishes for physical masculinity or for revenge on the man are difficult to classify on account of their multiplicity. It has also to be borne in mind that neurotic symptoms are not the sole expressions of unconscious origin which have to concern us here; we need only refer to the different forms in which the same repressed tendencies appear in dreams. As mentioned at the beginning, therefore, this investigation cannot pretend to give an exhaustive account of the forms of expression of the repressed castration complex, but rather to lay stress on certain frequent and instructive forms and especially those which have not hitherto been considered.

The *wish-fulfilment* which goes farthest in the sense of the female castration complex comprises those symptoms or dreams of neurotics which convert the fact of femininity into the opposite. The unconscious phantasies of the woman proclaim in such a case: I am the fortunate possessor of a penis and exercise the male function. Van Ophuijsen gives an example of this kind in his article on the 'masculine complex' of women. This case of the conscious phantasy from the youth of one of his patients gives us at first only an insight into the patient's still unrepressed active-homosexual wishes, but at the same time clearly demonstrates the foundation of neurotic symptoms which give expression to the same tendencies after they have become repressed. The patient in the evening would place herself between the lamp and the wall, and then would hold her finger against the lower part of her body in such a manner that her shadow portrayed the form of a penis on her. She thus did something very similar to what the two years old child did with the cigar.

In conjunction with this instructive example I mention the dream of a neurotic newly-married woman. She was an only child. Her parents had ardently desired a son and had in consequence cultivated the narcissism and particularly the masculinity wishes of their daughter. According to an expression of theirs she was to become quite 'a celebrated man'. In her youthful day-dreams she saw herself as a 'female Napoleon'; she began a glorious career as a female officer, advanced to the highest positions, and saw all the countries of Europe lying at her feet. After having thus shown herself superior to all the men in the world a man appeared at last who surpassed not only all men but also herself; she subjected herself to him. Marital relations in real life were accompanied by the most extreme resistance against assuming the feminine role; I shall mention symptoms relating to this later. I quote here one of my patient's dreams.

My husband seizes a woman, lifts up her clothes, finds a peculiar pocket and pulls out from it a hypodermic morphia syringe. She gives him an injection with this syringe and he is then carried away quite weak and miserable.

The woman in this dream is the patient herself who takes over the active role from the man. The possibility for this is afforded her by a concealed penis (syringe) with which she practices coitus on him. The weakened condition of the man signifies that he is killed by her assault.

Pulling out the syringe from the pocket suggests the male method of urinating, which seemed enviable to the patient in her childhood. It has, however, a further significance. At a meeting of the Berlin Psycho-Analytical Society Boehm drew attention to a common infantile sexual theory: the penis originally ascribed to both sexes is thought to be concealed in a cleft from which it can temporarily emerge.

Another patient, whose neurosis brought to expression the permanent divorce between masculinity and femininity in most manifold forms, stated that during sexual excitation she often had the feeling that something on her body swelled to an enormous size. The tendency of this sensation was obviously to delude herself that she possessed a penis.

In other patients the symptoms do not represent the complete wish-fulfilment in the sense of masculinity, but a corresponding expectation for the near or distant future. While the unconscious in the cases just described expresses the idea, 'I am a male', it here conceives the wish in the formula, 'I shall receive the "gift" one day, I absolutely insist upon that!'

The following conscious phantasy from the youth of a neurotic girl is perfectly typical of the unconscious content of many neurotic symptoms.

When the girl's elder sister menstruated for the first time she noticed that her mother and sister conversed together secretly. The thought flashed across her, 'Now my sister is certainly getting a penis'; therefore she herself will get one in due course. The reversal of the real state of affairs is here highly characteristic: the acquisition of the longed-for part of the body is put in place of the renewed 'castration' which the first menstruation signifies.

A neurotic patient in whom psychoanalysis revealed extraordinary narcissism one day showed the greatest resistance to treatment, and manifested many signs of defiance towards me which really referred to her deceased father. She left my consulting room in a state of violent negative transference. When she stepped into the street she caught herself saying impulsively: 'I *will not* be well until I have got a penis'. She thus expected this gift from me, as a substitute for her father, and made the effect of the treatment dependent upon it. Certain dreams of the patient had the same content as this idea which suddenly appeared from her unconscious. In these dreams being presented with something occurred in a double sense (to receive a child or a penis).

Compromises between impulse and repression occur in the sphere of the castration complex as elsewhere in the realm of psychopathology. In many cases the unconscious is content with a substitute-gratification, in place of the male organ and the full wish fulfilment by present or future possession.

A condition in neurotic women which owes one of its most important determinants to the castration complex is enuresis nocturna. The analogy to the determination of this symptom in male neurotics is striking. I mention, for example, a dream of a patient fourteen years old who suffered from this complaint. He was in a closet and urinating with manifest feelings of pleasure when he suddenly noticed that his sister was looking at him through the window. When a little boy he had actually demonstrated with pride before his sister his masculine way of urinating. This dream ending in enuresis shows the boy's pride in his penis, and enuresis in the female frequently rests on the wish to urinate in the male way. The dream represents this process in a disguised form and ended with a pleasurable emptying of the bladder.

Women who are prone to enuresis nocturna are regularly burdened with strong resistances against the female sexual functions. The infantile desire to urinate in the male position is associated with the well known interchange of urine and sperma, and of micturition and ejaculation. The unconscious tendency to wet the man with urine in sexual intercourse has its origin here.

Other substitute formations show a still greater displacement of the libido in that they are removed some distance from the genital region. When the libido for some reason or other has to turn away from the genital zone it is attracted to certain other erotogenic zones, the particular ones being chosen as the result of individual determinations. In some neurotic women the nose achieves the significance of a surrogate of the male genital. The not infrequent neurotic attacks of redness and swelling of the nose in women is conceived in the unconscious phantasy as an erection in the sense of masculinity wishes.

In other cases the eyes take over a similar role. Some neurotic women get an abnormally marked congestion of the eyes with every sexual excitation. In a certain measure this congestion is a normal and common phenomenon accompanying sexual excitation. However, in those women of whom we are speaking the condition is not simply a quantitative increase of the phenomenon for a short period, but a redness of the sclerotics accompanied by a burning sensation, while swelling persists for several days after each sexual excitation. In such cases we are justified in speaking of a conjunctivitis neurotica.

I have seen several women patients, troubled by many neurotic consequences of the castration complex, in whom this condition of the eyes was associated with a feeling of a fixed stare which they conceived to be an expression of their masculinity. In the unconscious the 'fixed stare' is often equivalent to an erection. I have already alluded to this symptom in an earlier article dealing with neurotic disturbances of the eyes.[2] In some cases the idea exists that the fixed stare will terrorise people. If we pursue the unconscious train of thought of these patients who identify the fixed stare with erection we can then understand the meaning of their anxiety. Just as male exhibitionists among other things seek to terrify women by the sight of the phallus, so these women unconsciously endeavour to attain the same effect by means of their fixed stare.

Some years ago a very neurotic young girl consulted me. The very first thing she did on entering my consulting room was to ask me straight out whether she had beautiful eyes. I was startled for a moment by this very unusual way of introducing oneself to a physician. She noticed my hesitation and then gave vent to a violent outburst of affect on *my* suggestion that she should first of all answer my questions. The whole conduct of the patient, whom I only saw a few times, made a methodical psychoanalysis impossible. I did not succeed even in coming to a clear diagnosis of the case, for certain characteristics of the clinical picture suggested a paranoid condition. Still I was able to obtain a few facts concerning the origin of a most striking symptom, which in spite of their incompleteness offered a certain insight into the structure of the condition.

The patient told me that she had experienced a great fright when a child. In a small town where she then lived a boa constrictor had broken out from a menagerie and could not be found. On passing through a park with her governess she thought the snake suddenly appeared before her. She became quite rigid with terror and ever since had been afraid that she might have a fixed stare.

It could not be decided whether this experience was a real one or whether it was wholly or partially a phantasy. The association, snake=rigidity, is familiar and comprehensible to us. We also recognise the snake as a male genital symbol. Fixity of the eye is then explicable from the identification, fixed eye=snake=phallus. The patient, however, protected herself against this masculinity wish of hers, and its place was taken by the compulsion to get every man to assure her that her eyes were beautiful, i.e. had feminine charms. If anyone hesitated to answer her question in the affirmative we have to assume that she was exposed to the danger of becoming overwhelmed by a male-sadistic impulse which was repressed with difficulty, and so fell into a state of anxiety at the rising tide of her masculinity.

I should like to point out here that these various observations by no means do justice to the great multiplicity of the symptoms belonging to this group. I supplement these examples, which illustrate the vicarious assumption by various parts of the body of the male genital role, by adding that objects which do not belong to the body can also be made use of for the same purpose, provided their form and use permits in any way a genital-symbolical utilisation. We may call to mind the tendency of neurotic women to use a syringe and to give themselves or relatives enemas.

There are numerous points of contact here with the normal expressions of the female castration complex, especially with typical female symptomatic acts. For example, thrusting the end of an umbrella into the ground may be mentioned; the great enjoyment many women obtain from using a hose for watering the garden is also characteristic, for here the unconscious experiences the ideal fulfilment of a childish wish.

Other women are less able or less inclined to find a substitute-gratification of the masculinity wishes in neurotic surrogates. Their symptoms give expression to a completely different attitude. They represent the male organ as something of secondary importance and unnecessary. Here belong all the symptoms and phantasies of *immaculate conception*. It is as though these women want to proclaim through their neurosis: 'I can also do it *alone*'. One of my patients experienced such a conception while in a dreamlike, hazy state of consciousness. She had had a dream once before in which she held a box with a crucifix in her hands; the identification with Mary is here quite clear. I constantly found the anal character traits particularly pronounced in neurotic women who showed these phenomena. In the idea, 'to be able to do it alone', is expressed a high degree of obstinacy which is also prominent in these patients. They wish, for example, to find everything in the psychoanalysis alone, without the help of the physician. They are as a rule women who through obstinacy, envy and self-overestimation destroy all relationships in their environment, even their whole life.

V

The symptoms we have described up to the present bear the character of positive wish-fulfilment in the sense of the infantile desire to be physically equal to the man. The last-mentioned forms of reaction, however, already begin to approximate to the *revenge type*. For in the refusal to acknowledge the significance of the male organ there is expressed, although in a very mitigated form, an emasculation of the man. We therefore arrive quite easily at the phenomena of the second group.

We regularly meet two tendencies in repressed form in these patients: the longing for revenge on the man, and the desire to take by force the longed-for organ, i.e. to rob the man of it.

One of my patients dreamed that she in common with other women carried round a gigantic penis which they had robbed from an animal. This reminds us of the neurotic impulse to steal. The so-called kleptomania is often traceable to the fact that a child feels injured or neglected in respect of proofs of love—which we have equated with gifts—or in some way feels disturbed in the gratification of its libido. It procures a substitute pleasure for the lost pleasure, and at the same time takes revenge on those who have caused it the supposed injury. Psychoanalysis shows that in the unconscious of our patients there exist the same impulses to take forcible possession of the 'gift' which has not been received.

Vaginismus is from a practical point of view the most important of the neurotic symptom serving the repressed phantasies of performing castration on the man. The tendency of vaginismus is not only to prevent intromission of the penis, but also in case of its intromission not to let it escape again, i.e. to retain it and thereby carry out castration on the man. The phantasy therefore culminates in robbing the man of his penis and appropriating it to oneself.

The patient who had produced the previously-mentioned dream of the morphia syringe showed a rare and complicated form of refusal of her husband at the commencement of their marriage. She suffered from an hysterical adduction of her thighs whenever her husband approached her. After this had been overcome in the course of a few weeks a high degree of vaginismus developed as a fresh symptom of refusal; the vaginismus only completely disappeared under psychoanalytic treatment.

The same patient, whose libido was very strongly fixed on her father, once had a short dream previous to her marriage, which she related to me in very remarkable words. She said that in the dream her father had been run over and had thereby 'lost some leg or other and his power'. The castration idea is here not only expressed by means of the 'leg' but also by the 'power'. Being run over is one of the most frequent castration symbols. One of my patients whose 'totem' was a dog dreamed how a dog was run over and lost a leg. The same symbol is found in a phobia that a definite male person may be run over and thereby lose an arm or a leg. One of my patients was the victim of this anxiety with reference to various male members of her family.

For many years and especially during the late war I have come across women who take particular erotic interest in men who have lost an arm or a leg by amputation or accident. These are women with particularly strong feelings of inferiority; their libido prefers a mutilated man rather than one who is physically intact; the mutilated man has also lost a limb. It is obvious that these women feel themselves physically closer to the mutilated man, they consider him a companion in distress and do not need to reject him with hate like the sound man. The interest of some women in Jewish men is explicable on the same grounds; the circumcision is looked upon as at any rate a partial castration, and so makes possible a transference of libido to the man. I know cases in which mixed marriages were contracted by women chiefly as a result of an unconscious motive of this nature. The same interest is also shown in men who are crippled in other ways and have thereby lost the masculine 'superiority'.

It was the psychoanalysis of a girl seventeen years old that gave me the strongest impression of the power of the castration complex. In this case there was an abundance of neurotic conversion phenomena, phobias, and obsessive impulses, all of which were connected with her disappointment at her femininity and with revenge phantasies against the male sex. The patient had been operated on for appendicitis some years previously.[3] The surgeon had given her the removed appendix preserved in a bottle of spirit, and this she now treasured as something sacred. Her ideas of being castrated centred round this specimen, and it also appeared in her dreams with the significance of the once possessed but now lost penis.[4] As the surgeon happened to be a relative of the patient it was easy for her to connect the 'castration' performed by him associatively with her father.

Among the patient's symptoms which rested on the repression of active castration wishes was a phobia which can be called *dread of marriage*. This anxiety was expressed in the strongest opposition to the idea of a future marriage, because the patient was afraid 'that she would have to do something terrible to her future husband'. The most difficult part of the analysis was to uncover an extreme refusal of genital erotism, and an extraordinary accentuation of mouth erotism in the form of phantasies which appeared compulsively. The idea of oral intercourse was firmly united with that of biting off the penis. This phantasy, which is frequently expressed in anxiety and phenomena of the most varied kinds, was in the present case accompanied by a number of other ideas of a terrifying nature. Psychoanalysis succeeded in removing this abundant production of morbid phantasy.

These kinds of anxiety prevent the person from having intimate union with the other sex, and thereby also from carrying out the unconsciously intended 'crime'. The patient is then the only person who has to suffer under those impulses, in the form of permanent abstinence and neurotic anxiety. This assumes a different form as soon as the active castration phantasy has become somewhat distorted and thereby unrecognisable to consciousness. The modified appearance of the phantasies makes possible stronger effects of these tendencies externally. Such a modification of the active castration tendency can take such a form as that the idea of robbing the man of his genital is abolished and the hostile purpose is displaced from the organ to its function; the aim is now to destroy the potency of the man. The wife's neurotic sexual aversion often has a repelling effect on the man's libido so that a disturbance of potency occurs.

A further modification of the aggressive tendency is expressed in an attitude of the woman to the man that is seen fairly frequently and which can be exceedingly painful to him; it is the tendency to *disappoint* the man. Disappointing signifies to excite expectations in a person and not fulfil them. In relations with the man this can occur through response up to a certain point followed by refusal. This behaviour is most frequently and significantly expressed in *frigidity* on the part of the woman. Disappointing other persons is a piece of unconscious tactics which we frequently find in the psychology of the neuroses and is especially pronounced in obsessional neurotics. These neurotics are unconsciously impelled towards violence and revenge, but on account of the contrary play of ambivalent forces these impulses are incapable of effectually breaking through. Because the hostility cannot express itself in actions these patients excite expectations of a pleasant nature in their environment which they do not subsequently fulfil. In the sphere of the female castration complex the tendency to disappoint can be represented in respect to its origin as follows:

First stage: I rob you of what you have because I lack it.
Second stage: I rob you of nothing: I even promise you what I have to give.
Third stage: I do not give you what I have promised.

In very many cases the frigidity is associated with the conscious readiness to assume the female role and acknowledge that of the man. The unconscious striving has in part the object of disappointing the man who is inclined to infer from the conscious readiness of his wife the possibility of mutual enjoyment; while there also exists in the frigid woman the tendency to demonstrate to herself and her partner that his ability signifies nothing.

If we penetrate to the deeper psychic layers we recognise how strongly the desire of the frigid woman to be male dominates in the unconscious. In a previous article I have attempted to demonstrate in conjunction with Freud's well known observations on frigidity[5] that this condition in the female sex is the exact analogue of a disturbance of potency in the man, namely, 'ejaculatio praecox'.[6] In both conditions the libido is attached to that erotogenic zone which has normally a similar significance in the opposite sex. In cases of frigidity the pleasurable sensation is as a rule situated in the clitoris and the vaginal zone has none. The clitoris, however, corresponds developmentally with the penis.

Frigidity is such an exceedingly widespread disturbance that it hardly needs description with examples. On the other hand, it is less well known that the condition appears in varying degrees. The highest degree, that of actual anaesthesia, is rare; in these cases the vaginal mucous membrane has lost all sensitiveness to touch, so that the male organ is not perceived in sexual intercourse, and its existence is therefore actually denied. The common condition is a relative disturbance of sensitivity; contact is perceived but is not pleasurable. In other cases a sensation of pleasure is felt but does not go on to orgasm, or, what is the same thing, the contractions of the female organ corresponding with the acme of pleasure are absent. It is these contractions that signify the complete and positive reaction of the woman to the male activity, the absolute affirmation of the normal relation of the sexes.

Some women desire gratification along normal paths but endeavour to make the act as brief and formal as possible. They refuse all enjoyment of any preliminary pleasure; especially do they behave after gratification as if nothing had happened that could make any impression on them, and turn quickly to some other subject of conversation, a book or occupation. These women thus give themselves up to the full physical function of the woman for a few fleeting moments only to disown it immediately afterwards.

It is an old and well known medical fact that many women only obtain normal sexual sensation after a child has been born. They become, so to speak, only female in the full sense by way of maternal feelings. The deeper connection of this is only to be comprehended by the castration complex. The child was even at an early period the 'gift' which was to compensate for the missed penis. It is now received in reality, and thus the 'wound' is at last healed. It is to be noted that in some women there exists a wish to get a child from a man against his will; we cannot fail to see in this the unconscious tendency to take the penis from the man and appropriate it—in the form of a child. The other extreme belonging to this group is represented by those women who wish to remain childless under all circumstances. They decline any kind of 'substitute', and would be constantly reminded of their femininity in the most disturbing manner if they had children.

A relative frigidity exists not only in the sense of the degree of capability of sensation, but also in the fact that some women are frigid with certain men and sensitive with others.

It will probably be expected that a marked activity on the part of the man is the most favourable condition to call forth sexual sensation in such relatively frigid women. This, however, is not always the case; on the contrary, there are many women in whom a humiliation of the man is just as essential a condition of love as is the humiliation of the woman to many neurotic men.[7] A single example may be given in illustration of this by no means rare attitude. I analysed a woman whose love-life was markedly polyandrous, and who was constantly anaesthetic if she had to acknowledge that the man was superior to her in some way or other. If, however, she had a quarrel with the man and succeeded in forcing him to give in to her, then her frigidity disappeared completely. Such cases show very clearly how necessary acknowledgement of the male genital function is as a condition of a normal love-life on the part of the woman. We here arrive at a source of the conscious and unconscious prostitution of women.

Frigidity is a necessary condition of the behaviour of the prostitute. Full sexual sensation binds the woman to the man, and only where this is lacking does the woman go from man to man, just like the continually ungratified Don Juan type of man who has constantly to change his love-object. The Don Juan avenges himself on all women for the disappointment which happened to him once on the part of the first woman in his life, and the prostitute avenges herself on every man for the gift she had expected from her father and did not receive. Her frigidity signifies a humiliation of all men and therefore a mass castration in the sense of her unconscious; her whole life is given up to this tendency.[8]

While the frigid woman unconsciously strives to diminish the importance of that part of the body denied her, there is another form of refusal of the man which strives for the same aim with the opposite means. In this form of refusal the man is nothing else than a sex organ and therefore consists only of coarse sensuality. Every other mental or physical quality is denied him. The effect is that the neurotic woman imagines that the man is an inferior being on account of his possession of a penis. Her self-respect is thereby enhanced, and she may even be pleased at being free from such inferiority. One of my patients who showed a very marked aversion to men had the obsessing hallucination of a very big penis at the sight of any man and in any situation. This vision brought to her mind again and again that there is nothing else in men than their genital organ, from which she turned away in disgust, but which at the same time represented something that greatly interested her unconscious. Certain phantasies connected with this vision were of a supplementary nature. In these the patient represented herself as though every opening of her body, even the body as a whole, was nothing else than a receptive female organ. The vision therefore contained a mixture of overestimation and depreciation of the male organ.

VI

We have already shown that the tendency to depreciate the importance of the male genital underlies a progressive sexual repression, and often appears outwardly as humiliation of men as a whole. In neurotic women this tendency is often shown by an instinctive avoidance of men who have pronounced masculine characteristics. They direct their love choice towards passive and effeminate men, and by living with them can daily renew the proof that their own activity is superior to the man's. Just like manifest homosexual women they love to represent the mental and physical differences between man and woman as insignificant. One of my patients when six years old had begged her mother to send her to a boy's school in boy's clothes; 'then no one will know that she is a girl'.

Besides the inclination to depreciate men there is also found a marked sensitiveness of the castration complex towards any situation which can awaken a feeling of inferiority, even if only remotely. Women with this attitude refuse to accept any kind of help from a man, and show the greatest disinclination to follow a man's example. A young woman betrayed her claims of masculinity, repressed with difficulty, by declining to walk along a street covered in deep snow behind her husband and make use of his footsteps. A further very significant characteristic of this lady may be mentioned here. When she was almost a child she had had a strong desire for independence, and in adolescence she was very jealous of the occupations of two women in particular: the cashier in her father's office, and the woman who swept the street in her native town. The cause of this attitude is obvious to the psychoanalyst. The cashier sweeps together money, the crossing-sweeper dirt, and both things have the same significance in the unconscious. There is here a marked turning away from genital sexuality in favour of the formation of anal character traits, a process which will be mentioned in another connection.

A characteristic behaviour of some children shows the strength of the disinclination to be reminded of one's own femininity by any impression. In little girls it not infrequently happens that they give up in favour of the stork fable knowledge they have already obtained of procreation and birth. The role bestowed upon them by nature is distinctly unwished-for. The stork tale has the advantage that in it children originate without the man's part being a more privileged one in respect of activity.

The most extreme degree of sensitiveness in the sense of the castration complex is found in certain cases of psychical depression in the female sex. Here the feeling of misfortune on account of their femininity exists wholly unrepressed; these women do not even succeed in working it off in a modified form. One of my patients complained about the complete uselessness of her life because she had been born a girl. She considered the superiority of men in all respects as obvious, and just for this reason felt it so tormentingly. She refused to compete with men in any sphere, and also rejected every feminine performance. In particular she declined the female erotic role, and equally so the male one. In consequence of this attitude all conscious eroticism was entirely strange to her; she even said that she was unable to imagine any erotic pleasure at all. Her resistance against female sexual functions assumed grotesque forms. She transferred her refusal to everything in the world that reminded her, if only remotely, of bearing fruit, propagation, birth, etc. She hated flowers and green trees, and found fruit disgusting. A mistake which she made many times was easily explicable from this attitude; she would read *'furchtbar'* ('frightful') instead of *'fruchtbar'* ('fruitful'). In the whole of nature only the winter in the mountains could give her pleasure; there was here nothing to remind her of living beings and their propagation, but only stones, ice and snow. She had the idea that in marriage the woman was quite of secondary importance, and an expression of hers clearly showed that this idea was based on the castration complex. She said that the ring—which was to her a hated female symbol—was not fit to be a symbol of marriage, and she suggested a nail as a substitute. The over-emphasis of masculinity here evidently developed from the penis envy of the little girl which appeared strikingly undisguised in the patient's adult age.

In many women the incapability of reconciling themselves to the lack of the male organ is expressed in neurotic horror at the sight of wounds. Every wound re-awakens in their unconscious the idea of the 'wound' received in childhood. Sometimes a definite feeling of anxiety occurs at the sight of wounds, and sometimes this sight or the mere idea of it causes a 'painful feeling in the lower part of the body'. The patient whom I mentioned above as having a complicated form of vaginismus spoke of her horror of wounds at the commencement of the psychoanalysis and before there had been any mention of the castration complex. She said that she could look at large and irregular wounds without being particularly affected. On the other hand, she could not bear to see a very small and somewhat open cut in her skin or on another person if the red colour of the flesh was visible in the depth of the cut; this gave her an intense pain in the genital region coupled with marked anxiety, 'as though something had been cut away there'. Similar sensations accompanied by anxiety are found in men with marked fear of castration. In many women it does not need the sight of a wound to cause phenomena of the kind described, but they also have an aversion, associated with marked affects, to the idea of surgical operations, even to knives. Some time ago a lady who was a stranger to me and who would not give her name rang me up on the telephone and asked me if I could prevent an operation that had been arranged for the next day. On my request for more information she told me she was to be operated on for a severe uterine haemorrhage due to myomata. When I told her it was not part of my work to prevent a necessary and perhaps life-saving operation she did not reply, but explained with affective volubility that she had always been 'hostile to all operations', adding, 'whoever is once operated on is for ever afterwards a cripple for life'. The senselessness of this exaggeration is comprehensible if we remember that that operation carried out in phantasy in early childhood makes the girl a 'cripple'.

VII

A tendency with which we are well acquainted and which has already been mentioned leads in the sphere of the female castration complex to modifications of the aversion, to conditional admission of that which is tabooed, and to compromise formations between impulse and repression.

In some of our patients we come across phantasies which refer to the possibility of a recognition of the man and to the formulation of conditions under which the patient, after their fulfilment, would be prepared to reconcile herself to her femininity. I mention first of all a condition I have met with many times; it runs: 'I could be content with my femininity if I were absolutely the most beautiful of all women'. All men would lie at the feet of the most beautiful woman, and the female narcissism would consider this power not a bad compensation for the defect so painfully perceived. It is in fact easier for a beautiful woman to assuage her castration complex than for an ugly one. However, the idea of being the most beautiful of all women does not have this effect in all cases. We are well acquainted with the expression of a woman, 'I should like to be the most beautiful of all women so that all men would adore me; then I would show them the cold shoulder'. In this case the craving for revenge is quite clear; this remark was made by a woman of an extremely tyrannical nature which was based on a wholly unsublimated castration complex.

However, the majority of women are less blunt, they are inclined to compromise and to satisfy themselves with relatively harmless expressions of their repressed hostility. In this connection we can understand a characteristic trait in the conduct of many women. Let us keep in view the fact that sexual activity is essentially associated with the male organ, that the woman is only in the position to excite the man's libido or respond to it, and that otherwise she is compelled to adopt a waiting attitude. In a great number of women we find resistance against being a woman displaced to this necessity of waiting. In marriage these women take a logical revenge upon the man in that they *keep him waiting* on all occasions in daily life.

There is another condition related to the above mentioned 'If I were the most beautiful woman'. In some women we find readiness to admit the male activity and their own passivity connected with the idea that the most manly (greatest, most important) man should come and desire them. We have no difficulty in recognising here the infantile desire for the father. I have previously mentioned an example of a phantastic form of this idea from one of my psychoanalyses. I was able to follow the development of a similar phantasy through different stages in the psychoanalysis of another patient. The original desire ran: 'I should like to be a man'. When this was given up, the patient wished to be 'the only woman' (at first 'the only woman of the father' was meant). When also this wish had to give way to reality the idea appeared: 'As a woman I should like to be unique.'

Certain compromise formations are of far greater practical importance, and though well known to psychoanalysts nevertheless merit special consideration in this connection. They concern the acknowledgement of the man, or to be more correct, his activity and the organ serving it, combined with definite limitations. Sexual relations with the man are endured, even wished-for, so long as the woman's own genital organ is avoided, or is, so to speak, considered to be non-existent. A displacement of libido to other erotogenic zones (mouth, anus) takes place, and a mitigation of feelings of discomfort originating in the castration complex is associated with this turning away of sexual interest from the genital organ. The body openings which are now at the disposal of the libido are not specifically female organs! Further determinants are found in the analysis of each of this kind of cases; one only need be mentioned, namely, the possibility of active castration through biting by means of the mouth. Oral and anal perversions in women are therefore to a considerable extent explicable in the light of the castration complex.

Among our patients we certainly have to deal more frequently with the negative counterpart of the perversions, i.e. with conversion symptoms which occur in relation to the specific erotogenic zones, than with the perversions themselves. Examples of this kind have already been mentioned above. I referred among other cases to that of a young girl who had the phobia of having to do something horrible to her husband in the event of her marriage. The 'horrible thing' turned out to be the idea of castration through biting. The case showed most clearly how displacement of the libido from the genital to the mouth zone gratifies very different tendencies simultaneously. In these phantasies the mouth serves equally for the desired reception of the male organ and for its destruction. Such experiences warn us not to be too ready to overestimate a single determinant. Although in the preceding presentation we have estimated the castration complex to be an important impelling force in the development of neurotic phenomena, we are not justified in over-valuing it in the way Adler has done when he one-sidedly represents the 'masculine protest' as an essential causa movens of the neuroses. Experience that is definite and is verified every day shows us that neurotics of both sexes who loudly proclaim and lay emphasis on the masculine tendency frequently conceal—though only superficially—intense female-passive desires. Psychoanalysis should constantly remind us of the over-determination of all psychical ideas; it has to reject as one-sided and fragmentary every psychological method of working which does not take into full account the influence of various factors on one another. In the present work I have collected material belonging to the castration complex from a great number of psychoanalyses. I expressly mention here that it is solely for reasons of clearness that I have only occasionally mentioned the expressions of the female-passive impulses which were lacking in none of my patients.

VIII

Women whose ideas and feelings are influenced and governed by the castration complex to an important degree—no matter whether consciously or unconsciously—*transplant the effect of this complex on to their children.* These women may influence the psychosexual development of their *daughters* either by speaking disparagingly of female sexuality to them, or by unconsciously giving them indications of their aversion to the man. The latter method is the more permanently effective one, because it tends to undermine the heterosexuality of the growing-up girl. On the other hand, the direct method of depreciation can evoke real effects of a shock, for instance, if a mother says to her daughter who is about to marry, 'What is coming now is disgusting'.

There are in particular those neurotic women whose libido has been displaced from the genital to the anal zone and who give expression to their disgust of the male body in this or similar manner. These women produce serious effects on their *sons* without foreseeing the result of their attitude. A mother with this kind of aversion to the male sex injures the narcissism of the boy. A boy in his early years is proud of his genital organs, he likes to exhibit them to his mother and expects her to admire them. He soon sees that his mother ostentatiously looks the other way, even if she does not give expression to her disinclination in words. These women are especially given to prohibiting masturbation on the grounds that it is disgusting for him to touch his genital organ. Whereas touching and even mentioning the penis is most carefully avoided by these women they tend to caress the child's buttocks, and cannot speak enough of the 'bottom', often getting the child to repeat this word; they also take an excessive interest in the child's defecatory acts. The boy is thus forced to an altered orientation of his libido. Either it is transferred from the genital to the anal zone, or the boy is impelled towards his own sex, his father in the first instance, and feels himself bound to his father by a bond which is quite comprehensible to us; at the same time he becomes a woman-hater, and later will be constantly ready to make very severe criticisms of the weaknesses of the female sex. This chronic influence of the mother's castration complex seems to me to be a cause of the castration fear in boys of greater importance than occasionally uttered threats of castration. I can produce abundant proofs of this view from my psychoanalyses of male neurotics. The mother's anal-erotism is the earliest and most dangerous enemy of the psychosexual development of children, the more so because the mother has more influence on them in the earliest years of life than the father.

To everyone of us who are practising psychoanalysts the question occurs at times whether the trifling number of individuals to whom we can give assistance justifies the great expenditure of time, labour and patience. The answer to this question is contained in the above exposition: If we succeed in freeing such a person from the defects of her psychosexuality, i.e. from the burdens of her castration complex, then we obviate the neuroses of children to a great extent, and thus help the coming generation. Our psychoanalytic activity is a quiet and little recognised work, and for this reason all the more attacked, but its effect on and beyond the individual seems to us an aim worthy of much labour.

Notes

[1] The character trait of envy is treated more in detail in an article by the author to appear shortly, 'Contributions to the Theory of the Anal Character' (1921), *Selected Papers of Karl Abraham* (London: Hogarth Press, 1927), 370-92.

[2] See 'Restrictions and Transformations of Scoptophilia in Psycho-Neurotics; with Remarks on Analogous Phenomena in Folk Psychology' (1914), *Selected Papers*, 169-234.

[3] The removal of the vermiform appendix in men also often stimulates their castration complex.

4 Another patient imagined she had a brother and had to remove his appendix.
5 *Three Essays on the Theory of Sexuality* (1905d), SE 7:221ff.
6 'Ejaculatio Praecox' (1917), *Selected Papers*, 280-98.
7 See Sigmund Freud, 'A Special Type of Choice of Object Made by Men' (1910h) and 'On the Universal Tendency to Debasement in the Sphere of Love' (1912d) (Contributions to the Psychology of Love I and II), SE 11:163-75 and 177-90.
8 The remarks of Dr. Theodor Reik in a discussion at the Berlin Psycho-Analytical Society have suggested this idea to me.

4

Origins and Growth of Object Love

Karl Abraham (1924)

Part 2 of 'A Short Study of the Development of the Libido', *Selected Papers of Karl Abraham*. London: Hogarth Press, 1927, pp 480-501.

This clinical piece by Abraham is the second part of his 1924 study, 'A Short Study of the Development of the Libido', which focuses on the psychosexual pathology of the narcissistic neuroses. While the first part is confined to the theory of the pregenital levels of the libido, the second part traces the development of the relation of individuals to their love objects.

Though it may appear that the detailed clinical observations related here are sometimes beside the point of femininity, they do however give a clear picture of the various manifestations of the castration complex. This actually leads Abraham to trace the genesis of penis envy to an oral fixation, a point Stärcke, in the paper included in this collection, had developed on the basis of an earlier piece by Abraham. Moreover, Abraham's observations on identification anticipate Freud's distinction between primary and secondary identification. In point of fact, if there is one article which is central to the controversy on female sexuality, this is the one: since all contributors either quote it or discuss it, and do so not only because of the frequently cited table surveying psychosexual development which is discussed in the conclusion.

* * *

In the first part of this study I have attempted to throw light on the psychology of certain pathological states of mind and to add something to our knowledge of the sexual life of the individual. But in doing this I have confined myself to the theory of the pregenital levels of the libido. That part of sexual theory deals with the transformations which the individual undergoes in regard to his sexual aim during the course of his psychosexual development. Since Freud's classical work on this subject[1] we are accustomed to distinguish the sexual *aims* of the individual from those processes which concern his relations to his sexual *object*. What we have so far said about the ontogenesis of object love does not sufficiently cover the field of facts. This is especially so in those pathological states which, in accordance with Freud, we group together under the name of the 'narcissistic neuroses'. In analysing them we meet with a number of psychosexual phenomena which our theory must take account of. And I propose in the following section to attempt to do this.

In thus tracing separately the development of the relation of the individual to his love-object we shall not overlook the close and manifold psychological connections which exist between it and the subject of our earlier investigations. Those connections will, on the contrary, become much more evident in this way than before. And just as in the previous section we were led to discuss at some length certain important aspects of object-relations, such, for instance, as ambivalence in man's instinctual life, so now there can be no question of treating particular subjects as isolated problems. And indeed we shall most easily be able to see in what respects the history of the development of object-love requires amplification if we begin by giving a short summary of the theory of the stages of libidinal organization.

We have recognized the presence of two different pleasurable tendencies in the anal-sadistic phase: a more primitive one of expelling the object (evacuation) and destroying it, and a later one of retaining and controlling it. Thus we have been led on empirical grounds to believe that there is a differentiation within the anal-sadistic phase which before had been supposed to be homogeneous. We have come to the conclusion that the melancholic patient regresses to the lower level of that phase but does not make a halt there. His libido tends towards a still earlier phase—the cannibalistic phase—in which his instinctual aim is to incorporate the object in himself. In his unconscious he identifies the love-object he has lost and abandoned with the most important product of bodily evacuation—with his faeces—and reincorporates it in his ego by means of the process we have called introjection. But he cannot, even by regressing so far, escape from the conflict of his ambivalent feelings. That conflict, on the contrary, increases in strength, until there begins to arise in him a tendency to regress to a still more primitive stage of libidinal development whose sexual aim is that of sucking. This stage we have considered as *pre-ambivalent*. Thus we have been led to distinguish two levels in the oral phase as well as in the anal one. Finally we have been able to observe a similar differentiation within the later, genital phase. And it is only the most recent of those two levels that we have been able to regard as free from ambivalence, or *post-ambivalent*.

By assuming that each of the three main phases of the libido is differentiated into two stages we have been able, so far at least, to account satisfactorily for the observed facts concerning the changes undergone by the individual in regard to his sexual aim. And we have also been able to find a more definite genetic connection between certain kinds of illness and certain levels of the libido than has hitherto been possible. But we will not try to conceal the very considerable gaps that still exist in our knowledge in this respect. For instance, we have up till now not succeeded in finding a connection of this sort for paranoic conditions. This is a point to which we shall return later

Up till now much less has been known about the development of object-love. Just as we have hitherto been accustomed to distinguish three phases in the development of the libido, so we have recognized three phases in the relationship of the individual to his object. And here once more it is to Freud that we owe the first discoveries of importance. He grouped the development of that relationship into an auto-erotic phase belonging to earliest infancy in which the individual has no object, a narcissistic phase in which the individual is his own love-object, and a phase in which there is object-love in the true sense of the word. In the following discussion I shall try to show how far we are able to add new knowledge to this part of our sexual theory.

The new contributions which I hope to be able to make are derived from a particular field of psychoanalytic empiricism, namely, from the study of the 'narcissistic neuroses' and of certain neuroses belonging to those levels of object-love which are closely related to the narcissistic neuroses in a certain respect

The manic-depressive cases whose analysis formed the groundwork of the first part of this study are of considerable assistance in helping us to solve our present problem also. At the time that I was analysing those cases it happened that I was also having two female patients under long treatment of whose neurotic condition I should like to give a brief account in these pages. The clinical picture they presented was quite different from melancholia, but it will soon become evident why I have placed them side by side with the latter.

The first of these patients, whom I shall call X, presented a very complicated clinical picture, and I shall only reproduce the most outstanding features of it. Foremost of these was a marked *pseudologia phantastica* dating back to her sixth year. Besides this, she had severe impulses of kleptomania going back to the same time. And lastly, she suffered from attacks of despair which could be occasioned by the slightest thing and which found utterance in uncontrollable fits of weeping of many hours' duration. This compulsive weeping had two main determinants. It was, in the first place, derived from her castration complex, and represented the loss of her masculinity with all that this involved, such as envy of her more favoured younger brother, and so on. During menstruation, which used to excite her castration complex in a typical way, she scarcely ever stopped crying.[2] The second determinant of her crying fits was connected with her relation to her father whose loss she was mourning, not in a real sense because he was dead, but in a psychological one. It was in connection with this psychological loss of him that the earliest symptoms of her neurosis had appeared. As a child she had early developed an especially strong transference love towards her father, but, as her analysis showed, it had suffered a sudden check in the first half of her sixth year. At that time she had been convalescing from an illness and had shared her parents' bedroom. There she had had an opportunity of seeing her mother and father having sexual intercourse, and of observing her father's body. This increased her scopophilic tendencies greatly, until they were overtaken by an intense repression. I should like to mention one especial consequence which those experiences had in her case in addition to those familiar to all analysts. This was that she complained of having lost all emotional contact with her father, and indeed of being unable to form any kind of mental image of him. She was conscious neither of affectionate feelings nor of sensual ones towards him. But we were able to infer from a quantity of neurotic material that she had a quite specialized compulsive interest in one particular part of his body, namely, his penis. He had ceased to exist for her as a whole person; only one part of him had remained, and this formed the object of her compulsive looking.[3] Besides this, she unconsciously identified herself now with him, now with his genitals, which had become for her his representative Her kleptomanic impulses were in a great measure derived from her active castration tendency directed against her father. The unconscious aim of her thefts was to rob him of his envied possession so as to have it herself or to identify herself with it. That those thefts were connected with the person of her father was made evident in many ways. For instance, she had on one occasion taken an enema tube out of his room and had used it—as a substitute for his male member—for anal-erotic purposes. She used to 'castrate' him in other ways, by taking money [*Vermögen*][4] out of his purse, and by stealing his pens, pencils, and other male symbols, as is so common in cases of kleptomania.

The patient's castration complex also proved to be an important motive of her *pseudologia*. Just as her kleptomanic impulses expressed the idea, 'I seize by force or fraud what has been withheld from me or taken away from me', we might formulate one of the main determinants of her lying in this way: 'I do possess that desired part of the body, and so I am equal to my father.' It is particularly interesting to learn from the patient that telling these imaginary facts gave her strong sexual excitement and a sensation as if something was growing and swelling out of her abdomen. This sensation was connected with a feeling of physical strength and activity; and in the same way the act of lying made her feel mentally powerful and superior to others.

Her relation to her father, as I have roughly sketched it, was in keeping with her attitude to the rest of her environment. She had no real mental contact whatever with anyone. Telling lies had for many years represented for her her sole mental relation with the external world.

As we have said, she had arrived at this position, so far removed from a regular and complete object-love, through a regression from such an object-love. She did nevertheless maintain some kind of relation to her objects, and she clung to them with the utmost tenacity. Further analysis of her kleptomania, together with analysis of one or two other cases, threw light on the nature of her peculiar and incomplete form of object-love. Her dreams and day-dreams contained ever recurring images of castration by means of biting. The aim of her phantasies was not to incorporate her love-object as a whole but to bite off and swallow a part of it and then to identify herself with the part. Such a partial incorporation of the object seems to occur in other cases of kleptomania as well. I will give another example.

A female patient whom I shall call Y was suffering from a grave neurosis whose most marked symptom was severe hysterical vomiting. In addition she exhibited very strong kleptomanic tendencies which in her case too were found to be determined by her castration complex. Her habit of stealing had grown up around an incorrigible inclination she had had in childhood to pull everything out with her hands, especially flowers and hair. But this impulse was itself a modification of a desire to bite off everything that 'stuck out'. Even when she was grown up she had phantasies of this kind. As soon as she got to know a man she had a compulsive idea of biting off his penis. Her neurotic vomiting was closely related to these oral-sadistic impulses. In her case, too, her father had lost all value for her as a person. Her libidinal interest was focused on his penis alone. And when he had died she too had been unable to feel any sorrow. But she had had a vivid phantasy of stealing his penis by biting it off, and of keeping it. In her day-dreams she used to have a great many phantasies of copulating with a penis 'without any man belonging to it'.

Another similarity between these two patients was that in each case the mother also was represented by only one part of her body, namely, her breasts. They had obviously been identified in the child's mind with the supposed penis of the female. She was alternatively represented by her buttocks, which in their turn stood for her breasts. The relation of this image to oral erotism (pleasure in biting) was more than evident, and could be supported by many examples, one of which I shall give. X once dreamed as follows: 'I was eating away at a piece of meat, tearing it with my teeth. At last I swallowed it. Suddenly I noticed that the piece of meat was the back part of a fur coat belonging to Frau N.'

It is not difficult to understand the 'back part' as a displacement from before backwards. In the same way we can understand the frequent symbolic use made of fur as an allusion to the female genital. Frau N.'s surname was in fact the name of an animal, and of an animal which frequently symbolized her mother in this patient's dreams.

'Displacement backwards' was a process that constantly occurred in the mental images of both patients. Both had a feeling of disgust at their mother, and in their phantasies and certain symptoms both likened her to the essence of all that is most disgusting, namely, excrement. Thus the mother was represented in imagination by a piece of the body that had left it, i.e. a penis, and faeces.

In both cases the libido had undergone a considerable degree of narcissistic regression, though by no means a complete one. What had happened was that—until analysis set this right—its capacity for object-love had been imperfectly developed in a certain respect or had regressed to a stage of imperfect development. The stage in question must have lain somewhere between narcissism and object-love. Another fact which was to be noticed about both cases, and which I later on observed in other persons, pointed in the same direction. This was that the libido was in an unmistakable state of ambivalence towards its object and showed a strong tendency to inflict injuries on it. Nevertheless, that destructive tendency had already been subjected to limitations. At this stage the sexual aim of the individual must have been to deprive his object of a part of its body, i.e. to attack its integrity without destroying its existence. We are put in mind of a child which catches a fly and, having pulled off a leg, lets it go again. We must once more emphasize the fact that the pleasure in biting is very markedly associated with this form of object-relation which had hitherto escaped our notice.

I have been able to ascertain the presence of similar psychological processes in the two manic-depressive patients about whom I have spoken in greater detail in the first part of this study. But the really valuable evidence for this only appeared when their gravest symptoms were beginning to pass off. So long as these were present the cannibalistic destructive tendencies of the libido manifested themselves in many ways. During the period of recovery one of the patients used very often to have a phantasy of biting off the nose, or the lobe of the ear or the breast, of a young girl whom he was very fond of. At other times he used to play with the idea of biting off his father's finger. And once, when he believed that I was not going to continue his analysis, he all of a sudden had the same thought about me. This idea of biting off a finger was found to have a great number of determinants besides its obvious significance of castration. What chiefly interests us here is the ambivalence expressed in the phantasy. For although in it the patient's physician—as the substitute of his father—was to be maimed by having a piece of his body bitten off, we must not see the hostile side of the phantasy only and overlook its friendly tendency which was expressed in the patient's desire to spare the existence of the object except for one part, and again in his desire to keep that part as his own property for ever. We may thus speak of an impulse of *partial incorporation* of the object. The patient just referred to once said that he would like to 'eat up' the young girl in question (whom he identified with his mother) 'mouthful by mouthful'. And the following incident will show how greatly occupied his mind was in this stage of his analysis with the idea of biting off things. On one occasion he was speaking about a man under whom he was working who represented both his father and his mother in his unconscious and towards whom he had an extremely ambivalent attitude. As often happened with him his free associations flowed over into phantasies of a markedly concrete kind, which would at times be interrupted by an affective 'blocking'. A 'blocking' of this nature occurred as he was speaking about his superior. In accounting for that stoppage in his associations he said, 'Now [i.e. in the phantasied situation] I must first tear out his beard with my teeth; I can't get any further till I've done that.' The patient was thus himself saying that there was no possible way of avoiding the intrusion of those phantasies which belonged unmistakably to the class of partial cannibalism.

Complete and unrestricted cannibalism is only possible on the basis of unrestricted narcissism. On such a level all that the individual considers is his own desire for pleasure. He pays no attention whatever to the interests of his object, and destroys that object without the least hesitation.[5] On the level of partial cannibalism we can still detect the signs of its descent from total cannibalism, yet nevertheless the distinction between the two is sharply marked. On that later level the individual shows the first signs of having some care for his object. We may also regard such a care, incomplete as it is, as the first beginnings of object-love in a stricter sense, since it implies that the individual has begun to conquer his narcissism. But we must add that on this level of development the individual is far from recognizing the existence of another individual as such and from 'loving' him in his entirety, whether in a physical or a mental way. His desire is still directed towards removing a part of the body of his object and incorporating it. This, on the other hand, implies that he has resigned the purely narcissistic aim of practising complete cannibalism.

Now that we have become alive to certain occurrences relating to infantile development, there will not be wanting confirmatory evidence obtained from the direct observation of the child. Our inquiries have, moreover, led us a certain distance forward into unknown country, and we are glad to come upon some traces of earlier exploration. Several years ago two psychoanalysts, whose reliability as observers is not open to question, have each independently added to our knowledge of the psychology of paranoic delusions of persecution. Both van Ophuijsen[6] and Stärcke[7] discovered during the course of their psychoanalytic practice that in paranoia the 'persecutor' can be traced back to the patient's unconscious image of the faeces in his intestines which he identifies with the penis of the 'persecutor', i.e. the person of his own sex whom he originally loved. Thus in paranoia the patient represents his persecutor by a part of his body, and believes that he is carrying it within himself. He would like to get rid of that foreign body but cannot.

I must admit that I did not at the time recognize the full importance of van Ophuijsen's and Stärcke's discovery. It was an isolated one, and did not fit easily into the general body of known facts, although the relations between paranoia and anal-erotism had already been recognized by Ferenczi. Now, however, it finds its place in a wider scheme and is thus seen to possess a very great significance.

When the paranoiac has lost his libidinal relations to his object and to all objects in general, he tries as far as he can to compensate for the loss which to him amounts to a destruction of the world. As we know since Freud's analysis of the case of Schreber, he proceeds to reconstruct his lost object. We may now add that in this process of reconstruction the paranoiac incorporates a part of his object. In doing this he undergoes much the same fate as the melancholiac who has introjected the whole of his object by a process of incorporation. Nor can he, either, escape his ambivalence in this way. Like the melancholiac, therefore, he tries to get rid of that part of his object which he has taken into himself. And on the psychosexual developmental level on which he is this can only be an anal process for him. To a paranoiac, therefore, the love-object is equivalent to faeces which he cannot get rid of. The introjected part of his love-object will not leave him, just as in the case of the melancholiac the object, which has been introjected *in toto*, continues to exercise its despotic power from within.

We have thus come to the conclusion that the melancholiac incorporates his abandoned love-object as a whole, whereas the paranoiac only introjects a part of his. In the latter case there is another alternative to be considered, namely, that this partial introjection need not be effected in an oral way but can be thought of as an anal process. Pending a more complete understanding of the situation we may put forward the view— though with all due hesitation—that in respect of its sexual aim the libido of the paranoiac regresses to the earlier of the two sadistic-anal stages, while in respect of its attitude towards its object it goes back to the stage of partial introjection. Whether that introjection takes place in an oral or an anal way must be left an open question. We meet with a similar state of affairs in melancholiacs during their period of convalescence. Nor can we as yet say why it is that in the latter case regular paranoic delusions are not formed. This difference may be due to the different effects of introjection according as it is total or partial in its extent, and oral or anal in its means. We shall have no certainty on this subject until we know more about the part played by the ego in those two forms of illness.

Another point to be noted in regard to the part of the body that has been introjected is that the penis is regularly assimilated to the female breast, and that other parts of the body, such as the finger, the foot, hair, faeces, and buttocks, can be made to stand for those two organs in a secondary way, as has already been shown.[8] If we suppose that there is such a stage of 'partial love' as we have depicted in the development of object-love, further facts are opened to us and we begin to understand a certain peculiarity of sexual perversions to which Sachs has recently drawn our attention once again:[9] I refer to the pervert's concentration of interest on certain bodily parts of his object, the choice of which often seems very curious to us. This peculiarity is most strikingly exhibited in the fetishist. To him the whole person is often only an accidental appendage to one particular part of his body which alone exercises an irresistible attraction over him. Many years ago, as I was attempting for the first time to investigate a case of foot and corset fetishism[10] by means of psychoanalysis, Freud suggested to me that I should introduce the idea of a partial repression so as to account for the phenomena in question. In the light of our present knowledge this psychological process, by means of which the greater part of the object is reduced to insignificance and excessive value is attached to the remaining part, is seen to be the consequence of a regression of the libido to this supposed stage of 'partial love'; and it ceases to be an isolated event found in a certain kind of illness, and falls into place among a large number of allied psychological phenomena. It is not the intention of this study to go more deeply into the symptoms of fetishism. But it may be useful to point out that those parts of the body on which the fetishist tends to concentrate his inclinations are the same as those we meet with as the objects of 'partial love'.

Our clinical observations have long since made us acquainted with a stage in the development of object-love in which the individual already spares his object in a great measure; and we meet with it again in the neuroses as a regressive phenomenon belonging to the sexual life of obsessional patients. In this stage the individual is not yet able to love anyone in the full sense of the word. His libido is still attached to a part of its object. But he has given up his tendency to incorporate that part. Instead, he desires to rule and possess it. Distant as the libido still is at this stage from the ultimate goal of its development, it has yet made an important step forward in so far as such a proprietorship is, as it were, *exteriorized*. Property no longer means that which the individual has incorporated by devouring. It is situated outside his body now. In this way its existence is recognized and safeguarded. This implies that the individual has accomplished an important piece of adaptation to the external world. Such a change has the greatest practical significance in a social sense. It makes possible for the first time joint ownership of an object; whereas the method of devouring the object could only secure it for one person alone.

This position of the libido in respect of its object has left traces in the forms of speech of various languages, as in the German word *besitzen*,[11] for instance, and in the Latin *possidere*. A person is thought of as *sitting on* his property, and thus as still keeping in close contact with it. This attitude can easily be observed in children. We often notice how a child will take an object that is specially dear to him to bed with him at night and will lie on top of it. In animals, too, and especially in dogs, the same thing can be seen They will endeavour to place an object in security by covering it with their bodies. I have noticed this in my own dog. As soon as a stranger came to stay in the house he would fetch his muzzle—an object, that is, that belonged exclusively to him—and would lie down upon it.[12]

Further psychoanalytic study of the obsessional neuroses will, no doubt, furnish us with more information concerning this stage of object-love. The especially intense nature of active and passive castration images in obsessional patients and their peculiar attitude to questions of possession make it seem very probable that there is a connection between that illness and the stage of partial love.

Psychoanalysis has taught us that the unconscious of the adult person contains many traces of the earlier stages of his psychosexual life. In the healthy person we come across such traces chiefly in his dreams. In the same way the stage of partial love leaves traces behind in the unconscious.

An example of this is seen in the familiar dreams about a tooth dropping out. Every analyst is aware of the manifold symbolic meaning of such a dream. The tooth that drops out symbolizes on the one hand castration, and on the other some person whom the dreamer knows and whose death he desires in the dream. Thus a near friend or relative is made equivalent to a part of the body which has to be expelled. We see at once the resemblance with the psychology of delusions of persecution. We should particularly note the ambivalence of the subject's feelings which is manifested in his identification of a person with a part of his own body. To compare another person with a part of one's own body which is the object of a specially high narcissistic estimation is without doubt a proof of exceptional love. In German we often call a loved person 'my heart' (*mein Herz*); and we say of a mother that she loves her child as the 'apple of her eye'. When a man likens someone to his tooth, as so often occurs in dreams, it is as much as to say that although he is loath to lose a part of himself he nevertheless can do without it since he possesses plenty more. Indeed, the dreamer often observes that the loss of his tooth or its extraction is quite painless; from which it may be inferred that the loss of that person would not be so very painful to him after all. Furthermore, we must not forget that underlying symbolic castration there is an unconscious wish for the loss of that part of the body upon which the narcissism of man is as a rule centred. The hostile significance of the comparison, however, is most clearly seen where the part employed as the equivalent of the person is excrement.

Thus it is clear that the stage of partial love has left traces behind it even in the mind of the healthy person. He represents the love-object that is cathected with his ambivalent feelings by a single part of its body, which he has introjected into his own.

As my two female patients, X and Y, whose case I have described, gradually approached a normal condition of object-love under the influence of psychoanalysis, they passed through a stage of development that seemed to be the next modification of the stage we have been discussing. As will be remembered, the patient X had been dominated by an idea which had constantly recurred in varying forms in her dreams and phantasies, and which was concerned with the acquisition of her father's penis; and we recollect that she had identified the whole of herself with that part of his body. At a certain point in her recovery, when she had pretty well overcome her kleptomanic impulses and her *pseudologia*, her phantasies took another form. As a particularly clear example of this later form, I may mention a dream she had in which she saw her father's body and noticed the absence of the pubic hair (a part of his body which had always stood for his genitals in a number of earlier dreams). Now, therefore, she was dreaming of her father as an entire person *except* for one part of his body. We are struck by the contrast between this and certain expressions of her neurosis that have been mentioned earlier. Before, when she had had a compulsion to stare at her father's genitals, her love interest had been turned away from all the rest of him. Now she was repressing what had then exercised a compulsive power in her consciousness.

I have come across dreams like the one above in other people. One patient, a woman, who had a strongly ambivalent attitude towards me, expressed her transference in a dream in which she represented me without any genitals. The hostile tendency—the desire to castrate her object— is obvious. But the dream had another determinant, which was to be found in her likening me to her father whom she was allowed to love but not to desire in a genital sense. She could only love her analyst, as her father's substitute, so long as the genital aspect was excluded. And the dream censorship took means accordingly to prevent her from overstepping the incest barrier.

Such a positive erotic attitude towards the object, but with the exclusion of the genitals, seems to be a typically hysterical expression of the incest prohibition. As early as in the first edition of his *Three Essays on the Theory of Sexuality*, Freud pointed out that hysterics reject the normal, genital sexual aim, and put in its place other, 'perverse' aims. We shall remain in agreement with his view in proposing to set up a stage of object-love with the exclusion of the genitals.[13] The rejection of the genital zone applies to the subject's own body as well as to that of his object. This situation is to a great extent responsible for two very general and, from a practical point of view, important symptoms—impotence in men and frigidity in women. In it the individual cannot love his object completely because of the presence of its genitals.

We know from the psychoanalysis of neurotics that such an inhibition of the libido in both sexes proceeds from the castration complex. In the man, anxiety about his own male organ and horror at the absence of any such organ in the female bring about the same result as is effected in the woman by her still unmastered pain at having been deprived of her genitals and by her castration desires directed against the male. We must not forget, too, that the genitals are more intensely cathected by narcissistic love than any other part of the subject's own body. Thus everything else in the object can be loved sooner than the genitals. On the level of the 'phallic' organization of the libido, as Freud calls it, the last great step in its development has obviously not yet been made. It is not made until the highest level of the libido–that which alone should be called the genital level–is attained. Thus we see that the attainment of the highest level of the organization of the libido goes hand in hand with the final step in the evolution of object-love.

The table appended below is intended to facilitate a survey of the various stages of sexual organization and of object-love which the individual traverses. I should like to make it quite clear that it is of a purely provisional nature and that it by no means implies that those stages are only six in number. We can compare it to a timetable of express trains in which only the larger stations at which they stop are given. The halting places that lie between cannot be marked in a summary of this kind. I should also like to say that the stages placed on the same horizontal level in each column do not necessarily coincide in time.

Stages of Libidinal Organization.	Stages of Object-love.	
VI. Final Genital Stage	Object-love	(Post-ambivalent)
V. Earlier Genital Stage (phallic)	Object-love with exclusion of genitals	
IV. Later Anal-sadistic Stage	Partial love	(Ambivalent)
III. Earlier Anal-sadistic Stage	Partial love with incorporation	
II. Later Oral Stage (cannibalistic)	Narcissism (total incorporation of object)	
I. Earlier Oral Stage (sucking)	Auto-erotism (wthout object)	(Pre-ambivalent)

The table gives a brief survey of the psychosexual development of man in two respects. It considers the movement of his libido in respect of his sexual aim and of his sexual object. Among other important phenomena belonging to this process of development there is one in especial that I have omitted to deal with, and that is the formation of the inhibitions of the instincts. I should therefore like to add a few short remarks on this subject.

We regard the earliest, auto-erotic stage of the individual as being still exempt from instinctual inhibitions, in accordance with the absence of any real object relations. In the stage of narcissism with a cannibalistic sexual aim the first evidence of an instinctual inhibition appears in the shape of morbid anxiety. The process of overcoming the cannibalistic impulses is intimately associated with a sense of guilt which comes into the foreground as a typical inhibitory phenomenon belonging to the third stage. The third stage, whose sexual aim is the incorporating of a part of the object, is left behind when feelings of pity and disgust arise in the individual and cut off this form of libidinal activity. In the next stage–that of object-love with the exclusion of the genitals–inhibition takes the form of feelings of shame. Finally, in the stage of real object-love we find social feelings of a superior kind regulating the instinctual life of the individual. This brief and generalized outline will serve to show that a further inquiry is needed into the origin of the inhibitions of the libido, but that psychoanalysis can doubtless give us the key to the solution of this problem as well.

I should only like to say a few more words about one event in that complicated process. In the stage of 'partial love with incorporation', as we have seen, the love-object is represented by one part of itself. The small child has an ambivalent attitude towards that part (penis, breast, excrement, etc.); that is, he desires it and rejects it at the same time. It is not until he has completely given up his tendency to incorporate objects–a change which, according to our scheme, does not happen until the fourth stage–that he adopts a contemptuous attitude towards those parts, and especially towards excrement. In this stage excrement becomes for him the representative of everything that he does not want to keep; so that he identifies the person whom he rejects with disgust with faeces (as in the case of X and Y). And the mere idea of putting excrement into the mouth is now the very essence of all that is disgusting. In certain illnesses we can observe a serious process of regression taking place in which the individual once more has as his sexual aim the eating of faeces. For in our unconscious we retain our original narcissistic estimation of the value of excrement.

I have already attempted in an earlier paper[14] to give some coherent account of the relation between the various forms of psychoneurosis and the different levels of libidinal development, as far as the state of our knowledge then permitted. My attempt was a very imperfect one and far from being a final explanation of the facts. Even at the present day we know almost as little as we did then; and we can only hope to have made an addition to our knowledge in two points, and that with every reserve.

In the first place we may assume that in melancholia the subject's capacity for object-love is especially poorly developed, so that if he falls ill his tendency to incorporate his object in a cannibalistic way gets the better of him–an occurrence which would coincide with a regression of his libido to the second stage as tabulated above. In the second place, it would seem that in paranoic states the libido has stopped in its regressive movement at the stage of partial incorporation (the third stage). This also seems to be true of kleptomanic conditions. And perhaps the main difference between the wish contained in each of those illnesses is that the kleptomaniac has taken as his sexual aim an *oral* incorporation of his object, while the paranoiac has made his its *anal* incorporation.

Only steady and persistent psychoanalytical work, especially in regard to the narcissistic psychoneuroses, can gradually give us a more complete view of man's psychosexual development. Meanwhile, until we have collected a greater number of thorough analyses to confirm and amplify the theoretic assumptions made in this paper, it may not be superfluous to consider the *prima facie* arguments in favour of those assumptions.

To begin with, we must remember that the results of our examination have been obtained by strictly empirical methods. I do not think that I have anywhere allowed myself to abandon the ground of empirical fact for that of speculative reasoning. At any rate I can say that I have never attempted to produce a complete and a well-rounded-off theory, but that on the contrary I have myself drawn attention to faults and shortcomings in my own suggestions.

In the next place, I should like to point out the simplicity of that process of development whose existence we have assumed. It follows along the same lines as the processes involved in organic growth: what was at first a *part* grows into a *whole* and what was at first a *whole* shrinks to a *part* and finally loses all value or continues its existence as a mere rudiment.

But we can carry this parallel with biological processes further still. We have long since learned to apply the biogenetic principle of organic life to the mental (psychosexual) development of man. Psychoanalysis is constantly finding confirmation of the fact that the individual recapitulates the history of his species in its psychological aspects as well. A great quantity of empirical data, however, warrants us in laying down yet another law concerning man's psychosexual development. This is that it lags a long way behind his somatic development, like a late version or repetition of that process. The biological model upon which the developmental processes discussed in this paper are based takes place in the earliest embryonic period of the individual, whereas the psychosexual processes extend over a number of years of his extrauterine life, namely, from his first year to the period of puberty.

If we turn to the field of embryology we can without difficulty recognize that there is an extensive similarity between the gradual development of man's psychosexual life, as we have examined it in this paper, and the organic development of his early embryonic life. In the first period of his extra-uterine life his libido is, according to our view, predominantly attached to the mouth as an erotogenic zone. The first vital relation of the infant to external objects consists in sucking up into its mouth a substance that is suitable for it and accessible to it. In its embryonic life, the first organ that is formed in connection with the earliest simple process of cell division is the so-called blastopore, an organ which is permanently retained and keeps its function in low forms of the animal world such as the Coelenterata.

It is a long time before the sexual organs (in the narrower sense of the word) of the child take over the leading part in its sexual life. Before this state is reached the intestinal canal, and especially the apertures at either end, becomes possessed of an important erotogenic significance, and sends out strong stimuli to the nervous system This state also has its prototype in the embryo. For a time there exists an open connection between the intestinal canal (rectum) and the caudal part of the neural canal *(canalis neurentericus).* The path along which stimuli may be transmitted from the intestinal canal to the nervous system might thus be said to be marked out organically.

But what is most clearly visible is the biological prototype of the child's oral-sadistic (cannibalistic) and anal-sadistic phases. Freud has already alluded to this fact; and I will quote the passage here:

> The sadistic-anal organization can easily be regarded as a continuation and development of the oral one. The violent muscular activity, directed upon the object, by which it is characterized, is to be explained as an action preparatory to eating. The eating then ceases to be a sexual aim and the preparatory action becomes a sufficient aim in itself. The essential novelty, as compared with the previous stage, is that the receptive passive function becomes disengaged from the oral zone and attached to the anal zone.[15]

He goes on to speak of parallel processes in the field of biology but does not specify which they are. In this connection I should like to lay particular stress on a striking parallel between the organic and the psychosexual development of the individual.

At first the blastopore is situated at the anterior end (cephalic end) of the primitive streak. In the embryos of certain animals we can observe that the original mouth opening closes up at the anterior end and becomes enlarged at the posterior end. In this way it gradually approaches the tail, which is in process of formation, and finally comes to rest there as the anus. This direct derivation of the anus from the blastopore appears as the biological prototype of that psychosexual process which Freud has described and which occurs somewhere about the second year of the life of the individual.

At about the same time as the anus is being formed in the embryo we can observe the muscular system of the body developing. In this process the jaw muscles are far in advance of the limb muscles. The development of the anus and of the jaws is closely connected. We may also remark that in extra-uterine life the jaw muscles are able to perform powerful and effective movements much earlier than other muscles, such as the muscles of the trunk or of the limbs.

We recognized as the fourth stage of the psychosexual development of the individual that in which he has as his sexual aim the retention and control of his object. Its correlate in biological ontogenesis is to be found in the formation of the intestinal mechanisms for retaining what has been taken into the body. These consist in constrictions and enlargements, annular contractures, branching passages, divagations ending blindly, manifold convolutions, and finally the voluntary and involuntary sphincter muscles of the anus itself. At the time that this complicated arrangement for the retention of objects is being formed there is as yet no sign of the appearance of the uro-genital apparatus.

We have seen that the genital organization of the libido falls into two stages which correspond to two stages in the development of object-love. Here once more the organic development of the individual supplies the model. The genital organs are at first 'indifferent', and it is only later on that they become differentiated into 'male' and 'female'. This applies to the generative glands as well as to the organs of copulation. In the same way we have detected a gradual process of differentiation in the psychosexual life of the individual.

Until a wider and more profound psychoanalytic knowledge shall have enabled us to come to valid conclusions concerning psychosexual development, I trust that the above instances of parallelism with biological processes may lend a certain support to my endeavour to give an account of the evolution of object-love in the human individual.

Notes

1 Sigmund Freud (1905d), *Three Essays on the Theory of Sexuality*, SE 7.

2 It may be mentioned in passing that this copious flow of tears represented her unconscious wish to urinate like a man.

3 This took the form of looking for the outline of his genitals underneath his clothes.

4 [= 'means', is also used in the sense of 'capacity', and thus comes to stand for 'sexual potency' in German. *Trans.*]

5 The cannibalism of primitive people after which we have named this phase of the infantile libido cannot be said to be unrestricted in this way. It is not at all the case that any one person can kill and eat any other. The selection of the victim has a strict affective determination.

6 'On the Origin of the Feeling of Persecution', *International Journal of Psycho-Analysis*, 1(1920):235-9

7 'The Reversal of the Libido-Sign in Delusions of Persecution', *International Journal of Psycho-Analysis*, 1(1920):231-4.

8 A remarkable parallel to this 'partial love' is seen in the 'partial identification' of the individual with his love-object, as Freud has briefly outlined it in his *Group Psychology and the Analysis of the Ego* (1921c), SE 18:107.

9 Hans Sachs (1923), 'On the Genesis of Perversions', *Psychoanalytic Quarterly*, 55(1986):477-88.

10 Cf. my earlier essay, 'Notes on the Analysis of a Case of Foot and Corset Fetishism', *Selected Papers of Karl Abraham* (London: Hogarth Press, 1927), 125.

11 [To possess.' *Sitzen* = to sit. *Trans.*]

12 We may compare with this the phantasies of little Hans (Freud, 'Analysis of a Phobia in a Five-Year-Old Boy' [1909b], SE 10) in which he takes the giraffe, who represents his mother, away from his father and then sits down upon it.

13 Such a stage of object-love with genital exclusion seems to coincide in time with Freud's 'phallic stage' in the psychosexual development of the individual, and moreover to have close internal relations with it. We may look upon hysterical symptoms as the obverse of those libidinal impulses which belong to object-love with genital exclusion and to the phallic organization.

14 See 'Contributions to a Discussion on Tic' (1921), *Selected Papers of Karl Abraham* (London: Hogarth Press, 1927), 323-5.

15 Cf. 'From the History of an Infantile Neurosis' (1918b), SE 17.

5

The Psychology of Women in Relation to the Functions of Reproduction

Helene Deutsch (1924)

International Journal of Psycho-Analysis 6(1925):405-418.

Originally presented before the Eighth International Psycho-Analytical Congress held in Salzburg in April 1924, 'The Psychology of Women in Relation to the Functions of Reproduction' was published in English in 1925.

In this paper Deutsch endorses and expands Freud's views about sexual development in relation to erogenous zones. What she shows here is how one becomes a woman, i.e., how the switch in valuation of the female genital occurs and how this event relates to the function of reproduction; and it emerges that for Deutsch, 'woman ' means the 'phallic mother'.

The starting point of the paper is that the development of the infantile libido to the normal heterosexual object choice is more difficult in women: the little girl has to give up a masculinity bound up with the clitoris and, in the difficult transition from the phallic phase (whose importance is emphasized) to the vaginal phase, she has to discover a new organ 'in her own person' through a passive and masochistic submission to the penis. The truly feminine attitude to the vagina finds its origins in the oral activity of the child at the breast. This, Deutsch posits, reflects the whole psychological difference displayed by the mature woman in her relations with the object-world, since the psychic significance of coitus lies in the repetition and mastery of the trauma of a symbolic form of castration; incorporating the penis repeats the trauma of weaning.

According to Deutsch, phallic narcissism centred on the clitoris gives way to a vaginal phase whereby the vagina becomes the maternal receptacle: the vagina, which represents the child, becomes the woman's 'ego in miniature.' Thus, as the object of maternal libido, the partner becomes the child; and in coitus the penis takes on the role of the breast, and the vagina the passive role of the sucking mouth.

The libidinal investment of the vagina derives from the entire body, on one hand, and specifically from the clitoris on the other. The greater importance of the investment of the whole body in women also explains the tendency for women to retain a relatively greater degree of polymorphous perversity.

Finally, one should note Deutsch's claim that for woman the sexual act is divided into two phases: orgasm and labour. Female orgasm is seen as a 'missed labour' and labour as an 'orgy of masochistic pleasure' that duplicates male ejaculation.

* * *

Psychoanalytic research discovered at the very outset that the development of the infantile libido to the normal heterosexual object-choice is in women rendered difficult by certain peculiar circumstances.

In males the path of this development is straightforward, and the advance from the 'phallic' phase does not take place in consequence of a complicated 'wave of repression', but is based upon a ratification of that which already exists and is accomplished through ready and willing utilization of an already urgent force. The essence of the achievement lies in the mastery of the Oedipus attitude which it connotes, and in overcoming the feelings of guilt bound up with this.

The girl, on the other hand, has in addition to this a two-fold task to perform: (1) she has to renounce the masculinity attaching to the clitoris; (2) in her transition from the 'phallic' to the 'vaginal' phase she has to discover a new genital organ.

The man attains his final stage of development when he discovers the vagina in the world outside himself and possesses himself of it sadistically. In this his guide is his own genital organ, with which he is already familiar and which impels him to the act of possession.

The woman has to discover this new sexual organ *in her own person*, a discovery which she makes through being masochistically subjugated by the penis, the latter thus becoming the guide to this fresh source of pleasure.

The final phase of attaining to a definitively feminine attitude is not gratification through the sexual act of the infantile desire for a penis, but full realization of the vagina as an organ of pleasure—an exchange of the desire for a penis for the real and equally valuable possession of a vagina. This newly-discovered organ must become for the woman 'the whole ego in miniature', a 'duplication of the ego', as Ferenczi[1] terms it when speaking of the value of the penis to the man.

In the following paper I shall try to set forth how this change in the valuation of a person's own genital organ takes place and what relation it bears to the function of reproduction in women.

We know how the different organizations of libido succeed one another and how each successive phase carries with it elements of the previous ones, so that no phase seems to have been completely surmounted but merely to have relinquished its central role. Along each of these communicating lines of development the libido belonging to the higher stages tends regressively to revert to its original condition, and succeeds in so doing in various ways.

The consequence of this oscillation of libido between the different forms taken by it in development is not only that the higher phases contain elements of the lower ones, but, conversely, that the libido on its path of regression carries with it constituents of the higher phases which it interweaves with the earlier ones, a process which we recognize subsequently in phantasy-formation and symptoms.

Thus the first or oral phase is auto-erotic, that is to say, it has no object either narcissistically, in the ego, or in the outside world. And yet we know that the process of weaning leaves in the Ucs[2] traces of a narcissistic wound. This is because the mother's breast is regarded as a part of the subject's own body and, like the penis later, is cathected with large quantities of narcissistic libido. Similarly, the oral gratification derived from the act of sucking leads to discovering the mother and to finding the first object in her.

The mysterious, heterosexual part of the little girl's libido finds its first explanation already in the earliest phase of development. To the tender love which she devotes to her father ('the sheltering male') as the nearest love-object side by side with the mother is added a large part of that sexual libido which, originating in the oral zone, in the first instance cathected the maternal breasts. Analysis of patients shows us that in a certain phase of development the Ucs equates the paternal penis with the maternal breast as an organ of suckling. This equation coincides with the conception of coitus (characteristic of this phase) as a relation between the mouth of the mother and the penis of the father and is extended into the theory of oral impregnation. The passive aim of this phase is achieved through the mucous membrane of the mouth zone, while the active organ of pleasure is the breast.

In the sadistic-anal phase the penis loses its significance (for phantasy-life) as an organ of suckling and becomes an organ of mastering. Coitus is conceived of as a sadistic act; in phantasies of beating, as we know, the girl either takes over the role of the father, or experiences the act masochistically in identification with the mother.

In this phase the passive aim is achieved through the anus, while the column of faeces becomes the active organ of pleasure, which, like the breast in the first phase, belongs at one and the same time to the outside world and to the subject's own body. By a displacement of cathexis the faeces here acquire the same narcissistic value as the breast in the oral phase. The birth-phantasy of this phase is that of the 'anal child'.

We are familiar with the biological analogy between the anus and the mouth; that between the breast and the penis as active organs arises from their analogous functions.

One would suppose it an easy task for feminine libido in its further development to pass on and take possession of the third opening of the female body—the vagina. Biologically, in the development of the embryo, the common origin of anus and vagina in the cloaca has already foreshadowed this step. The penis as an organ of stimulation and the active agent for this new erotogenic zone perhaps attains its function by means of the equation: breast=column of faeces=penis.

The difficulty lies in the fact that the bisexual character of development interposes between anus and vagina the masculine clitoris as an erotogenic zone. In the 'phallic' phase of development the clitoris attracts to itself a large measure of libido, which it relinquishes in favour of the 'feminine' vagina only after strenuous and not always decisive struggles. Obviously, this transition from the 'phallic' to the 'vaginal' phase (which later coincides with what Abraham[3] terms the 'postambivalent') must be recognized as the hardest task in the libidinal development of the woman.

The penis is already in the early infantile period discovered auto-erotically. Moreover, its exposed position makes it liable to stimulation in various ways connected with the care of the baby's body, and thus it becomes an erotogenic zone before it is ready to fulfil its reproductive function. All three masturbatory phases are dominated by this organ.

The clitoris (which is in reality so inadequate a substitute for the penis) assumes the importance of the latter throughout the whole period of development. The hidden vagina plays no part. The child is unaware of its existence, possibly has mere vague premonitions of it. Every attempt to pacify the little girl's envy of the penis with the explanation that she also has 'something' is rightly doomed to complete failure; for the possession of something which one neither sees nor feels cannot give any satisfaction. Nevertheless, as a zone of active energy the clitoris lacks the abundant energy of the penis; even in the most intense masturbatory activity it cannot arrogate to itself such a measure of libido as does the latter organ. Accordingly the primal distribution of libido over the erotogenic zones is subject to far less modification than in the male, and the female, owing to the lesser tyranny of the clitoris, may all her life remain more *'polymorph-pervers'*, more infantile; to her more than to the male 'the whole body is a sexual organ'. In the wave of development occurring at puberty this erotogenicity of the whole body increases, for the libido which is forced away from the clitoris (presumably by way of the inner secretions) flows back to the body as a whole. This must be of importance in the later destiny of the woman, because in this way she is regressively set back into a state in which, as Ferenczi[4] shows, she 'cleaves to intra-uterine existence' in sexual things.

In 'transformations which take place at puberty' (and during the subsequent period of adolescence) libido has therefore to flow towards the vagina from two sources: (1) from the whole body, especially from those erotogenic zones that have the most powerful cathexis, (2) from the clitoris, which has still to some extent retained its libidinal cathexis.

The difficulty lies in the fact that the clitoris is not at all ready to renounce its role, that the conflict at puberty is associated with the traumatic occurrence of menstruation; and this not only revives the castration-wound but at the same time represents, both in the biological and the psychological sense, the disappointment of a frustrated pregnancy. The periodic repetition of menstruation every time recalls the conflicts of puberty and reproduces them in a less acute form.

At the same time there is no doubt that the whole process of menstruation is calculated to exercise an eroticizing and preparatory influence upon the vagina.

The task of conducting the libido to the vagina from the two sources which I have mentioned devolves upon the activity of the penis, and that in two ways.

First, libido must be drawn from the whole body. Here we have a perfect analogy to the woman's breast, which actively takes possession of the infant's mouth and so centres the libido of the whole body in this organ. Just so does the vagina, under the stimulus of the penis and by a process of displacement 'from above downwards', take over the passive role of the sucking mouth in the equation: penis=breast. This oral, sucking activity of the vagina is indicated by its whole anatomical structure (with their corresponding terms).

The second operation accomplished by the penis is the carrying-over of the remaining clitoris-libido to the vagina. This part of the libido still takes a 'male' direction, even when absorbed by the vagina; that is to say, the clitoris renounces its male function in favour of the penis that approaches the body from without.

As the clitoris formerly played its 'masculine' part by identification with the paternal penis, so the vagina takes over its role (that of the clitoris) by allowing one part of its functions to be dominated by an identification with the penis of the partner.

In certain respects the orgastic activity of the vagina is wholly analogous to the activity of the penis. I refer to the processes of secretion and contraction. As in the man, we have here an 'amphimixis' of urethral and anal tendencies—of course greatly diminished in degree. Both these component-instincts develop their full activity only in that 'extension' of the sexual act, pregnancy and parturition.

We see then that one of the vaginal functions arises through identification with the penis, which in this connection is regarded as a possession of the subject's own body. Here the psychic significance of the sexual act lies in the repetition and mastery of the castration-trauma.

The truly passive, feminine attitude of the vagina is based upon the oral, sucking activity discussed above.

In this function coitus signifies for the woman a restoring of that first relation of the human being with the outside world, in which the object is orally incorporated, introjected; that is to say, it restores that condition of perfect unity of being and harmony in which the distinction between subject and object was annulled. Thus the attainment of the highest, genital, 'post-ambivalent' (Abraham) phase signifies a repetition of the earliest, pre-ambivalent phase.

In relation to the partner the situation of incorporating is a repetition of sucking at the mother's breast; hence incorporation amounts to a repetition and mastery of the trauma of weaning. In the equation penis=breast, and in the sucking activity of the vagina, coitus realizes the fulfilment of the phantasy of sucking at the paternal penis.

The identifications established between the two partners in the preparatory act (Ferenczi) now acquire a manifold significance, identification with the mother taking place in two ways: (1) through equating the penis with the breast, (2) through experiencing the sexual act masochistically, i.e. through repeating that identification with the mother which belongs to the phase of a sadistic conception of coitus.

Through this identification, then, the woman plays in coitus the part of mother and child simultaneously—a relation which is continued in pregnancy, when one actually is both mother and child at the same time.

As the object of maternal libido in the act of suckling, the partner therefore becomes the child, but at the same time the libido originally directed towards the father must be transferred to the partner (according to the equation: penis=organ of suckling and to the conception of coitus as a sadistic act of mastery). This shows us that ultimately coitus represents for the woman incorporation (by the mouth) of the father, who is made into the child and then retains this role in the pregnancy which occurs actually or in phantasy.

I arrived at this identification-series, which is complicated and may seem far-fetched, as a result of all the experience which I have had of cases of frigidity and sterility.

Ferenczi's 'maternal regression' is realized for the woman in equating coitus with the situation of sucking. The last act of this regression (return into the uterus), which the man accomplishes by the act of introjection in coitus, is realized by the woman in pregnancy in the complete identification between mother and child. In my opinion the mastery of 'the trauma of birth', which Rank[5] has shown to be so important, is accomplished by the woman above all in the actively repeated act of parturition, for to the Ucs carrying and being carried, giving birth and being born, are as identical as giving suck and sucking.

This conception of coitus reflects the whole psychological difference displayed by men and women in their relation to the object-world. The man actively takes possession of some piece of the world and in this way attains to the bliss of the primal state. And this is the form taken by his tendencies to sublimation. In the act of incorporation passively experienced the women introjects into herself a piece of the object-world which she then absorbs.

In its role of organ of sucking and incorporation the vagina becomes the receptacle not of the penis but of the child. The energy required for this function is derived not from the clitoris, but, as I said before, from the libidinal cathexis of the whole body, this libido being conducted to the vagina by channels familiar to us. The vagina now itself represents the child, and so receives that cathexis of narcissistic libido which flows on to the child in the 'extension' of the sexual act. It becomes the 'second ego', the ego in miniature, as does the penis for the man. A woman who succeeds in establishing this maternal function of the vagina by giving up the claim of the clitoris to represent the penis has reached the goal of feminine development, *has become a woman.*

In men the function of reproduction terminates with the act of introjection, for with them that function coincides with the relief from sexual tension by ejaculation.

Women have to perform in two phases the function which men accomplish in a single act; nevertheless the first act of incorporation contains elements which indicate the tendency to get rid of the germ-plasm by expulsion, as is done by the male in coitus. Orgasm in the woman appears not only to imply identification with the man but to have yet another motive; it is the expression of the attempt to impart to coitus itself in the interest of the race the character of parturition (we might call it a 'missed labour'). In animals the process of expulsion of the products of reproduction very often takes place during the sexual act in the female as well as in the male.

In the human female this process is not carried through, though it is obviously indicated and begun in the orgastic function; it terminates only in the second act, that of parturition. The process therefore is a *single* one, which is merely divided into two phases by an interval of time. As the first act contains (in orgasm) elements of the second, so the second is permeated by the pleasure-mechanisms of the first. I even assume that the act of parturition contains the acme of sexual pleasure owing to the relief from stimulation by the germ-plasm. If this be so, parturition is a process of 'autotomy' analogous to ejaculation (Ferenczi), requiring, however, the powerful stimulus of the matured foetus in order that it may function. This reverses the view which Groddeck first had the courage to put forward, at the Hague Congress, that parturition is associated with pleasure owing to its analogy with coitus. It would rather seem that coitus acquires the character of a pleasurable act mainly through the fact that it constitutes an attempt at and beginning of parturition. In support of my view I would cite the following considerations.

Freud[6] has told us that the sadistic instincts of destruction reach their fullest development when the erotic sexual instincts are put out of action. This happens after their tension has been relieved in the act of gratification. The death-instinct has then a free hand and can carry through its claims undisturbed. A classical instance of this is furnished by those lower animals in which the sexual act leads to death.

This applies to the fertilizing male, but repeats itself *mutatis mutandis* in the female also, when the fertilized ovum is expelled after a longer or shorter interval during which it has matured in the maternal body. There are many species of animals, e.g. certain spiders, in which the females perish when they have fulfilled the function of reproduction. If the liberation of the death-instinct is a consequence of the gratification of sexual trends, it is only logical to assume that this gratification reaches its highest point in the female only in the act of parturition.

In actual fact parturition is for the woman an orgy of masochistic pleasure, and the dread and premonition of death which precede this act are clearly due to a perception of the menace of the destructive instincts about to be liberated.

Conditions of insanity sometimes met with after delivery are characterized by a specially strong tendency to suicide and murderous impulses towards the newly-born child.

These facts in my opinion confirm my assumption that parturition constitutes for women the termination of the sexual act, which was only inaugurated by coitus, and that the ultimate gratification of the erotic instinct is analogous to that in men and takes place at the moment when soma and germ-plasm are separated.

The interval in time between the two acts is filled by complicated processes in the economy of the libido.

The object incorporated in coitus is introjected physically and psychically, finds its extension in the child, and persists in the mother as a part of her ego.

Thus we see that the mother's relation to the 'child' as a libidinal object is two-fold: on the one hand it is worked out within the ego in the interaction of its different parts; on the other hand it is the extension of all those object-relations which the child embodies in our identification-series. For even while the child is still in the uterus its relation to the mother is partly that of an object belonging to the outside world, such as it ultimately becomes.

The libido which in the act of incorporation has regressed to the earliest stage of development seeks out all the positions which it had abandoned, and the harmonious state of identity between subject and object does not always remain so harmonious in relation to the child as object.

The ambivalent tendencies of later phases of development, which have already manifested themselves in coitus, become stronger during pregnancy. The ambivalent conflict which belongs to the 'later oral phase of development' finds expression in the tendency to expel again (orally) the object which has been incorporated.

This manifests itself in vomiting during pregnancy and in the typical eructations and peculiar cravings for food, etc.

The regressive elements of the sadistic-anal phase find expression in the hostile tendencies to expulsion manifested in the pains which appear long before delivery. If these predominate over the tendencies to retain the foetus, the result is miscarriage. We recognize these elements again in the transitory, typically anal, changes in the character of pregnant women. The old equation, child=faeces, is in this phase revived in the Ucs, owing to the child's position in the body as something belonging to that body and yet destined to be severed from it.

In the oral incorporation a quantity of narcissistic libido has already flowed to the child as a part of the subject's own ego. Similarly the libidinal relation in the identification, child=faeces, is again a narcissistic one.

But as faeces become for children, in reaction against their original narcissistic overestimation of them, the essence of what is disgusting, so in this phase of pregnancy there arise typical feelings of disgust, which become displaced from the child to particular kinds of food, situations, etc.

It is interesting that all these sensations disappear in the fifth month of pregnancy with the quickening of the child. The mother's relation to it is now determined in two directions. In the first place that part of her own body which is moving to and fro and vigorously pulsing within her is equated with the penis; and her relation to the child, which is still rooted in the depths of her narcissism, is now raised to a higher stage of development, namely, the 'phallic'. At the same time the child gives proof through a certain developing independence that it belongs to the outside world and in this way enters more into an object-relation to the mother.

I have tried thus briefly to reveal in the state of pregnancy deposits of all the phases of development. I shall now return to the mother-child relation that I mentioned before, which begins with the process of incorporation, makes the child a part of the subject's own ego and works itself out within that ego.

In this process the libidinal relations to the child are formed as follows: in the process of introjection the quantities of libido sent out to the partner in the sexual act flow back to the subject's narcissism. This is a very considerable contribution, for, as I have shown, in effecting a cathexis of the partner libido was drawn from the old father-fixation and mother-fixation.

The libido thus flowing into the ego constitutes the secondary narcissism of the woman as a mother, for, though it is devoted to the object (the child), that object represents at the same time a part of her ego. The change in the ego of the pregnant woman which follows on the process of introjection is a new edition of a process which has already taken place at a previous time: the child becomes for her the incarnation of the ego-ideal which she set up in the past. It is now for the second time built up by introjecting the father.

The narcissistic libido is displaced on to this newly erected super-ego, which becomes the bearer of all those perfections once ascribed to the father. A whole quantity of object-libido is withdrawn from its relations to the outside world and conducted to the child as the super-ego. Thus the process of sublimation in the woman is effected through her relation to her child.

The man measures and controls his ego-ideal by his productions through sublimation in the outside world. To the woman, on the other hand, the ego-ideal is embodied in the child, and all those tendencies to sublimation which the man utilizes in intellectual and social activity she directs to the child, which in the psychological sense represents for the woman her sublimation product. Hence the relation, mother-child, in pregnancy has more than one determinant. Since the child in the uterus becomes a part of the ego and large quantities of libido flow to it, the libidinal cathexis in the ego is heightened, narcissism is increased, and that primal condition is realized in which there was as yet no distinction between ego-libido and object-libido.

This primal condition, however, is disturbed by two factors: (1) by a process of sublimation the child becomes the super-ego, and our experience in other directions teaches us that this may enter into vigorous opposition to the ego; (2) the child is at the same time an object belonging to the outside world, in relation to which the ambivalent conflicts of all phases of libidinal development are stirred up.

Our observations enable us to distinguish two characteristic types of women according to their mental reactions to pregnancy. There are a number of women who endure their pregnancy with visible discomfort and depression. A similar unfavourable change takes place in their bodily appearance: they become ugly and shrunken, so that as the child matures they actually change into a mere appendage to it, a condition highly uncomfortable for themselves. The other type consists of those women who attain during pregnancy their greatest physical and psychical bloom.

In the first case the woman's narcissism has been sacrificed to the child. On the one hand the super-ego has mastered the ego, and on the other the child as a love-object has attracted to itself such a large measure of ego-libido that the ego is impoverished. Possibly this explains those states of melancholia which occur during pregnancy.

In the other type of woman the distribution of libido during pregnancy is different. That part of the libido which has now been withdrawn from the outside world is directed towards the child as a part of the ego. This can happen only when the formation of the super-ego is less powerful and the child is regarded less as an object and more as a part of the ego. When this is so the result is a heightening of the secondary narcissism, which is expressed in an increased self-respect, self-satisfaction, etc.

It seems as though we may conclude from these remarks that that unity, mother—child, is not so completely untroubled as we might suppose.

The original harmony of the primal state, inaugurated in the process of introjection during the sexual act, is soon disturbed by manifestations of ambivalence towards the child in the uterus. From this point of view parturition appears as the final result of a struggle which has long been raging. The stimulus which proceeds from the foetus becomes insupportable and presses for discharge. Every hostile impulse which has already been mobilized during pregnancy reaches its greatest intensity in this decisive battle. Finally the incorporated object is successfully expelled into the outside world.

We have seen that the introjected object takes the place of the ego-ideal in the restored unity of the ego. When projected into the outside world it retains this character, for it continues to embody the subject's own unattained ideals. This is the psychological path by which, as Freud[7] recognized, women attain from narcissism to full object-love.

The final 'maternal regression' takes place in pregnancy through identification with the child: 'the trauma of birth' is mastered through the act of parturition.

Having regard to this identity of mother and child, we may perhaps draw certain conclusions from the mother's frame of mind as to the mental condition of the child. This of course undergoes amnesia, and then is only vaguely hinted at in dreams, phantasies, etc.

In actual fact the woman feels as though the world were out of joint and coming to an end; she has a sense of chaotic uneasiness, a straining, bursting sensation displaced from the avenues of birth to her head, and with these feelings is associated an intense dread of death. Possibly here we have a complete repetition of the anxiety attaching to the trauma of birth and a discharge of it by means of actual reproduction. That which men endeavour to attain in coitus and which impels them to laborious sublimations women attain in the function of reproduction.

It is known that in the dreams of pregnant women there very often appears a swimming child. This child may always be recognized as the dreamer herself, endowed with some quality which makes her, or in child-hood made her, particularly estimable in her own eyes—it is as it were an illustration of the formation of the ego-ideal in relation to the child. The birth-phantasies of women who are already mothers prove on thorough investigation to represent details of two separate births interwoven into one: the birth of the subject herself (never recalled to memory) and the delivery of a child.

The mental state of the woman after delivery is characterized by a feeling of heavy loss. After a short phase in which the sense of victorious termination of the battle preponderates, there arises a feeling of boundless emptiness and disappointment, certainly analogous to the feeling of a 'lost Paradise' in the child which has been expelled.

This blank is filled only when the first relation to the child as an object in the outside world is ultimately established. The supposition that this relation is already present during the act of delivery itself is borne out by the observation which Rank[8] has already made in another connection, namely, that mothers who are in a state of narcosis during delivery have a peculiar feeling of estrangement towards their children. These mothers do not go through the phase of emptiness and disappointment, but on the other hand their joy in the child is not so intense as when delivery has taken place naturally. The child which is perceived by their senses is regarded as something alien.

This factor of loss clearly contributes to the joy of finding the child again. Apart from this, it is precisely this last factor of 'severance' which completes the analogy with coitus. The vaginal passage constitutes a frontier where the child is for the last time a part of the subject's own body and at the same time is already the object which has been thrust out. Here we have a repetition of the coitus-situation, in which the object was still felt to be a piece of the outside world but, being introjected, was on the border-line between the outside world and the ego.

Although the child has been hailed after delivery as an object belonging to the outside world, the bliss of the primal state, the unity of subject and object, is nevertheless re-established in lactation. This is a repetition of coitus, rendered with photographic faithfulness, the identification being based on the oral incorporation of the object in the act of sucking. Here again we have the equation: penis = breast. As in the first instance the penis took possession of one of the openings of the woman's body (the vagina), and in the act of mastery created an erotogenic centre, so now the nipple in a state of erection takes possession of the infant's mouth. As in coitus the erotogenicity of the whole body was attracted to the vagina, so here the whole disseminated libido of the newly-born infant is concentrated in the mouth. That which the semen accomplished in the one instance is accomplished in the other by the jet of milk. The identification made in childish phantasy between the mother's breast and the father's penis is realized a second time: in coitus the penis takes on the role of the breast, while in lactation the breast becomes the penis. In the identification-situation the dividing line between the partners vanishes, and in this relation, mother-child, the mother once more annuls the trauma of weaning.

The identification, penis=breast, threw light on a remarkable disturbance in lactation which I had the opportunity of observing analytically. A young mother with a very ambivalent attitude towards her child was obliged to give up suckling it, although she wished to continue and her breasts were functioning excellently. But what happened was that in the interval between the child's meals the milk poured out in a stream, so that the breast was empty when she wished to give it to the child. The measures she took to overcome this unfortunate condition recalled the behaviour of men suffering from ejaculatio praecox, who convulsively endeavour to hasten the sexual act but are always overtaken by their infirmity. In the same way this woman tried to hasten the feeding of the child, but with the same ill success—it was always too late. The analysis of this disturbance was traced to a urethral source in her, as in ejaculatio praecox in the man. In a disturbance of lactation more frequently met with, namely, the drying up of the secretion, the other (anal) components of the process undoubtedly predominate.

The relation between the genital processes and lactation finds very characteristic expression at the moment when the child is put to the breast. Sometimes there is even a convulsion in the uterus, as though it were terminating its activity only now when it resigns it to the breast.

So the act of reproduction, begun in oral incorporation, completes the circle by representing the same situation at the end as at the beginning.

The whole development of the libido is rapidly revived and run through once more, the effect of the primal traumata is diminished by repetitive acts, and the work of sublimation is accomplished in relation to the child. But for the bisexual disposition of the human being, which is so adverse to the woman, but for the clitoris with its masculine strivings, how simple and clear would be her way to an untroubled mastering of existence!

Notes

[1] Sándor Ferenczi (1924), *Thalassa, a Theory of Genitality* (Albany, NY: Psychoanalytic Quarterly Inc., 1938).

[2] [This has been adopted as the English rendering of *Ubw*, Pcs as that of *Vbw*, Cs as that of *Bw*, and Pcpt-Cs (perception-consciousness) as that of *W.Bw. Translator.*]

[3] Karl Abraham (1924), 'A Short Study of the Development of the Libido, Viewed in the Light of Mental Disorders', *Selected Papers of Karl Abraham* (London: Hogarth Press, 1927), 418-501. See Part 2, 'Origins and Growth of Object Love', reprinted above.

[4] *Thalassa.*
[5] Otto Rank (1924), *The Trauma of Birth* (London: Paul, Trench, Trubner, 1929).
[6] Sigmund Freud (1923*b*), *The Ego and the Id*, SE 19:3.
[7] Sigmund Freud (1914*c*), 'On Narcissism: an Introduction', SE 14:69.
[8] *The Trauma of Birth.*

The Flight from Womanhood: The Masculinity-Complex in Women, as Viewed by Men and Women

Karen Horney (1925)

International Journal of Psycho-Analysis 7 (1926):324-39

This paper was first read under the title 'A Woman's Thoughts on the Masculinity Complex in Women' at a meeting of the Berlin Society on 31st October 1925. It was published in German and in English in 1926.
While appearing to endorse Freud's mature views on male and female sexuality, described in such places as 'The Infantile Genital Organization of the Libido' and 'Some Psychical Consequences of the Anatomical Differences between the Sexes', Horney questions here the supremacy of the male point of view in the analytic field of inquiry. She disputes the version of the little girl as a castrated little man and posits a womanly relation to the father as the origin of the castration complex which is resolved through identifying with the masculine position. She introduces the term 'primary' penis envy in relation to mere anatomical difference which, in her view, is reinforced by a realization of the privileges of the boy in connection with urethral eroticism, the scopophilic drive, and masturbation. She then distinguishes a secondary formation in which women reject their female functions and take flight from womanhood by seeking refuge in an unconscious desire to be a man. Horney argues that the reason this flight is encountered so frequently in women is that it offers the girl a way of repudiating libidinal wishes and fantasies concerning the father.

* * *

In some of his latest works Freud has drawn attention with increasing urgency to a certain one-sidedness in our analytical researches. I refer to the fact that till quite recently the mind of boys and men only was taken as the object of investigation.

The reason for this is obvious. Psycho-analysis is the creation of a male genius, and almost all those who have developed his ideas have been men. It is only right and reasonable that they should evolve more easily a masculine psychology and understand more of the development of men than of women.

A momentous step towards the understanding of the specifically feminine was made by Freud himself in discovering the existence of penis envy, and soon after the work of van Ophuijsen and Abraham showed how large a part this factor plays in the development of women and in the formation of their neuroses. The significance of penis envy has been extended quite recently by the hypothesis of the 'phallic phase'. By this we mean that in the infantile genital organization in both sexes only one genital organ, namely the male, plays any part, and that it is just this which distinguishes the infantile organization from the final genital organization of the adult.[1] According to this theory, the clitoris is conceived of as a phallus, and we assume that little girls as well as boys attach to the clitoris in the first instance exactly the same value as to the penis.[2]

The effect of this phase is partly to inhibit and partly to promote the subsequent development. Helene Deutsch has demonstrated principally the inhibiting effects. She is of opinion that, at the beginning of every new sexual function (e.g. at the beginning of puberty, of sexual intercourse, of pregnancy and child-birth), this phase is re-animated and has to be overcome every time before feminine attitude can be attained. Freud has elaborated her exposition on the positive side, for he believes that it is only penis envy and the overcoming of it which gives rise to the desire for a child and thus forms the love-bond to the father.[3]

The question now arises whether these hypotheses have helped to make our insight into feminine development (insight which Freud himself has stated to be unsatisfactory and incomplete) more satisfactory and clearer.

Science has often found it fruitful to look at long familiar facts from a fresh point of view. Otherwise there is a danger that we shall involuntarily continue to classify all new observations amongst the same clearly defined groups of ideas.

The new point of view of which I wish to speak came to me by way of philosophy, in some essays by Georg Simmel.[4] The point which Simmel makes there and which has been in many ways elaborated since, especially from the feminine side,[5] is this: Our whole civilization is a masculine civilization. The State, the laws, morality, religion and the sciences are the creation of men. Simmel by no means deduces from these facts, as is commonly done by other writers, an inferiority in women, but he first of all gives considerable breadth and depth to this conception of a masculine civilization:

> The requirements of art, patriotism, morality in general and social ideas in particular, correctness in practical judgement and objectivity in theoretical knowledge, the energy and the profundity of life—all these are categories which belong as it were in their form and their claims to humanity in general, but in their actual histor-

ical configuration they are masculine throughout. Supposing that we describe these things, viewed as absolute ideas, by the single word 'objective', we then find that in the history of our race the equation objective = masculine is a valid one.

Now Simmel thinks that the reason why it is so difficult to recognize these historical facts is that the very standards by which mankind has estimated the values of male and female nature are 'not neutral, arising out of the difference of the sexes, but in themselves essentially masculine.'

We do not believe in a purely 'human' civilization, into which the question of sex does not enter, for the very reason that prevents any such civilization from in fact existing, namely, the (so to speak) naïve identification of the concept 'human being'[6] and the concept 'man',[7] which in many languages even causes the same word to be used for the two concepts. For the moment I will leave it undetermined whether this masculine character of the fundamentals of our civilization has its origin in the essential nature of the sexes or only in a certain preponderance of force in men, which is not really bound up with the question of civilization. In any case this is the reason why in the most varying fields inadequate achievements are contemptuously called 'feminine', while distinguished achievements on the part of women are called 'masculine' as an expression of praise.

Like all sciences and all valuations, the psychology of women has hitherto been considered only from the point of view of men. It is inevitable that the man's position of advantage should cause objective validity to be attributed to his subjective, affective relations to the woman, and according to Delius[8] the psychology of women hitherto does actually represent a deposit of the desires and disappointments of men.

An additional and very important factor in the situation is that women have adapted themselves to the wishes of men and felt as if their adaptation were their true nature. That is, they see or saw themselves in the way that their men's wishes demanded of them; unconsciously they yielded to the suggestion of masculine thought.

If we are clear about the extent to which all our being, thinking and doing conform to these masculine standards, we can see how difficult it is for the individual man and also for the individual woman really to shake off this mode of thought.

The question then is how far analytical psychology also, when its researches have women for their object, is under the spell of this way of thinking, in so far as it has not yet wholly left behind the stage in which frankly and as a matter of course masculine development only was considered. In other words, how far has the evolution of women, as depicted to us to-day by analysis, been measured by masculine standards and how far therefore does this picture not fail to present quite accurately the real nature of women.

If we look at the matter from this point of view our first impression is a surprising one. The present analytical picture of feminine development (whether that picture be correct or not) differs in no case by a hair's breadth from the typical ideas which the boy has of the girl.

We are familiar with the ideas which the boy entertains. I will therefore only sketch them in a few succinct phrases, and for the sake of comparison will place in a parallel column our ideas of the development of women.

The Boy's Ideas:	*Our Ideas of Feminine Development:*
Naïve assumption that girls as well as boys possess a penis.	For both sexes it is only the male genital which plays any part.
Realization of the absence of the penis.	Sad discovery of the absence of the penis.
Idea that the girl is a castrated, mutilated boy.	Belief of the girl that she once possessed a penis and lost it by castration.
Belief that the girl has suffered punishment which also threatens him.	Castration is conceived of as the infliction of punishment.
The girl is regarded as inferior.	The girl regards herself as inferior. Penis envy.
The boy is unable to imagine how the girl can ever get over this loss or envy.	The girl never gets over the sense of deficiency and inferiority and has constantly to master afresh her desire to be a man.
The boy dreads her envy.	The girl desires throughout life to avenge herself on the man for possessing something which she lacks.

The existence of this over-exact agreement is certainly no criterion of its objective correctness. It is quite possible that the infantile genital organization of the little girl might bear as striking a resemblance to that of the boy as has up till now been assumed.

But it is surely calculated to make us think and take other possibilities into consideration. For instance, we might follow Georg Simmel's train of thought and reflect whether it is likely that female adaptation to the male structure should take place at so early a period and in so high a degree that the specific nature of a little girl is overwhelmed by it. Later I will return for a moment to the point that it does actually seem to me probable that this infection with a masculine point of view occurs in childhood. But it does not seem to me clear off-hand how everything bestowed by nature could be thus absorbed into it and leave no trace. And so we must return to the question I have already raised: whether the remarkable parallelism which I have indicated may not perhaps be the expression of a one-sidedness in our observations, due to their being made from the man's point of view.

Such a suggestion immediately encounters an inner protest, for we remind ourselves of the sure ground of experience upon which analytical research has always been founded. But at the same time our theoretical scientific knowledge tells us that this ground is not altogether trustworthy, but that all experience by its very nature contains a subjective factor. Thus, even our analytical experience is derived from direct observation of the material which our patients bring to analysis in free associations, dreams and symptoms and from the interpretations which we make or the conclusions which we draw from this material. Therefore, even when the technique is correctly applied, there is in theory the possibility of variations in this experience.

Now, if we try to free our minds from this masculine mode of thought, nearly all the problems of feminine psychology take on a different appearance.

The first thing that strikes us is that it is always, or principally, the genital difference between the sexes which has been made the cardinal point in the analytical conception and that we have left out of consideration the other great biological difference, namely, the different parts played by men and by women in the function of reproduction.

The influence of the man's point of view in the conception of motherhood is most clearly revealed in Ferenczi's extremely brilliant genital theory.[9]

His view is that the real incitement to coitus, its true, ultimate meaning for both sexes, is to be sought in the desire to return to the mother's womb. During a period of contest man acquired the privilege of really penetrating once more, by means of his genital organ, into a uterus. The woman, who was formerly in the subordinate position, was obliged to adapt her organization to this organic situation and was provided with certain compensations. She had to 'content herself' with substitutes of the nature of phantasy and above all with harbouring the child, whose bliss she shares. At the most, it is only in the act of birth that she perhaps has potentialities of pleasure which are denied to the man.[10]

According to this view the psychic situation of a woman would certainly not be a very pleasurable one. She lacks any real primal impulse to coitus, or at least she is debarred from all direct—even if only partial—fulfilment. If this is so, the impulse towards coitus and pleasure in it must undoubtedly be less for her than for the man. For it is only indirectly, by circuitous ways, that she attains to a certain fulfilment of the primal longing—i.e. partly by the roundabout way of masochistic conversion and partly by identification with the child which she may conceive. These, however, are merely 'compensatory devices'. The only thing in which she ultimately has the advantage over the man is the, surely very questionable, pleasure in the act of birth.

At this point I, as a woman, ask in amazement, and what about motherhood? And the blissful consciousness of bearing a new life within oneself? And the ineffable happiness of the increasing expectation of the appearance of this new being? And the joy when it finally makes its appearance and one holds it for the first time in one's arms? And the deep pleasurable feeling of satisfaction in suckling it and the happiness of the whole period when the infant needs her care?

Ferenczi has expressed the opinion in conversation that in that primal period of conflict which ended so grievously for the female, the male as victor imposed upon her the burden of motherhood and all that it involves.

Certainly, regarded from the standpoint of the social struggle, motherhood *may* be a handicap. It is certainly so at the present time, but it is much less certain that it was so in times when human beings were closer to nature.

Moreover, we explain penis envy itself by its biological relations and not by social factors; on the contrary, we are accustomed without more ado to construe the woman's sense of being at a disadvantage socially as the rationalization of her penis envy.

But from the biological point of view woman has in motherhood, or in the capacity for motherhood, a quite indisputable and by no means negligible physiological superiority. This is most clearly reflected in the unconscious of the male psyche in the boy's intense envy of motherhood. We are familiar with this envy as such, but it has hardly received due consideration as a dynamic factor. When one begins, as I did, to analyse men only after a fairly long experience of analysing women, one receives a most surprising impression of the intensity of this envy of pregnancy, child-birth and motherhood, as well as of the breasts and of the act of suckling.

In the light of this impression derived from analysis one must naturally enquire whether an unconscious masculine tendency to depreciation is not expressing itself intellectually in the above mentioned view of motherhood? This depreciation would run as follows: In reality women do simply desire the penis; when all is said and done motherhood is only a burden which makes the struggle for existence harder, and men may be glad that they have not to bear it.

When Helene Deutsch writes that the masculinity-complex in women plays a much greater part than the femininity-complex in man, she would seem to overlook the fact that the masculine envy is clearly capable of more successful sublimation than the penis envy of the girl, and that it certainly serves as one, if not as the essential, driving force in the setting-up of cultural values.

Language itself points to this origin of cultural productivity. In the historic times which are known to us this productivity has undoubtedly been incomparably greater in men than in women. Is not the tremendous strength in men of the impulse to creative work in every field precisely due to their feeling of playing a relatively small part in the creation of living beings, which constantly impels them to an over-compensation in achievement?

If we are right in making this connection we are confronted with the problem why no corresponding impulse to compensate herself for her penis envy is found in woman? There are two possibilities; either the envy of the woman is absolutely less than that of the man or it is less successfully worked off in some other way. We could bring forward facts in support of either supposition.

In favour of the greater intensity of the man's envy we might point out that an actual anatomical disadvantage on the side of the woman exists only from the point of view of the pregenital levels of organization.[11] From that of the genital organization of adult women there is no disadvantage, for obviously the capacity of women for coitus is not less but simply other than that of men. On the other hand, the part of the man in reproduction is ultimately less than that of the woman.

Further, we observe that men are evidently under a greater necessity to depreciate women than conversely. The realization that the dogma of the inferiority of women had its origin in an unconscious male tendency could only dawn upon us after a doubt had arisen whether in fact this view were justified in reality. But if there actually are in men tendencies to depreciate women behind this conviction of feminine inferiority, we must infer that this unconscious impulse to depreciation is a very powerful one.

Further, there is much to be said in favour of the view that women work off their penis envy less successfully than men from a cultural point of view. We know that in the most favourable case this envy is transmuted into the desire for a husband and child, and probably by this very transmutation it forfeits the greater part of its power as an incentive to sublimation. In unfavourable cases, however, as I shall presently show in greater detail, it is burdened with a sense of guilt instead of being able to be employed fruitfully, whilst the man's incapacity for motherhood is probably felt simply as an inferiority and can develop its full driving power without inhibition.

In this discussion I have already touched on a problem which Freud has recently brought into the foreground of interest:[12] namely, the question of the origin and operation of the desire for a child. In the course of the last decade our attitude towards this problem has changed. I may therefore be permitted to describe briefly the beginning and the end of this historical evolution.

The original hypothesis[13] was that penis envy gave a libidinal reinforcement both to the wish for a child and the wish for the man, but that the latter wish arose independently of the former. Subsequently the accent became more and more displaced on to the penis envy, till in his most recent work on this problem Freud expressed the conjecture that the wish for the child arose only through penis envy and the disappointment over the lack of the penis in general, and that the tender attachment to the father came into existence only by this circuitous route—by way of the desire for the penis and the desire for the child.

This latter hypothesis obviously originated in the need to explain psychologically the biological principle of heterosexual attraction. This corresponds to the problem formulated by Groddeck, who says that it is natural that the boy should retain the mother as a love-object, 'but how is it that the little girl becomes attached to the opposite sex?'[14]

In order to approach this problem we must first of all realize that our empirical material with regard to the masculinity-complex in women is derived from two sources of very different importance. The first is the direct observation of children, in which the subjective factor plays a relatively insignificant part. Every little girl who has not been intimidated displays penis envy frankly and without embarrassment. We see that the presence of this envy is typical and understand quite well why this is so; we understand how the narcissistic mortification of possessing less than the boy is reinforced by a series of disadvantages arising out of the different pregenital cathexes: the manifest privileges of the boy in connection with urethral erotism, the scopophilic instinct, and onanism.[15]

I should like to suggest that we should apply the term *primary* to the little girl's penis envy which is obviously based simply on the anatomical difference.

The second source upon which our experience draws is to be found in the analytical material produced by adult women. Naturally it is more difficult to form a judgement on this, and there is therefore more scope for the subjective element. We see here in the first instance that penis envy operates as a factor of enormous dynamic power. We see patients rejecting their female functions, their unconscious motive in so doing being the desire to be male. We meet with phantasies of which the content is: 'I once had a penis; I am a man who has been castrated and mutilated', from which proceed feelings of inferiority and which have for after-effect all manner of obstinate hypochondriacal ideas. We see a marked attitude of hostility towards men, sometimes taking the form of depreciation and sometimes of a desire to castrate or maim them, and we see how the whole destinies of certain women are determined by this factor.

It was natural to conclude—and especially natural because of the male orientation of our thinking—that we could link these impressions on to the primary penis envy and to reason *a posteriori* that this envy must possess an enormous intensity, an enormous dynamic power, seeing that it evidently gave rise to such effects. Here we overlooked the fact, more in our general estimation of the situation than in details, that this desire to be a man, so familiar to us from the analyses of adult women, had only very little to do with that early, infantile, primary penis envy, but that it is a secondary formation embodying all that has miscarried in the development towards womanhood.

From beginning to end my experience has proved to me with unchanging clearness that the Oedipus complex in women leads (not only in extreme cases where the subject has come to grief, but *regularly*) to a regression to penis envy, naturally in every possible degree and shade. The difference between the outcome of the male and the female Oedipus complexes seems to me in average cases to be as follows. In boys the mother as a sexual object is renounced owing to the fear of castration, but the male role itself is not only affirmed in further development but is actually overemphasized in the reaction to the fear of castration. We see this clearly in the latency and prepubertal period in boys and generally in later life as well. Girls, on the other hand, not only renounce the father as a sexual object but simultaneously recoil from the feminine role altogether.

In order to understand this flight from womanhood we must consider the facts relating to early infantile onanism, which is the physical expression of the excitations due to the Oedipus complex.

Here again the situation is much clearer in boys, or perhaps we simply know more about it. Are these facts so mysterious to us in girls only because we have always looked at them through the eyes of men? It seems rather like it when we do not even concede to little girls a specific form of onanism but without more ado describe their autoerotic activities as male; and when we conceive of the difference, which surely must exist, as being that of a negative to a positive, i.e. in the case of anxiety about onanism, that the difference is that between a castration threatened and castration that has actually taken place! My analytical experience makes it most decidedly possible that little girls have a specific feminine form of onanism (which incidentally differs in technique from that of boys), even if we assume that the little girl practises exclusively clitoral masturbation, an assumption which seems to me by no means certain. And I do not see why, in spite of its past evolution, it should not be conceded that the clitoris legitimately belongs to and forms an integral part of the female genital apparatus.

Whether in the early phase of the girl's genital development she has organic vaginal sensations is a matter remarkably difficult to determine from the analytical material produced by adult women. In a whole series of cases I have been inclined to conclude that this is so and later I shall quote the material upon which I base this conclusion. That such sensations should occur seems to me theoretically very probable for the following reasons. Undoubtedly the familiar phantasies that an excessively large penis is effecting forcible penetration, producing pain and haemorrhage and threatening to destroy something, go to show that the little girl bases her Oedipus phantasies most realistically (in accordance with the plastic concrete thinking of childhood) on the disproportion in size between father and child. I think too that both the Oedipus phantasies and also the logically ensuing dread of an internal, i.e. vaginal injury go to show that the vagina as well as the clitoris must be assumed to play a part in the early infantile genital organization of women.[16] One might even infer from the later phenomena of frigidity that the vaginal zone has actually a stronger cathexis (arising out of anxiety and attempts at defence) than the clitoris, and this because the incestuous wishes are referred to the vagina with the unerring accuracy of the unconscious. From this point of view frigidity must be regarded as an attempt to ward off the phantasies so full of danger to the ego. And this would also throw a new light on the unconscious pleasurable feelings which, as various authors have maintained, occur at parturition or, alternatively, on the dread of childbirth. For (just because of the disproportion between the vagina and the baby and because of the pain to which this gives rise) parturition would be calculated to a far greater extent than subsequent sexual intercourse to stand to the unconscious for a realization of those early incest-phantasies, a realization to which no guilt is attached. The female genital anxiety, like the castration-dread of boys, invariably bears the impress of feelings of guilt and it is to them that it owes its lasting influence.

A further factor in the situation, and one which works in the same direction, is a certain consequence of the anatomical difference between the sexes. I mean that the boy can inspect his genital to see whether the dreaded consequences of onanism are taking place; the girl, on the other hand, is literally in the dark on this point and remains in complete uncertainty. Naturally this possibility of a reality-test does not carry weight with boys in cases where the castration-anxiety is acute, but in the slighter cases of fear, which are practically more important because they are more frequent, I think that this difference is very important. At any rate the analytical material which has come to light in women whom I have analysed has led me to conclude that this factor plays a considerable part in feminine mental life and that it contributes to the peculiar inner uncertainty so often met with in women.

Under the pressure of this anxiety the girl now takes refuge in a fictitious male role.

What is the economic gain of this flight? Here I would refer to an experience which probably all analysts have had: they find that the desire to be a man is generally admitted comparatively willingly and that, when once it is accepted, it is clung to tenaciously, the reason being the desire to avoid the realization of libidinal wishes and phantasies in connection with the father. Thus the wish to be a man subserves the repression of these feminine wishes or the resistance against their being brought to light. This constantly recurring, typical experience compels us, if we are true to analytical principles, to conclude that the phantasies of being a man were at an earlier period devised for the very purpose of securing the subject against libidinal wishes in connection with the father. The fiction of maleness enabled the girl to escape from the female role now burdened with guilt and anxiety. It is true that this attempt to deviate from her own line to that of the male inevitably brings about a sense of inferiority, for the girl begins to measure herself by pretensions and values which are foreign to her specific biological nature and confronted with which she cannot but feel herself inadequate.

Although this sense of inferiority is very tormenting, analytical experience emphatically shows us that the ego can tolerate it more easily than the sense of guilt associated with the feminine attitude, and hence it is undoubtedly a gain for the ego when the girl flees from the Scylla of the sense of guilt to the Charybdis of the sense of inferiority.

For the sake of completeness I will add a reference to the other gain which, as we know, accrues to women from the process of identification with the father which takes place at the same time. I know of nothing with reference to the importance of this process itself to add to what I have already said in my earlier work.

We know that this very process of identification with the father is one answer to the question why the flight from feminine wishes in regard to the father always leads to the adoption of a masculine attitude. Some reflections connected with what has already been said reveals another point of view which throws some light on this question.

We know that, whenever the libido encounters a barrier in its development, an earlier phase of organization is regressively activated. Now, according to Freud's latest work, penis envy forms the preliminary stage to the true object-love for the father. And so this train of thought suggested by Freud helps us to some comprehension of the inner necessity by which the libido flows back precisely to this preliminary stage whenever and in so far as it is driven back by the incest-barrier.

I agree in principle with Freud's notion that the girl develops towards object-love by way of penis envy, but I think that the nature of this evolution might also be pictured differently.

For when we see how large a part of its strength accrues to primary penis envy only by retrogression from the Oedipus complex, we must resist the temptation to interpret in the light of penis envy the manifestations of so elementary a principle of nature as that of the mutual attraction of the sexes.

Whereupon, being confronted with the question how we should conceive psychologically of this primal, biological principle, we should again have to confess ignorance. Indeed, in this respect the conjecture forces itself more and more strongly upon me that perhaps the causal connection may be the exact converse and that it is just the attraction to the opposite sex, operating from a very early period, which draws the libidinal interest of the little girl to the penis. This interest, in accordance with the level of development reached, acts at first in an auto-erotic and narcissistic manner, as I have described before. If we view these relations thus, fresh problems would logically present themselves with regard to the origin of the male Oedipus complex, but I wish to postpone these for a later paper. But, if penis envy were the first expression of that mysterious attraction of the sexes, there would be nothing to wonder at either when analysis discloses its existence in a yet deeper layer than that in which the desire for a child and the tender attachment to the father occur. The way to this tender attitude towards the father would be prepared not simply by disappointment in regard to the penis but in another way as well. We should then instead have to conceive of the libidinal interest in the penis as a kind of 'partial love', to use Abraham's term.[17] Such love, he says, always forms a preliminary stage to true object-love. We might explain the process too by an analogy from later life: I refer to the fact that admiring envy is specially calculated to lead to an attitude of love.

With regard to the extraordinary ease with which this regression takes place I must mention the analytical discovery[18] that in the associations of female patients the narcissistic desire to possess the penis and the object-libidinal longing for it are often so interwoven that one hesitates as to the sense in which the words 'desire for it'[19] are meant.

One word more about the castration-phantasies proper, which have given their name to the whole complex because they are the most striking part of it. According to my theory of feminine development I am obliged to regard these phantasies also as a secondary formation. I picture their origin as follows: when the woman takes refuge in the fictitious male role her feminine genital anxiety is to some extent translated into male terms—the fear of vaginal injury becomes a phantasy of castration. The girl gains by this conversion, for she exchanges the uncertainty of her expectation of punishment (an uncertainty conditioned by her anatomical formation) for a concrete idea. Moreover, the castration-phantasy too is under the shadow of the old sense of guilt—and the penis is desired as a proof of guiltlessness.

Now these typical motives for flight into the male role—motives whose origin is the Oedipus complex—are reinforced and supported by the actual disadvantage under which women labour in social life. Of course we must recognize that the desire to be a man, when it springs from this last source, is a peculiarly suitable form of rationalization of those unconscious motives. But we must not forget that this disadvantage is actually a piece of reality and that it is immensely greater than most women are aware of.

Georg Simmel says in this connection that 'the greater importance attaching to the male sociologically is probably due to his position of superior strength', and that historically the relation of the sexes may be crudely described as that of master and slave. Here, as always, it is 'one of the privileges of the master that he has not constantly to think that he is master, whilst the position of the slave is such that he can never forget it'.

Here we probably have the explanation also of the under-estimation of this factor in analytical literature. In actual fact a girl is exposed from birth onwards to the suggestion—inevitable, whether conveyed brutally or delicately—of her inferiority, an experience which must constantly stimulate her masculinity complex.

There is one further consideration. Owing to the hitherto purely masculine character of our civilization it has been much harder for women to achieve any sublimation which should really satisfy their nature, for all the ordinary professions have been filled by men. This again must have exercised an influence upon women's feelings of inferiority, for naturally they could not accomplish the same as men in these masculine professions and so it appeared that there was a basis in fact for their inferiority. It seems to me impossible to judge to how great a degree the unconscious motives for the flight from womanhood are reinforced by the actual social subordination of women. One might conceive of the connection as an interaction of psychic and social factors. But I can only indicate these problems here, for they are so grave and so important that they require a separate investigation.

The same factors must have quite a different effect on the man's development. On the one hand they lead to a much stronger repression of his feminine wishes, in that these bear the stigma of inferiority; on the other hand it is far easier for him successfully to sublimate them.

In the foregoing discussion I have put a construction upon certain problems of feminine psychology which in many points differs from the views hitherto current. It is possible and even probable that the picture I have drawn is one-sided from the opposite point of view. But my primary intention in this paper was to indicate a possible source of error arising out of the sex of the observer, and by so doing to make a step forward towards the goal which we are all striving to reach: to get beyond the subjectivity of the masculine or the feminine standpoint and to obtain a picture of the mental development of woman which shall be truer to the facts of her nature—with its specific qualities and its differences from that of man—than any we have hitherto achieved.

Notes

[1] Sigmund Freud (1923e), 'The Infantile Genital Organization: An Interpolation into the Theory of Sexuality', SE 19:141-5.

[2] Helene Deutsch, *Zur Psychoanalyse der weiblichen Sexualfunktionen* (Vienna: Internationaler psychoanalytischer Verlag, 1925).

[3] Sigmund Freud (1925j), 'Some Psychical Consequences of the Anatomical Distinction Between the Sexes', SE 19:243-58.

[4] Georg Simmel, *Philosophische Kultur* (Leipzig: Alfred Kröner Verlag, 1919).

[5] Cf. in particular Mathilde and Mathias Vaerting, *The Dominant Sex: a Study in the Sociology of Sex Differentiation* (London: Allen & Unwin, 1923).

[6] German '*Mensch*'.

[7] German '*Mann*'.

[8] Delius, *Vom Erwachen der Frau*.

[9] Sándor Ferenczi (1924), *Thalassa, a Theory of Genitality* (Albany, NY: Psychoanalytic Quarterly Inc., 1938).

[10] Helene Deutsch, *Psychoanalyse der weiblichen Sexualfunktionen*, and Georg Groddeck (1923), *The Book of the It* (New York: International Universities Press, 1976).

[11] Karen Horney (1923), 'On the Genesis of the Castration Complex in Women' *International Journal of Psycho-Analysis* , 5(1924): 50-65.

[12] Sigmund Freud (1925j), 'Some Psychical Consequences of the Anatomical Distinction between the Sexes', SE 19:243-58.

[13] Sigmund Freud (1917c), 'On Transformations of Instinct as Exemplified in Anal Erotism', SE 17:127-33.

[14] *The Book of the It.*

[15] I have dealt with this subject in greater detail in my paper 'On the Genesis of the Castration Complex in Women'.

[16] Since the possibility of such a connection occurred to me I have learnt to construe in this sense, i.e. as representing the dread of vaginal injury, many phenomena which I was previously content to interpret as castration-phantasies in the male sense.

[17] Karl Abraham (1924), 'A Short Study of the Development of the Libido', *Selected Papers of Karl Abraham* (London: Hogarth Press, 1927), 418-501. See Part 2, 'Origins and Growth of Object Love', reprinted above.

[18] Sigmund Freud referred to this in his (1918a) *The Taboo of Virginity*, SE 11:193-208.

[19] German '*Haben-Wollen*'.

7

A Contribution to the Problem of Libidinal Development of the Genital Phase in Girls

by Josine Müller (1925)

International Journal of Psycho-Analysis 13(1932):361-68f.

Josine Müller's paper was read at a meeting of the German Psycho-Analytical Society on 10th November 1925. The author died suddenly at the close of the year 1930, and this piece was published posthumously in 1932 with an introduction by Carl Müller-Braunschweig, her husband.

Like Horney, Josine Müller argues that the vagina has a greater significance than any other erotogenic zone: since libidinal cathexis of the vagina occurs during the infantile genital period, it makes no sense to privilege the clitoris as erotic site. On the basis of the observation of children and of the analysis of patients she demonstrates that there is a 'vigorous instinctual impulse' associated with the vagina. She links the repression of this impulse with penis envy and clitoral excitation with urethral fantasies. Worth noting is that Müller lays particular stress upon Horney's distinction between primary and secondary penis envy.

* * *

The following paper by the late Josine Müller, who died suddenly and unexpectedly on December 30, 1930, contains some important conclusions about 'a libidinal cathexis of the vagina during the infantile genital period'. The author reports that she found this cathexis precisely in women who later proved frigid and in whom the clitoris had special emphasis. The present communication was read at a meeting of the German Psycho-Analytical Society on November 10, 1925. It is really a précis of the main thesis of a comprehensive work left by the author on the 'study of femininity in the infant in the light of the illnesses of women of the narcissistic type'—a work which I hope later to get published. The book will contain *in extenso* both the material upon which the ideas in this article were based, and also further material collected by Josine Müller in her last five years, which has thoroughly confirmed her view.

- *Carl Müller-Braunschweig*

At a meeting of the Berlin Society on October 31, 1925, Frau Horney read a paper entitled: 'A Woman's Thoughts on the Masculinity-Complex in

Women'. This paper, which will shortly appear in the *Zeitschrift*,[1] leads me to draw attention to the following conjectures. It is my belief that libidinal cathexis of the vagina occurs during the infantile genital period more frequently than has hitherto been supposed and that it causes the vagina to assume a far greater significance than any other erotogenic zone. This occurs just in those subjects who in later life prove frigid in sexual intercourse, in whom the clitoris is especially emphasized and who are burdened with a strong castration complex and masculine character-traits. In this paper I want to limit the discussion to the libidinal cathexis of the two female genital organs. I will refer to thought processes and phantasies only in so far as they offer a key to the subject's preference for clitoral rather than vaginal pleasure, or when it is necessary to touch on the relation of the genital impulses to the castration complex. Two kinds of material will be drawn on: first, direct observation of children, and secondly, the impressions received from the analyses of patients. As regards the latter, the question which has occurred to me is this: if we analyse the subject's castration complex and trace back her perception of the clitoris to her earliest childhood, do we not regularly get a sense of yet another factor which leads us to infer that, in early life, she was aware of instinctual demands associated with the vagina, but very soon repressed them, together with the idea of the special libidinal object and aim connected with them? And further, that, though repressed, this perception permanently troubled the child's consciousness and found negative expression in a general uncertainty of will, instinct and perception?

With regard to the direct observation of children I am basing my remarks on the following recollections, dating from the period of my hospital work and the years when I was in general practice. It quite often happened that mothers consulted me about their little daughters of from two to five years old, whom they brought to see me, stating that the children had made themselves ill through playing with the vagina. I have a specially clear recollection of two such children, one nearly three and the other four years old. Often, examination revealed a reddening of the entrance to the vagina and a slight vaginal discharge. In such cases the physician will first call to mind the fact that when girls are suffering from threadworms it sometimes happens that these, on leaving the bowel, pass into the vagina and set up irritation there, causing the child to rub the part with her fingers.[2] While undoubtedly this is a cause of masturbation in many cases, there are others in which there is no demonstrable external cause, and such children, instead of receiving medical treatment, become the victims of the usual exhortations and threats. Now we know that only the most obvious sexual activities of children are observed by those who bring them up and by physicians. Children who practise vaginal masturbation in a masked form are not detected. Some, for instance, jerk up and down and rock to and fro in their seats, or stimulate the vagina by contracting and relaxing the surrounding muscles. Nor are those children observed who are ready on the very slightest check to conceal their activities, *or even to repress* the instinctual impulse concerned. Nevertheless, if we question physicians, we find a remarkable number of cases of the above kind, though each doctor thinks that his cases are exceptions. Analysts, too, have given me some striking instances. Frau M. Klein referred me to the cases she had already reported from her analyses of children (cf. her remarks at the Würzburg Conference, 1924, and her companion-paper to that of Frau Horney). Boehm gave an instance from the analysis of an adult, who at the age of from five to seven years (like Frau Klein's patient) used to masturbate by drawing the hem of her chemise backwards and forwards, thus pressing on the region of the vagina. Hárnik cited two analyses of adult, frigid women, in whom the clitoris was peculiarly sensitive to stimulation. One of the two knew that, when she was three years old, a hairpin had to be extracted from her vagina by a physician, and the other remembered having practised vaginal masturbation at the age of fifteen. Thus, notwithstanding a conscious libidinal cathexis of the vagina at puberty, she had been able to repress the impulses connected with that organ and to give the preference to the clitoris. To judge by the analyses I myself have conducted, I think it improbable that she could have done this, unless *a path had already been prepared for the later repression in the infantile period.* I myself have a most striking case to quote from my own observation. I hope to include it, with others less obvious, in a full clinical communication on this subject.

There were elements in my analytical material which made me feel certain that children repress, more frequently than we have supposed, an original, instinctual impulse associated with the vagina in favour of a later preference for the clitoris. Before I go more closely into the material, however, let me put before you certain theoretical considerations. Let us consider the hypothetical case of a little girl who, during the genital phase, has become aware of an excitation, perhaps not at first differentiated, of both the clitoris and the vagina. Subsequently, experiences of some sort force her to withdraw her attention from the vaginal part of the excitation and to repress the idea of any aim associated with it. We now realize the importance of the fact that girls have two genital organs: in our hypothetical case, the girl is not obliged wholly to abandon the genital level again; it will already be a great help to her if she succeeds in strengthening the libidinal cathexis of the clitoris; and the more essential it is to withdraw attention from the vagina, the greater the clitoral hypercathexis will have to be. Hence, such a hypercathexis may indicate that the instinctual impulse associated with the vagina was originally specially vigorous.

Now the repression may not be very successful, and I think in fact that it is likely to fail just in so far as clitoral pleasure enables the child to remain on the genital level and saves her from regressing in any great measure to lower levels. But if the repression is thus unsuccessful, one consequence will be that the vaginal excitation will be easily roused again. It will then be met with a fresh effort of repression, but will at any rate threaten to enter consciousness in the form of a sense of guilt, attaching itself most readily to clitoral masturbation, and will tend, moreover, to produce a feeling of general uncertainty of will, instinct and perception. It is inevitable that the defence against intense sensations which mark the very nature of the subject's sex should arouse a sense of inferiority pervading her psychic life; and this will ally itself with the feelings of inferiority which have their origin in penis-envy. On the other hand, the same process of defence will cause preference to be given to such ideas, capacities and activities as can be linked up with the instinctual impulses which remain in the child's consciousness. Clitoral excitations seem to be akin to urethral pleasure and to evoke phantasies containing urethral components, and, conversely, urethral phantasies seem to be apt to induce clitoral excitation. These phantasies are of an active, aggressive character and contain an identification with the man (father) in his sexual role.

We shall expect that in the hypothetical case worked out above the hypercathexis of the clitoris will make it difficult for the child to give up clitoral masturbation even when the latency period sets in, i.e. when the sexual excitation becomes less urgent. At the same time the ill-repressed vaginal impulse, with its infantile goal, will equally persist in the unconscious. On the other hand, just because the child retains the libidinal cathexis of the whole genital, penis-envy will have its full effect.

This last factor only comes into action as a cramping disturbance of the subject's life at the close of puberty or at latest when she enters into a sexual relation, if the fresh flood of sexual impulses fails to overcome her renewed attempts at repression and to make her conscious of vaginal desires, so setting her will in the direction of a recognized central goal of instinctual gratification. In such cases the infantile goal persists in the unconscious. The ego cannot identify itself with this unconscious will and feels secure only when *warding off* genital impulses, whilst other ego-wishes cannot come to terms with the genital desires. Instead of facing the outside world in her own right as an independent observer, the woman is compelled to avoid everything that might awaken her feminine approach to the world, and anxiously to associate herself with the man's way of seeing things. In connection with this renewed identification with the man, I may say that material which I have collected from a number of analyses of little girls between the ages of five and twelve shows how, on the one hand, the final forms of infantile gratification of instinct are warded off and vaginal masturbation recurs at puberty, while, on the other, the phantasies lose their infantile form and take on that which is to persist in later life. This then, largely unconscious as it is, becomes the controlling factor in the woman's life, which proves to be a constant attempt to identify herself with an *ideal* man.

Finally, I would like to say something about the normal self-regard of women, as, on the whole, it ultimately reasserts itself in the face of their penis-envy. I would not in any way minimize the enormous importance of the little girl's wish for the penis; I would merely bring to bear on it some considerations arising from the general nature of human instinctual demands. I have arrived at my present view chiefly by observing how frigid women, whose self-feeling is rendered morbidly sensitive through anxiety since it is perpetually jeopardized by their castration complex, pass into a state of more tranquil self-consciousness as soon as their frigidity begins to be dispelled. This observation has suggested the question: how can the castration complex ever be destroyed if there is very little prospect of any external change in the subject's sexual life?

I imagine that the self-regard of every human being depends very largely on his capacity to satisfy central instinctual impulses and to use them as a basis for satisfactory relations with other people. In the child the genital theme has not yet attained to the central and dominating place in life, but in the case of the adolescent, if his self-regard is to be finally and firmly established, it is essential that those genital tendencies which are proper to his or her sex shall secure clear acceptance by his ego. With some women, however, vaginal impulses are from the outset shut off from conscious perception and remain infantile in aim, whilst their behaviour is nevertheless governed by unconscious vaginal wishes with an infantile goal. In such cases, then, it is inevitable that the woman's behaviour should lead her into discord with her ego-feeling in so far as this is instinctually reinforced by clitoral impulses, and that the conflict which convulses her genital desires themselves should seriously undermine her self-regard. If she makes a fresh attempt at repression by over-emphasizing her masculine attitude and the impulses associated with the clitoris, she will become all the more sensitive to penis-envy. If, on the contrary, the vaginal impulses are admitted to consciousness and given full satisfaction, she will naturally be diverted from her penis-envy. Experience shows that women with the mere capacity (apart from the opportunity) for complete vaginal gratification are better able to fill men's places than frigid women, and at the same time better able to avoid pitting themselves against men in situations in which the woman is bound to be the inferior, thus reviving their castration complex. In this connection I have found Frau Horney's distinction between primary and secondary penis-envy important.

As to the clinical aspect of this problem, I will content myself with indicating in what sort of cases it arises and what are the salient points which confront us. The patients in question are women between the ages of twenty and forty, suffering from hysteria or obsessional neurosis and marked by frigidity or vaginal spasm.

In a few cases, moreover, an attitude of vigorous opposition had prevented the vagina from ever being touched after puberty, either in coitus or in examination, whilst yet marked functional disturbances (such as almost total absence of menstruation, vaginal spasm, etc.), were present up to the beginning of the analysis, but were cleared up by the analysis.

It may be said of these cases, and moreover of their whole life, that the periods when the promptings of sexuality are more urgent cannot be sharply delimited from the other periods of life. The infantile instinctual impulses perturb these children until they are about seven years old. After that age the impulses are subjected to a new type of repression, but the repressive forces soon have to be marshalled against the first renewed onslaughts of sexual instinct at puberty (in the tenth and eleventh years of life). The beginning of the menstrual periods is often accepted with remarkable indifference or may be deferred to an unusually late age, sometimes till the girl's nineteenth year. The ailments belonging to the period of puberty are very troublesome and never really clear up (e.g. symptoms of chlorosis at the age of thirty-five). In women of this type the climacteric begins early and is very prolonged (ten years). I have not had cases of this in analysis, but I have treated such patients in my general practice, sometimes over a period of years, and I have found that for ten to fifteen years after menstruation has ceased, they are subject either to grave chronic depression or, at least, to various typical climacteric troubles, such as variable moods, hyperaemia and outbreaks of perspiration.

I have come to believe that, in these cases, not only is the castration complex extremely active but the repressing forces are engaged in another struggle, which to a certain extent reinforces that complex, a struggle to repress a libidinal cathexis of the vagina which was already making itself felt in infancy. My reasons for thinking so are as follows:

1   If we study the little girl's experiences and phantasies, between, say, her eighth and her eleventh year, these show evidence that she is struggling to free herself from vaginal wishes and arming herself against a relapse into these at the time of puberty.

2   Unless it is because defensive mechanisms have already been set up against the perception of a libidinal cathexis of the female genital organs, it is difficult to see how we get the presence of serious symp-

toms of dysmenorrhoea, or complete indifference to the onset of menstruation, without any awareness of those voluptuous sensations which are normally associated with a congestion of the female sexual organs with blood. We might perhaps more easily understand the postponement of menstruation, sometimes for years after it should have begun, as due to continued failure to effect a libidinal cathexis which the subject had not in fact managed to accomplish previously.

3   Just at this period, when they have the greatest need for care, some young girls show a strong desire to perform special feats of strength and to be particularly active; this attitude of mind, when analysed, usually reveals a potent masculinity or castration complex. Much has been said in this connection about the defence set up against the passive role in sexual life. If analysis is carried further, however, we come upon a different attitude, which one of my patients called 'the fear of feeling afraid'. In her case a particular transference-situation enabled us to trace this form of anxiety to an infantile situation (of which we were already aware) in which she had experienced and stifled a vaginal impulse, passive in its aim and directed towards her father.

4   We know how marriage tends to break down the woman's previous ego-consciousness, and

5   We often find in analysis that, behind the patient's identification with a man, there lies the direct wish to be overpowered and ravished. Both these are points which offer support to the present suggestion.

I hope that, when I have the opportunity to present my material *in extenso*, I shall be able, if not to prove the thesis from which I started, at least to show that it is based on a strong probability.

Notes
[1] See 'The Flight from Womanhood', above.
[2] For instance, we find the following statement in the *Lehrbuch der speziellen Pathologie und Therapie der inneren Krankheiten*, by Strümpell (16th Edition, 1907, vol. 1, p. 684): 'In girls it is not uncommon for the oxyures to stray into the vagina and there, too, a violent irritation is set up, which sometimes acts as an incitement to masturbation'.

8

The Genesis of the Feminine Super-Ego

Carl Müller-Braunschweig (1926)

International Journal of Psycho-Analysis 7(1926):359-62

The article starts with two interrelated questions: what in the little girl is equivalent to castration anxiety? And how does she form a super-ego of sufficient strength to 'oppose and overcome' her Oedipal wishes? Müller-Braunschweig's answers highlight the passivity of a certain feminine attitude, which he links to the little girl's unconscious knowledge of the passivity of the vagina. He is critical of Freud and characterizes Freud's view of early sexuality as starting from a masculine position.

Müller-Braunschweig argues for a type of sexual unconscious essentialism where there is a feminine id in girls which desires to be overpowered in contrast to a masculine id in boys which demands to overpower and penetrate the woman. The crucial difference between the two sexes is as follows. Assuming that the ego is always concerned with activity, there is a conjunction of aims between masculine ego and masculine id, whereas the drive towards activity of the feminine ego is at odds with the passive aim of the feminine id, which leads to the reaction formation of the feminine super-ego. It is this passive attitude of the little girl that Müller-Braunschweig considers to be the female equivalent of castration anxiety.

* * *

According to Freud the Oedipus complex of a boy is wrecked on castration anxiety. The presupposition here is that a boy seeks to take his father's place, is threatened in consequence with the loss of his penis, and tries to put himself in the place of his mother. The male child, in order to save himself from castration, identifies himself with the authority of the parents, especially with that of the father, and of the incest-prohibition associated with the father's personality. By this identification he builds up his super-ego, which spurs him on and gives him the power to oppose and overcome the Oedipus wishes.

The question is: What takes the place of castration anxiety in the case of a girl? Does she possess anything equivalent to this, giving her power in the same degree to form a super-ego? According to Freud, the influences of education and of threatened loss of affection have far more effect in driving a girl to abandon the Oedipus complex and form a super-ego than on a boy.

Now I believe I can show that it is probable that a girl possesses something which can be regarded as perhaps completely equivalent to a boy's castration anxiety. I find this equivalent in the infantile femininity of a little girl, and, as compared with a boy's, in the more pronounced masochistic and passive attitude that is contained in it from the outset. This view is based, it is true, on a certain rectification of the conception we have hitherto held, namely, that the original type of sexuality in the female child is masculine.

I have the impression that we have not only emphasised this too exclusively, but have considered it as too primary. I believe rather that already at a very early stage expression is given in a little girl's mind to her feminine nature, and that the mode of this expression corresponds to an unconscious knowledge of the passive part of the female genital apparatus, i.e. of the vagina; further, that the penis envy indicates a reaction-formation (though also a very early one) against this knowledge and against the passive attitude.

In order to form a proper estimate of this, we must refer to an important relation that the two great systems in the mind—the ego and the id—bear to one another. From the outset the function and endeavour of the ego is to be active, all the more because it has a lifelong difficulty in achieving a full and fruitful activity, since, indeed, it really never reaches and never can reach, in this regard, a satisfying result. The differentiation of the ego from the id must be placed at a very early period; and at this point there begins the struggle of the ego for activity against the claims of the id. It has to rise up and defend itself from the exactions of the id, and escape from the danger of being overmastered by it.

The relation of the ego to its id, however, reveals an important difference between the two sexes. The demand of the masculine id, so far as its sexual striving is concerned, tends, as it develops, towards overpowering the woman, while the demand of the feminine id, on the other hand, tends towards being overpowered by the man.

This means that the ego, in its concern for activity, can find in the masculine sexual striving which has an active purpose a support, a trend in the direction of its own aims; while in the feminine trend which is directed towards a passive aim it must see an opposing force, a danger, and not a support. This noteworthy difference in the relation of the ego to the masculine and the feminine id is of the most decisive importance for the question we are considering.

If we are right in asserting that a little girl shows so soon a primary, passive attitude corresponding to an unconscious knowledge of the passive part of her genital apparatus, then this passive attitude constitutes an equivalent to the castration anxiety of a boy. As the latter finds protection against the threatened passivity (of castration) in the increased activity of the ego that results from the formation of the super-ego, so a girl, by establishing the reaction-formation of the super-ego, finds protection against the incestuous trend that also appears as a danger to her ego because it involves her being overpowered.

If she were to yield to the incestuous trend, the result would be a danger of violation by her father and of the loss of her mother's love. In addition there would also be a loss of the father's love, in so far as a girl sees in him a judge, a ruler, and a representative of every law-giving power.

In the case of a girl the reaction-formation of the super-ego finds ground already prepared, which is lacking—at least in the same sense—in the case of a boy, viz.: the penis-envy, or, better, the penis-phantasy. This we have already suggested as the first reaction-formation against the primary, passive, masochistic attitude of a girl which is regarded as a danger by the infantile ego. The female child's phantasy of the possession of a penis continues to exist unconsciously beneath the conscious, rationalizing idea that she once possessed a penis 'only' it has been taken away, and is an expression of the need to cancel out the primary feminine attitude. This cancelling reaction-formation of the penis-ideal is essential for the feminine ideal-ego; on this foundation the girl's super-ego can be established later on.

If we emphasize the indestructible feminine phantasy of the possession of a penis, and if we admit, as we ought to do, the psychical reality of the imagined penis in the case of a girl alongside the corporeal reality of the penis in the case of the boy, then we can speak positively of a feminine castration anxiety as well as of a masculine. Many adult women, in their parapraxes and dreams, behave entirely 'as if' they possess a member, the loss of which they have constantly to fear. This 'deprivation-anxiety' connected with the possible loss of a penis is, unless I am deceived, at least as great as the castration anxiety of men; indeed it is, if anything, greater.

This dreaded loss of an imagined penis is the infantile precursor, and later on the nucleus, of the loss of the feminine super-ego, an ego-formation which provides security against the passively feminine wish to be violated already adumbrated in infancy. This wish—regarded always in the light of the ego's tendencies to activity and independence—signifies for the ego a greater danger than the actively-masculine wish to violate; for this can be regarded by the ego as a danger only in special circumstances, e.g. when it exists simultaneously with a conflict against an overpowering rival (the castrating father) or with a passively homosexual attitude. Apart from such complications it tends in the same direction as the activity of the ego.

The infantile ego, which is confronted with the task of overcoming the Oedipus complex, is, in comparison with the ego of the adult, still weak and only in process of formation. Yet it finds itself faced with greater difficulties than those with which the adult has to deal; for though the sexual impulses of the infantile ego are actually weaker than those of the adult, yet they are relatively stronger. The principal objects towards which they are directed, and by which they are roused, are the all-powerful parents. Hence there comes into being a relation of the ego to the id, which, so far as concerns the greatness of the danger threatening the ego from the id, can never be found again at any later period. A boy is guided by the danger of castration, a girl by that of violation by the overpowering father. Both protect themselves against these dangers by the reaction-formation of the super-ego. No urgency of equal importance exists any longer in adult life.

A large number of questions arise from what has been submitted here: What are the empirical foundations and the theoretical supports for the assertion of a primary infantile passively-feminine attitude? What place is to be given to this conception in the theory of the stages of libidinal organization? What significance, in this connection, has the phallic stage of organization for a girl? Does the penis-wish exist only as a reaction-formation, or is there also a primary form of it? Has it one or several meanings? What is the relation of the developmental sequence penis-wish—child-wish to the attitude of a girl to her father?[1] What significance for the formation of the super-ego have the actively-masculine and the passively-feminine trends in the processes of identification and desexualization, and what is their relation to the psychical systems? Limits of space, however, compel us to content ourselves with what has been said, and to await a further opportunity for consideration of all these conclusions and hypotheses.[2]

Notes

[1] Cf. Sigmund Freud (1925j), 'Some Psychical Consequences of the Anatomical Distinction between the Sexes', SE 19:243-58.

[2] After reading in manuscript a paper by Karen Horney, 'The Flight from Womanhood', which she read some time ago before the Berlin Society [reprinted above], I cannot omit a reference to the fact that, while there is considerable difference between her work and mine and even occasional contradiction, several striking and gratifying points of agreement are to be noticed. E.g. in her paper a girl's 'dread of vaginal injury' is paralleled by the boy's castration-anxiety, and a girl's violation-anxiety is 'the equivalent of a boy's castration-anxiety'; her idea also that the 'masculine phantasy' is a security against libidinal wishes towards the father partly coincides with my conception of the 'penis-phantasy' as a reaction-formation against the wishes to be violated by the father that expose the ego to danger. This agreement seems to me all the more noteworthy from the fact that both of us not only support our statements by independent observations made in the course of analytic practice, but evidently reach our common ground by following individually lines of thought that are quite different.

9

The Early Development of Female Sexuality

Ernest Jones (1927)

International Journal of Psycho-Analysis 8(1927):459-72

First presented at the Tenth International Congress of Psycho-Analysis in Innsbruck on 1st September 1927, Jones's paper appeared in print in October of the same year.

Jones starts with Freud's now well known claim about the inadequacy of psychoanalytic knowledge regarding female sexuality. He sides with Horney in seeing the cultural bias against women as one of the reasons for this inadequacy and he puts forward his own claim concerning the phallocentric bias of male analysts. Jones explores two questions. The first is the very same question that Carl Müller-Braunschweig (see above) had raised in the same journal the previous year: what, in women, corresponds to the fear of castration? His second question is: what differentiates the path of homosexual women from that of heterosexual women?

Jones has two major objections to the notion of castration: first that the psychoanalytic concept of castration is equated with the abolition of sexuality, as opposed to a partial threat to sexual enjoyment; and second that penis envy in women is partial and secondary, from which he concludes that the threat of castration is also partial and secondary. In the place of castration, Jones proposes another concept, 'aphanisis', for the total and permanent loss of the capacity for sexual enjoyment. In his view, this is the real 'bedrock' of the neuroses. Along with Deutsch and Klein, interestingly enough, Jones argues that while no woman escapes penis envy, it only plays a small role in neurosis.

In his version of psychosexual developmental stages, Jones construes Freud's phallic phase as a secondary, defensive construction rather than as a phase in its own right. Also, he claims that the Oedipus conflict is resolved in the same way for boys and girls: both either give up their love-object or their own sex. The latter choice yields two types of homosexuality in women, both marked in their fixation to the oral-sadistic stage. The first type is characterized by an intense oral eroticism, dependence on women and disinterest in men; the second type is characterized by sadism, a wish to obtain recognition of her male attributes and resentment towards men, played out in castrating (biting) fantasies.

* * *

Freud has more than once commented on the fact that our knowledge of the early stages in female development is much more obscure and imperfect than that of male development, and Karen Horney has forcibly, though justly, pointed out that this must be connected with the greater tendency to bias that exists on the former subject. It is probable that this tendency to bias is common to the two sexes, and it would be well if every writer on the subject kept this consideration in the foreground of his mind throughout. Better still, it is to be hoped that analytic investigation will gradually throw light on the nature of the prejudice in question and ultimately dispel it. There is a healthy suspicion growing that men analysts have been led to adopt an unduly phallocentric view of the problems in question, the importance of the female organs being correspondingly underestimated. Women have on their side contributed to the general mystification by their secretive attitude towards their own genitals and by displaying a hardly disguised preference for interest in the male organ.

The immediate stimulus to the investigation on which the present paper is mainly based was provided by the unusual experience, a couple of years ago, of having to analyse at the same time five cases of manifest homosexuality in women. The analyses were all deep ones and lasted from three to five years; they have been completed in three of the cases and carried to a far stage in the other two. Among the numerous problems thus aroused two particular ones may serve as a starting point for the considerations I wish to bring forward here. They were: what precisely in women corresponds with the fear of castration in men? and what differentiates the development of homosexual from that of heterosexual women? It will be noticed that these two questions are closely related, the word 'penis' indicating the point of connection between them.

A few clinical facts about these cases may be of interest, though I do not propose to relate any casuistic material. Three of the patients were in the twenties and two in the thirties. Only two of the five had an entirely negative attitude towards men. It was not possible to establish any consistent rule in respect of their conscious attitude towards the parents: all varieties occurred, negative towards the father with either negative or positive towards the mother, and vice versa. In all five cases, however, it proved that the unconscious attitude towards both parents was strongly ambivalent. In all cases there was evidence of an unusually strong infantile fixation in regard to the mother, this being definitely connected with the oral stage. This was always succeeded by a strong father fixation, whether it was temporary or permanent in consciousness.

The first of the two questions mentioned above might also be formulated as follows: when the girl feels that she has already suffered castration, what imagined future event can evoke dread proportionate to the dread of castration? In attempting to answer this question, i.e. to account for the fact that women suffer from dread at least as much as men, I came to the conclusion that the concept 'castration' has in some respects hindered our appreciation of the fundamental conflicts. We have here in fact an example of what Horney has indicated as an unconscious bias from approaching such studies too much from the male point of view. In his illuminating discussion of the penis complex in women, Abraham[1] had remarked that there was no reason for not applying the word 'castration' there as well as with men, for wishes and fears about the penis of a parallel order occur in both. To agree with this statement, however, does not involve overlooking the differences in the two cases, nor should it blind us to the danger of importing into the one considerations with which we are already familiar in the other. Freud has justly remarked in connection with the pregenital precursors of castration (weaning and defecation, pointed out by Stärcke and myself respectively) that the psychoanalytical concept of castration, as distinguished from the corresponding biological one, refers definitely to the penis alone—the testicles at most being included in addition.

Now the fallacy to which I wish to draw attention here is this. The all-important part normally played in male sexuality by the genital organs naturally tends to make us equate castration with the abolition of sexuality altogether. This fallacy often creeps into our arguments even though we know that many men wish to be castrated for, among others, erotic reasons, so that their sexuality certainly does not disappear with the surrender of the penis. With women, where the whole penis idea is always partial and mostly secondary in nature, this should be still more evident. In other words, the prominence of castration fears among men tends sometimes to make us forget that in both sexes castration is only a *partial* threat, however important a one, against sexual capacity and enjoyment as a whole. For the main blow of total extinction we might do well to use a separate term, such as the Greek word 'aphanisis'.

If we pursue to its roots the fundamental fear which lies at the basis of all neuroses we are driven, in my opinion, to the conclusion that what it really signifies is this aphanisis, the total, and of course permanent, extinction of the capacity (including opportunity) for sexual enjoyment. After all, this is the consciously avowed intention of most adults towards children. Their attitude is quite uncompromising: children are not to be permitted *any* sexual gratification. And we know that to the child the idea of indefinite postponement is much the same as that of permanent refusal. We cannot, of course, expect that the unconscious, with its highly concrete nature, will express itself for us in these abstract terms, which admittedly represent a generalization. The nearest approach to the idea of aphanisis that we meet with clinically is that of castration and of death thoughts (conscious dread of death and unconscious death wishes). I may cite here an obsessional case in a young man which illustrates the same point. He had substituted as his *summum bonum* the idea of aesthetic enjoyment for that of sexual gratification, and his castration fears took the form of apprehension lest he should lose his capacity for this enjoyment, behind them being of course the concrete idea of the loss of the penis.

From this point of view we see that the question under discussion was wrongly put. The male dread of being castrated may or may not have a precise female counterpart, but what is more important is to realize that this dread is only a special case and that both sexes ultimately dread exactly the same thing, aphanisis. The mechanism whereby this is supposed to be brought about shows important differences in the two sexes. If we neglect for the moment the sphere of auto-erotism—on the justifiable ground that conflicts here owe their main importance to the subsequent allo-erotic cathexis of it—and thus confine our attention to allo-erotism itself, we may say that the reconstructed train of thought in the male is somewhat as follows: 'I wish to obtain gratification by committing a particular act, but I dare not do so because I fear that it would be followed by the punishment of aphanisis, by castration that would mean for me the permanent extinction of sexual pleasure'. The corresponding thought in the female, with her more passive nature, is characteristically somewhat different: 'I wish to obtain gratification through a particular experience, but I dare not take any steps towards bringing it about, such as asking for it and thus confessing my guilty wish, because I fear that to do so would be followed by aphanisis'. It is, of course, plain that this difference is not only not invariable, but is in any event only one of degree. In both cases there is activity, though it is more overt and vigorous with the male. This is not, however, the main difference in accent: a more important one depends on the fact that, for obvious physiological reasons, the female is much more dependent on her partner for her gratification than is the male on his. Venus had much more trouble with Adonis, for example, than Pluto with Persephone.

The last consideration mentioned provides the biological reason for the most important psychological differences in the behaviour and attitude of the sexes. It leads directly to a greater dependence (as distinct from desire) of the female on the willingness and moral approbation of the partner than we usually find with the male, where the corresponding sensitiveness occurs in respect of another, authoritative male. Hence, among other things, the more characteristic reproaches and need for reassurance on the woman's part. Among the important social consequences the following may be mentioned. It is well known that the morality of the world is essentially a male creation and—what is much more curious—that the moral ideals of women are mainly copied from those of men. This must certainly be connected with the fact, pointed out by Helene Deutsch,[2] that the super-ego of women is, like that of men, predominantly derived from reactions to the father. Another consequence, which brings us back to our main discussion, is that the mechanism of aphanisis tends to differ in the two sexes. Whereas with the male this is typically conceived of in the active form of castration, with the female the primary fear would appear to be that of separation. This can be imagined as coming about through the rival mother intervening between the girl and the father, or even through her sending the girl away for ever, or else through the father simply with-holding the desired gratification. The deep fear of being deserted that most women have is a derivative of the latter.

At this point it is possible to obtain from the analysis of women a deeper insight than from that of men into the important question of the relation between privation and guilt, in other words into the genesis of the super-ego. In his paper on the passing of the Oedipus complex Freud suggested that this happened in the female as the direct result of continued disappointment (privation), and we know that the super-ego is as much the heir of this complex in the female as in the male where it is the product of the guilt derived from the dread of castration. It follows, and my analytical experience fully confirms the conclusion,[3] that sheer privation comes, of course in both sexes, to have just the same meaning as deliberate deprivation on the part of the human environment. We thus reach the formula: *Privation is equivalent to frustration.* It is even likely that, as may be inferred from Freud's remarks on the passing of the female Oedipus complex, privation alone may be an adequate cause for the genesis of guilt. To discuss this further would take us too far into the structure of the super-ego and away from the present theme, but I should like just to mention a view I have reached which is sufficiently germane to the latter. It is that guilt, and with it the super-ego, is as it were artificially built up for the purpose of protecting the child from the stress of privation, i.e. of ungratified libido, and so warding off the dread of aphanisis that always goes with this; it does so, of course, by damping down the wishes that are not destined to be gratified. I even think that the external disapproval, to which the whole of this process used to be ascribed, is largely an affair of exploitation on the child's part; that is to say, non-gratification primarily means danger, and the child projects this into the outer world, as it does with all internal dangers, and then makes use of any disapproval that comes to meet it there (*moralisches Entgegenkommen*) to signalize the danger and to help it in constructing a barrier against this.

To return once more to the young girl, we are faced with the task of tracing the various stages in development from the initial oral one. The view commonly accepted is that the nipple, or artificial teat, is replaced, after a little dallying with the thumb, by the clitoris as the chief source of pleasure, just as it is with boys by the penis. Freud[4] holds that it is the comparative unsatisfactoriness of this solution which automatically guides the child to seek for a better external penis, and thus ushers in the Oedipus situation where the wish for a baby[5] gradually replaces that for a penis. My own analyses, as do Melanie Klein's 'early analyses', indicate that in addition to this there are more direct transitions between the oral and the Oedipus stages. It would seem to me that the tendencies derived from the former stage bifurcate early into clitoris and fellatio directions, i.e. into digital plucking at the clitoris and fellatio phantasies respectively; the proportion between the two would naturally be different in different cases, and this may be expected to have fateful consequences for the later development.

We have now to follow these lines of development in closer detail, and I will first sketch what I conceive to be the more normal mode of development, that leading to heterosexuality. Here the sadistic phase sets in late, and so neither the oral nor the clitoris stage receives any strong sadistic cathexis. In consequence, the clitoris does not become associated with a particularly active masculine attitude (thrusting forward, etc.), nor on the other hand is the oral-sadistic phantasy of biting off the male penis at all highly developed. The oral attitude is mainly a sucking one and passes by the well-known developmental transition into the anal stage. The two alimentary orifices thus constitute the receptive female organ. The anus is evidently identified with the vagina to begin with, and the differentiation of the two is an extremely obscure process, more so perhaps than any other in female development; I surmise, however, that it takes place in part at an earlier age than is generally supposed. A variable amount of sadism is always developed in connection with the anal stage and is revealed in the familiar phantasies of anal rape which may or may not pass over into beating phantasies. The Oedipus relationship is here in full activity; and the anal phantasies, as we shall show later, are already a compromise between libidinal and self-punishment tendencies. This mouth-anus-vagina stage, therefore, represents an identification with the mother.

What in the meantime has been the attitude towards the penis? It is likely enough that the initial one is purely positive,[6] manifested by the desire to suck it. But penis-envy soon sets in and apparently always. The primary, so to speak auto-erotic, reasons for this have been well set out by Karen Horney[7] in her discussion of the part played by the organ in urinary, exhibitionistic, scopophilic and masturbatory activities. The wish to possess a penis as the male does passes normally, however, into the wish to share his penis in some coitus-like action by means of the mouth, anus or vagina. Various sublimations and reactions show that no woman escapes the early penis-envy stage, but I fully agree with Karen Horney,[8] Helene Deutsch,[9] Melanie Klein,[10] and other workers in their view that what we meet with clinically as penis-envy in the neuroses is only in small part derived from this source. We have to distinguish between what may perhaps be termed pre-Oedipus and post-Oedipus penis-envy (more accurately, auto-erotic and allo-erotic penis-envy), and I am convinced that clinically the latter is much the more significant of the two. Just as masturbatory and other auto-erotic activities owe their main importance to reinvestment from allo-erotic sources, so we have to recognize that many clinical phenomena depend on the defensive function of regression, recently insisted on by Freud.[11] It is the privation resulting from the continued disappointment at never being allowed to share the penis in coitus with the father, or thereby to obtain a baby, that reactivates the girl's early wish to possess a penis of her own. According to the theory put forward above, it is this privation that is primarily the unendurable situation, the reason being that it is tantamount to the fundamental dread of aphanisis. Guilt, and the building-up of the super-ego, is, as was explained above, the first and invariable defence against the unendurable privation. But this is too negative a solution in itself; the libido must come to expression somehow as well.

There are only two possible ways in which the libido can flow in this situation, though both may, of course, be attempted. The girl must choose, broadly speaking, between sacrificing her erotic attachment to her father and sacrificing her femininity, i.e. her anal identification with the mother. Either the object must be exchanged for another one or the wish must be; it is impossible to retain both. Either the father or the vagina (including pregenital vaginas) must be renounced. In the first case feminine wishes are developed on the adult plane—i.e. diffuse erotic charm (narcissism), positive vaginal attitude towards coitus, culminating in pregnancy and child-birth—and are transferred to more accessible objects. In the second case the bond with the father is retained, but the object-relationship in it is converted into identification, i.e. a penis complex is developed.

More will be said in the next section about the precise way in which this identification defence operates, but what I should like to lay stress on at the moment is the interesting parallelism thus established, already hinted at by Horney,[12] between the solutions of the Oedipus conflict in the two sexes. The boy also is threatened with aphanisis, the familiar castration fear, by the inevitable privation of his incest wishes. He also has to make the choice between changing the wish and changing the object, between renouncing his mother and renouncing his masculinity, i.e. his penis. We have thus obtained a generalization which applies in a unitary manner to boy and girl alike: *faced with aphanisis as the result of inevitable privation, they must renounce either their sex or their incest*; what cannot be retained, except at the price of neurosis, is hetero-erotic and allo-erotic incest, i.e. an incestuous object-relationship. In both cases the situation of prime difficulty is the simple, but fundamental, one of union between penis and vagina. Normally this union is made possible by the overcoming of the Oedipus complex. When, on the other hand, the solution of inversion is attempted every effort is made to avoid the union, because it is bound up with the dread of aphanisis. The individual, whether male or female, then identifies his sexual integrity with possessing the organ of the opposite sex and becomes pathologically dependent on it. With boys this can be done either by using their mouth or anus as the necessary female organ (towards either a man or a masculine woman) or else by vicariously adopting the genitalia of a woman with whom they identify themselves; in the latter case they are dependent on the woman who carries the precious object and develop anxiety if she is absent or if anything in her attitude makes the organ difficult of access. With girls the same alternative presents itself, and they become pathologically dependent on either possessing a penis themselves in their imagination or on having unobstructed access to that of the man with whom they have identified themselves. If the 'condition of dependence' (cf. Freud's phrase '*Liebesbedingung*') is not fulfilled the individuals, man or woman, approach an aphanistic state or, in looser terminology, 'feel castrated'. They alternate, therefore, between potency on the basis of inverted gratification and aphanisis. To put it more simply, they either have an organ of the opposite sex or none at all; to have one of their own sex is out of the question.

We have next to turn to the second of our two questions, the difference in the development of heterosexual and homosexual women. This difference was indicated in our discussion of the two alternative solutions of the Oedipus conflict, but it has now to be pursued in further detail. The divergence there mentioned—which, it need hardly be said, is always a matter of degree—between those who surrender the position of their object-libido (father) and those who surrender the position of their subject-libido (sex), can be followed into the field of homosexuality itself. One can distinguish two broad groups here. (1) Those who retain their interest in men, but who set their hearts on being accepted by men as one of themselves. To this group belongs the familiar type of women who ceaselessly complain of the unfairness of women's lot and their unjust ill-treatment by men. (2) Those who have little or no interest in men, but whose libido centres on women. Analysis shows that this interest in women is a vicarious way of enjoying femininity; they merely employ other women to exhibit it for them.[13]

It is not hard to see that the former group corresponds with the class in our previous division where the sex of the subject is surrendered, while the latter group corresponds with those who surrender the object (the father), replacing him by themselves through identification. I will amplify this condensed statement for the sake of greater clarity. The members of the first group exchange their own sex, but retain their first love-object; the object-relationship, however, becomes replaced by identification, and the aim of the libido is to procure recognition of this identification by the former object. The members of the second group also identify themselves with the love-object, but then lose further interest in him; their external object-relationship to the other woman is very imperfect, for she merely represents their own femininity through identification, and their aim is vicariously to enjoy the gratification of this at the hand of an unseen man (the father incorporated in themselves).

Identification with the father is thus common to all forms of homosexuality, though it proceeds to a more complete degree in the first group than in the second, where, in a vicarious way, some femininity is after all retained. There is little doubt that this identification serves the function of keeping feminine wishes in repression. It constitutes the most complete denial imaginable of the accusation of harbouring guilty feminine wishes, for it asserts, 'I cannot possibly desire a man's penis for my gratification, since I already possess one of my own, or at all events I want nothing else than one of my own'. Expressed in terms of the theory developed earlier in this paper, it assures the most complete defence against the aphanistic danger of privation from the non-gratification of the incest wishes. The defence is in fact so well designed that it is little wonder that indications of it can be detected in all girls passing through the Oedipus stage of development, though the extent to which it is retained later is extremely variable. I would even venture the opinion that when Freud postulated a 'phallic' stage in female development corresponding with that in the male, i.e. a stage in which all the interest appears to relate to the male organ only with obliteration of the vaginal or pre-vaginal organs, he was giving a clinical description of what may be observed rather than a final analysis of the actual libidinal position at that stage; for it seems to me likely that the phallic stage in normal girls is but a mild form of the father-penis identification of female homosexuals, and, like it, of an essentially secondary and defensive nature.

Horney[14] has pointed out that for a girl to maintain a feminine position and to accept the absence of a penis in herself often signifies not only the daring to have incestuous object-wishes, but also the phantasy that her physical state is the result of a castrating rape once actually performed by the father. The penis identification, therefore, implies a denial of both forms of guilt, the wish that the incestuous deed may happen in the future and the wish-fulfilment phantasy that it has already happened in the past.

She further points out the greater advantage that this heterosexual identification presents to girls than to boys, because the defensive advantage common to both is strengthened with the former by the reinforcement of narcissism derived from the old pre-Oedipus sources of envy (urinary, exhibitionistic and masturbatory) and weakened with the latter by the blow to narcissism involved in the acceptance of castration.

As this identification is to be regarded as a universal phenomenon among young girls, we have to seek further for the motives that heighten it so extraordinarily and in such a characteristic way among those who later become homosexual. Here I must present my conclusions on this point even more briefly than those on the former ones. The fundamental—and, so far as one can see, inborn—factors that are decisive in this connection appear to be two—namely, an unusual intensity of oral erotism and of sadism respectively. These converge in an *intensification of the oral-sadistic stage*, which I would regard, in a word, as *the central characteristic of homosexual development in women.*

The sadism shows itself not only in the familiar muscular manifestations, with the corresponding derivatives of these in character, but also in imparting a specially active (thrusting) quality to the clitoris impulses, which naturally heightens the value of any penis that may be acquired in phantasy. Its most characteristic manifestation, however, is to be found in the oral-sadistic impulse forcibly to wrench the penis from the man by the act of biting. When, as is often found, the sadistic temperament is accompanied by a ready reversal of love to hate, with the familiar ideas of injustice, resentment and revenge, then the biting phantasies gratify both the desire to obtain a penis by force and also the impulse to revenge themselves on the man by castrating him.

The high development of the oral erotism is manifested in the numerous ways well known through the researches of Abraham[15] and Edward Glover;[16] they may be positive or negative in consciousness. A special feature, however, to which attention should be called is the importance of the tongue in such cases. The identification of tongue with penis, with which Flugel[17] and I[18] have dealt at length, reaches with some female homosexuals a quite extraordinary degree of completeness. I have seen cases where the tongue was an almost entirely satisfactory substitute for the penis in homosexual activities. It is evident that the nipple fixation here implied favours the development of homosexuality in two ways. It makes it harder for the girl to pass from the fellatio position to that of vaginal coitus, and it also makes it easier to have recourse once more to a woman as the object of libido.

A further interesting correlation may be effected at this point. The two factors mentioned above of oral erotism and sadism appear to correspond very well with the two classes of homosexuals. Where the oral erotism is the more prominent of the two the individual will probably belong to the second group (interest in women) and where the sadism is the more prominent to the first group (interest in men).

A word should be said about the important factors that influence the *later* development of female homosexuality. We have said that, to protect herself against aphanisis, the girl erects various barriers, notably penis identification, against her femininity. Prominent among these is a strong sense of guilt and condemnation concerning feminine wishes; most often this is for the greater part unconscious. As an aid to this barrier of guilt the idea is developed of 'men' (i.e. the father) being strongly opposed to feminine wishes. To help her own condemnation of it she is forced to believe that all men in their hearts disapprove of femininity. To meet this comes the unfortunate circumstance that many men do really evince disparagement of women's sexuality together with dread of the female organ. There are several reasons for this, into which we need not enter here; they all centre around the male castration complex. The homosexual woman, however, seizes with avidity on any manifestations of this attitude and can be means of them sometimes convert her deep belief into a complete delusional system. Even in milder forms it is quite common to find both men and women ascribing the whole of the supposed inferiority of women[19] to the social influences which the deeper tendencies have exploited in the way just indicated.

I will conclude with a few remarks on the subjects of dread and punishment among women in general. The ideas relating to these may be connected mainly with the mother or mainly with the father. In my experience the former is more characteristic of the heterosexual and the latter more of the homosexual. The former appears to be a simple retaliation for the death wishes against the mother, who will punish the girl by coming between her and the father, by sending the girl away for ever, or by in any other way seeing to it that her incestuous wishes remain ungratified. The girl's answer is partly to retain her femininity at the cost of renouncing the father and partly to obtain vicarious gratification of her incest wishes in her imagination through identification with the mother.

When the dread mainly relates to the father the punishment takes the obvious form of his withholding gratification of her wishes, and this rapidly passes over into the idea of his disapproval of them. Rebuff and desertion are the common conscious expressions of this punishment. If this privation takes place on the oral plane the answer is resentment and castrating (biting) phantasies. If it takes place on the later anal plane the outcome is rather more favourable. Here the girl manages to combine her erotic wishes with the idea of being punished in a single act—namely, of anal-vaginal rape; the familiar phantasies of being beaten are, of course, a derivative of this. As was remarked above, this is one of the ways in which incest gets equated with castration, so that the penis phantasy is a protection against both.

We may now *recapitulate the main conclusions* reached here. For different reasons both boys and girls tend to view sexuality in terms of the penis alone, and it is necessary for analysts to be sceptical in this direction. The concept 'castration' should be reserved, as Freud pointed out, for the penis alone and should not be confounded with that of 'extinction of sexuality', for which the term 'aphanisis' is proposed. Privation in respect of sexual wishes evokes with the child the fear of aphanisis, i.e. is equivalent to the dread of frustration. Guilt arises rather from within as a defence against this situation than as an imposition from without, though the child exploits any *moralisches Entgegenkommen* in the outer world.

The oral-erotic stage in the young girl passes directly into the fellatio and clitoris stages, and the former of these then into the anal-erotic stage; the mouth, anus and vagina thus form an equivalent series for the female organ. The repression of the incest wishes results in regression to the pre-Oedipus, or auto-erotic, penis-envy as a defence against them. The penis-envy met with clinically is principally derived from this reaction on the allo-erotic plane, the identification with the father essentially representing denial of femininity. Freud's 'phallic phase' in girls is probably a secondary, defensive construction rather than a true developmental stage.

To avoid neurosis both the boy and the girl have to overcome the Oedipus conflict in the same way: they can surrender either the love-object or their own sex. In the latter, homosexual solution they become dependent on imagined possession of the organ of the opposite sex, either directly or through identification with another person of that sex. This yields the two main forms of homosexuality.

The essential factors that decide whether a girl will develop the father-identification in such a high degree as to constitute a clinical inversion are specially intense oral erotism and sadism, which typically combine in an intense oral-sadistic stage. If the former of these two factors is the more prominent one the inversion takes the form of dependence on another woman, with lack of interest in men; the subject is male, but enjoys femininity also through identification with a feminine woman whom she gratifies by a penis substitute, most typically the tongue. Prominence of the second factor leads to occupation with men, the wish being to obtain from them recognition of the subject's male attributes; it is this type that shows so often resentment against men, with castrating (biting) phantasies in respect of them.

The heterosexual woman dreads the mother more than the homosexual woman does, whose dread centres around the father. The punishment feared in the latter case is withdrawal (desertion) on the oral level, beating on the anal one (rectal assault).

Notes

1 Karl Abraham (1922), 'Manifestations of the Female Castration Complex', above.

2 Helene Deutsch, *Zur Psychoanalyse der weiblichen Sexualfunktionen* (Vienna: Internationaler psychoanalytischer Verlag, 1925).

3 This was reached partly in conjunction with Mrs. Riviere, whose views are expounded in another context, in 'Symposium on Child-Analysis' (1927). See her *The Inner World and Joan Riviere* (London: Karnac Books, 1991), 80-7.

4 Sigmund Freud (1925*j*), 'Some Psychical Consequences of the Anatomical Distinction between the Sexes', SE 19:256.

5 Little is said throughout this paper about the wish for a baby because I am mainly dealing with early stages. I regard the wish as a later derivative of the anal and phallic trends.

6 Helene Deutsch, *Zur Psychoanalyse der weiblichen Sexualfunktionen*, records an interesting observation in a girl-child of eighteen months who viewed a penis with apparent indifference at that time, and who only later developed affective reactions.

7 Karen Horney (1923), 'On the Genesis of the Castration Complex in Women', *International Journal of Psycho-Analysis*, 5(1924):52-4.

8 Karen Horney, 'Genesis', 64.

9 Helene Deutsch, *Psychoanalyse der weiblichen Sexualfunktionen*, 16-18.

10 Melanie Klein, communications to the British Psycho-Analytical Society.

11 Sigmund Freud (1926*d*), *Inhibitions, Symptoms and Anxiety*, SE 20:105.

12 Karen Horney, 'Genesis', 64.

13 For the sake of simplicity an interesting third form is omitted in the text, but should be mentioned. Some women obtain gratification of feminine desires provided two conditions are present: (1) that the penis is replaced by a surrogate such as the tongue or finger, and (2) that the partner using this organ is a woman instead of a man. Though clinically they may appear in the guise of complete inversion, such cases are evidently nearer to the normal than either of the two mentioned in the text.

14 'Genesis', 64.

15 Karl Abraham (1916), 'The First Pregenital Stage of the Libido' *Selected Papers of Karl Abraham* (London: Hogarth Press, 1927), 248-79.

16 Edward Glover, 'Notes on Oral Character Formation', *International Journal of Psycho-Analysis*, 6(1925):131.

17 J. C. Flugel, 'A Note on the Phallic Significance of the Tongue', *International Journal of Psycho-Analysis*, 6(1925):209.

18 Ernest Jones, *Essays in Applied Psycho-Analysis*, 1923, ch. viii.

19 Really, their inferiority as women.

10

Early Stages of the Oedipus Conflict

Melanie Klein (1927)

International Journal of Psycho-Analysis 9(1928):167-80

Klein's article differs from the other pieces collected here in that it is based upon analysis with children rather than recollections of childhood by adults. Read at the Tenth International Psycho-Analytical Congress, Innsbruck, September 3, 1927, this paper was first published in 1928.

The article synthesises and endorses the ideas of authors whose views on the Oedipus complex were very different from Freud's. Klein mentions the work of Horney and Deutsch, but Abraham could well be added to the list. Klein argues that there exists a primary, 'incorporative', femininity in both sexes, based on an early identification with the mother. In the case of the little girl, it is the receptive and passive aims of the oral and anal phases that determine the girl's turning towards the father.

For Klein, the Oedipus complex occurs much earlier than it does for Freud, prompted as it is by the frustrations experienced by the child at weaning. The Oedipal situation is then reinforced as a result of the frustrations experienced during toilet training. It follows that penis envy is, as for Horney, a secondary formation. In attributing a much greater influence on the Oedipus complex to pregenital conflicts, Klein downplays the role of the anatomical difference between the sexes in the development of female sexuality.

The primary femininity Klein discusses here is grounded on the anal-sadistic level and imparts to this level a new content with two aims: the desire for children and the jealousy aroused by the prospect of future siblings. A third object of the boy's oral-sadistic tendencies is the womb that contains the penis, in other words, the mother as castrator. *This dread of the mother, Klein argues, gives rise to a femininity complex in men which goes together with an asocial and sadistic attitude of contempt—the mask of 'anxiety and ignorance'.*

The end of the paper focuses on the development of girls. Like Deutsch and Abraham, she argues that the genital development of the woman finds its completion in the successful shift of oral libido onto the genital. Unlike them though, she also argues that the arousal of vaginal sensations is contemporaneous with the Oedipus complex.

* * *

In my analyses of children, especially of children between the ages of three and six, I have come to a number of conclusions of which I shall here present a summary.

I have repeatedly alluded to the conclusion that the Oedipus complex comes into operation earlier than is usually supposed. In my last paper, 'The Psychological Principles of Early Analysis',[1] I discussed this subject in greater detail. The conclusion which I reached there was that the Oedipus tendencies are released in consequence of the frustration which the child experiences at weaning, and that they make their appearance at the end of the first and the beginning of the second year of life; they receive reinforcement through the anal frustrations undergone during training in cleanliness. The next determining influence upon the mental processes is that of the anatomical difference between the sexes.

The boy, when he finds himself impelled to abandon the oral and anal positions for the genital, passes on to the aim of *penetration* associated with possession of the penis. Thus he changes not only his libido-position, but its aim, and this enables him to retain his original love-object. In the girl, on the other hand, the *receptive* aim is carried over from the oral to the genital position: she changes her libido-position, but retains its aim, which has already led to disappointment in relation to her mother. In this way receptivity for the penis is induced in the girl, who then turns to the father as her love-object.

The very onset of the Oedipus wishes, however, already becomes associated with incipient dread of castration and feelings of guilt.

The analysis of adults, as well as of children, has familiarized us with the fact that the pregenital instinctual impulses carry with them a sense of guilt, and it was thought at first that the feelings of guilt were of subsequent growth, displaced back on to these tendencies, though not originally associated with them. Ferenczi assumes that, connected with the urethral and anal impulses, there is a 'kind of physiological forerunner of the super-ego', which he terms 'sphincter-morality'. According to Abraham, anxiety makes its appearance on the cannibalistic level, while the sense of guilt arises in the succeeding early anal-sadistic phase.

My findings lead rather further. They show that the sense of guilt associated with pregenital fixation is already the direct effect of the Oedipus conflict. And this seems to account satisfactorily for the genesis of such feelings, for we know the sense of guilt to be simply a result of the introjection (already accomplished or, as I would add, in process of being accomplished) of the Oedipus love-objects: that is, a sense of guilt is a product of the formation of the super-ego.

The analysis of little children reveals the structure of the super-ego as built up of identifications dating from very different periods and strata in the mental life. These identifications are surprisingly contradictory in character, over-indulgence and excessive severity existing side by side. We find in them, too, an explanation of the severity of the super-ego, which comes out specially plainly in these infant analyses. It does not seem clear why a child of, say, four years old should set up in his mind an unreal, phantastic image of parents who devour, cut and bite. But it is clear why in a child of about *one year* old the anxiety caused by the beginning of the Oedipus conflict takes the form of a dread of being devoured and destroyed. The child himself desires to destroy the libidinal object by biting, devouring and cutting it, which leads to anxiety, since awakening of the Oedipus tendencies is followed by introjection of the object, which then becomes one from which punishment is to be expected. The child then dreads a punishment corresponding to the offence: the super-ego becomes something which bites, devours and cuts.

The connection between the formation of the super-ego and the pregenital phases of development is very important from two points of view. On the one hand, the sense of guilt attaches itself to the oral and anal-sadistic phases, which as yet predominate; and, on the other, the super-ego comes into being while these phases are in the ascendant, which accounts for its sadistic severity.

These conclusions open up a new perspective. Only by strong repression can the still very feeble ego defend itself against a super-ego so menacing. Since the Oedipus tendencies are at first chiefly expressed in the form of oral and anal impulses, the question of which fixations will predominate in the Oedipus development will be mainly determined by the degree of the repression which takes place at this early stage.

Another reason why the direct connection between the pregenital phase of development and the sense of guilt is so important is that the oral and anal frustrations, which are the prototypes of all later frustrations in life, at the same time signify *punishment* and give rise to anxiety. This circumstance makes the frustration more acutely felt, and this bitterness contributes largely to the hardship of all subsequent frustrations.

We find that important consequences ensue from the fact that the ego is still so little developed when it is assailed by the onset of the Oedipus tendencies and the incipient sexual curiosity associated with them. Still quite undeveloped intellectually, it is exposed to an onrush of problems and questions. One of the most bitter grievances which we come upon in the unconscious is that this tremendous questioning impulse, which is apparently only partly conscious and even so far as it is conscious 01cannot yet be expressed in words, remains unanswered. Another reproach follows hard upon this, namely, that the child could not understand words and speech. Thus his first questions go back beyond the beginnings of his understanding of speech.

In analysis both these grievances give rise to an extraordinary amount of hate. Singly or in conjunction they are the cause of numerous inhibitions of the epistemophilic impulse: for instance, the incapacity to learn foreign languages, and, further, hatred of those who speak a different tongue. They are also responsible for direct disturbances in speech, etc. The curiosity which shows itself plainly later on, mostly in the fourth or fifth year of life, is not the beginning, but the climax and termination, of this phase of development, which I have also found to be true of the Oedipus conflict in general.

The early feeling of *not knowing* has manifold connections. It unites with the feeling of being incapable, impotent, which soon results from the Oedipus situation. The child also feels this frustration the more acutely because he *knows nothing* definite about sexual processes. In both sexes the castration complex is accentuated by this feeling of ignorance.

The early connection between the epistemophilic impulse and sadism is very important for the whole mental development. This instinct, roused by the striving of the Oedipus tendencies, at first mainly concerns itself with the mother's womb, which is assumed to be the scene of all sexual processes and developments. The child is still dominated by the anal-sadistic libido-position which impels him to wish to *appropriate* the contents of the womb. He thus begins to be curious about what it contains, what it is like, etc. So the epistemophilic instinct and the desire to take possession come quite early to be most intimately connected with one another and at the same time with the sense of guilt aroused by the incipient Oedipus conflict. This significant connection ushers in a phase of development in both sexes which is of vital importance, hitherto not sufficiently recognized. It consists of a very early identification with the mother.

The course run by this 'femininity' phase must be examined separately in boys and in girls, but, before I proceed to this, I will show its connection with the previous phase, which is common to both sexes.

In the early anal-sadistic stage the child sustains his second severe trauma, which strengthens his tendency to turn away from the mother. She has frustrated his oral desires, and now she also interferes with his anal pleasures. It seems as though at this point the anal deprivations cause the anal tendencies to amalgamate with the sadistic tendencies. The child desires to get possession of the mother's faeces, by penetrating into her body, cutting it to pieces, devouring and destroying it. Under the influence of his genital impulses, the boy is beginning to turn to his mother as love-object. But his sadistic impulses are in full activity, and the hate originating in earlier frustrations is powerfully opposed to his object-love on the genital level. A still greater obstacle to his love is his dread of castration by the father, which arises with the Oedipus impulses. The degree in which he attains to the genital position will partly depend on his capacity for tolerating this anxiety. Here the intensity of the oral-sadistic and anal-sadistic fixations is an important factor. It affects the degree of hatred which the boy feels towards the mother; and this, in its turn, hinders him to a greater or lesser extent in attaining a positive relation to her. The sadistic fixations exercise also a decisive influence upon the formation of the super-ego, which is coming into being whilst these phases are in the ascendant. The more cruel the super-ego the more terrifying will be the father as castrator, and the more tenaciously in the child's flight from his genital impulses will he cling to the sadistic levels, from which his Oedipus tendencies in the first instance then also take their colour.

In these early stages all the positions in the Oedipus development are cathected in rapid succession. This, however, is not noticeable, because the picture is dominated by the pregenital impulses. Moreover, no rigid line can be drawn between the active heterosexual attitude which finds expression on the anal level and the further stage of identification with the mother.

We have now reached that phase of development of which I spoke before under the name of the 'femininity phase'. It has its basis on the anal-sadistic level and imparts to that level a new content, for faeces are now equated with the child that is longed for, and the desire to rob the mother now applies to the child as well as to faeces. Here we can discern two aims which merge with one another. The one is directed by the desire for children, the intention being to appropriate them, while the other aim is motivated by jealousy of the future brothers and sisters whose appearance is expected and by the wish to destroy them in the womb. A third object of the boy's oral-sadistic tendencies in the mother's womb is the father's penis.

As in the castration complex of girls, so in the femininity complex of the male, there is at bottom the frustrated desire for a special organ. The tendencies to steal and destroy are concerned with the organs of conception, pregnancy and parturition, which the boy assumes to exist in the womb, and further with the vagina and the breasts, the fountain of milk, which are coveted as organs of receptivity and bounty from the time when the libidinal position is purely oral.

The boy fears punishment for his destruction of his mother's body, but, besides this, his fear is of a more general nature, and here we have an analogy to the anxiety associated with the castration wishes of the girl. He fears that his body will be mutilated and dismembered, and amongst other things castrated. Here we have a direct contribution to the castration complex. In this early period of development the mother who takes away the child's faeces signifies also a mother who dismembers and castrates him.

Not only by means of the anal frustrations which she inflicts does she pave the way for the castration complex: in terms of psychic reality she *is* also already the *castrator*.

This dread of the mother is so overwhelming because there is combined with it an intense dread of castration by the father. The destructive tendencies whose object is the womb are also directed with their full oral- and anal-sadistic intensity against the father's penis, which is supposed to be located there. It is upon his penis that the dread of castration by the father is focussed in this phase. Thus the femininity phase is characterized by anxiety relating to the womb and the father's penis, and this anxiety subjects the boy to the tyranny of a super-ego which devours, dismembers and castrates and is formed from the image of father and mother alike.

The aims of the incipient genital libido-positions are thus crisscrossed by and intermingled with the manifold pregenital tendencies. The greater the preponderance of sadistic fixations the more does the boy's identification with his mother correspond to an attitude of rivalry towards the woman, with its blending of envy and hatred; for on account of his wish for a child he feels himself at a disadvantage and inferior to the mother.

Let us now consider why the femininity complex of men seems so much more obscure than the castration complex in women, with which it is equally important.

The amalgamation of the desire for a child with the epistemophilic impulse enables a boy to effect a displacement on to the intellectual plane; his sense of being at a disadvantage is then concealed and over-compensated by the superiority he deduces from his possession of a penis, which is also acknowledged by girls. This exaggeration of the masculine position results in excessive protestations of masculinity. In her paper entitled 'Notes on Curiosity',[2] Mary Chadwick, too, has traced the man's narcissistic over-estimation of the penis and his attitude of intellectual rivalry towards women to the frustration of his wish for a child and the displacement of this desire on to the intellectual plane.

A tendency to excess in the direction of aggression, which very frequently occurs, has its source in the femininity complex. It goes with an attitude of contempt and 'knowing better', and is highly asocial and sadistic; it is partly conditioned as an attempt to mask the anxiety and ignorance which lie behind it. In part it coincides with the boy's protest (originating in his fear of castration) against the feminine role, but it is rooted also in his dread of his mother, whom he intended to rob of the father's penis, her children and her female sexual organs. This excessive aggression unites with the pleasure in attack which proceeds from the direct, genital Oedipus situation, but it represents that part of the situation which is by far the more asocial factor in character-formation. This is why a man's rivalry with women will be far more asocial than his rivalry with his fellow-men, which is largely prompted through the genital position. Of course the quantity of sadistic fixations will also determine the relationship of a man to other men when they are rivals. If, on the contrary, the identification with the mother is based on a more securely established genital position, on the one hand his relation to women will be positive in character, and on the other the desire for a child and the feminine component, which play so essential a part in men's work, will find more favourable opportunities for sublimation.

In both sexes one of the principal roots of inhibitions in work is the anxiety and sense of guilt associated with the femininity phase. Experience has taught me, however, that a thorough analysis of this phase is, for other reasons as well, important from a therapeutic point of view, and should be of help in some obsessional cases which seem to have reached a point where nothing more could be resolved.

In the boy's development the femininity phase is succeeded by a prolonged struggle between the pregenital and the genital positions of the libido. When at its height, in the third to the fifth year of life, this struggle is plainly recognizable as the Oedipus conflict. The anxiety associated with the femininity phase drives the boy back to identification with the father; but this stimulus in itself does not provide a firm foundation for the genital position, since it leads mainly to repression and over-compensation of the anal-sadistic instincts, and not to overcoming them. The dread of castration by the father strengthens the fixation to the anal-sadistic levels. The degree of constitutional genitality also plays an important part as regards a favourable issue, i.e. the attainment of the genital level. Often the outcome of the struggle remains undecided, and this gives rise to neurotic troubles and disturbances of potency.[3] Thus the attainment of complete potency and reaching the genital position will in part depend upon the favourable issue of the femininity phase.

I will now turn to the development of girls. As a result of the process of weaning, the girl-child has turned from the mother, being impelled more strongly to do so by the anal deprivations she has undergone. The genital now begins to influence her mental development.

I entirely agree with Helene Deutsch,[4] who holds that the genital development of the woman finds its completion in the successful displacement of oral libido on to the genital. Only, my results lead me to believe that this displacement begins with the first stirrings of the genital impulses and that the oral, receptive aim of the genital exercises a determining influence in the *girl's turning to the father*. Also I am led to conclude that not only an unconscious awareness of the vagina, but also sensations in that organ and the rest of the genital apparatus, are aroused as soon as the Oedipus impulses make their appearance. In girls, however, onanism does not afford anything like so adequate an outlet for these quantities of excitation as it does in boys. Hence the accumulated lack of satisfaction provides yet another reason for more complications and disturbances of female sexual development. The difficulty of obtaining complete gratification by onanism may be another cause, besides those indicated by Freud, for the girl's repudiation of the practice, and may partly explain why, during her struggle to give it up, manual masturbation is generally replaced by pressing the legs together.

Besides the receptive quality of the genital organ, which is brought into play by the intense desire for a new source of gratification, envy and hatred of the mother who possesses the father's penis seem, at the period when these first Oedipus impulses are stirring, to be a further motive for the little girl's turning to the father. His caresses have now the effect of a seduction and are felt as 'the attraction of the opposite sex'.[5]

In the girl identification with the mother results directly from the Oedipus impulses: the whole struggle caused in the boy by his castration anxiety is absent in her. In girls as well as boys this identification coincides with the anal-sadistic tendencies to rob and destroy the mother. If identification with the mother takes place at a stage at which the oral- and anal-sadistic tendencies predominate, dread of a primitive maternal super-ego will lead to the repression and fixation of this phase and interfere with further genital development. Dread of the mother, too, impels the little girl to give up identification with her, and identification with the father begins.

The little girl's epistemophilic impulse is first roused by the Oedipus complex; the result is that she discovers her lack of a penis. She feels this lack to be a fresh cause of hatred of the mother, but at the same time her sense of guilt makes her regard it as a punishment. This embitters her frustration in this direction, and it, in its turn, exercises a profound influence on the whole castration complex.

This early grievance about the lack of a penis is greatly magnified later on, when the phallic phase and the castration complex are in full swing. Freud has stated that the discovery of the lack of a penis causes the turning from the mother to the father. My findings show, however, that this discovery operates only as a reinforcement in this direction, since it follows on a very early stage in the Oedipus conflict, and is succeeded by the wish for a child, by which it is actually replaced in later development. I regard the deprivation of the breast as the most fundamental cause of the turning to the father.

Identification with the father is less charged with anxiety than that with the mother; moreover, the sense of guilt towards her impels to overcompensation through a fresh love-relation with her. Against this new love-relation with her there operates the castration complex which makes a masculine attitude difficult, and also the hatred of her which sprang from the earlier situations. Hate and rivalry of the mother, however, again lead to abandoning the identification with the father and turning to him as the object to be secured and loved.

The little girl's relation with her mother causes that to her father to take both a positive and a negative direction. The frustration undergone at his hands has as its very deepest basis the disappointment already suffered in relation to the mother; a powerful motive in the desire to possess him springs from the hatred and envy against the mother. If the sadistic fixations remain predominant, this hatred and its over-compensation will also materially affect the woman's relation to men. On the other hand, if there is a more positive relation to the mother, built up on the genital position, not only will the woman be freer from a sense of guilt in her relation to her children, but her love for her husband will be strongly reinforced, since for the woman he always stands at one and the same time for the mother who gives what is desired and for the beloved child. On this very significant foundation is built up that part of the relation which is connected exclusively with the father. At first it is focussed on the act of the penis in coitus. This act, which also promises gratification of the desires that are now displaced on to the genital, seems to the little girl a most consummate performance.

Her admiration is, indeed, shaken by the Oedipus frustration, but unless it is converted into hate, it constitutes one of the fundamental features of the woman's relation to the man. Later, when full satisfaction of the love-impulses is obtained, there is joined with this admiration the great gratitude ensuing from the long-pent-up deprivation. This gratitude finds expression in the greater feminine capacity for complete and lasting surrender to a love-object, especially to the 'first love'.

One way in which the little girl's development is greatly handicapped is the following. Whilst the boy does in reality *possess* the penis, in respect of which he enters into rivalry with the father, the little girl has only the *unsatisfied* desire for motherhood, and of this, too, she has but a dim and uncertain, though a very intense, awareness.

It is not merely this uncertainty which disturbs her hope of future motherhood. It is weakened far more by anxiety and sense of guilt, and these may seriously and permanently damage the maternal capacity of a woman. Because of the destructive tendencies once directed by her against the mother's body (or certain organs in it) and against the children in the womb, the girl anticipates retribution in the form of destruction of her own capacity for motherhood or of the organs connected with this function and of her own children. Here we have also one root of the constant concern of women (often so excessive) for their personal beauty, for they dread that this too will be destroyed by the mother. At the bottom of the impulse to deck and beautify themselves there is always the motive of *restoring* damaged comeliness, and this has its origin in anxiety and sense of guilt.[6]

It is probable that this deep dread of the destruction of internal organs may be the psychic cause of the greater susceptibility of women, as compared with men, to conversion-hysteria and organic diseases.

It is this anxiety and sense of guilt which is the chief cause of the repression of feelings of pride and joy in the feminine role, which are originally very strong. This repression results in depreciation of the capacity for motherhood, at the outset so highly prized. Thus the girl lacks the powerful support which the boy derives from his possession of the penis, and which she herself might find in the anticipation of motherhood.

The girl's very intense anxiety about her womanhood can be shown to be analogous to the boy's dread of castration, for it certainly contributes to the checking of her Oedipus impulses. The course run by the boy's castration anxiety concerning the penis which *visibly* exists is, however, different; it might be termed more *acute* than the more chronic anxiety of the girl concerning her internal organs, with which she is necessarily less familiar. Moreover, it is bound to make a difference that the boy's anxiety is determined by the paternal and the girl's by the maternal super-ego.

Freud has said that the girl's super-ego develops on different lines from that of the boy. We constantly find confirmation of the fact that jealousy plays a greater part in women's lives than in men's, because it is reinforced by deflected envy of the male on account of the penis. On the other hand, however, women especially possess a great capacity, which is not based merely on an over-compensation, for disregarding their own wishes and devoting themselves with self-sacrifice to ethical and social tasks. We cannot account for this capacity by the blending of masculine and feminine traits which, because of the human being's bisexual disposition, does in individual cases influence the formation of character, for this capacity is so plainly maternal in nature. I think that, in order to explain how women can run so wide a gamut from the most petty jealousy to the most self-forgetful loving-kindness, we have to take into consideration the peculiar conditions of the formation of the feminine super-ego. From the early identification with the mother in which the anal-sadistic level so largely preponderates, the little girl derives jealousy and hatred and forms a cruel super-ego after the maternal imago. The super-ego which develops at this stage from a father-identification can also be menacing and cause anxiety, but it seems never to reach the same proportions as that derived from the mother identification. But the more the identification with the mother becomes stabilized on the genital basis, the more will it be characterized by the devoted kindness of an indulgent mother-ideal. Thus this positive affective attitude depends on the extent to which the maternal mother-ideal bears the characteristics of the pregenital or of the genital stage. But when it comes to the active conversion of the emotional attitude into social or other activities, it would seem that it is the paternal ego-ideal which is at work. The deep admiration felt by the little girl for the father's genital activity leads to the formation of a paternal super-ego which sets before her active aims to which she can never fully attain. If, owing to certain factors in her development, the incentive to accomplish these aims is strong enough, their very impossibility of attainment may lend an impetus to her efforts which, combined with the capacity for self-sacrifice which she derives from the maternal super-ego, gives a woman, in individual instances, the capacity for very exceptional achievements on the intuitive plane and in specific fields.

The boy, too, derives from the feminine phase a maternal super-ego which causes him, like the girl, to make both cruelly primitive and kindly identifications. But he passes through this phase to resume (it is true, in varying degrees) identification with the father. However much the maternal side makes itself felt in the formation of the super-ego, it is yet the paternal super-ego which from the beginning is the decisive influence for the man. He too sets before himself a figure of an exalted character upon which to model himself, but, because the boy *is* 'made in the image of' his ideal, it is not unattainable. This circumstance contributes to the more sustained and objective creative work of the male.

The dread of injury to her womanhood exercises a profound influence on the castration complex of the little girl, for it causes her to over-estimate the penis which she herself lacks; this exaggeration is then much more obvious than is the underlying anxiety about her own womanhood. I would remind you here of the work of Karen Horney, who was the first to examine the sources of the castration complex in women in so far as those sources lie in the Oedipus situation.

In this connection I must speak of the importance for sexual development of certain early experiences in childhood. In the paper which I read at the Salzburg Congress in 1924, I mentioned that when observations of coitus take place at a later stage of development they assume the character of traumata, but that if such experiences occur at an early age they become fixated and form part of the sexual development. I must now add that a fixation of this sort may hold in its grip not only that particular stage of development, but also the super-ego which is then in process of formation, and may thus injure its further development. For the more completely the super-ego reaches its zenith in the genital stage the less prominent will the sadistic identifications be in its structure and the more surely will an ethically fine personality be developed and greater possibilities of mental health be secured.

There is another kind of experience in early childhood which strikes me as typical and exceedingly important. These experiences often follow closely in time upon the observations of coitus and are induced or fostered by the excitations set up thereby. I refer to the sexual relations of little children with one another, between brothers and sisters or playmates, which consist in the most varied acts: looking, touching, performing excretion in common, fellatio, cunnilingus and often direct attempts at coitus. They are deeply repressed and have a cathexis of profound feelings of guilt. These feelings are mainly due to the fact that this love-object, chosen under the pressure of the excitation due to the Oedipus conflict, is felt by the child to be a substitute for the father or mother or both. Thus these relations, which seem so insignificant and which apparently no child under the stimulus of the Oedipus development escapes, take on the character of an Oedipus relation actually realized, and exercise a determining influence upon the formation of the Oedipus complex, the subject's detachment from that complex and upon his later sexual relations. Moreover, an experience of this sort forms an important fixation point in the development of the super-ego. In consequence of the need for punishment and the repetition compulsion, these experiences often cause the child to subject himself to sexual traumata. In this connection I would refer you to Abraham,[7] who showed that experiencing sexual traumata is one part of the sexual development of children. The analytic investigation of these experiences, during the analysis of adults as well as of children, to a great extent clears up the Oedipus situation in its connection with early fixations and is therefore important from the therapeutic point of view.

To sum up my conclusions: I wish above all to point out that they do not, in my opinion, contradict the statements of Professor Freud. I think that the essential point in the additional considerations which I have advanced is that I date these processes earlier and that the different phases (especially in the initial stages) merge more freely in one another than was hitherto supposed.

The early stages of the Oedipus conflict are so largely dominated by pregenital phases of development that the genital phase, when it begins to be active, is at first heavily shrouded and only later, between the third and fifth years of life, becomes clearly recognizable. At this age the Oedipus complex and the formation of the super-ego reach their climax. But the fact that the Oedipus tendencies begin so much earlier than we supposed, the pressure of the sense of guilt which therefore falls upon the pregenital levels, the determining influence thus exercised so early upon the Oedipus development on the one hand and that of the super-ego on the other, and accordingly upon character-formation, sexuality and all the rest of the subject's development—all these things seem to me of great and hitherto unrecognized importance. I found out the therapeutic value of this knowledge in the analyses of children, but it is not confined to these. I have been able to test the resulting conclusions in the analysis of adults and have found not only that their theoretical correctness was confirmed, but that their therapeutic importance was established.

Notes

[1] Melanie Klein (1926), in *Love, Guilt and Reparation and Other Works 1921-1945* (New York: Macmillan, 1975), 128-38.

[2] *Internationale Zeitschrift für Psychoanalyse*, 11(1925); abstract in *International Journal of Psycho-Analysis* 6(1925).

[3] Cf. here Wilhelm Reich, *Die Funktion des Orgasmus; zur Psychopathologie und zur Soziologie des Geschlechtslebens* (Vienna: Internationaler Psychoanalytischer Verlag, 1927).

[4] Helene Deutsch, *Zur Psychoanalyse der weiblichen Sexualfunktionen* (Vienna: Internationaler psychoanalytischer Verlag, 1925)

[5] We regularly come across the unconscious reproach that the mother has seduced the child whilst tending it. The explanation is that at the period when she had to minister to its bodily needs the Oedipus tendencies were awaking.

[6] Cf. J. Hárnik's paper at the Tenth Psycho-Analytical Congress at Innsbruck in 1927, 'Die ökonomischen Beziehungen zwischen dem Schuldgefühl und dem weiblichen Narzissmus', *Internationale Zeitschrift für Psychoanalyse* 14(1928); 'The Economic Relations between the Sense of Guilt and Feminine Narcissism', *Psychoanalytic Review* , 15 (1928):94-95.

[7] Karl Abraham, *Selected Papers on Psycho-Analysis* (London: Hogarth, 1927).

11

The Evolution of the Oedipus Complex in Women

Jeanne Lampl de Groot (1928)

International Journal of Psycho-Analysis 9(1928):332-45

Jeanne Lampl de Groot emphasises the importance of the girl's attachment to the mother prior to her encountering the castration complex. She thus considers the castration complex in girls to be a secondary formation that succeeds an earlier 'negative Oedipus complex' in which the girl's mother is her love object and the father her rival. Further, it is only from the negative Oedipus complex that the castration complex derives its psychic significance. Such emphasis on this early negative complex, she argues, might throw more light on disturbances encountered in the mental life of women, for instance, the denial of sexual desire and frigidity. This 'object relations' approach which stresses the early attachment to the mother is supported by two cases, one of whom had earlier been in treatment with van Ophuijsen. It is this study that Freud has in mind when he refers to Lampl de Groot in his 1931 paper, 'Female Sexuality'.

* * *

One of the earliest discoveries of psychoanalysis was the existence of the Oedipus complex. Freud found the libidinal relations to the parents to be the centre and the acme of the development of childish sexuality and soon recognized in them the nucleus of the neuroses. Many years of psychoanalytical work greatly enriched his knowledge of the developmental processes in this period of childhood; it gradually became clear to him that in both sexes there is both a positive and a negative Oedipus complex and that at this time the libido finds physical outlet in the practice of onanism. Hence the Oedipus complex makes its appearance only when the phallic phase of libido development is reached and, when the tide of infantile sexuality recedes, that complex must pass in order to make way for the period of latency during which the instinctual tendencies are inhibited in their aim. Nevertheless, in spite of the many observations and studies by Freud and other authors, it has been remarkable how many obscure problems have remained for many years unsolved.[1]

It seemed that one very important factor was the connection between the Oedipus and the castration complexes, and there were many points about this which were obscure. Again, understanding of the processes in male children has been carried much further than with the analogous processes in females. Freud ascribed the difficulties in elucidating the early infantile love-relations to the difficulty of getting at the material relating to them: he thought that this was due to the profound repression to which these impulses are subjected. The greater difficulty of understanding these particular mental processes in little girls may arise on the one hand from the fact that they are in themselves more complicated than the analogous processes in boys and, on the other, from the greater intensity with which the libido is repressed in women. Horney thinks that another reason is that, so far, analytical observations have been made principally by men.

In 1924 and 1925 Freud published two works which threw much light on the origin of the Oedipus complex and its connection with the castration complex. The first of these, 'The Dissolution of the Oedipus Complex',[2] shows what happens to that complex in little boys. It is true that several years previously in the 'History of an Infantile Neurosis'[3] and again, in 1923, in the paper entitled 'A Seventeenth-Century Demonological Neurosis',[4] its fate in certain individual cases had been described. But in 'The Dissolution of the Oedipus Complex' we have the general application and the theoretical appreciation of this discovery and also the further conclusions to be deduced from it. The result arrived at in this paper is as follows: the Oedipus complex in male children receives its death blow from the castration complex, that is to say, that both in the positive and the negative Oedipus attitude the boy has to fear castration by his father, whose strength is superior to his own. In the first case castration is the punishment for the inadmissible incest wish and, in the second, it is the necessary condition of the boy's adopting the feminine role in relation to his father. Thus, in order to escape castration and to retain his genital he must renounce his love-relations with both parents. We see the peculiarly important part which this organ plays in boys and the enormous psychic significance it acquires in their mental life. Further, analytic experience has shown how extraordinarily difficult it is for a child to give up the possession of the mother, who has been his love-object since he was capable of object-love at all. This reflection leads us to wonder whether the victory of the castration complex over the Oedipus complex, together with the narcissistic interest in the highly prized bodily organ, may not be due also to yet another factor, namely, the tenacity of this first love-relation. Possibly, too, the following train of thought may have some significance: If the boy gives up his ownership of the penis, it means that the possession of the mother (or mother-substitute) becomes for ever impossible to him. If, however, forced by the superior power of that far stronger rival, his father, he renounces the fulfilment of his desire, the way remains open to him at some later period to fight his father with greater success and to return to his first love-object, or, more correctly, to her substitute. It seems not impossible that this knowledge of a future chance of fulfilling his wish (a knowledge probably phylogenetically acquired and, of course, unconscious) may be a contributing motive in the boy's temporary renunciation of the prohibited love-craving. This would also explain why before, or just at the beginning of, the latency period a little boy longs so intensely to be 'big' and 'grown-up'.

In this work, then, Freud largely explains the connections between the Oedipus and the castration complex in little boys, but he does not tell us much that is new about the same processes in little girls. Hence his paper, published in 1925, 'Some Psychical Consequences of the Anatomical Distinction between the Sexes',[5] throws all the more light on the fate of the early infantile love-impulses of the little girl. Freud holds that in girls the Oedipus complex (he is speaking of the attitude which for the girl is positive: love for the father and rivalry with the mother) is a secondary formation, first introduced by the castration complex; that is to say, that it arises after the little girl has become aware of the difference between the sexes and has accepted the fact of her own castration. This theory throws a new light on many hitherto obscure problems. By this assumption Freud explains many later developmental characteristics, various differences in the further vicissitudes of the Oedipus complex in girls and in boys, and in the super-ego formation in the two sexes, and so forth.

Nevertheless, even after this connection has been discovered, there are several problems which remain unsolved. Freud mentions that, when the castration complex has become operative in the girl, that is, when she has accepted her lack of the penis and therewith become a victim of penis envy, 'a loosening of the tender relation with the mother as love-object' begins to take place.[6] He thinks that one possible reason for this may be the fact that the girl ultimately holds her mother responsible for her own lack of the penis and, further, quotes a historical factor in the case, namely, that often jealousy is conceived later on against a second child who is more beloved by the mother. But, Freud says, 'we do not very clearly understand the connection'.[7] According to him another remarkable effect of penis envy is the girl's struggle against onanism, which is more intense than that of the boy and which, in general, still makes itself felt at a later age. Freud's view is that the reason why the little girl revolts so strongly against phallic onanism is the blow dealt to her narcissism in connection with her penis envy: she suspects that in this matter it is no use to compete with the boy and therefore it is best not to enter into rivalry with him. This statement gives rise to the involuntary thought: How should the little girl who never possessed a penis and therefore never knew its value from her own experience, regard it as so precious?

Why has the discovery of this lack in herself such far-reaching mental consequences and, above all, why should it begin to produce a mental effect at a certain moment, when it is probable that the bodily difference between herself and little boys has already been perceived countless times without any reaction? Probably the little girl produces pleasurable physical sensations in the clitoris in the same way and presumably with the same degree of intensity as the boy does in the penis, and perhaps she feels them in the vagina too. About this latter fact we received a communication by Josine Müller in the German Psycho-Analytical Society, and I have been told of it by an acquaintance, the mother of two little girls. Why, then, should there be this mental reaction in the girl to the discovery that her own member is smaller than the boy's or is lacking altogether? I should like to try whether the following considerations, which have been suggested to me by experiences in my analytic practice (to be narrated hereafter), may bring us a little nearer to answering these questions.

I think that several points will be clearer to us if we consider the previous history of the castration complex or penis envy in little girls. But, before doing so, it will be advisable to examine once more the analogous process in boys. As soon as the little boy is capable of an object-relation he takes as his first love-object the mother who feeds and tends him. As he passes through the pregenital phases of libidinal development he retains always the same object. When he reaches the phallic stage he adopts the typical Oedipus attitude, i.e. he loves his mother and desires to possess her and to get rid of his rival, the father. Throughout this development the love-object remains the same. An alteration in his love-attitude, an alteration characteristic of his sex, occurs at the moment when he accepts the possibility of castration as a punishment threatened by his powerful father for these libidinal desires of his. It is not impossible, indeed it is very probable, that the boy, even before he reaches the phallic stage and adopts the Oedipus attitude which coincides with it, has perceived the difference between the sexes by observing either a sister or a girl play-fellow. But we assume that this perception has no further significance to him. If, however, such a perception occurs when he is already in the Oedipus situation and has recognized the possibility of castration as a punishment with which he is threatened, we know how great its significance may be in his mind. The child's first reaction is an endeavour to deny the actuality of castration and to hold very tenaciously to his first love-object. After violent inward struggles, however, the little fellow makes a virtue of necessity; he renounces his love-object in order to retain his penis. Possibly he thus ensures for himself the chance of a renewed and more successful battle with his father at some later date—a possibility which I suggested earlier in this paper. For we know that, when the young man reaches maturity, he succeeds in wresting the victory from his father, normally in relation to a mother-substitute.

Now what happens in the little girl? She, too, takes as her first object-love the mother who feeds and tends her. She, too, retains the same object as she passes through the pregenital phases of libidinal evolution. She, too, enters upon the phallic stage of libido development. Moreover, the little girl has a bodily organ analogous to the little boy's penis, namely, the clitoris, which gives her pleasurable feelings in masturbation. Physically she behaves exactly like the little boy. We may suppose that in the psychic realm also children of either sex develop up to this point in an entirely similar manner; that is to say, that girls as well as boys, when they reach the phallic stage enter into the Oedipus situation, i.e. that which for the girl is negative. She wants to conquer the mother for herself and to get rid of the father. Up to this point, too, a chance observation of the difference between the sexes may have been without significance; now, however, a perception of this sort is fraught with serious consequences for the little girl. It strikes her that the boy's genital is larger, stronger and more visible than her own and that he can use it actively in urinating, a process which for the child has a sexual significance. When she makes this comparison, the little girl must feel her own organ to be inferior. She imagines that hers was once like the boy's and that it has been taken from her as a punishment for her prohibited love-cravings in relation to the mother. At first the little girl tries, as does the boy, to deny the fact of castration or to comfort herself with the idea that she will still grow a genital. The acceptance of castration has for her the same consequences as for the boy. Not only does her narcissism suffer a blow on account of her physical inferiority, but she is forced to renounce the fulfilment of her first love-longings. Now at this point the difference in the psychic development of the two sexes sets in, in connection, that is, with the perception of the anatomical difference between male and female. To the boy castration was only a threat, which can be escaped by a suitable modification of behaviour. To the girl it is an accomplished fact, which is irrevocable, but the recognition of which compels her finally to renounce her first love-object and to taste to the full the bitterness of its loss. Normally, the female child is bound at some time to come to this recognition: she is forced thereby completely to abandon her negative Oedipus attitude, and with it the onanism which is its accompaniment. The object-libidinal relation to the mother is transformed into an identification with her; the father is chosen as a love-object, the enemy becomes the beloved. Now, too, there arises the desire for the child in the place of the wish for the penis. A child of her own acquires for the girl a similar narcissistic value to that which the penis possesses for the boy; for only a woman, and never a man, can have children.

The little girl, then, has now adopted the positive Oedipus attitude with the very far-reaching after-results of which we are so familiar. Freud has explained more than once that there is no motive for the shattering of the positive Oedipus complex in the female such as we have in the threat of castration in the case of the boy. Hence, the female Oedipus complex vanishes only gradually, is largely incorporated in the normal development of the woman, and explains many of the differences between the mental life of women and of men.

We may now sum up by saying that the little girl's castration complex (or her discovery of the anatomical difference between the sexes) which, according to Freud, ushers in and renders possible her normal, positive Oedipus attitude, has its psychic correlative just as that of the boy, and it is only this correlative which lends it its enormous significance for the mental evolution of the female child. In the first years of her development as an individual (leaving out of account the phylogenetic influences which, of course, are undeniable) she behaves exactly like a boy not only in the matter of onanism but in other respects in her mental life: in her love-aim and object-choice she is actually a little man. When she has discovered and fully accepted the fact that castration has taken place, the little girl is forced once and for all to renounce her mother as love-object and therewith to give up the active, conquering tendency of her love-aim as well as the practice of clitoral onanism. Perhaps here, too, we have the explanation of a fact with which we have long been familiar, namely, that the woman who is wholly feminine does not know object-love in the true sense of the word: she can only 'let herself be loved'. Thus it is to the mental accompaniments of phallic onanism that we must ascribe the fact that the little girl normally represses this practice much more energetically and has to make a far more intense struggle against it than the boy. For she has to forget with it the first love-disappointment, the pain of the first loss of a love-object.

We know how often this repression of the little girl's negative Oedipus attitude is wholly or partly unsuccessful. For the female as well as for the male child it is very hard to give up the first love-object: in many cases the little girl clings to it for an abnormally long time. She tries to deny the punishment (castration) which would inevitably convince her of the forbidden nature of her desires. She firmly refuses to give up her masculine position. If later her love-longing is disappointed a second time, this time in relation to the father who does not give way to her passive wooing of his love, she often tries to return to her former situation and to resume a masculine attitude. In extreme cases this leads to the manifest homosexuality of which Freud gives so excellent and clear an account in 'A Case of Female Homosexuality'.[8] The patient about whom Freud tells us in this work made a faint effort on entering puberty to adopt a feminine love attitude but, later in the period of puberty, she behaved towards an elder woman whom she loved exactly like a young man in love. At the same time she was a pronounced feminist, denying the difference between man and woman; thus she had gone right back to the first, negative phase of the Oedipus complex.

There is another process which is perhaps commoner. The girl does not entirely deny the fact of castration, but she seeks for over-compensation for her bodily inferiority on some plane other than the sexual (in her work, her profession). But in so doing she represses sexual desire altogether, that is, remains sexually unmoved. It is as if she wished to say: 'I may not and cannot love my mother, and so I must give up any further attempt to love at all'. Her belief in her possession of the penis has then been shifted to the intellectual sphere; there the woman can be masculine and compete with the man.

We may observe as a third possible outcome that a woman may form relationships with a man, and yet remain nevertheless inwardly attached to the first object of her love, her mother. She is obliged to be frigid in coitus because she does not really desire the father or his substitute, but the mother. Now these considerations place in a somewhat different light the phantasies of prostitution so common amongst women. According to this view they would be an act of revenge, not so much against the father as against the mother. The fact that prostitutes are so often manifest or disguised homosexuals might be explained in analogous fashion as follows: the prostitute turns to the man out of revenge against the mother, but her attitude is not that of passive feminine surrender but of masculine activity; she captures the man on the street, castrates him by taking his money and thus makes herself the masculine and him the feminine partner in the sexual act.

I think that in considering these disturbances in the woman's development to complete femininity we must keep two possibilities in view. Either the little girl has never been able wholly to give up her longing to possess her mother and thus has formed only a weak attachment to her father, or she has made an energetic attempt to substitute her father for her mother as love-object but, after suffering a fresh disappointment at his hands, has returned to her first position.

In the paper 'Some Psychical Consequences of the Anatomical Distinction between the Sexes', Freud draws attention to the fact that jealousy plays a far greater part in the mental life of women than in that of men. He thinks that the reason for this is that in the former jealousy is reinforced by deflected penis envy. Perhaps one might add that a woman's jealousy is stronger than a man's because she can never succeed in securing her first love-object, while the man, when he grows up, has the possibility of doing so.

In another paragraph Freud traces the phantasy 'a child is being beaten' ultimately to the masturbation of the little girl when in the phallic phase. The child which is beaten or caressed is at bottom the clitoris (i.e. the penis); the being beaten is on one hand the punishment for the forbidden genital relation and on the other a regressive substitute for it. But in this phase the punishment for prohibited libidinal relations is precisely castration. Thus the formula 'a child is being beaten' means 'a child is being castrated'. In the phantasies in which the child beaten is a stranger the idea of its being castrated is intelligible at the first glance. It means: 'No one else shall have what I have not got'. Now we know that in the phantasies of puberty, which are often greatly metamorphosed and condensed, the child beaten by the father always represents as well the girl herself. Thus she is constantly subjecting herself to castration, for this is the necessary condition of being loved by the father; she is making a fresh effort to get clear of her old love-relations and reconcile herself to her womanhood. In spite of the many punishments, pains and tortures which the hero has to undergo, the phantasies always end happily⁹ i.e. the sacrifice having been made the passive, feminine love is victorious. Sometimes this immolation permits the return to masturbation, the first forbidden love-tendency having been duly expiated. Often, however, onanism remains none the less prohibited, or it becomes unconscious and is practised in some disguised form, sometimes accompanied by a deep sense of guilt. It seems as though the repeated submission to the punishment of castration signifies not only the expiation due to the feelings of guilt but also a form of wooing the father, whereby the subject experiences also masochistic pleasure.

To sum up what I have said above: in little boys who develop normally the positive Oedipus attitude is by far the more prevalent, for by adopting it the child through his temporary renunciation of the mother-object can retain his genital and perhaps ensure for himself thereby the possibility of winning later in life a mother-substitute; if he adopted the negative attitude, it would mean that he must renounce both from the outset. Little girls, however, normally pass through both situations in the Oedipus complex: first the negative, which occurs under precisely the same conditions as in boys, but which they are compelled finally to abandon when they discover and accept the fact of their castration. Now, the girl's attitude changes; she identifies herself with the lost love-object and puts in its place her former rival, the father, thus passing into the positive Oedipus situation. Thus, in female children the castration complex deals a death blow to the negative Oedipus attitude and ushers in the positive Oedipus complex.

This view confirms Freud's hypothesis that the (positive) Oedipus complex in women is made possible and ushered in by the castration complex. But, in contradistinction to Freud, we are assuming that the castration complex in female children is a secondary formation and that its precursor is the negative Oedipus situation. Further, that it is only from the latter that the castration complex derives its great psychic significance, and it is probably this negative attitude which enables us to explain in greater detail many peculiarities subsequently met with in the mental life of women.

I am afraid it will be objected that all this looks like speculation and is lacking in any empirical basis. I must reply that this objection may be just as regards part of what I have said, but that nevertheless the whole argument is built up on a foundation of practical experience, although unfortunately this is still but meagre. I shall now give a short account of the material which has led me to my conclusions.

Some time ago I was treating a young girl who had been handed over to me by a male colleague. He had analysed her for some years already, but there were certain difficulties connected with the transference which resisted solution. This girl had suffered from a somewhat severe hysterical neurosis. Her analysis had already been carried a good way. The normal, positive Oedipus complex, her rivalry with her sister and her envy of her younger brother's penis had been dealt with thoroughly, and the patient had understood and accepted them. Many of her symptoms had disappeared, but nevertheless she remained to her great regret unfit for work. When she came to me, the unresolved, ambivalent transference to the male analyst was playing a principal part in the situation. It was difficult to determine which was the stronger: her passionate love or her no less passionate hate. I knew this patient personally before she came to me for treatment, and the analysis began with a strong positive transference to me. Her attitude was rather that of a child who goes to its mother for protection. But after a short time a profound change began to take place. The patient's behaviour became first rebellious and hostile and soon, behind this attitude, there was revealed a very deep-seated and wholly active tendency to woo my love. She behaved just like a young man in love, displaying, for instance, a violent jealousy of a young man whom she suspected of being her rival in real life. One day she came to analysis with the idea that she would like to read all Freud's writings and become an analyst herself. The obvious interpretation which we tried first, namely, that she wanted to identify herself with me, proved inadequate. A series of dreams showed an unmistakable desire to get rid of my own analyst, to 'castrate' him and take his place, so as to be able to analyse (possess) me. In this connection the patient remembered various situations in her childhood when her parents quarrelled and she assumed a defensive and protective attitude towards her mother, and also times when they displayed mutual affection and she detested her father and wished to have her mother to herself. The analysis had long ago revealed a strong positive attachment to the father and also the experience which put an end to this. As a child the patient slept in a room next to her parents' and was in the habit of calling them at night when she had to urinate; of course, the intention was to disturb them. At first she generally demanded that her mother should come but, later on, her father.

She said that, when she was five years old, this once happened again and her father came to her and quite unexpectedly boxed her ears. From that moment the child resolved to hate him. The patient produced yet another recollection: when she was four years old she dreamt that she was lying in bed with her mother beside her and that she had a sense of supreme bliss. In her dream her mother said: 'That is right, that is how it ought to be'. The patient awoke and found that she had passed urine in bed; she was greatly disappointed and felt very unhappy.

She had various recollections of the time when she still slept in her parents' room. She said she used often to awake in the night and sit up in bed. These recollections are a fairly certain indication that she observed her parents' coitus. The dream she had as a child may very well have been dreamt after such an observation. It clearly represents coitus with her mother, accompanied by a sense of bliss. Even in later life urethral erotism played a particularly important part in this patient. Her disappointment on awaking showed that she was already conscious of her inability to possess her mother: she had long ago discovered the male genital in her younger brother. The bed-wetting can be construed either as a substitute for or a continuation of masturbation; the dream shows how intense must have been her emotional relation to her mother at that time. Hence it is clear that the patient, after the disappointment with her father (the box on the ears) tried to return to the earlier object, whom she had loved at the time of the dream, i.e. to her mother. When she grew up she made a similar attempt. After an unsuccessful love affair with a younger brother of her father's she had for a short time a homosexual relation. This situation was repeated in her analysis when she came from the male analyst to me.

This patient stated that she had had a special form of the beating phantasy when she was from eight to ten years old. She described it as 'the hospital phantasy'. The gist of it was as follows: A large number of patients went to a hospital to get well. But they had to endure the most frightful pains and tortures. One of the most frequent practices was that they were flayed alive. The patient had a feeling of shuddering pleasure when she imagined their painful, bleeding wounds. Her associations brought recollections of how her younger brother sometimes pushed back the foreskin of his penis, whereupon she saw something red, which she thought of as a wound. The method of cure in her phantasy was therefore obviously a representation of castration. She identified herself on one occasion with the patients, who at the end always got well and left the hospital with great gratitude. But generally she had a different role. She was the protecting, compassionate Christ, who flew over the beds in the ward, in order to bring relief and comfort to the sick people. In this phantasy, which reveals its sexual-symbolic character in the detail of *flying*, the patient is the man who alone possesses his mother (for Christ was born without a father), but who finally, in order to atone for the guilt and to be able to reach God the Father, offered the sacrifice of crucifixion (castration). After we broke off the analysis, which the patient gave up in a state of negative transference, a reaction to the disappointment of her love, she tried to translate this phantasy into reality by deciding to become a nurse. After a year, however, she abandoned this new profession for her earlier one, which was more masculine in character and much more suited to her temperament. Gradually, too, her feelings of hate towards me disappeared.

I had a second patient in whom I discovered similar processes with regard to the transference. In the first two months of treatment this patient produced very strong resistances. She acted the part of a naughty, defiant child and would utter nothing but monotonous complaints to the effect that she was forsaken and that her husband treated her badly. After we had succeeded in discovering that her resistance arose from feelings of hate towards me, due to envy and jealousy, the full, positive, feminine Oedipus attitude gradually developed in her—there entered into it both love for the father and the wish for a child. Soon, too, penis envy began to show itself. She produced a recollection from her fifth or sixth year. She said that she had once put on her elder brother's clothes and displayed herself proudly to all and sundry. Besides this she had made repeated efforts to urinate like a boy. At a later period she always felt that she was very stupid and inferior and thought that the other members of her family treated her as if this were the case. During puberty she conceived a remarkably strong aversion from every sort of sexual interest. She would listen to none of the mysterious conversations in which her girlfriends joined. She was interested only in intellectual subjects, literature, etc. When she married she was frigid. During her analysis she experienced a desire to have some profession; this stood to her for being male. But her feelings of inferiority forbade any real attempt to compass this ambition. Up to this point the analysis had made splendid progress. The patient had one peculiarity: she remembered very little, but she enacted all the more in her behaviour. Envy and jealousy and the desire to do away with the mother were repeated in the most diverse guises in the transference. After this position had been worked through, a new resistance presented itself; we discovered behind it deep homosexual desires having reference to myself. The patient now began to woo my love in a thoroughly masculine manner. The times of these declarations of love, during which in her dreams and phantasies she always pictured herself with a male genital, invariably coincided with some active behaviour in real life. They alternated, however, with periods in which her behaviour was wholly passive. At such times the patient was once more incapable of anything; she failed in everything, suffered from her inferiority and was tortured with feelings of guilt. The meaning of this was that every time she conquered the mother, she was impelled to castrate herself in order to get free from her sense of guilt. Her attitude to masturbation also was noteworthy. Before analysis she had never consciously practised this habit; during the period when she was being treated she began clitoral masturbation. At first this onanism was accompanied by a strong sense of guilt; later, at times when her love-wishes in relation to her father were most vehemently manifested, the feelings of guilt abated. They were succeeded by the fear that the onanism might do her some physical harm: 'weaken her genitals'. At the stage when she was in love with me the sense of guilt reappeared and she gave up masturbating, because this fear became in her mind a certainty. Now this 'weakening' of the genital organs signified castration. Thus the patient constantly oscillated between a heterosexual and homosexual love. She had a tendency to regress to her first love-relation—with the mother— and at this stage tried to deny the fact of castration. To make up, however, she had to refrain from onanism and sexual gratification of any kind. She could not derive satisfaction from her husband, because she herself really wanted to be a man in order to be able to possess the mother.

Thus, in both the cases which I have quoted it was plain that behind the woman's positive Oedipus attitude there lay a negative attitude, with the mother as love-object, which revealed itself later in the analysis and therefore had been experienced at an earlier stage of development. Whether this evolution is typical cannot, of course, be asserted with any certainty from the observation of two cases. I should be inclined to believe that in other female patients the Oedipus complex has had a similar previous history, but I have not been able to gather enough material from their analyses to establish this beyond question. The phase of the negative Oedipus attitude, lying, as it does, so far back in the patient's mental history, cannot be reached until the analysis has made very considerable progress. Perhaps with a male analyst it may be very hard to bring this period to light at all. For it is difficult for a female patient to enter into rivalry with the father-analyst, so that possibly treatment under these conditions cannot get beyond the analysis of the positive Oedipus attitude. The homosexual tendency, which can hardly be missed in any analyses, may then merely give the impression of a later reaction to the disappointment experienced at the father's hands. In our cases, however, it was clearly a regression to an earlier phase—one which may help us to understand better the enormous psychic significance that the lack of a penis has in the erotic life of women. I do not know whether in the future it will turn out that my exposition in this paper explains only the development of these two patients of mine. I think it not impossible that it may be found to have a more general significance. Only the gathering of further material will enable us to decide this question.

Notes

[1] Karl Abraham (1922), 'Manifestations of the Female Castration Complex', above; Franz Alexander, 'The Castration Complex in the Formation of Character', *International Journal of Psycho-Analysis*, 4(1923):11-42; Helene Deutsch, *Zur Psychoanalyse der weiblichen Sexualfunktionen* (Vienna: Internationale psychoanalytischer Verlag, 1925); Karen Horney (1923), 'On the Genesis of the Castration Complex in Women', *The International Journal of Psycho-Analysis*, 5(1924):50-65; 'The Flight from Womanhood', above; Jean van Ophuijsen, 'Contributions to the Masculinity Complex in Women', above.

[2] Sigmund Freud (1924*d*), SE 19:173-9.

[3] Sigmund Freud (1918*b*), 'From the History of an Infantile Neurosis', SE 17:1-122.

[4] Sigmund Freud (1923*d*), SE 19:67-105.

[5] Sigmund Freud (1925*j*), SE 19:241-58.

[6] SE 19:254.

[7] SE 19:254.

[8] Sigmund Freud (1920*a*), 'The Psychogenesis of a Case of Homosexuality in a Woman', SE 18:145-72.

[9] Cf. Anna Freud (1922), 'The Relation of Beating Phantasies to a Day Dream', *International Journal of Psycho-Analysis*, 4(1923):89-102.

12

Womanliness as a Masquerade

Joan Riviere (1929)

International Journal of Psycho-Analysis 9(1929):303-13

Joan Riviere's 'Womanliness as a Masquerade', published in 1929, is one of the most frequently referred to papers in this collection.

The title of the paper takes its cue from the dreams that an analysand, whose history is summed up here, had of people putting on masks in order to avert disaster and injury. Riviere first offers a synopsis of Jones's essay 'The Early Development of Female Sexuality' (with its rough schema of heterosexual, homosexual and 'intermediate' types) to introduce her analysand, 'a particular type of intellectual woman', who, as one of Jones's intermediate types, is principally heterosexual in development but also displays strong features of the other sex. Riviere's suggestion is that women who wish for masculinity may put on a mask of womanliness to avert anxiety and the retribution feared from men. The case study is given in support of this claim: womanliness is assumed and worn as a mask both to hide the possession of masculinity and to avert the reprisals expected if found guilty of the crime (cf. her analogy with the thief).

The paper is of particular interest, for it erases the distinction between genuine womanliness and masquerade. It also raises the question of 'the essential nature of fully developed femininity', a question lurking everywhere in the controversy, yet never properly addressed.

Both masquerade and womanliness are used as a device for avoiding anxiety, Riviere argues. They should therefore not be seen as primary modes of sexual enjoyment. If one sketches the early libido development of womanliness as a mask, one finds that the womanly woman's reactions to both men and women lies in the little girl's reaction to her parents during the oral biting-sadistic phase. In its content, the womanly woman's fantasy in relation to the father is similar to the normal Oedipal one, the difference being that it is predicated on sadism. Because she has 'killed' her mother, she is also excluded from enjoying what the mother had, and what she does obtain from her father, she has to extort.

For Riviere, as for Deutsch and Jones, fully developed womanhood originates in the oral-sucking stage, the source of primary gratification , i.e., receiving a child from the father (via nipple, milk, penis, semen). The acceptance of castration is partly determined by the overestimation of the object in the oral-sucking phase, but mainly by the renunciation of sadistic castration wishes during the later oral-biting phase. Thus full heterosexuality coincides here with that of genitality. What makes a female homosexual, then, is the degree of sadism and anxiety involved in castration.

* * *

Every direction in which psychoanalytic research has pointed seems in its turn to have attracted the interest of Ernest Jones, and now that of recent years investigation has slowly spread to the development of the sexual life of women, we find as a matter of course one by him among the most important contributions to the subject. As always, he throws great light on his material, with his peculiar gift both clarifying the knowledge we had already and also adding to it fresh observations of his own.

In his paper on 'The Early Development of Female Sexuality'[1] he sketches out a rough scheme of types of female development, which he first divides into heterosexual and homosexual, subsequently subdividing the latter homosexual group into two types. He acknowledges the roughly schematic nature of his classification and postulates a number of intermediate types. It is with one of these intermediate types that I am to-day concerned. In daily life types of men and women are constantly met with who, while mainly heterosexual in their development, plainly display strong features of the other sex. This has been judged to be an expression of the bisexuality inherent in us all; and analysis has shown that what appears as homosexual or heterosexual character-traits, or sexual manifestations, is the end-result of the interplay of conflicts and not necessarily evidence of a radical or fundamental tendency. The difference between homosexual and heterosexual development results from differences in the degree of anxiety, with the corresponding effect this has on development. Ferenczi pointed out a similar reaction in behaviour,[2] namely, that homosexual men exaggerate their heterosexuality as a 'defence' against their homosexuality. I shall attempt to show that women who wish for masculinity may put on a mask of womanliness to avert anxiety and the retribution feared from men.

It is with a particular type of intellectual woman that I have to deal. Not long ago intellectual pursuits for women were associated almost exclusively with an overtly masculine type of woman, who in pronounced cases made no secret of her wish or claim to be a man. This has now changed. Of all the women engaged in professional work to-day, it would be hard to say whether the greater number are more feminine than masculine in their mode of life and character. In University life, in scientific professions and in business, one constantly meets women who seem to fulfil every criterion of complete feminine development. They are excellent wives and mothers, capable housewives; they maintain social life and assist culture; they have no lack of feminine interests, e.g. in their personal appearance, and when called upon they can still find time to play the part of devoted and disinterested mother-substitutes among a wide circle of relatives and friends. At the same time they fulfil the duties of their profession at least as well as the average man. It is really a puzzle to know how to classify this type psychologically.

Some time ago, in the course of an analysis of a woman of this kind, I came upon some interesting discoveries. She conformed in almost every particular to the description just given; her excellent relations with her husband included a very intimate affectionate attachment between them and full and frequent sexual enjoyment; she prided herself on her proficiency as a housewife. She had followed her profession with marked success all her life. She had a high degree of adaptation to reality, and managed to sustain good and appropriate relations with almost everyone with whom she came in contact.

Certain reactions in her life showed, however, that her stability was not as flawless as it appeared; one of these will illustrate my theme. She was an American woman engaged in work of a propagandist nature, which consisted principally in speaking and writing. All her life a certain degree of anxiety, sometimes very severe, was experienced after every public performance, such as speaking to an audience. In spite of her unquestionable success and ability, both intellectual and practical, and her capacity for managing an audience and dealing with discussions, etc., she would be excited and apprehensive all night after, with misgivings whether she had done anything inappropriate, and obsessed by a need for reassurance. This need for reassurance led her compulsively on any such occasion to seek some attention or complimentary notice from a man or men at the close of the proceedings in which she had taken part or been the principal figure; and it soon became evident that the men chosen for the purpose were always unmistakable father-figures, although often not persons whose judgement on her performance would in reality carry much weight. There were clearly two types of reassurance sought from these father-figures: first, direct reassurance of the nature of compliments about her performance; secondly, and more important, indirect reassurance of the nature of sexual attentions from these men. To speak broadly, analysis of her behaviour after her performance showed that she was attempting to obtain sexual advances from the particular type of men by means of flirting and coquetting with them in a more or less veiled manner. The extraordinary incongruity of this attitude with her highly impersonal and objective attitude during her intellectual performance, which it succeeded so rapidly in time, was a problem.

Analysis showed that the Oedipus situation of rivalry with the mother was extremely acute and had never been satisfactorily solved. I shall come back to this later. But beside the conflict in regard to the mother, the rivalry with the father was also very great. Her intellectual work, which took the form of speaking and writing, was based on an evident identification with her father, who had first been a literary man and later had taken to political life; her adolescence had been characterized by conscious revolt against him, with rivalry and contempt of him. Dreams and phantasies of this nature, castrating the husband, were frequently uncovered by analysis. She had quite conscious feelings of rivalry and claims to superiority over many of the 'father-figures' whose favour she would then woo after her own performances! She bitterly resented any assumption that she was not equal to them, and (in private) would reject the idea of being subject to their judgement or criticism. In this she corresponded clearly to one type Ernest Jones has sketched: his first group of homosexual women who, while taking no interest in other women, wish for 'recognition' of their masculinity from men and claim to be the equals of men, or in other words, to be men themselves. Her resentment, however, was not openly expressed; publicly she acknowledged her condition of womanhood.

Analysis then revealed that the explanation of her compulsive ogling and coquetting—which actually she was herself hardly aware of till analysis made it manifest—was as follows: it was an unconscious attempt to ward off the anxiety which would ensue on account of the reprisals she anticipated from the father-figures after her intellectual performance. The exhibition in public of her intellectual proficiency, which was in itself carried through successfully, signified an exhibition of herself in possession of the father's penis, having castrated him. The display once over, she was seized by horrible dread of the retribution the father would then exact. Obviously it was a step towards propitiating the avenger to endeavour to offer herself to him sexually. This phantasy, it then appeared, had been very common in her childhood and youth, which had been spent in the Southern States of America; if a Negro came to attack her, she planned to defend herself by making him kiss her and make love to her (ultimately so that she could then deliver him over to justice). But there was a further determinant of the obsessive behaviour. In a dream which had a rather similar content to this childhood phantasy, she was in terror alone in the house; then a Negro came in and found her washing clothes, with her sleeves rolled up and arms exposed. She resisted him, with the secret intention of attracting him sexually, and he began to admire her arms and to caress them and her breasts. The meaning was that she had killed father and mother and obtained everything for herself (alone in the house), became terrified of their retribution (expected shots through the window), and defended herself by taking on a menial role (washing clothes) and by *washing off* dirt and sweat, guilt and blood, everything she had obtained by the deed, and 'disguising herself' as merely a castrated woman. In that guise the man found no stolen property on her which he need attack her to recover and, further, found her attractive as an object of love. Thus the aim of the compulsion was not merely to secure reassurance by evoking friendly feelings towards her in the man; it was chiefly to make sure of safety by masquerading as guiltless and innocent. It was a compulsive reversal of her intellectual performance; and the two together formed the 'double-action' of an obsessive act, just as her life as a whole consisted alternately of masculine and feminine activities.

Before this dream she had had dreams of people putting masks on their faces in order to avert disaster. One of these dreams was of a high tower on a hill being pushed over and falling down on the inhabitants of a village below, but the people put on masks and escaped injury!

Womanliness therefore could be assumed and worn as a mask, both to hide the possession of masculinity and to avert the reprisals expected if she was found to possess it—much as a thief will turn out his pockets and ask to be searched to prove that he has not the stolen goods. The reader may now ask how I define womanliness or where I draw the line between genuine womanliness and the 'masquerade'. My suggestion is not, however, that there is any such difference; whether radical or superficial, they are the same thing. The capacity for womanliness was there in this woman—and one might even say it exists in the most completely homosexual woman—but owing to her conflicts it did not represent her main development, and was used far more as a device for avoiding anxiety than as a primary mode of sexual enjoyment.

I will give some brief particulars to illustrate this. She had married late, at twenty-nine; she had had great anxiety about defloration, and had had the hymen stretched or slit before the wedding by a woman doctor. Her attitude to sexual intercourse before marriage was a set determination to obtain and experience the enjoyment and pleasure which she knew some women have in it, and the orgasm. She was afraid of impotence in exactly the same way as a man. This was partly a determination to surpass certain mother-figures who were frigid, but on deeper levels it was a determination not to be beaten by the man.[3] In effect, sexual enjoyment was full and frequent, with complete orgasm; but the fact emerged that the gratification it brought was of the nature of a reassurance and restitution of something lost, and not ultimately pure enjoyment. The man's love gave her back her self-esteem. During analysis, while the hostile castrating impulses towards the husband were in process of coming to light, the desire for intercourse very much abated, and she became for periods relatively frigid. The mask of womanliness was being peeled away, and she was revealed either as castrated (lifeless, incapable of pleasure), or as wishing to castrate (therefore afraid to receive the penis or welcome it by gratification). Once, while for a period her husband had had a love-affair with another woman, she had detected a very intense identification with him in regard to the rival woman. It is striking that she had had no homosexual experiences (since before puberty with a younger sister); but it appeared during analysis that this lack was compensated for by frequent homosexual dreams with intense orgasm.

In every-day life one may observe the mask of femininity taking curious forms. One capable housewife of my acquaintance is a woman of great ability, and can herself attend to typically masculine matters. But when, e.g. any builder or upholsterer is called in, she has a compulsion to hide all her technical knowledge from him and show deference to the workman, making her suggestions in an innocent and artless manner, as if they were 'lucky guesses'. She has confessed to me that even with the butcher and baker, whom she rules in reality with a rod of iron, she cannot openly take up a firm straightforward stand; she feels herself as it were 'acting a part', she puts on the semblance of a rather uneducated, foolish and bewildered woman, yet in the end always making her point. In all other relations in life this woman is a gracious, cultured lady, competent and well-informed, and can manage her affairs by sensible rational behaviour without any subterfuges. This woman is now aged fifty, but she tells me that as a young woman she had great anxiety in dealings with men such as porters, waiters, cabmen, tradesmen, or any other potentially hostile father-figures, such as doctors, builders and lawyers; moreover, she often quarrelled with such men and had altercations with them, accusing them of defrauding her and so forth.

Another case from every-day observation is that of a clever woman, wife and mother, a University lecturer in an abstruse subject which seldom attracts women. When lecturing, not to students but to colleagues, she chooses particularly feminine clothes. Her behaviour on these occasions is also marked by an inappropriate feature: she becomes flippant and joking, so much so that it has caused comment and rebuke. She has to treat the situation of displaying her masculinity to men as a 'game', as something *not real*, as a 'joke'. She cannot treat herself and her subject seriously, cannot seriously contemplate herself as on equal terms with men; moreover, the flippant attitude enables some of her sadism to escape, hence the offence it causes.

Many other instances could be quoted, and I have met with a similar mechanism in the analysis of manifest homosexual men. In one such man with severe inhibition and anxiety, homosexual activities really took second place, the source of greatest sexual gratification being actually masturbation under special conditions, namely, while looking at himself in a mirror dressed in a particular way. The excitation was produced by the sight of himself with hair parted in the centre, wearing a bow tie. These extraordinary 'fetishes' turned out to represent a *disguise of himself* as his sister; the hair and bow were taken from her. His conscious attitude was a desire to *be* a woman, but his manifest relations with men had never been stable. Unconsciously the homosexual relation proved to be entirely sadistic and based on masculine rivalry. Phantasies of sadism and *'possession of a penis'* could be indulged only while reassurance against anxiety was being obtained from the mirror that he was safely 'disguised as a woman'.

To return to the case I first described. Underneath her apparently satisfactory heterosexuality it is clear that this woman displayed well-known manifestations of the castration complex. Horney was the first among others to point out the sources of that complex in the Oedipus situation; my belief is that the fact that womanliness may be assumed as a mask may contribute further in this direction to the analysis of female development. With that in view I will now sketch the early libido-development in this case.

But before this I must give some account of her relations with women. She was conscious of the rivalry of almost any woman who had either good looks or intellectual pretensions. She was conscious of flashes of hatred against almost any woman with whom she had much to do, but where permanent or close relations with women were concerned she was none the less able to establish a very satisfactory footing. Unconsciously she did this almost entirely by means of feeling herself superior in some way to them (her relations with her inferiors were uniformly excellent). Her proficiency as a housewife largely had its root in this. By it she surpassed her mother, won her approval and proved her superiority among rival 'feminine' women. Her intellectual attainments undoubtedly had in part the same object. They too proved her superiority to her mother; it seemed probable that since she reached womanhood her rivalry with women had been more acute in regard to intellectual things than in regard to beauty, since she could usually take refuge in her superior brains where beauty was concerned.

The analysis showed that the origin of all these reactions, both to men and to women, lay in the reaction to the parents during the oral-biting sadistic phase. These reactions took the form of the phantasies sketched by Melanie Klein[4] in her Congress paper, 1927. In consequence of disappointment or frustration during sucking or weaning, coupled with experiences during the primal scene which is interpreted in oral terms, extremely intense sadism develops towards both parents.[5] The desire to bite off the nipple shifts, and desires to destroy, penetrate and disembowel the mother and devour her and the contents of her body succeed it. These contents include the father's penis, her faeces and her children—all her possessions and love-objects, imagined as within her body.⁶ The desire to bite off the nipple is also shifted, as we know, on to the desire to castrate the father by biting off his penis. Both parents are rivals in this stage, both possess desired objects; the sadism is directed against both and the revenge of both is feared. But, as always with girls, the mother is the more hated, and consequently the more feared. She will execute the punishment that fits the crime—destroy the girl's body, her beauty, her children, her capacity for having children, mutilate her, devour her, torture her and kill her. In this appalling predicament the girl's only safety lies in placating the mother and atoning for her crime. She must retire from rivalry with the mother, and if she can, endeavour to restore to her what she has stolen. As we know, she identifies herself with the father; and then she uses the masculinity she thus obtains by *putting it at the service of the mother*. She becomes the father, and takes his place; so she can 'restore' him to the mother. This position was very clear in many typical situations in my patient's life. She delighted in using her great practical ability to aid or assist weaker and more helpless women, and could maintain this attitude successfully so long as rivalry did not emerge too strongly. But this restitution could be made on one condition only; it must procure her a lavish return in the form of gratitude and 'recognition'. The recognition desired was supposed by her to be owing for her self-sacrifices; more unconsciously what she claimed was recognition of her *supremacy* in *having* the penis to give back. If her supremacy were not acknowledged, then rivalry became at once acute; if gratitude and recognition were withheld, her sadism broke out in full force and she would be subject (in private) to paroxysms of oral-sadistic fury, exactly like a raging infant.

In regard to the father, resentment against him arose in two ways: (1) during the primal scene he took from the mother the milk, etc., which the child missed; (2) at the same time he gave to the mother the penis or children instead of to her. Therefore all that he had or took should be taken from him by her; he was castrated and reduced to nothingness, like the mother. Fear of him, though never so acute as of the mother, remained; partly, too, because his vengeance for the death and destruction of the mother was expected. So he too must be placated and appeased. This was done by masquerading in a feminine guise for him, thus showing him her 'love' and guiltlessness towards him. It is significant that this woman's mask, though transparent to other women, was successful with men, and served its purpose very well. Many men were attracted in this way, and gave her reassurance by showing her favour. Closer examination showed that these men were of the type who themselves fear the ultra-womanly woman. They prefer a woman who herself has male attributes, for to them her claims on them are less.

At the primal scene the talisman which both parents possess and which she lacks is the father's penis; hence her rage, also her dread and helplessness.[7] By depriving the father of it and possessing it herself she obtains the talisman—the invincible sword, the 'organ of sadism'; he becomes powerless and helpless (her gentle husband), but she still guards herself from attack by wearing towards him the mask of womanly subservience, and under that screen, performing many of his masculine functions herself—'for him'—(her practical ability and management). Likewise with the mother: having robbed her of the penis, destroyed her and reduced her to pitiful inferiority, she triumphs over her, but again secretly; outwardly she acknowledges and admires the virtues of 'feminine' women. But the task of guarding herself against the woman's retribution is harder than with the man; her efforts to placate and make reparation by restoring and using the penis in the mother's service were never enough; this device was worked to death, and sometimes it almost worked her to death.

It appeared, therefore, that this woman had saved herself from the intolerable anxiety resulting from her sadistic fury against both parents by creating in phantasy a situation in which she became supreme and no harm could be done to her. The essence of the phantasy was her *supremacy* over the parent-objects; by it her sadism was gratified, she triumphed over them. By this same supremacy she also succeeded in averting their revenges; the means she adopted for this were reaction-formations and concealment of her hostility. Thus she could gratify her id-impulses, her narcissistic ego and her super-ego at one and the same time. The phantasy was the main-spring of her whole life and character, and she came within a narrow margin of carrying it through to complete perfection. But its weak point was the megalomanic character, under all the disguises, of the necessity for supremacy. When this supremacy was seriously disturbed during analysis, she fell into an abyss of anxiety, rage and abject depression; before the analysis, into illness.

I should like to say a word about Ernest Jones' type of homosexual woman whose aim is to obtain 'recognition' of her masculinity from men. The question arises whether the need for recognition in this type is connected with the mechanism of the same need, operating differently (recognition for services performed), in the case I have described. In my case direct recognition of the possession of the penis was not claimed openly; it was claimed for the reaction-formations, though only the possession of the penis made them possible. Indirectly, therefore, recognition was none the less claimed for the penis. This indirectness was due to apprehension lest her possession of a penis *should be* 'recognized', in other words 'found out'. One can see that with less anxiety my patient too would have openly claimed recognition from men for her possession of a penis, and in private she did in fact, like Ernest Jones' cases, bitterly resent any lack of this direct recognition. It is clear that in his cases the primary sadism obtains more gratification; the father has been castrated, and shall even acknowledge his defeat. But how then is the anxiety averted by these women? In regard to the mother, this is done of course by denying her existence. To judge from indications in analyses I have carried out, I conclude that, first, as Jones implies, this claim is simply a displacement of the original sadistic claim that the desired object, nipple, milk, penis, should be instantly surrendered; secondarily, the need for recognition is largely a need for absolution. Now the mother has been relegated to limbo; no relations with her are possible. Her existence appears to be denied, though in truth it is only too much feared. So the guilt of having triumphed over both can only be absolved by the father; if he sanctions her possession of the penis by acknowledging it, she is safe. By *giving* her recognition, he *gives* her the penis and to her instead of to the mother; then she has it, and she may have it, and all is well. 'Recognition' is always in part reassurance, sanction, love; further, it renders her supreme again. Little as he may know it, to her the man has admitted his defeat. Thus in its content such a woman's phantasy-relation to the father is similar to the normal Oedipus one; the difference is that it rests on a basis of sadism. The mother she has indeed killed, but she is thereby excluded from enjoying much that the mother had, and what she does obtain from the father she has still in great measure to extort and extract.

These conclusions compel one once more to face the question: what is the essential nature of fully-developed femininity? What is *das ewig Weibliche*? The conception of womanliness as a mask, behind which man suspects some hidden danger, throws a little light on the enigma. Fully-developed heterosexual womanhood is founded, as Helene Deutsch and Ernest Jones have stated, on the oral-sucking stage. The sole gratification of a primary order in it is that of receiving the (nipple, milk) penis, semen, child from the father. For the rest it depends upon reaction-formations. The acceptance of 'castration', the humility, the admiration of men, come partly from the overestimation of the object on the oral-sucking plane; but chiefly from the renunciation (lesser intensity) of sadistic castration-wishes deriving from the later oral-biting level. 'I must not take, I must not even ask; it must be *given* me'. The capacity for self-sacrifice, devotion, self-abnegation expresses efforts to restore and make good, whether to mother or to father figures, what has been taken from them. It is also what Radó has called a 'narcissistic insurance' of the highest value.

It becomes clear how the attainment of full heterosexuality coincides with that of genitality. And once more we see, as Abraham first stated, that genitality implies attainment of a *post-ambivalent* state. Both the 'normal' woman and the homosexual desire the father's penis and rebel against frustration (or castration); but one of the differences between them lies in the difference in the degree of sadism and of the power of dealing both with it and with the anxiety it gives rise to in the two types of women.

Notes

[1] See above.

[2] Sándor Ferenczi (1916), 'The Nosology of Male Homosexuality (Homoerotism)', *First Contributions to Psycho-Analysis* (London: Hogarth, 1952), 296-318.

[3] I have found this attitude in several women analysands and the self-ordained defloration in nearly all of them (five cases). In the light of Freud's 'Taboo of Virginity' (SE 11:193-208), this latter symptomatic act is instructive.

[4] 'Early Stages of the Oedipus Conflict', above.

[5] Ernest Jones, 'Early Development of Female Sexuality', above, regards an intensification of the oral-sadistic stage as the central feature of homosexual development in women.

[6] As it was not essential to my argument, I have omitted all reference to the further development of the relation to children.

[7] Cf. M. N. Searl, 'Danger Situations of the Immature Ego', Oxford Congress, 1929, *International Journal of Psycho-Analysis*, 10(1929):423-5.

The Significance of Masochism in the Mental Life of Women

Helene Deutsch (1929)

International Journal of Psycho-Analysis 11(1930):48-60

'The Significance of Masochism in the Mental Life of Women' was first read at the Eleventh International Psycho-Analytical Congress on 27th July 1929 at Oxford. It appeared in English one year later.

Deutsch examines here 'the genesis of femininity', i.e., the feminine, passive and masochistic disposition, in the mental life of women by focusing on the relation of the function of 'feminine instinct' to the function of reproduction. She also discusses the related topic of frigidity.

Although Deutsch first sums up and reinforces Freud's views on the masculinity complex, particularly about erotogenicity and the supremacy of the phallic zone, she then shifts her argument towards an investigation of woman's 'anatomical destiny'. Deutsch's question is, 'What, then, does happen to the actively directed cathexis of the clitoris in the phase when that organ ceases to be valued as the penis?' Her answer is that the hitherto active-sadistic libido attached to the clitoris regressively cathects points in the pregenital development while it is deflected (also regressively) towards masochism and gives rise to the masochistic fantasy of castration (which is identified with rape and parturition). This, she argues, is the foundation of the passive-feminine disposition which determines the development of femininity. Frigidity arises out of the vicissitudes of this infantile masochistic libidinal development while the girl's identification with motherhood is masochistic in character.

* * *

Part 1
Feminine Masochism and its Relation to Frigidity

In the analysis of women we became familiar with the masculinity complex before we learnt much about the 'femininity' which emerges from the conflicts accompanying development. The reasons for this later recognition were various. First of all, analysis comes to know the human mind in its discords rather than in its harmonies, and, when we turn the microscope of observation upon the woman, we see with special distinctness that the main source of her conflicts is the masculinity which she is destined to subdue. It followed that we were able to recognize the 'masculine' element in women earlier and more clearly than what we may term the nucleus of their 'femininity'. Paradoxical as it may sound, we approached the feminine element with greater interest when it formed part of a pathological structure and, as a foreign body, attracted a closer attention. When we encountered in men that instinctual disposition which we designate feminine and passive-masochistic, we recognized its origin and the weighty consequences it entailed. In the case of women we discovered that, even in the most feminine manifestations of their life—menstruation, conception, pregnancy and parturition—they had a constant struggle with the never wholly effaced evidences of the bisexuality of their nature. Hence, in my earlier writings[1] I showed with what elemental force the masculinity complex flares up in the female reproductive functions, to be once more subdued.

My aim in this paper is different. I want to examine the genesis of 'femininity', by which I mean the feminine, passive-masochistic disposition in the mental life of women. In particular I shall try to elucidate the relation of the function of feminine instinct to the function of reproduction, in order that we may first of all clarify our ideas about sexual inhibition in women, that is to say, about frigidity. The discussion will concern itself with theoretical premises rather than with the clinical significance of frigidity.

But first let us return to the masculinity complex. No one who has experience of analysis can doubt that female children pass through a phase in their libidinal evolution, in which they, just like boys, having abandoned the passive oral and anal cathexes, develop an erotogenicity which is actively directed to the clitoris as in boys to the penis. The determining factor in the situation is that, in a certain phase, sensations in the organs, which impel the subject to masturbate, tend strongly towards the genital and effect cathexis of that zone which in both sexes we have called the 'phallic'.

Penis envy would never acquire its great significance were it not that sensations in the organs, with all their elemental power, direct the child's interest to these regions of the body. It is this which first produces the narcissistic reactions of envy in little girls. It seems that they arrive only very gradually and slowly at the final conclusion of their investigations: the recognition of the anatomical difference between themselves and boys. So long as onanism affords female children an equivalent pleasure they deny that they lack the penis, or console themselves with hopes that in the future the deficiency will be made good. A little girl, whom I had the opportunity of observing, reacted to the exhibitionistic aggression of an elder brother with the obstinate and often repeated assertion: 'Susie has got one', pointing gaily to her clitoris and labia, at which she tugged with intense enjoyment. The gradual acceptance of the anatomical difference between the sexes is accompanied by conflicts waged round the constellation which we term penis envy and masculinity complex.

We know that, when the little girl ceases to deny her lack of the penis and abandons the hope of possessing one in the future, she employs a considerable amount of her mental energy in trying to account for the disadvantage under which she labours. We learn from our analyses what a large part the sense of guilt connected with masturbation commonly plays in these attempts at explanation. The origin of these feelings of guilt is not quite clear, for they already exist in the phase in which the Oedipus complex of the little girl does not seem as yet to have laid the burden of guilt upon her.[2]

Direct observation of children shows beyond question that these first onanistic activities are informed with impulses of a primary sadistic nature against the outside world.[3] Possibly a sense of guilt is associated with these obscure aggressive impulses. It is probable that the little girl's illusion that she once had a penis and has lost it is connected with these first, sadistic, active tendencies to clitoral masturbation. Owing to the memory-traces of this active function of the clitoris, it is subsequently deemed to have had in the past the actual value of an organ equivalent to the penis. The erroneous conclusion is then drawn: 'I once did possess a penis.'

Another way in which the girl regularly tries to account for the loss is by ascribing the blame for it to her mother. It is interesting to note that, when the father is blamed for the little girl's lack of a penis, castration by him has already acquired the libidinal significance attaching to this idea in the form of the rape phantasy. Rejection of the wish that the father should have been the aggressor generally betokens, even at this early stage, that rejection of the infantile feminine attitude to which I shall recur.

In his paper 'Some Consequences of the Anatomical Difference between the Sexes', Freud sees in the turning of the little girl to her father as a sexual object a direct consequence of this anatomical difference. In Freud's view, development from the castration to the Oedipus complex consists in the passing from the narcissistic wound of organ inferiority to the compensation offered: that is to say, there arises the desire for a child. This is the source of the Oedipus complex in girls.

In this paper I shall follow up the line of thought thus mapped out by Freud. After the phallic phase, where the boy renounces the Oedipus complex and phallic masturbation, there is intercalated in the girl's development a phase which we may call 'post-phallic'; in this the seal is set upon her destiny of womanhood. Vaginal cathexis, however, is as yet lacking.

In spite of my utmost endeavours, I am unable to confirm the communications that have been made with reference to vaginal pleasure-sensations in childhood. I do not doubt the accuracy of these observations, but isolated exceptions in this case prove little. In my own observations I have had striking evidence in two instances of the existence of vaginal excitations and vaginal masturbation before puberty. In both, seduction with defloration had occurred very early in life.[4] If there were in childhood a vaginal phase, with all its biological significance, it surely could not fail to appear as regularly in our analytical material as do all the other infantile phases of development. I think that the most difficult factor in the 'anatomical destiny' of the woman is the fact that at a time when the libido is still unstable, immature and incapable of sublimation, it seems condemned to abandon a pleasure-zone (the clitoris as a phallic organ) without discovering the possibility of a new cathexis. The narcissistic estimation of the non-existent organ passes smoothly (to use a phrase of Freud's) 'along the symbolic equation: penis=child, which is mapped out for it'. But what becomes of the dynamic energy of the libido which is directed towards the object and yearns for possibilities of gratification and for erotogenic cathexes?

We must also reflect that the wish-phantasy of receiving a child from the father—a phantasy of the greatest significance for the future of a woman—is, nevertheless, in comparison with the reality of the penis, for which it is supposed to be exchanged, a very unreal and uncertain substitute. I heard of the little daughter of an analyst mother who, at the time when she was experiencing penis envy, was consoled with the prospect of having a child. Every morning she woke up to ask in a fury: 'Hasn't the child come *yet*?' and no more accepted the consolation of the future than we are consoled by the promise of Paradise.

What, then, does happen to the actively directed cathexis of the clitoris in the phase when that organ ceases to be valued as the penis? In order to answer this question we may fall back on a familiar and typical process. We already know that, when a given activity is denied by the outside world or inhibited from within, it regularly suffers a certain fate—it turns back or is deflected. This seems to be so in the instance before us: the hitherto active-sadistic libido attached to the clitoris rebounds from the barricade of the subject's inner recognition of her lack of the penis and, on the one hand, regressively cathects points in the pregenital development which it had already abandoned, while, on the other hand, and most frequently of all, it is deflected in a regressive direction towards masochism. In place of the active urge of the phallic tendencies, there arises the masochistic phantasy: 'I want to be castrated', and this forms the erotogenic masochistic basis of the feminine libido. Analytic experience leaves no room for doubt that the little girl's first libidinal relation to her father is masochistic, and the masochistic wish in its earliest distinctively feminine phase is: 'I want to be castrated by my *father.*'[5]

In my view this turning in the direction of masochism is part of the woman's 'anatomical destiny', marked out for her by biological and constitutional factors, and lays the first foundation of the ultimate development of femininity, independent as yet of masochistic reactions to the sense of guilt. The original significance of the clitoris as an organ of activity, the masculine-narcissistic protest: 'I won't be castrated' are converted into the desire: 'I want to be castrated.' This desire assumes the form of a libidinal, instinctual trend whose object is the father. The woman's whole passive-feminine disposition, the entire genital desire familiar to us as the rape-phantasy, is finally explained if we accept the proposition that it originates in the castration complex. *My view is that the Oedipus complex in girls is inaugurated by the castration complex.* The factor of pleasure resides in the idea of a sadistic assault by the love-object and the narcissistic loss is compensated by the desire for a child, which is to be fulfilled through this assault. When we designate this masochistic experience by the name of the wish for castration, we are not thinking merely of the biological meaning—the surrender of an organ of pleasure (the clitoris)—but we are also taking into account the fact that the whole of this deflection of the libido still centres on that organ. The onanism belonging to this phase and the masochistic phantasy of being castrated (raped) employ the same organ as the former active tendencies. The astonishing persistency of the feminine castration complex (including all the organic vicissitudes with which is associated a flow of blood) as we encounter it in the analyses of our female patients is thus explained by the fact that this complex contains in itself not only the masculinity complex, but also the whole infantile set towards femininity.

At that period there is a close connection between the masochistic phantasies and the wish for a child, so that the whole subsequent attitude of the woman towards her child (or towards the reproductive function) is permeated by pleasure-tendencies of a masochistic nature.

We have an illustration of this in the dream of a patient whose subsequent analysis unequivocally confirmed what had been hinted in the manifest content of her dream; this occurred in the first phase of her analysis before much insight had been gained.

> Professor X. and you (the analyst) were sitting together. I wanted him to notice me. He went past my chair and I looked up at him and he smiled at me. He began to ask me about my health, as a doctor asks his patient; I answered with reluctance. All of a sud-

den he had on a doctor's white coat and a pair of obstetrical forceps in his hand. He said to me: 'Now we'll just have a look at the
little angel.' I clearly saw that they were obstetrical forceps, but I
had the feeling that the instrument was to be used to force my legs
apart and display the clitoris. I was very much frightened and
struggled. A number of people, amongst them you and a trained
nurse, were standing by and were indignant at my struggling.
They thought that Professor X. had specially chosen *me* for a kind
of experiment, and that I ought to submit to it. As everyone was
against me, I cried out in impotent fury: 'No, I will not be operated on, you shall not operate on me.'

Without examining the dream more closely here, we can see in its
manifest content that castration is identified with rape and parturition,
and the dream-wish which excites anxiety is as follows: 'I want to be castrated (raped) by my father and to have a child'—a three-fold wish of a
plainly *masochistic character*.

The first, infantile identification with the mother is always, independently of the complicated processes and reactions belonging to the sense
of guilt, *masochistic*, and all the active birth-phantasies, whose roots lie in
this identification, are of a bloody, painful character, which they retain
throughout the subject's life.[6]

In order to make my views on frigidity intelligible I had to preface
them with these theoretical considerations.

I will now pass on to discuss those forms of frigidity which bear the
stamp of the masculinity complex or penis envy. In these cases the woman
persists in the original demand for possession of a penis and refuses to
abandon the phallic organization. Conversion to the feminine-passive attitude, the necessary condition of vaginal sensation, does not take place.

Let me mention briefly the danger of the strong attachment of all sexual phantasies to clitoris-masturbation. I think I have made it clear that the
clitoris has come to be the executive organ, not only of active but of passive masochistic phantasies. By virtue of its past phase of masculine activity, a kind of organ-memory constitutes it the great enemy of any transference of pleasure-excitation to the vagina. Moreover, the fact that the whole
body receives an increased cathexis of libido (since it has failed to find its
focus) brings it about that, in spite of an often very vehement manifestation of the sexual instinct, the libido never attains to its centralized form of
gratification.

In far the largest number of cases, feminine sexual inhibition arises out
of the vicissitudes of that infantile-masochistic libidinal development
which I have postulated. These vicissitudes are manifold, and every form

they assume may lead to frigidity. For instance, as a result of the repression of the masochistic tendencies a strong narcissistic cathexis of the feminine ego may be observed. The ego feels that it is threatened by these tendencies, and takes up a narcissistic position of defence. I believe that, together with penis envy, this is an important source of so-called feminine narcissism.

Akin to this reaction of repression is another reaction-formation which Karen Horney calls 'the flight from femininity', and of which she has given a very illuminating description. This flight from the incest-wish is, in my view, a shunning not only of the incestuous object (Horney), but most of all of the masochistic dangers threatening the ego which are associated with the relation to this object. Escape into identification with the father is at the same time a flight from the masochistically determined identification with the mother. Thus there arises the masculinity complex, which I think will be strong and disturbing in proportion as penis envy has been intense and the primary phallic active tendencies vigorous.

Repression of the masochistic instinctual tendencies may have another result in determining a particular type of object-choice later in life. The object stands in antithesis to the masochistic instinctual demands and corresponds to the requirements of the ego. In accordance with these the woman chooses a partner whose social standing is high or whose intellectual gifts are above the average, often a man whose disposition is rather of an affectionate and passive type. The marriage then appears to be peaceful and happy, but the woman remains frigid, suffering from an unsatisfied longing—the type of the 'misunderstood wife'. Her sexual sensibility is bound up with conditions whose fulfilment is highly offensive to her ego. How often do such women become the wretched victims of a passion for men who ill-treat them, thus fulfilling the women's unconscious desires for castration or rape.

I have also observed how frequently—indeed, almost invariably—women whose whole life is modelled on the lines of masculine sublimation-tendencies are markedly masochistic in their sexual experiences. They belong to that reactive masculine type which yet has failed to repress its original masochistic instinctual attitude. My experience is that the prospect of cure in these cases of relative frigidity, in which sexual sensation depends on the fulfilment of masochistic conditions, is very uncertain. It is peculiarly difficult to detach these patients from the said conditions and, when analysis has given them the necessary insight, they have consciously to choose between finding bliss in suffering or peace in renunciation.

The analyst's most important task is, of course, the abolition of the sexual inhibition in his patients, and the attainment of instinctual gratification. But sometimes, when the patient's instincts are so unfortunately fixed and yet there are good capacities for sublimation, the analyst must have the courage to smooth the path in the so-called 'masculine' direction and thus make it easier for the patient to renounce sexual gratification.

There are women who have strong sexual inhibition and intense feelings of inferiority, the origin of which lies in penis envy. In such cases it is evidently the task of analysis to free these patients from the difficulties of the masculinity complex and to convert penis envy into the desire for a child, i.e. to induce them to adopt their feminine role. We can observe that during this process the 'masculine aims' become depreciated and are given up. Nevertheless we often find that, if we can succeed in making it easier for such women to sublimate their instincts in the direction of 'masculine tendencies' and so to counter the sense of inferiority, the capacity for feminine sexual sensibility develops automatically in a striking manner. The theoretical explanation of this empirically determined fact is self-evident.

It is but rarely in analytic practice that we meet with such cases of conditioned frigidity as I have described or indeed with any cases of frigidity unaccompanied by pathological symptoms, i.e. of sexual inhibition without symptoms of suffering. When such a patient comes to us, it is generally at the desire of the husband, whose narcissism is wounded, and who feels uncertain of his masculinity. The woman, actuated by her masochistic tendencies, has renounced the experience of gratification for herself, and, as a rule, her desire to be cured is so feeble that the treatment is quite unsuccessful.

As we know, hysteria which expresses itself in symptom-formation is extraordinarily capricious and varied as regards the nature of the sexual inhibition displayed. One type of hysterical patient is driven by an ever-lasting hunger for love-objects, which she changes without inhibition: her erotic life appears free, but she is incapable of genital gratification. Another type is monogamous and remains tenderly attached to the love-object, but without sexual sensibility; she exhibits other neurotic reactions which testify to her morbid state. Such women often dissipate the sexual excitation in the fore-pleasure, either owing to the strong original cathexis of the pregenital zones or because by a secondary and regressive reaction they are endeavouring to withhold the libido from the genital organ which prohibitions and their own anxiety have barricaded off. Here one often receives the impression that all the sense organs, and indeed the whole female body, are more accessible to sexual excitation than is the vagina, the organ apparently destined for it. But conversion symptoms turn out to be the seat of false sexual cathexes. Behind the hysterical, pleasure-inhibiting, genital anxiety we discover the masochistic triad: castration, rape and parturition. The fixation of these wish-phantasies to the infantile object here becomes, as we know, the motive factor in the neuroses. If this attachment is resolved by analysis, sexual sensibility as a rule develops.

In touching briefly on the question of frigidity accompanying phobias and obsessions, mention must be made of the remarkable fact that in these cases the sexual disturbance is emphatically not in direct ratio to the severity of the neurosis. There are patients who remain frigid long after they have overcome their anxiety, and even after they have got rid of the most severe obsessional symptoms, and the converse is also true. The uncertainty of obsessional neurosis—in so far as the genital capacity of female patients is concerned—is most plainly manifested in certain cases (several of which have come under my observation) in which the most violent orgasm may result from hostile masculine identifications. The vagina behaves like an active organ, and the particularly brisk secretion is designed to imitate ejaculation.

At the beginning of this paper I endeavoured to show that the masochistic triad constantly encountered in the analyses of women corresponds to a definite phase of feminine libidinal development and represents, so to speak, the last act in the drama of the vicissitudes of the 'feminine castration complex'. In neurotic diseases, however, we meet above all with the reactions of the sense of guilt, and hence we find this primary-libidinal feminine masochism already so closely interwoven and interlocked with the moral masochism, originating under pressure of the sense of guilt, that we miss the significance of that which is in origin libidinal. Thus many obscure points in connection with the feminine castration complex become clearer if we recognize that, behind the castration anxiety, there is further the repressed masochistic wish characteristic of a definite infantile phase of development in the normal feminine libido.

The task of psychoanalysis is to resolve the conflicts of the individual existence. The instinctual life of the individual, which is the object of analytical scrutiny, strives towards the ultimate goal, amidst conflicts and strange vicissitudes, of *attainment of pleasure*. The preservation of the race lies outside these aims, and, if there be a deeper significance in the fact that the same means are employed to achieve the racial aim as to subserve the pleasure-tendency of man's instincts, that significance is outside the scope of our individualistic task.

Here I think we have a fundamental and essential difference between 'feminine' and 'masculine'. In the woman's mental life there is *something* which has nothing at all to do with the mere fact of whether she has or has not actually given birth to a child. I refer to the psychic representatives of motherhood which are here long before the necessary physiological and anatomical conditions have developed in the girl. For the tendency of which I am speaking the attaining of the child is the main goal of existence, and in woman the exchange of the racial aim for the individual one of gratification may take place largely at the expense of the latter. No analytical observer can deny that in the relation of mother to child—begun in pregnancy and continued in parturition and lactation—libidinal forces come into play which are very closely allied to those in the relation between man and woman.

In the deepest experience of the relation of mother to child it is masochism in its strongest form which finds gratification in the bliss of motherhood.

Long before she is a mother, long after the possibility of becoming one has ended, the woman has ready within her the maternal principle, which bids her take to herself and guard the real child or some substitute for it.

In coitus and parturition the masochistic pleasure of the sexual instinct is very closely bound up with the mental experience of conception and giving birth; just so does the little girl see in the father, and the loving woman in her beloved—a child. For years I have traced out in analyses this most intimate blending of the sexual instinct with that of the reproductive function in women, and always the question has hovered before my mind: When does the female child begin to be a woman and when a mother? Analytic experience has yielded the answer: *Simultaneously*, in that phase when she turns towards masochism, as I described at the beginning of this paper. Then, at the same time as she conceives the desire to be castrated and raped, she conceives also the phantasy of receiving a child from her father. From that time on, the phantasy of parturition becomes a member of the masochistic triad and the gulf between instinctual and the reproductive tendencies is bridged by masochism. The interruption of the little girl's infantile sexual development by the frustration of her desire for the child gives to the sublimation-tendencies of the woman a very definite stamp of masochistic maternity. If it is true that men derive the principal forces which make for sublimation from their sadistic tendencies, then it is equally true that women draw on the masochistic tendencies with their imprint of maternity. In spite of this symbiosis, the two opposite poles, the sexual instinct and the reproductive function, may enter into conflict with one another. When this occurs, the danger is the greater in proportion as the two groups of tendencies are in close proximity.

Thus, a woman may commandeer the whole of her masochistic instinctual energy for the purpose of direct gratification and abandon sublimation in the function of reproduction. In the relation of the prostitute to the *souteneur* we have such an unadulterated product of the feminine masochistic instinctual attitude.

At the opposite end of the pole, yet drawing upon the same source, we have the *mater dolorosa*, the whole of whose masochism has come to reside in the relation of mother to child.

From this point I return to my original theme. There is a group of women who constitute the main body figuring in the statistics which give the large percentage of frigidity. The women in question are psychically healthy, and their relation to the world and to their libidinal object is positive and friendly. If questioned about the nature of their experience in coitus, they give answers which show that the conception of orgasm as something to be experienced by themselves is really and truly foreign to them. During intercourse what they feel is a happy and tender sense that they are giving keen pleasure and, if they do not come of a social environment where they have acquired full sexual enlightenment, they are convinced that coitus as a sexual act is of importance only for the man. In it, as in other relations, the woman finds happiness in tender, maternal giving.

This type of woman is dying out and the modern woman seems to be neurotic if she is frigid. Her sublimations are further removed from instinct and therefore, while on the one hand they constitute a lesser menace to its direct aims, they are, on the other, less well adapted for the indirect gratification of its demands. I think that this psychological change is in accordance with social developments and that it is accompanied by an increasing tendency of women towards masculinity. Perhaps the women of the next generation will no longer submit to defloration in the normal way and will give birth to children only on condition of freedom from pain.

And then in after-generations they may resort to infibulation and to refinements in the way of pain—ceremonials in connection with parturition. It is this masochism—the most elementary force in feminine mental life—that I have been endeavouring to analyse.

Possibly I have succeeded in throwing light on its origin and, above all, on its importance and its application in the function of reproduction. This employing of masochistic instinctual forces for the purpose of race-preservation I regard as representing in the mental economy an act of sublimation on the part of the woman. In certain circumstances it results in the withdrawal from the direct gratification of instinct of the energy involved and in the woman's sexual life becoming characterized by frigidity without entailing any such consequences as would upset her mental balance and give rise to neurosis.

Let me now at the close of my paper give its main purport: *Women would never have suffered themselves throughout the epochs of history to have been withheld by social ordinances on the one hand from possibilities of sublima-*

tion, and on the other from sexual gratifications, were it not that in the function of reproduction they have found magnificent satisfaction for both urges.

Notes

1 Helene Deutsch, *Zur Psychoanalyse der weiblichen Sexualfunktionen* (Vienna: Internationaler psychoanalytischer Verlag, 1925).

2 Sigmund Freud (1925*j*), 'Some Psychical Consequences of the Anatomical Distinction Between the Sexes', SE 19:243-58. The argument in this paper of Freud's is that the Oedipus complex does not develop in girls until after the phase of phallic onanism. Cf. also Helene Deutsch, *Psychoanalyse der weiblichen Sexualfunktionen*.

3 In his paper on 'The Economic Problem of Masochism' (1924*c*), SE 19:157-70, Freud points out that the important task of the libido is to conduct into the outside world the instinct of destruction primarily inherent in living beings, transforming it into the 'instinct of mastery'. This is effected by means of the organ of motility, the muscular system. It appears to me that part of these destructive tendencies remains attached to the subject's own person in the earliest form of masturbation, which has as yet no libidinal object, and that it is thus intercalated between organic pleasure and motor discharge into the outside world. At any rate I have been able with some degree of certainty to establish the fact that children who are specially aggressive and active have a particularly strong urge to masturbation. (I am speaking here of the earliest masturbation, which is as yet autoerotic.) We see too that in little children frustration may provoke an outburst of rage and at the same time attempts at masturbation.

4 Even if further observations should prove the occurrence of vaginal sensations in childhood, the subsequent cathexis of the vagina as a sex organ would still seem to be scarcely affected by the question of whether it had transitorily been a zone of excitation, very soon repressed so as to leave scarcely a trace, or whether it were only in later years of development that it assumed for the first time the role of the genital apparatus. The same difficulties arise in either case.

5 That 'feminine' masochism has its origin in this regressive deflection of the libido is clear evidence of the identity of 'erotogenic' and 'feminine' masochism.

6 In the second section of this paper I will revert to the part that the sense of guilt plays in feminine masochistic phantasies. In the present argument I am indicating the purely libidinal origin of feminine masochism, as determined by the course of evolution.

14

The Pregenital Antecedents of the Oedipus Complex

Otto Fenichel (1931)

International Journal of Psycho-Analysis 12(1931):141-66

Fenichel's article first appeared in English in 1931. It is very much a synthesis of what has been said on the importance of preoedipal matters linking the castration complex and the Oedipus complex from the point of view of object-relations.

Fenichel starts from the Freudian premise that the Oedipus complex is the nucleus not just of the neuroses but of the unconscious. But interestingly enough he opposes both Freud and Klein with regard to the timing and development of the Oedipus complex. On the basis of his own findings in case studies of adult analysands, he disagrees with Klein and attempts to distinguish between pregenital and autoerotic tendencies from the point of view of object relations.

He initially raises the question how the Oedipus complex, properly so-called, evolves from its pregenital preliminary phases. But it soon becomes apparent that the real focus of the paper is in the more specific question how the change in aim and object of females' pregenital relations, which is necessary for entry to the Oedipus complex, comes about.

Fenichel sums up the analytical picture regarding the influence of pregenital factors on the Oedipus complex, then gives an account of three case histories (one of a bisexual and ambivalent-sadistic case and two cases of hysteria), draws some theoretical conclusions from the material with regard to the change of object in women, and proceeds to comment on and compare with each other the views of Freud, Horney, Lampl de Groot and Jones on the topic. Ultimately he confirms Freud's views and reinforces the Freudian consensus, briefly arguing with Deutsch (concerning the change of object) and with Abraham (concerning the shift in, or primacy of, erotogenic zones).

Thus, Fenichel offers clinical observations that might illustrate the various pregenital phases of the Oedipus complex and hopefully solve the debate around the issue of femininity, particularly with regard to the shift in the choice of object and erogenous zone. What he emphasizes is that the pregenital material (oral or anal) accounts for the different phases of sexuality. Furthermore, all demands and frustrations of sexuality are bound up with the mother-child relationship. Like Deutsch, he follows Abraham, particularly concerning the concept of the anal child. The mother is here the castrating mother, which also explains why he disagrees with Lampl de Groot on the issue of the little girl's phallicism.

The question underlying the argument, then, is not: what does woman want?, but rather: what does mother want? The mother is the anal 'other', and the castrating mother would thus be the equivalent of the 'primal' mother of a parallel text to Totem and Taboo.

* * *

I

The Oedipus complex has been called by Freud 'the nuclear complex' of the neuroses, and we may go further and say that it is the nuclear complex of the unconscious of mankind in general. Every single analysis provides fresh evidence of this fact, if we except those cases of extreme malformation of character which resemble a life-long psychosis and in which a true Oedipus complex has never become crystallized, either because the subject's object-relations were destroyed root and branch at an earlier period, or because such relations never existed at all. However strong may be one's theoretical convictions on the point, it comes as a fresh surprise every time when we find that final solution and cure in an analysis which has remained obscure depend invariably on the deepening of our knowledge of the Oedipus complex.

Freud holds that it is in the fourth or fifth year of life that the Oedipus complex reaches its zenith, that is, that this coincides with the attainment of the *phallic* level of organization.[1] We know that (as is in accordance with this hypothesis) the content of the complex is the wish for *genital* union with the parent of the opposite sex, together with a jealous hatred of the parent of the subject's own sex. Melanie Klein states that she has found in the analyses of children that the complete Oedipus complex is already established at a far earlier period.[2] This view contradicts our experience of the analyses of adults. It is undoubtedly true that at a far earlier period the child is attached to the parent of the opposite sex, and feels jealousy and hatred towards the other parent. But these preliminary phases differ in certain fundamental points from the Oedipus complex at the time of its zenith. (We have an exact analogy in the difference between the preliminary phases of the super-ego—not sufficiently differentiated by M. Klein— and the consolidated super-ego established after the passing of the Oedipus complex.)[3] These preliminary phases have contents (not genital) other than those of the true Oedipus complex; they are still competing with auto-erotic tendencies; the jealous hatred still exists without conflict side by side with love for the parent of the subject's own sex. Moreover, these preliminary phases are by no means always comprised in one single 'complex'. Thus it is certain that pregenital object-relations exist, and it would be a fundamental error to imagine that 'pregenital' and 'auto-erot-ic' are synonymous terms. Similarly, the *objects* of these pregenital relations will be pre-eminently the parents. The *content* of these relations was first described by Freud[4] and later by Abraham[5] who, as the result of his close study of persons with pregenital fixations, gave an exact and systematic description in the 'Origins and Growth of Object-Love'. Let me recall this to your minds by quoting his main headings: total incorporation, partial incorporation, partial love without incorporation, post-ambivalent love.

Abraham also established the fundamental facts about the causes and mechanisms of the advance from one stage of object-relationship to that immediately above it.[6] The question now before us is a more special one. How is the true Oedipus complex evolved from the pregenital preliminary phases? Or—to take the descriptive standpoint first—where and how are its pregenital antecedents reflected in the Oedipus complex? In answer to this question, psychoanalysis can begin by producing an abundance of one special kind of material, namely, the results of regression. They are illuminating but also very confusing. All neurotics suffer from having fended off the Oedipus complex by some inappropriate method, and so having failed to master it. But, in contrast to hysterics, persons suffering from obsessional neurosis and other mental diseases are characterized by the fact that they try to evade that complex by reverting to earlier modes of gratification and regressively substituting for it something pregenital. They may do this so completely that their later acquirements seem wholly to disappear, and to judge by his instinctual behaviour, the patient seems to be altogether at a pre-Oedipus stage (as in many psychoses). Or the regression may be less complete and behind the pregenital facade it may be possible to reveal the presence of the forbidden Oedipus wishes. This mode of defence is facilitated by two factors: (*a*) the subject's constitution, (*b*) some experience which causes fixation during the pregenital period. It is true that persons who have regressed produce an abundance of material by means of which they amalgamate the Oedipus complex with the pregenital object-relations, and it would be carrying coals to Newcastle if we cited particular examples. But we also called this material 'confusing' because it is only with the greatest difficulty that we can recognize which of the numerous 'pregenital' traits in the Oedipus wishes of these patients is a subsequent, regressive distortion and which represents the residue of their real, original, pregenital experience, and so gave a characteristic tinge to their Oedipus wishes when first these arose in childhood. Naturally, if a man suffers from obsessive impulses to kill his mother and cut off his own penis, we have no difficulty in recognizing in the first impulse the regressive distortion of the wish to have sexual intercourse with the mother, and in the second, the super-ego's demand that this wish be punished. Or,

again, if a woman is afraid that a snake may come up out of the water-closet, analysis can show that the anxiety once took another form, namely, that
the snake might be hidden in her bed, and that it signifies the father's
penis, the idea of which has been connected with anal-erotism by a process
of defensive regression. Neither phenomenon would be possible, had not
the male patient at some time had sadistic impulses and the female had
sexual sensations in the water-closet. But at first they still give us no hint
as to how long *before* the shattering of the Oedipus complex its own pregenital antecedents were reflected in that complex itself. For *every* Oedipus
complex has such antecedents. Little indications, vestiges of these
antecedents, characteristics of the complex may prove its origin from the
pregenital material, like the trade mark 'Made in Germany', which Freud
uses as a metaphor in another context. If so, we may conclude that precisely these traits will probably be of great importance in the formation of
the subject's character (pregenital tingeing of the super-ego). But perhaps
we shall acquire more reliable material in this connection from just the
types which are not regressive, i.e. normal people and hysterics, but also—
in a far more pronounced form—from persons with faulty development of
character and from psychopaths, whose Oedipus complex, owing to the
specially strong pregenital fixation, had from the very beginning a pregenital tinge.

In women the transition from the pregenital relations to the Oedipus
complex involves not only the change of aim, which we have so far considered, but a change of object. The first pregenital object—the mother—
has to be exchanged for the father. As we know, this change of object has
been made the subject of a lively discussion, in which very different and
sometimes contradictory views have been expressed.[7]

These questions are further complicated by the fact of bisexuality
which sometimes causes men to change their object, like women, and
women to fail to change it. We learn from Freud that with every human
being we have to reckon on the presence of the *complete* Oedipus complex,
i.e. not only that of the subject's own sex but that of the opposite sex.[8] The
normal solution is that the relation of the subject to the parent of his or her
own sex passes into an identification, while the relation to the other parent passes into object-love. We know that this normal solution often breaks
down wholly or in part and that total or partial 'errors of sexual identification'[9] take place. It is very common to meet with isolated features of
such erroneous identifications. They may cause the Oedipus complex to
betray from the very beginning characteristics of an original ambivalence,
which will be marked in proportion as a person is sadistic (i.e. suffering
from pregenital fixation), ambivalent and bisexual.

It may be asked: What is the typical way in which the object-relations
of the pregenital period are reflected in the Oedipus complex? The answer

is that it will vary greatly in normal and in pathological cases; we know something, but of much we are ignorant. Supposing that we make a dogmatic statement of the points on which all psychoanalytical writers are agreed. They hold that the following features of the Oedipus complex are influenced by pregenital factors:

1 the Oedipus prohibitions by the earlier prohibitions of auto-erotism;
2 the dread of castration by the dread of the loss of the mother's breast and of faeces;
3 the little girl's love for her father by her pregenital relations with her father;
4 the idea of the penis by that of the mother's breast and of faeces;
5 the wish for a child by the desire for a penis and, hence, for faeces;
6 the conception of coitus by that of total oral incorporation.

The following points are disputed:

1 the causes and mechanisms of the change of love-object in women;
2 the relation of oral to genital sexuality;[10]
3 the relation between receiving and surrendering (cf. Abraham's subdivision of the oral and anal levels of organization[11] and Ferenczi's view on the 'amphimixis' of pregenital instinctual impulses[12]).

Satisfactory answers to all these questions can be given only after exhaustive analysis of very many instances, which must exclude the regressive factor as far as possible in order to bring to light the true genesis. Perhaps the analyses of children may throw some light on the subject. In adults the most important material is very hard to come by and can be understood only after very long and deep analyses.

In the following article I want simply to make a modest contribution to the collection of such material. I will give an account of three cases, all of which were under analytic treatment for two or three years. Naturally it is neither possible nor necessary to communicate the whole of the case-histories. In each case I will quote exclusively the historical material relevant to our problems. The first case is not a typical one: it is that of a faulty character-development, peculiarly bisexual, ambivalent and sadistic (manifestly masochistic). But on the other hand it affords a remarkable mass of material. A strongly developed Oedipus complex proves to be essentially based on pregenital factors (whereas a markedly anal-sadistic attitude is found in obsessional neurotics to have its main basis in the Oedipus complex). The two other instances I shall quote are cases of hysteria and will show us what part of the material contributed by the first case can be utilized in normal psychology as well.

II

In a short communication about the interpretation of a dream which consisted solely of the word 'bees', I have already given some account[13] of the form and structure of the symptoms of the first patient, a man thirty-six years old. He suffered from various difficulties of character, the most important of which were marked moral masochism and a neurotic inability to take up a profession. His Oedipus complex was very clearly developed and, manifestly, it dominated his life. For years he had lived with a woman considerably older than himself, and he remained attached to her in the most irrational fashion. He had come to know her through 'rescuing' her from financial straits. In accordance with the principle of exogamy he appeared to have selected a woman as unlike his mother as possible, but nevertheless, in spite of their totally different environments, the two women had many traits in common and also the same name. During the analysis, the figure of this woman was at times indistinguishable in dreams and phantasies from that of the mother, but all the same, before analysis, the patient was quite unconscious that she was a mother-substitute, as he was unconscious of any affective attachment to his real mother. On the other hand, conscious hatred of his tyrannical father and the perpetually fruitless struggle with him formed the main content of the patient's life. The vehemence and fury of the death-wishes against the father, which broke out during the analysis, were almost beyond description. Moreover, the patient's inability to take up a profession proved at the outset to be due to his violent hatred of his father. 'He must give me his money' was the *leitmotif* of this life. His lack of a profession and his whole mode of life, which at times was very like that of a swindler, he justified by the expectation (amounting almost to a delusion) that before long he would draw a winning lottery ticket. He was a passionate devotee of lotteries and behaved as if 'luck' were a father on whom he had a claim: 'You *must* give me all the money'. (The form his demand took was derived from an incident during puberty, when his father once won in a lottery.) The first stratum which the analysis of his hate revealed was that of an unconscious love of his father, concealed under the hate. It manifested itself in 'fits of remorse' in contrast to his rebellious attitude (which invariably occurred when his father had *really* sent him money), in a disguised form in various day-dreams and, above all, in the transference to the analyst, which, although completely positive, was a pure father-transference. (I will discuss later why hate did not enter into the transference, or at least only to a relatively small extent.) As the patient was constantly requiring money and his mode of life kept him dependent on his father, his love was naturally of a demanding, sadistic character, its aim being to extort money and presents from his father. In the unconscious, corresponding to this love there was the full negative Oedipus complex—his jealousy of his brothers (one of his childhood recollections was that a bishop had once kissed one of the brothers but not the patient himself), dreams in which men pierced him with spears or locomotives ran over him, etc.; and, finally, the form taken by his castration-anxiety left no doubt of the interpretation that he wished to have coitus with his father and have a child by him. The main content of his anxiety was that he was being eaten up from inside by little animals in his body and being robbed of his penis. Experiences in connection with gonorrhoea (bacteria) and morbid growths ('cancer' = the animal 'crab')[14] had determined the form of this anxiety, the unconscious content of which followed the lines of the oral theory of conception: 'When one conceives a child in the sexual act' (thought of in terms of the oral theory) 'one is devoured from within by little animals' (children, spermatozoa, embryos) 'which, when birth takes place, eat their way out through the penis'.

The image the patient had in mind of the animals living inside the body was that of oxyuria (anal) and these he pictured like macaroni, which had been his favourite food when he was a very young child. Let me give a few examples of his excessive anal and oral fixations: (*a*) (*anal*) His whole life was dominated by his completely irrational libidinal relation to money. Even as an adult he occasionally failed to retain his stools. During puberty he had once evacuated on to a piece of newspaper and kept it for months. (*b*) (*oral*) He displayed a large number of the character-traits which Abraham[15] described as 'oral': in matters of 'getting' and 'giving' he was quite undisciplined. He attached particular importance to good food. He was markedly interested in words. 'To take money from one's father' meant also 'to be nourished by one's father'. He conceived of passive homosexual intercourse orally, as consisting either of sucking or biting off the penis. At the same time there were various traits which indicated identification with his father. For instance, he lived with a woman who was a mother-substitute (when this was interpreted to him, it had actually the effect of a trauma); he wanted to draw a winning ticket like his father and he was exceedingly fond of travelling, which was traceable to the desire to elope with his mother. An unusually intense love for his home and his part of the country proved to represent his love for his mother, or, as could be inferred from relatively early associations, his grandmother.

Now let me give the most essential historical facts in this case and, first of all, those concerned with the period of puberty. The strong, diffused sexual excitation (for, from the beginning, genitality was weak) had for its object a servant whose name was the same as that of the patient's mother. Later on he learnt that his father had had relations with this girl and that she had a child by him. There, then, was the whole constellation of the Oedipus complex: the father had 'taken away' the woman from the patient. The *motif* of 'taking away' governed his whole erotic life. His childhood was characterized by his ambivalent attitude towards his father, who was severe and used to beat him and forbid things he wanted, and by the failure of his attempts at a father-identification and, further, by his completely repressed, pregenital love for his mother. The idea of sucking the penis concealed the more deeply repressed idea of sucking at the breast. (The dream of the bees.) In his dreams and phantasies his grandmother kept appearing with increasing frequency and with the suggestion that her authority was equal to his mother's. Finally we discovered the fundamental, primal history of the case. On account of his mother's illness the boy had been separated from her soon after his birth and sent to his grandmother's, where he was fed by a wet nurse. At first the patient said that he was there for the first six months of his life. He said, too, that he was very much spoilt there and was given such quantities of macaroni to eat that his stomach was all puffed out and, when he went home, the doctor put him on a strict diet. He then did not speak for a whole year, so that he was supposed to be dumb, till at the end of a year he astonished the whole family by suddenly uttering a complete sentence (a complaint against his brothers). Now this seemed quite incredible. No child of six months could eat so much macaroni or lose, out of defiance, the power of speech, once acquired. By means of further analysis and objective information we were finally able to correct the patient's account. He had stayed with his grandmother not for six months but for eighteen months and, during that whole period, he was fed at the nurse's breast. During the second half of the time his grandmother spoilt him greatly in other oral ways (macaroni). When he went back to his parents this paradise of spoiling was left behind, and there followed a sudden and radical frustration. The breast which gave him milk so lavishly suddenly vanished, and so did the macaroni and the women who fulfilled the child's every wish. To *this* frustration the patient, who could already speak a little, responded by going on strike and refusing to speak for a year. The character of this sudden frustration is shown most clearly in a remark of his father's, when the patient during his analysis asked him about his recollections of this time. 'You did nothing but scream "Macaroni, macaroni", but I soon broke you of that! I used to give you a whipping every day!' The memories which

came up in analysis and, above all, the patient's dreams testified to the correctness of the father's recollection.

The fact that the child was first spoilt—by women (mother-equiva-
lents)—and then suddenly made to undergo frustration—by his father—
on the oral (and, as we may add, the anal) level, caused the pregenital fixation which coloured his whole life. The result where the Oedipus complex was concerned was that his wish for his mother remained essentially
oral. We have an illustration of this in a dream which occurred when the
analysis was already well advanced. 'I was walking along with a parcel
under each arm. I knew that my father was dead. The parcels opened and
I saw that they were full of macaroni'. Thus the longed-for death of the
father gave him the opportunity of oral gratification, as it might give
another the opportunity for sexual intercourse with the mother. In close
relation to this dream there occurred others, which gave the patient a great
shock: in these he was having coitus with his mother. The effect of his early
experiences upon the negative Oedipus complex was that he demanded of
his father, though the latter forbade the things the child desired, that the
father himself should restore what he had taken away—namely, oral or
anal gratification. The instinctual impulse originally directed towards the
mother was transferred to the father, and the frustration which had meanwhile been inflicted imparted to it a sadistic, rebellious character, so that
the love of the negative Oedipus complex expressed itself as follows: 'You
took it away from me and you must give it back!' The instinctual aim was
still that of partial incorporation: the parts incorporated were represented
by the 'little animals' and had a different significance in the different mental strata: milk, money (faeces), semen and also the penis. (During an illness of his father's the patient had the following dream, arising from an
actual experience of his own impotence: 'One of my teeth was loose'. The
tooth represented in the first place the father—its shakiness his illness and
the death-wish against him. But, further, it stood for the father's penis,
incorporated orally by the patient, the latent dream-thought being: 'Give
me your penis, so that I can satisfy the woman with it, if I cannot with my
own'.)

Now it became plain why the transference to the analyst was always
so positive. The analyst was the good father who fulfilled these demands
of the negative Oedipus complex. The *interpretations* given, the *words* spoken during the analytic hour, represented to the patient the oral gratification he longed for.

Whilst the central point in the patient's life appeared to be the inward
coming to terms with his father (the moral masochism corresponded to the
sadism whose real object was the father but had been turned against the
subject's own ego), the deeper, original heterosexual attitude betrayed

itself in two ways. First, it enabled the patient to make himself in some sense independent of his tyrannical father by going abroad and placing himself in an environment the very reverse of that at home, while both his brothers remained in their father's business, continuing to react in unison, in a neurotic fashion, not only to their father-imago but to the father in person. My patient, in contrast to them, had made the inalienable discovery of the existence of another world, independent of his father. But he had a false idea of his world! He anticipated with complete confidence that it would be a paradise, where the ideal woman and the winning ticket alike would be his. Since reality was no such paradise, his neurotic reaction was to turn away from it and once more to make his father responsible for the fact that his life abroad did not resemble his life with his grandmother in his early infancy. He was in despair when all he wanted did not drop into his mouth of its own accord and, at the same time, he held the unwavering belief that it *must* do so. His real attitude towards women was almost entirely pregenital. During the analysis his father died, and the patient's reaction was a very considerable regression to narcissism which manifested itself chiefly in organic neurotic symptoms. These demonstrated his helplessness—a sick man cannot look after himself; he *must* have a father or (still further back in the subject's mind) a nursing mother. But the symptoms signified, besides, a continuation on narcissistic ground of the ambivalent conflict of which his father was the object. His attitude to the diseased organs of his body, which represented the introjected father, was in detail identical with his earlier attitude to his father. The analysis of these symptoms revealed that he practised phallic onanism in his early childhood and that the habit was interrupted by a threat of castration. Owing to the marked pregenital fixation this threat was construed as a repetition of the oral traumas. The threatened loss of the penis was not merely regressively *represented* by the loss of the grandmother (= home) and of fostering care; it was from the beginning only a special case of this general frustration.

To sum up: the history is as follows: pregenital fixation to the mother (nurse, grandmother); bitter disappointment by the father followed by a two-fold reaction: (*a*) fixation of the heterosexual object-relation and hence of the subsequently established Oedipus complex on the pregenital level, (*b*) a rebellious turning towards the father, characterized by features of the previous heterosexual relation, which were now displaced on to the father; the development, by reaction, of a marked sadism; all this resulting in a most radically pregenital fixation of the negative Oedipus complex as well as the positive.

III

A woman patient of thirty-six came to be analysed on account of various neurotic symptoms which were serious but did not handicap her too badly in her work. This was hard work, a 'man's job', for she held a responsible post as a manager. Prominent in her case also was the influence of a strong, unsolved Oedipus complex. This was specially evident in her erotic relationships, in which typical 'conditions for a love-relation' mentioned by Freud were clearly present: namely, the pre-requisite of an 'injured third party', the series of similar figures, the love for superiors.[16] When she grew up, her relation to her old father was one of specially warm friendship; its unconscious erotic sources soon came to light in analysis. There was no open hostility between her and her mother, but the fact that, deep down, she passionately detested many things in the latter was not far from consciousness. Analysis revealed in a most striking manner her infantile wish to get a child from her father (longings at Christmas time, acts of losing other 'substitutes' and gifts and much besides). Her case, then, seemed to fit into the scheme of hysteria, where the patient comes to grief over the Oedipus complex, but without regression. Her behaviour in the transference represented in typical fashion the wrecking of her Oedipus wishes and her reactions to the frustrations of that period. On the idea: 'If I can't have my father, I will take whoever comes first' she had built up a strong harlot-complex, in accordance with which she experienced from time to time a violent eruption of erotic excitement, which she relieved principally by onanism and which was in complete contrast to her usually calm and self-controlled nature. Onanism had been practised by her without interruption during the latency-period and was accompanied by manifestly masochistic phantasies (of being beaten). Here analysis was able relatively early to show that there was a 'reversal', an underlying powerful unconscious sadism: she identified herself in phantasy with the person doing the beating—her masturbation took an active-masculine form (pulling at the labia)—she developed a strong hate-attachment to lovers who had disappointed her, and phantasies of revenge evoked the outbursts of erotic excitement of which I have spoken. She had also a perverse inclination—a special pleasure in cunnilingus—which seemed to spring from a tendency to abase men. In order to make her case clearer I will quote some of the material from her childhood. Her ideal of a calm, self-controlled person she derived from her father, an official of upright character. Affectionate and conscientious but of an obsessional type, he not merely preached but practised extreme self-control and calm reasonableness. The sudden outbursts of sensuality were such as she had seen in little girls she played with, but she could never get rid of the feeling that her own mother was a very sensual person. Thus sensual wishes relating to her father had to be repressed with special force, and the more so because once he had found her masturbating and had beaten her, which was quite unlike him. Her tender attachment to him, then, caused her to reject all sensuality. The repressed sensual feelings joined forces with the hostile attitude which was her reaction to them: there were vehement reproaches of her father for his 'cold reasonableness', his lack of understanding of behaviour actuated by elementary instinctual forces. During and after puberty this latter reproach took the sublimated form that he had no sympathy with her literary ambitions. An enormous transference-resistance when her compositions were for the first time to be subjected to analysis—the determination 'not to be robbed' of them—was the first clear indication of castration-anxiety. The sensuality characterized by hostility to her father soon took a homosexual direction. Once, shortly after puberty, she had actually performed a homosexual act with a friend and it had roused a deep disgust in her. It turned out that, as a child, she had played sexual games with this friend and, especially, that the two little girls had always gone to the water-closet together. Her subsequent homosexual inclinations and her attraction to the 'injured' wives of men she loved seemed, like the harlot-phantasies whose volcanic character they shared, to be the reactions of revenge to disappointments at the hands of men. At last there emerged a repressed memory of a nurse who was dismissed because she always took the patient into bed with her, and we thought that the prominence of the homosexual attitude was connected with the reality of these childhood experiences as contrasted with the phantastic nature of the sexual wishes relating to the father. It seemed that, as in the case of homosexuality in a woman of which Freud[17] gives an account, the homosexual attitude meant a declaration to the father: 'If you are not willing, I don't want you!' Finally, I must mention that a masochistic trait in the patient's character fortified itself principally with self-reproaches (certainly exaggerated) on the ground that she had harmed her father with advice on money matters during the period of inflation of the currency.

For a long time nothing was said about the mother. There were only hints that the patient disliked her more than she knew; in dreams she sometimes appeared as the 'bad mother', a witch or castrator. We did not get any further in this direction till the analysis reached the pregenital period. And here I must first say something about the patient's penis-envy.

In many respects her behaviour was masculine and her work was that of a man. In the structure of her character penis-envy had been displaced upwards; she took every opportunity of competing with men in the field of intellect. We discovered that the father-identification underlying this attitude was still being utilized in *wooing* her father. She wanted to prove to him by it that she was equal or superior to her only brother, who was older than she. It seemed at first as though her real penis-envy had reference to this brother, as was indicated by numbers of memories which gradually emerged and which we traced to the comparison between his powers of urination and her own. We succeeded, too, in bringing to light phantasies of a hidden penis of her own, or one which might perhaps appear again; finally, a day-dream, in which she lived with a child which was born by parthenogenesis, showed that she phantasied herself not only the mother but the father of the child and the latter itself as her penis. She could not urinate so well as her brother and was not allowed, as he was, to do it when out walking? Very well: she would concentrate her ambition on another bodily power—she could retain her urine longer. This retention—'self-control'—was in accordance with her father's ego-ideal, or the ego-ideal based on her father's character, which required above all things 'self-command'. The outbreaks of sensuality and the masturbation were the psychic equivalent of incontinence. The inclination to masturbate had to be suppressed like the desire to pass urine or evacuate faeces at an inconvenient time. Later, the patient still tried to suppress the habit, at least in part, endeavouring, when masturbating, at any rate to prevent herself from breathing in gasps. This gave rise to various symptoms and forms of anxiety (dread of suffocation). We then discovered that, whereas we had long supposed that her brother must have put her to shame by his possession of a penis while she had none, the humiliating episode had really taken place in another connection and referred to the equivalent power of continence. She had once been given an enema and, midway between her bed and the chamber, evacuation had taken place and her brother, who was standing by, had laughed at her. This proof of incontinence was felt by her as the deepest humiliation and taken as evidence that she had been castrated. In the history of her childhood it appeared that a change occurred in her character in connection with an intestinal illness which she had at the age of three: she had been a quiet and docile child, but now became peevish and tiresome. This had various determinants and amongst them was the fact that she regarded the illness as a humiliation, on account of the incontinence of faeces associated with it. Here is a symbolic equation: to be ill=to be incontinent=to be castrated, and to this experience she responded with the change in her character. The reason why the episode of incontinence shamed her so profoundly was that she had been trained in habits of cleanliness at a remarkably early age—ostensibly without any difficulty and by her mother alone. One significance of cunnilingus was the cancelling of the humiliation inflicted on her by her brother: it meant that he recognized the value of the dirty and incontinent anus—the genital which has no penis.

In connection with this material, memories of her third year at last emerged, from which we learnt something of the methods employed by her mother in training her in cleanliness and also how long that training had lasted. Up till the time of the patient's illness her mother had always gone with her to the water-closet (the games with the friend were screen-memories). She used to urge her daughter with much talk to defecate and used to praise her when she did her business well, and especially when the stool was well-formed. It was all done in such a way that the child understood clearly that her mother took a libidinal interest in these acts. Undoubtedly she herself also derived pleasure from them and in this way she formed what may be called an anal-erotic association with her mother. The repression of these scenes had as its counterpart the feeling that her mother, in contrast to her father, was very sensual. Actually, she was never allowed to say a word in his presence about these anal concerns, and he himself was most particular that the children should never notice his going to the water-closet. Thus the child probably very soon had the feeling that he disapproved of the closet-association with her mother. The pregenital fixation to the latter was inhibited by two experiences. The first, which reappeared in a dream, was that she noticed in the water-closet that blood was flowing from her mother, and this made the little girl think of a bloody punishment for the delights of the closet. The second experience was the illness I have mentioned. We discovered that not only her incontinence but also the nature of the stool, which was unformed on account of diarrhoea, wounded her narcissism severely. ('I am not creating anything—no child'). It happened that her father reproached her mother, saying 'Whatever did you give the child to eat?' or some such words, whereupon the little girl came to the conclusion that her mother had made her ill—i.e. sensual enjoyment with the mother made her ill, incontinent, castrated her: 'It would have been better to obey my father who always disapproved of it'. The mother was the witch who seduced one and gave pleasure, but the pleasure was fatal. The idea that her mother had given her something bad to eat brought us to the analysis of the oral attachment to the mother which existed before the anal period. A screen-memory from the time before the illness was that she was drinking milk out of a bottle. It turned out that this was the last occasion on which she drank any milk before her illness and her father suspected it of being the cause of the trouble. She thought then: 'Mother has poisoned me with milk'. In connection with the memory of cows' udders and the confusion between udder and penis, the idea then emerged: 'She has given me urine to drink'. It turned out that once, when the child was at the same age of three, her mother let her fall in the bath, i.e. nearly killed her (to drown [*ertränken*] = to give a noxious drink to [*schlecht tränken*]). It was to this incident that her fear of suffocation could be traced). From the idea of poisoning a succession of transitory oral symptoms led back to the idea of drinking purulent fluid, and this was finally linked up with the objective information that the mother had had to wean the child because she herself developed mastitis. Thus, the pregenital attachment to the mother ended with the verdict: 'What we did was wrong. Father never did anything like that'. She was doubtful as to whether the disastrous result would be a punishment by the father (as was indicated by the earliest memories of him, dating from before her illness—how he intervened when the little girl was 'hurt') or whether it would happen automatically, i.e. through her mother's fault, in which case he would be the rescuer rather than the avenger.

Now there was another point to be cleared up about the idea: mother = witch. The patient had an increasingly strong feeling that her mother was a *vampire* and meant to suck her dry for her own pleasure. The only thing which could give rise to this idea of 'sucking out what was inside' was the mother's encouraging words when the child's stool was well formed. The mother, then, had robbed her daughter of the well formed stool, i.e. by a familiar equation, of the penis. Material derived from dreams and symptoms did in fact suggest the hypothesis that, immediately before she fell ill, the child had happened to see an erect penis. 'Sucking dry' was the form in which the mother performed the act of castration. The harlot-phantasies—so closely related to homosexuality—corresponded amongst other things to the idea that the harlot, forced into coitus to the point of exhaustion, was 'sucked dry' by the men. In a second screen-memory from the time immediately preceding her illness (a memory which we evoked at the same time as we discussed that of the scene about the milk) she was walking between two boys and shouldering a shovel. This meant: 'Before my illness I still had my penis'.

Now for the first time we were able to understand the deeper strata of her Oedipus complex. In her dread of her mother she turned to her father for help—her attitude being ambivalent from the outset, for she feared her father would punish her. But unconsciously she could imagine only *one* form of help: he must give back what she had lost through her mother's fault. For a time the patient changed her method of masturbation, and this gave her a deep sense of guilt, so that she refused to speak of it in analysis. Finally, however, she admitted that she was practising vaginal masturbation, by means of objects, and that these were always made of glass. Analysis showed that this referred to the enemas given to her by her father, and so the infantile wish was reconstructed that he should put the whole apparatus into her rectum. In the anal sense this meant: 'He ought to give me a *formed* stool (penis, child) not a motion like diarrhoea (fluid injection).' This meant: 'He ought to give me back the stool—the penis—

which my mother has stolen from me'. In the patient's mental history this idea came to her in connection with the motion of the hand. She remembered playing that her father's hand was a 'child', and she recounted a phantasy of being raped by five men—who were the five fingers. The prototype of this 'rape' by the hand was undoubtedly the enema-syringe. Her demands that what she had lost should be replaced by the father's body were met with refusal on his part. Thereupon her oral-anal sadism was turned against him: just like the patient in the first case I quoted, she demanded of the father partial incorporation. In accordance with her experiences she constructed the sexual theory that her mother sucked her father dry, and she began to wish that she could do exactly the same. *This* was the root of her active behaviour and her sadism. The Oedipus complex was built up on an unconscious partial love, together with the idea of incorporation; the mouth and the anus gave place to the vagina, while the child was substituted for faeces and penis. The break-up of the Oedipus complex followed the lines of that of the pregenital mother-fixation: just as, then, the patient had reached the conclusion that her mother 'sucked her dry', so, now, she felt that her father's intellectual type of character, with its aloofness from instinctual behaviour, implied a 'theft of the finest capabilities', a kind of 'drying-up'. The periodic, nymphomanic obsessional masturbation in which she indulged was *mainly* determined by *these* pregenital components of the Oedipus complex. The unconscious phantasy accompanying the act was as follows: 'I am biting off—or sucking out—my father's penis, so that I shall have a penis and a child, and *he* will die'. This oral-sadistic trait was the cause of the patient's deep sense of guilt: her masochism represented the same tendency directed against her own ego. Her sadism she directed not only against her father but also against the child stolen from him.—As a child she had feared being poisoned or sucked dry by her mother (i.e. orally castrated and destroyed): so, unconsciously and in identification with the vampire-mother, did she wish, by biting off and sucking out, to destroy the child which she would steal from the father's body. The deepest strata in her Oedipus complex were represented in the following phantasies: (*a*) that of biting off a penis and so killing it—eating something 'dead'—having something 'dead' inside her and so perishing (the principal phantasy about her intestinal illness in childhood); (*b*) that of having something 'half dead' inside her, which could be saved by medical intervention (this was the principal phantasy of the unconscious wish for cure: that the analyst should draw forth and make manifest the penis which was inside her and excited her to masturbation).

To sum up: The mental history of this patient was as follows—pregenital fixation to the mother, first of an oral and then of an anal character;

bitter disappointment by the mother (prototype: mastitis; later, illness conceived of as castration); turning towards the father; substitutes demanded from him, with a transferring to him of tendencies and ambivalent feelings originally relating to the mother; formation of the Oedipus complex, coloured by this sequence. In this case, as in the first quoted, sadism was called forth by frustration, and the castration-anxiety, originally having reference to the mother, was displaced on to the father.

IV

I shall be able to give a somewhat shorter account of the third case. The patient was a woman of forty-four, with a neurotic character-formation and symptoms which were mainly those of anxiety-hysteria. Her character was dominated by a castration complex of excessive strength. An early identification with her father, of which I shall presently speak in greater detail, caused her largely to ignore her femininity: she regarded her menstrual periods as the most profound humiliation and shame. She had formerly had a very active sexual life, the principal feature of which was that she led men on in a wholly narcissistic fashion to make love to her, in order somehow to disappoint them in the end. She yielded herself only when she was the 'stronger', when for instance the man had burst into tears. Active castration-phantasies played a prominent role; she counted it a triumph when a man had a premature ejaculation and was therefore 'helpless'. What she aimed at was to put men as sexual beings to shame, to refuse them and then to say: 'If they were so feeble that they could not seduce me, it serves them right'. Naturally, in the transference her analysis also became a ceaseless contest for the mastery and she was constantly on the look-out for opportunities to make a fool of the analyst. Men who were no match for her were the objects of her derision. But not only the men—she mocked specially at the penis itself. It struck her as grotesque and made her laugh when she caught sight of it. Of course, this mockery had its origin in resentment and masked a vehement penis-envy.[18]

This behaviour becomes immediately more comprehensible when we learn that in this woman the whole Oedipus complex was nothing but an object of phantasy in a different sense from that in which this is true of other people. She had never known her father. He died the day she was born. And so no man was the right one. The only right one would be the father of her phantasy, the fairy-prince coming from the beyond. She had endless phantasies of 'salvation' and anxiety about her Christianity constituted the most powerful resistance in her analysis.

Her father died the day she was born. Here was reason enough for her identifying herself with him early and very widely. The mystical union with him, representing at one and the same time sexual intercourse and identification, was conceived of as oral union, as communion She had an abundance of dreams and phantasies about devouring fragments of corpses, about fruit-trees growing on graves, about oral impregnation, eating faeces, etc. The hysterical symptoms were mainly oral. She suffered from cravings of hunger and from loss of appetite, and she felt obliged to avoid various kinds of food: must not eat any meat or, above all, any fish and so on. (Fish had a 'soul' and therefore represented her father.) She had pains in the region of the diaphragm, and it turned out that, as a child, she had thought that the word 'Zwerchfell' (diaphragm) was the same as 'Zwergfell' (literally, 'dwarf's skin') and had pictured a little dwarf sitting inside and making a noise. She suffered from a dread of poisoning which, just as Weiss[19] has maintained, turned out to be dread of the introjected object. A further account of these symptoms would be interesting but is irrelevant to our present subject. To sum up: the purely phantastic Oedipus complex was characterized at all levels of libidinal development by total or partial incorporation, and the object introjected had to be interpreted, according to the stage of the analysis, as father, child, faeces or penis.

The two principal real sexual experiences of her childhood corresponded to these ideas. On one occasion she had performed fellatio with a little boy and with another boy she had often played at 'slaughter' and experienced sexual excitement.

The manifest anxiety was the most prominent feature in the clinical picture. In accordance with her real attitude towards men this anxiety proved to be, first, a dread of being the 'under-dog', secondly, the expression of inhibited aggressive impulses against men and, at bottom, an overpowering dread of the loss of love. Her behaviour gave cause enough for the fear that all men would desert her. On the other hand, she was aggressive towards men because they were disposed to leave her in the lurch.

The further the analysis advanced, and the more completely the infantile amnesias were dispelled, the clearer did it become that her real experiences with men were relatively unimportant and that the chief object which influenced her real character-formation was the one parent whom she knew—her mother. She was a 'posthumous child', and her brothers and sisters were many years older than she. In her enormous craving for tenderness the only person to whom she could turn was her mother. But here, from the very outset, she had every reason for her great fear of 'loss of love', for the mother's attitude towards this posthumous child, all that her husband had left her, was from the beginning highly ambivalent. The father had died of a mental disorder. The child often heard that she had been by no means a welcome arrival. She also heard her mother deplore her little daughter's ugliness and say: 'We thought that the child would turn out an idiot.' So she could not help hating her mother and the fiercest ambivalent conflicts were inevitable. Her aggressive tendencies manifested themselves in the way in which she caused her mother anxiety: the talion law decreed that she herself should suffer anxiety because of this, all her life long.

During analysis she remembered a forgotten Aunt Ottilie, and we were able to see that her transference-behaviour really had reference to a woman—ultimately to her mother—and that all real men were only screen-figures for the latter. It was to her mother that her longing for tenderness, and also her hatred, her aggressive impulses and her active castration-tendency were directed.

The great traumas of her life, which led to her neurotic illness, were the birth of her own daughter and that of a daughter to her lover by a strange woman. She always felt that her own daughter was ugly, all wrong—it was not the child of her own phantasy-father. Above all she feared retribution: 'My child will actually do to me what I wished to do to my mother.' A second cause of her neurosis was the feeling of injury: 'The other woman has the child, not I.' This led us to the discovery that the principal wrongs from which she had felt she suffered in her childhood were: 'Other children have a father and I haven't. Other children have a penis and I haven't'. It is certain that she held her mother responsible for both these disadvantages. We are accustomed to find the Oedipus complex in normal women taking the following form: 'My mother has taken my father away from me.' In this case there was a special meaning: 'My mother let my father die'. The main content of the ideas which caused her anxiety was that when someone dies, the other people are unmoved and just let him die. We had reason to assume that, even as a child, she suspected that her father's mental illness was the result of venereal disease; it followed that her mother had killed the father. In the 'mystic union' she received into herself the father whom her mother had slain. Her anxiety-attacks had also an exhibitionistic meaning—a reproach levelled at her mother: 'Look, this is how my mother is the death of me!' The mother was guilty, too, of the child's lack of the penis; the 'mystic union' restored the father and therewith the penis (obsessional thoughts about Christ's penis, etc.). When she demonstrated her helplessness, in an anxiety attack, she was disclosing her lack of the penis, with an implicit reproach against her mother; on real occasions of exhibition she repeatedly had such attacks, in order to demonstrate her helplessness—the fact that she had been castrated—and to accuse her mother.

Certain obsessional symptoms concealed under the patient's anxiety-hysteria led to the conclusion that, behind the thoughts of castration there were older, hidden, anal thoughts. It is true that at this point regressive factors obscured the picture. Later, she gave greater prominence to anal than to urethral functions, because in the former she could compete with boys. At the same time thorough analysis of her very complicated anal erotism showed beyond any doubt that she also made the quite primitive accusation against her mother of bothering too much about her daughter's anal concerns and destroying all pleasure in them. As in the case quoted earlier, the idea of the mother as castrator had, as substructure, the idea of her as the person who stole the child's faeces. But here again there was ambivalence: even when she was grown up, she could imagine no greater proof of love than that her lover should empty the bed-pan when she was ill. The symptom-picture which I have described makes it abundantly clear that an oral phase preceded this anal ambivalence, but I am not able to give exact particulars about the time when she was an infant at the breast.

To sum up: the patient's mental history is as follows: Pregenital (first oral and then anal) love for the mother; from the outset disappointments by the mother; aggressive reactions against her and an increased anxiety relating to loss of love; repression of aggressive impulses; anxiety still further increased; the turning to the father is possible only in phantasies—real men are, in fact, a screen for the figure of the mother. Sadism is once more a reaction to frustrations. The castration-anxiety originally having reference to the mother was subsequently displaced on to men.

V

Supposing that we now attempt to draw some theoretical conclusions from the material that we have amassed, the first point which strikes us after our discussion of the two last, female, cases is what may be learnt from them on the disputed question of 'the change of object in women'. Let us try to sum up briefly the principal points in the views held on this subject by various authors. Freud found that the little girl's discovery that she lacks a penis is felt as a purely narcissistic injury, for which she holds her mother responsible, and that it causes her to go over to the father, by way of the symbolic equation: penis = child. Freud urged analysts to investigate whether this were so in every case. K. Horney laid special stress on precisely the opposite situation, holding that little girls and women in whom there is manifestly a very marked penis-envy utilize that envy and their 'masculinity' in general *secondarily* as a defence against an already developed Oedipus complex. This is a finding which does not necessarily contradict Freud's. J. Lampl de Groot, starting from Freud's view, supplements it with a suggestion which, if it could be substantiated, would be of the utmost importance. She holds that the penis-envy of the period prior to the Oedipus complex is not narcissistic at all but is in the fullest sense masculine and phallic: the little girl really begins as a little boy and desires a penis in order to be able to have coitus with the mother. According to this view, the positive Oedipus complex in little girls would regularly be preceded by the negative.

The view which our two female cases obviously confirm first of all is that of Freud. Both patients were in the first instance attached to the mother (but *pregenitally* attached), both went over to the father and to the desire for a child, as a reaction to disappointments by the mother. In both the discovery of the lack of a penis played an important part, and both undoubtedly held the mother responsible for it. But, we must hasten to add, the idea: 'My mother has castrated me' seemed to be co-ordinated with other frustrations—to be only *one* factor among many. In one case, side by side with the reproach that the patient had been castrated by the mother were the further reproaches that the mother had poisoned her (oral), robbed her of her strength (anal). In the other, the idea that the mother had robbed the father existed from the outset side by side with that of castration, and besides, here again, we came upon important oral and anal frustrations. It chanced that all three patients were the youngest members of their families; otherwise we should certainly have found that the birth of younger brothers or sisters was a crucial instance of disillusionment. We can see immediately from our material that, amongst the disappointments emanating from the mother, the lack of a penis must play, economically, the most important part. This is very probable even when we only consider the matter theoretically. Of the co-ordinated disappointments which come through the mother those which are oral and anal affect both sexes equally. But the experience of 'castration' is one which affects the female sex only. If, then, females are impelled by these disappointments to change their love-object, while males are not so impelled (for the male case quoted is exceptional in this respect), the crucial instance of disappointment must be that connected with the lack of the penis, and it must be this which operates, in conjunction with constitutional biological factors. At all events our cases go to prove that, in females, the act of castration is originally attributed to the mother and that female sexuality is built up on a basis of partial incorporation, on the idea: 'My mother has stolen it; my father must give it back'.

Of course, the view put forward by K. Horney, that a more superficial penis-envy may act as a screen and defence for deeper Oedipus wishes, is not to be called in question, for it expresses a situation met with every day in our analytical experience. For instance, in our last case, the 'masculinity'-symptoms, so ostentatiously presented, were a screen for phantasies of mystic union with the father. But these facts tell us nothing of the possibility of a primitive narcissistic penis-envy, prior to and beyond all Oedipus wishes. Jones is right when he speaks of a pre- and a post-Oedipus penis-envy. But nothing in our material bore out the suppositions of J. Lampl de Groot. The original mother-attachments were, most markedly, exclusively pregenital. The fact that in one case this attachment was not, or not altogether, feminine and receptive but had for its aim the idea of giving the mother something or letting her take it away does not make it possible to call it a masculine, genital attachment. It is true that in the other case also there were masculine-genital wishes, having reference to the mother—e.g. the patient wished to place her own leg between her mother's thighs—but they arose at a much later, 'post-Oedipus' period, long after a secondary identification with the father had taken place. So the cases quoted by J. Lampl-de Groot do not appear to be typical.

Actually, then, the Oedipus complex is influenced by the pregenital attachment to the mother, and its break-up by the earlier break-up of that object-relation.

Let us once more sum up and compare our findings in the three cases schematically:

Case I.—Pregenital attachment to the mother—disappointment by the father—(a) fixation of heterosexuality (of the Oedipus complex), (b) turning towards the father: pregenital tendencies having reference to the mother are carried over to the father and there is a sadistic reaction.

Case II.—Pregenital attachment to the mother—disappointment by the mother—turning to the father: pregenital tendencies having reference to the mother are carried over to the father and there is a sadistic reaction.

Case III.—Pregenital attachment to the mother—chronic disappointment by the father: since he is no longer actually in existence (a) introversion takes place, (b) many pregenital tendencies having reference to the mother are carried over to real men and there is a sadistic reaction.

The second and third cases are doubtless more typical than the first. To judge by what I have recounted of them they seem characteristic instances of the development of the Oedipus complex in women. The subject's bisexuality manifests itself in the varying degrees in which the relation with the father is clouded by the importation of hate-tendencies really relating to the mother. The first case is more complicated. If it had taken a typically masculine course, the boy would probably have reacted to the disappointment by his father by turning to his mother with redoubled vehemence. Instead, however, it developed along the feminine line: that of turning to the father, after the disappointment, and transferring to him tendencies relating to the mother. We must suppose that this happened because the mother of his earliest days was replaced by his nurse and grandmother and then, later, these two were no longer present. There was also, no doubt, a special constitutional bisexual factor.

In conclusion, let us consider in the light of the material at our disposal the problems of the pregenital antecedents of the Oedipus complex, referred to at the beginning of this paper. The points upon which, as we said, all analysts are unanimous have certainly received fresh confirmation.

1   The Oedipus prohibition reflects the pregenital prohibition: in Case I, the loss of the environment associated with the grandmother remained, throughout the patient's life, the principal disaster with which he felt himself threatened; in Case II, beneath the father's commands of self-control ('being dried up') was the basic pregenital idea of 'being sucked dry'; in Case III, the overpowering dread of loss of love—originally, of the mother's love, conceived of in pregenital terms—was throughout life the chief content of the patient's anxiety. In the main we have dealt only with the material of the pregenital *object-relations* and have disregarded the question of auto-erotism, from which we might have learnt still more on these points.

2   In Case I, the castration-anxiety really always remained oral, while in Cases II and III it was built up out of the dread of losing faeces and the mother's breast.

3   In all three cases there was originally a pregenital attachment to the mother, and characteristics of this attachment were imported into the relation with the father.

4   In all three cases the introjected object in the unconscious ideas of 'partial incorporation' could represent equally the penis, faeces and the mother's breast.

5   In the cases of the two female patients it was particularly clear that the desire for a child was built up out of penis-envy and the longing for a well-formed stool.

6   In the 'eruptions' of sensuality in Case II it was easy to recognize the longing for oral incorporation as the basis of the wish for coitus.

Now, as regards the points which we said were 'disputed': With the first, the question of the change of love-object in women, we have already dealt at length. As regards the relation of oral to genital sexuality we were able in all three cases to demonstrate the feminine, *direct* transition of the incorporation-wishes from the oral to the vagina l level by way of the anal. This is a notion which Helene Deutsch[20] also puts forward. Obviously the three hollow organs simply succeed one another, as e.g. in Case II, where the coitus-wish was the direct successor of an anal incorporation-wish (enema-syringe). In this sense Jones speaks of an 'equivalent series' of female organs. It is plain that the active-phallic libido, about which we could say nothing directly, is evolved from the active excretion-components of anal sexuality, just as feminine libido is evolved from the receptive-retention-components. This brings us to the third and last point: the relation between retention and excretion. Our own findings would seem to testify to these tendencies' alternating with, or possibly succeeding one another in *every* erotogenic zone (in Abraham's[21] sense of the term) rather than to the localization in the urethra of all pleasure in excretion and in the anus of all pleasure in retention as postulated by Ferenczi in his theory of amphimixis.[22] Pure genitality seems to exist as independently as urethral and anal erotism. Only because it flowers later does it retain so many of those traces of pregenital origin which are derived from an earlier period. The object-relations were begun in that period, and therefore at their genital zenith they still bear vestiges of their origin.

Notes

[1] Sigmund Freud (1924*d*), 'The Dissolution of the Oedipus Complex', SE 19:173-9.

[2] 'Early Stages of the Oedipus Conflict', above.

[3] Cf. Melanie Klein (1927), 'Symposium on Child-Analysis', in her *Love, Guilt and Reparation and Other Works 1921-1945* (New York: Macmillan, 1975), 139-69.

[4] In various passages.

[5] Karl Abraham (1924), 'A Short Study of the Development of the Libido, Viewed in the Light of Mental Disorders', *Selected Papers of Karl Abraham* (London: Hogarth Press, 1927), 480-501. See Part 2, 'Origins and Growth of Object Love', reprinted above.

[6] 'Development of the Libido'.

[7] Sigmund Freud (1925*j*), 'Some Psychical Consequences of the Anatomical Distinction between the Sexes', SE 19:243-58; Karen Horney, 'The Flight from Womanhood', above; Jeanne Lampl de Groot, 'The Evolution of the Oedipus Complex in Women', above; Ernest Jones, 'The Early Development of Female Sexuality', above.

[8] Sigmund Freud (1923*b*), *The Ego and the Id*, SE 19:3-66.

[9] Wilhelm Reich: *Der triebhafter Charakter* (Vienna: Internationaler Psychoanalytischer Verlag, 1925).

[10] Cf. Otto Rank, 'The Genesis of Genitality', *Psychoanalytic Review*, 13(1926):129-44; Wilhelm Reich, *Der triebhafter Charakter*; Otto Fenichel (1925), 'Introjection and the Castration Complex', *Collected Papers of Otto Fenichel* (New York: Norton, 1953), 1:39-70.

[11] Karl Abraham, 'Development of the Libido'.

[12] Sándor Ferenczi (1924), *Thalassa, a Theory of Genitality* (Albany, NY: Psychoanalytic Quarterly Inc., 1938).

[13] Otto Fenichel (1927), 'Examples of Dream Analysis', *Collected Papers of Otto Fenichel* (New York: Norton, 1953), 1:123-7.

[14] In German the same word '*Krebs*' is used for both.

[15] Karl Abraham, 'Psycho-Analytical Studies on Character-Formation', chapters 13 to 16 of his *Selected Papers*.

[16] Sigmund Freud (1910*h*), 'A Special Type of Choice of Object Made by Men', SE 11:165-75.

[17] Sigmund Freud (1920*a*), 'The Psychogenesis of a Case of Homosexuality in a Woman', SE 18:147-72.

[18] Cf. Otto Fenichel (1928), 'The Long Nose', *Collected Papers*, 1:155-7

[19] Edoardo Weiss, 'The Delusion of being Poisoned in the Light of Introjective and Projective Procedures', *Archives of Psychoanalysis*, 1(1926):226-8.

[20] Helene Deutsch, *Zur Psychoanalyse der weiblichen Sexualfunktionen* (Vienna: Internationaler psychoanalytischer Verlag, 1925)

[21] Karl Abraham, 'Development of the Libido'.

[22] Sándor Ferenczi (1924), *Thalassa, a Theory of Genitality* (Albany, NY: Psychoanalytic Quarterly Inc., 1938).

15

On Female Homosexuality

Helene Deutsch (1932)

Psychoanalytic Quarterly 1(1932):484-510
Authorized translation by Edith B. Jackson

In this paper, which is based on eleven case studies of female homosexuality, Deutsch traces the genesis of female homosexuality. She considers that sexual inversion is a return to the primary fixation to the mother caused by a flight from the father and is a regressive relation along active/passive (rather than masculine/feminine) lines. Here more than ever before Deutsch emphasises the little girl's attachment to hatred for the mother.

The analysis revolves around the castration complex. Unlike van Ophuijsen, Deutsch talks about an exaggerated penis envy rather than a 'masculinity complex'. In her view, the female homosexual's sexual excitement is bound up with the maternal prohibition and with the consequent intense aggressive impulses towards the mother.

In all of the cases examined, she argues, the mother-child relation at pregenital levels dominates the perverse relationship with the love object. Thus, the little girl who feels rejected by her father because of denial, disappointment or anxiety, turns back to the mother for protection and peace. A subsequent direct prohibition of masturbation and interference with the activity unleashes the daughter's hostility against the disciplinary mother. It is, besides, through phallic masturbation that the affective discovery of the anatomical deficiency occurs.

Deutsch throws into relief the dangers of the passive phase. There is first a libidinal masochistic danger due to the expectation that the father might fulfil the daughter's wishes, secondly a danger of losing the newly chosen object because of a refusal on the father's part, and thirdly dangers of narcissistic injury of the ego libido resulting from the realization of the lack of penis.

Deutsch endorses the views of both Freud and Jones about the disposition to female homosexuality in the oral-sadistic phase.

* * *

This paper is based on the experience gained from the more or less profound analysis of eleven cases of female homosexuality. I should like, first of all, to stress the fact that none of these eleven women presented physical signs which might indicate that there had been a constitutional deviation, physiologically, in the direction of masculinity. The signs of accentuated bisexual disposition mentioned in this paper refer to forerunners of what, in later development, we usually call masculinity. These preliminary stages, however, appear to have no physical correlates, or at any rate none that can be determined, for the patients showed no physical signs of masculinity. There are, to be sure, certain homosexual types whose personality, mental and physical, including the secondary sexual characteristics, are of the type which is appropriate to the other sex; but none of my patients belonged to this type.

The first of the eleven cases of female homosexuality was analyzed twelve years ago. Although the patient was aware of her sexual inversion, she did not indulge in homosexual practices; she knew that her erotic potentialities and fantasies were directed towards members of her own sex, and she would unequivocally become sexually excited when she embraced and kissed certain women. Towards these women, she was faithful and monogamous; her relations with them were purely platonic and remained platonic even when she knew that the women had a perverse tendency like her own. There was no particular type of woman which especially attracted her. The women were not in any instance of a masculine type, and she herself was blond and feminine. She felt no hostility towards men, had a number of male friends, and accepted their favours and courtship without protestation. She had married a man of outspoken masculine appearance, and had several children by him to whom she gave a maternal, even if not excessively warm, response.

She was unable to explain why her homosexuality had not developed in a more active and urgent way; she only knew that her inhibitions against it were too strong—inhibitions which she rationalized on the basis of social shyness, family duty, and fear of psychic subjugation. She could trace her love response to women as far back as puberty, when it began in a typically adolescent way, directed towards teachers and other individuals more or less in authority. I cannot remember whether she characterized these individuals as particularly strict; in any event she was dominated by two feelings: a feeling of being sheltered, and, on the other hand, a feeling of fear of the individual in question. She was never really in love with a man. She had been attracted to her husband originally because she saw in him an exceptionally active and masculine personality. She was disappointed in marriage from the outset because, as she says, in this very relationship her husband failed to come up to her expectations. He lacked passion and was unaggressive particularly in sexual matters, and in other situations as well he failed her when she was most counting on his activity.

The patient came into analysis on account of neurotic difficulties. She had suffered for years from depressions and feelings of anxiety with a particular ideational content: she could not find the courage to assume the fitting authoritative attitude towards women in her employ. As a matter of fact, she expected a great deal of her servants and was upset when they failed to meet her demands, but she was quite unable to give them orders, much less to reprimand them. In situations which required this of her, she was overcome with timidity and anxiety in the presence of the person to be reproved. With every change in the personnel, and the consequent anticipation of a new woman in the household, her anxiety and conflict were greatly intensified. In these situations, moreover, she quite consciously reproached her husband for his lack of zeal in protecting and supporting her.

In recent years, her depressions had become more and more frequent and were intimately associated with the danger of suicide. The patient had already made a number of unsuccessful suicidal attempts; the last one had brought her to the verge of death. It happened that the physician called to her rescue was a close friend of mine, and he assured me that her intention to commit suicide had been genuine.

The patient's analysis for months revolved about the castration complex. At the time of this analysis—twelve years ago—the assumption of a castration complex in women was not such a matter of course as it is today. During the analysis I was so fascinated by the material dealing with this theme, that I was tempted to consider the castration complex the nucleus of her neurosis as well as of her perversion. She was so full of penis envy that it appeared even in her relation to her little boys whose penis she cut off in dreams and fantasies. Even though the patient was dominated by marked sadistic tendencies, her conscious personality was more reactive in character. That is to say, she was kind and gentle and showed unmistakable obsessional neurotic traits, such as exaggerated decorum and propriety. Her transference to me was very pronounced and was characteristic of that type whose actions as well as conscious responses over a long period of time reveal nothing except tenderness, respect and a feeling of safety. The patient was very happy and felt as if she had at last found a kind, understanding mother, who was making up to her all that her own mother had denied her. Her mother had been a stern and distant individual whom the patient had quite consciously hated all her life. After her mother's death (which occurred several years before the analysis began) the patient had a severe depression, during which she made one of her attempts at suicide.

The patient had several attacks of depression during the course of the analysis, following one another at short intervals. They were always accompanied by characteristic dreams and brought to light definite material. I discussed these dreams at the time—twelve years ago—at a meeting of the Vienna Psychoanalytic Society in a brief communication, under the title of *Mutterleibsträume und Selbstmordideen* (Uterus Dreams and Suicidal Ideas). Without presenting these dreams in detail, I may state that they contained practically everything we know about uterine symbolism; they were dreams of dark holes and crevices in which the patient crawled, dreams of comfortable dark places in which the dreamer felt at home and in which she lingered with a feeling of peace and redemption. These dreams appeared at a time when the patient was weighed down by conscious urges to kill herself, and was insisting that if it were not for her relation to me and her confidence in me, no power in the world could restrain her from committing suicide. One special dream-picture kept reappearing in the dreams: the patient saw herself as an infant swaddled with strips of tape or bandages. Her associations to this dream-picture made it clear that two hazy memories were emerging in these dreams. One referred to her last suicidal attempt (with poison): she awoke from a deep loss of consciousness while still strapped to the stretcher; she saw the doctor with a kind smile on his face, leaning over her, realized that he had saved her life (which was quite true) and thought, 'This time you saved me, but after all you can't give me any real help.'

Another set of associations led to the memory of a dangerous operation which her mother had undergone. The patient remembered seeing her mother, wrapped up as she herself was to be later, transported to the operating-room on a stretcher.

Starting from this memory the analysis led to an aggressive, murderous hate against the mother, which up to this point had been repressed, but which now became the central theme of the analysis. After about eight months' analysis childhood memories began to appear, and these turned out to be the nucleus of her neurosis as well as the nucleus of her perversion. The memories went back to the time between the patient's fourth and sixth years when she was masturbating to an alarming extent—at least from the mother's point of view. It was impossible to decide whether this masturbation really exceeded the normal amount, nor could we determine the content of the fantasies which, presumably, had accompanied the masturbation. But it is a fact, according to the patient's statement, that the mother resorted to the following method of checking the patient's masturbation: she bound the patient's hands and feet, strapped them to the crib, and said, as she stood looking on, 'Now play if you can!' This aroused two reactions in the little girl. One was ungovernable rage against her mother, which was prevented by the fetters from discharge in motor activity. The other was intense sexual excitement, which she tried to satisfy by rubbing her buttocks against the bedding, regardless of her mother's presence, or perhaps to vent her spite on her mother.

The most dreadful thing in this scene, for her, was the fact that her father, summoned by the mother, was a passive witness and did not offer to help his little girl despite his tender affection for her.

This memory was recovered in the analysis while the patient was associating to the following dream:

> She saw herself behind the bars in a police station, accused of some sort of sexual offence—apparently brought in from the street on suspicion of being a prostitute. The police sergeant, a kindly man, stood on the other side of the railing and did nothing to help her.

This is an almost direct repetition of the childhood situation.

The patient stopped masturbating after this childhood scene, and with this renunciation for a long while repressed her sexuality. At the same time, she repressed her hatred for her mother, to which she had in reality never given full expression. I do not believe that the scene with her mother, which occurred in the patient's childhood, was traumatic in the sense of causing the patient's later attitude. But concentrated in it were all of the tendencies which had a determining influence on her whole sexual life. Her reproach—that her mother had forbidden her to masturbate—would certainly have been present even without this scene. The hate reaction against her mother, in accordance with the patient's sadistic constitution, was also to be seen in other childhood situations, as well as the reproach that her father did not protect her from her mother. But this scene brought all of these tendencies to the boiling point, as it were, and so became the prototype for later events.

From this time on, all sexual excitement was bound up with the maternal prohibition and with the most intense aggressive impulses toward the mother. Her whole psychic personality resisted these hate impulses, and as a reaction to them there awakened in her an intense sense of guilt towards her mother, which led to a transformation of the hate into a masochistic libidinal attitude. It is, therefore, comprehensible that the patient should reply to the direct question, why she had never yielded to a homosexual attachment, with the answer that she was afraid of becoming subjugated to the sexual partner. She was, indeed, afraid of being masochistically attached to her mother. It will also become clear why she was afraid of the women in her employ and why she chided her husband for not adequately protecting her.

Even though, during her analysis, the patient manifested an exaggerated penis envy, it did not stand in the centre of her personality, either characterologically or in her behaviour towards men. She was not a woman with a 'masculinity complex'. However, it seems that this had not always been the case, for in her childhood before the eventful experience and also during puberty, there had been periods in which infallible signs of strongly developed masculine activity could be demonstrated. Especially at puberty many of her interests were quite unusual for a young girl in her social class at the time. This streak of masculinity was splendidly sublimated at the time, and indeed throughout her life. Yet a not inconsiderable part persisted and burdened her psychic economy, as dreams and certain inferiority feelings, etc., clearly showed.

I was very much tempted to assume that the patient was living out her masculinity in her homosexuality. But in this very point she failed to fulfil my analytic expectations, and presented me with a problem at the time which I could understand only years later. In order to adhere to a somewhat chronological order and present the facts as I learned them, I shall, for the time being, discontinue theoretical formulations.

After the above-mentioned part of the analysis had been worked through (after eight months) the father made his first real appearance as a topic of analytic material, and at the same time all of the impulses belonging to the Oedipus complex were revived, starting with the chief, unremitting, reproach against the father that he had been too inactive to love his daughter. I should like to emphasize the fact that even at that time it was clear to me that the hate against her mother and the libidinal desire for her were much older than the Oedipus complex.

I hoped that the patient's libidinal future would shape up more satisfactorily with a revival of the father relationship, especially when this relationship had been retouched and corrected. I referred her to an analyst of the fatherly type. Unfortunately, the transference did not advance beyond respect and sympathy, and the analysis was interrupted after a short time. About a year later I met the patient and saw that she had become a vivid, radiant person. She told me that her depressions had entirely disappeared. The wish to die which had been almost continuously present and her nostalgia had apparently receded completely. At last she had found happiness in a particularly congenial and uninhibited sexual relationship with a woman. The patient, who was intelligent and conversant with analysis, informed me that their homosexual relationship was quite consciously acted out as if it were a mother-child situation, in which sometimes one, sometimes the other played the mother—a play with a double cast, so to speak. Moreover, the satisfactions sought in this homosexual love play involved chiefly the mouth and the external genitalia. No 'male-female' contrast appeared in this relationship; the essential contrast was that of activity and passivity. The impression gained was that the feeling of happiness lay in the possibility of being able to play *both* roles.

The result of her analysis was evident. Everything that had come to the surface so clearly in the analytic transference was now detached from the person of the analyst and transferred to other women. The gratifications denied her in the analytic situation could now be found in the relationship with the new objects. It was evident that the overcoming of her hostility toward the analyst had brought with it the overcoming of her anxiety and, consequently, a positive libidinal relationship to women could appear in place of the anxiety and hostility which had caused the neurotic symptoms—only, of course, after the mother-substitute object had paid off the infantile grievances by granting her sexual satisfactions. The analytic treatment had not brought about the further and more favourable solution of the mother attachment, that is, a renunciation of her homosexuality and an inclination towards men. Here I should like to interrupt my discussion and present some of the other analyzed cases before continuing with the theoretical considerations. For the sake of completeness, it may be added that after the analysis the patient made no more suicidal attempts; but I have heard that the old difficulties with women in her employ have recently begun again. I suppose that some disturbances in the love relationship occurred, which probably resulted in a neurotic reaction. But in any case there has been no suggestion of the depressions as they were before the analysis.

In the course of the last three years I have analyzed several cases of female homosexuality—cases in which the perversion was more manifest than in the one just described. Analysis with them began, so to speak, where this patient's analysis left off. All of them were in a more or less consciously recognized mother-child relationship with their love object. Sexual satisfaction was obtained in all these cases from the following practices: close embrace, mutual sucking at the nipples, genital and (more prominently) anal masturbatory stimulation, and intense mutual cunnilingus. Of special interest is the prominence given to the double role in these cases also.

One of these patients had divided the double role between two types of objects: one type, represented by an insignificant, needy young girl, who would take the part of the child; the other by an older, very active and very authoritative woman with whom the patient herself played the part of the child. The latter type of relationship usually began when the patient, who was very active and professionally ambitious, entered into a sublimated relationship with the woman, remained for a short time in a scarcely noticeable attitude of competition (of which she became conscious only through analysis), and then began to fail in her work in a clearly neurotic way, so that she would be in a subordinate position to the particular woman in question. For example, the end-result of writing a technical article, which had been undertaken jointly, was that the patient—perhaps the more gifted of the two—would play the part of a secretary in editing the work. If sexual approaches were made during work of this kind, the role of active seducer was always conceded to the other woman.

From the life history and the analysis, I shall select only the material needed for the theoretical considerations to be presented later.

The patient belonged to a very large family; she had many sisters and two brothers, of whom only one, four years her senior, played a part in her life story. When she was only nine months old, a new sister arrived, a competitor who disputed her right to the mother's breast. She suffered, in early childhood, from all sorts of oral symptoms, from which it was possible to reconstruct a situation which might be described as 'oral envy'. She remained for a long time in a competitive relation to this sister, to whom, even in childhood, she gave precedence—an evident overcompensation. For instance, she recounted in the analysis that very early in childhood, she had heard that when there is such a slight difference in age and such a striking resemblance between two sisters as there was between her and her sister, only one of them could marry and have children. She thus retired from the feminine role in favour of her sister; and in adolescence, when her parents were divorced after the birth of the last child, she waived her claim to the father to the advantage of the other children and remained with her mother.

Very early in childhood, the patient developed reaction formations to aggressive tendencies which, before the birth of the next sister (when she was six), were suggestive of obsessional neurosis; they did not, however, develop to any great degree. At any rate, during her mother's pregnancy at that time, she reproached herself bitterly because she did not feel as kindly disposed towards her mother and the expected baby as her younger sister Erna did; she was convinced that the latter prayed every morning for the well-being of the mother and child.

The analysis uncovered strong aggression against the mother,[1] especially against the *pregnant* mother, and against the newborn child. The life of the patient and her whole character had developed, as it turned out, under the pressure of an attempt to dispel thoughts of killing her mother and the child. The reaction recurred afresh at the two following pregnancies of her mother—the children again were both girls; and only after the birth of her youngest sister, when the patient was twelve years old, did her psychical situation change. When she was very young, the patient always thought of her father as a mysterious, strange and powerful man, in whose presence one could not help feeling timid and anxious; but her attitude gradually changed, for the father had acquired a heart affection which finally incapacitated him for work. The family was thus involved in material difficulties, and with this stimulus, the patient took over the father's role herself, and gave free play to fantasies in which she held good positions and supported the family. As a matter of fact, by dint of hard work she later realized these fantasies.

In spite of the identification with her father, and in spite of the fact that she envied her brother's masculinity, she did not take the competitive attitude toward her youngest sister that she had taken to the other sisters when they were born. She was, on the contrary, highly pleased with the role of being a 'little mother' and claimed the child entirely for herself. In this situation, she was behaving quite normally as far as the Oedipus complex was concerned. The analysis showed that this positive Oedipus attitude was reached only because she had dethroned her father from his position of supreme and unapproachable power, and that only then could she overcome the intense fear of the masochistic, sexual experience which she desired.

My experience substantiates my assumption that this change of object—the libidinal turning away from the mother to the father—is accomplished with more difficulty, the more aggressive and sadistic are the predominating dispositions in the little girl, not only because the change of object is hindered by the active strivings, but also because the change into the passive attitude must, in cases of this type, assume a marked masochistic character and be repudiated by the ego as dangerous.

Our patient had certainly attained the normal Oedipus situation, as her puberty clearly showed, but the ensuing rivalry with her mother provided fresh fuel for the old pre-Oedipal aggression. This intensified her sense of guilt, which could be relieved only by means of a new overcompensation—renunciation of her father and definite persistence in her mother attachment.

To reduce the psychological basis of this relationship to a formula, we might say: 'I do not hate you; I love you. It is not true that you have refused me the breast and given it to my youngest (so to speak, pre-Oedipal) sister; you gave it to me, and, therefore, I do not need to kill you and the child. It is not true that I have killed the child, for I myself am the child whom you love and suckle.' This fundamental attitude toward the mother is reflected not only in the form of the direct oral satisfaction in homosexual intercourse with the young girl (see above), but also in the above-mentioned submissive, passive attitude to the elder love-partner.

It must be noted that homosexuality as stated in the above formula as yet does not involve the Oedipus situation, and is a continuation of and a reaction to the pre-Oedipal situation.

However, the type of relationship which the patient had with the young girl corresponds not only to the active part of the original mother-child relationship—in which she makes a typical identification with the nourishing mother—but quite clearly makes use of new elements taken from the Oedipus situation. The young girl is always a surrogate for her youngest sister—toward whom she actually had assumed a maternal role as a lifelong sublimation—but she is unsublimatedly homosexual with her love object, a relatively unknown young girl. In this relationship, she is at times the mother who suckles her child (or the father's child), and at times the suckled child herself. In this sexual experience she is able to transform the hate of her mother into love, for she is given the mother's breast; at the same time, she can be the active, suckling mother and thereby transform the aggression against her mother into activity.

At this point I should like to report some of the dreams which occurred in this patient's analysis, and from abundant material I shall select those which offer confirmation for the above statements even in the *manifest* dream content. One dream ran as follows:

> The patient sees herself on the street with her younger sister. She is pregnant. She is in a hurry to reach a house which she sees in front of her. In the middle of the front of this house is a large projecting bay-window with one of the windows open. This is her mother's room; she wants to get there to give birth to her child. She is very much afraid that she will lose the child on the street, that is, that she will miscarry before she reaches the house. She expresses this fear to her sister, and then really does miscarry in the street.

The dream was readily explained by the patient's actual situation at the time. The day before the dream, she had been visited by a young friend, living in another city, whom she had not seen since the beginning of the analysis. This friend was really a homosexual object after the pattern of her youngest sister. They slept together, and the patient held her in her arms, pressed closely against her. But before there was any sexual release, she was upset by an uneasy feeling that the gratification of her homosexual wishes might possibly interfere with the analysis. She therefore made the friend leave the bed—lost her, as it were, out of her arms—in order not to disturb her relationship with me. It is clear that the pregnancy in the dream—the condition in which she has the child with her (within her)—is equated with her experience of the sexual embrace. The longing for her pregnant mother in the dream, which appears as a uterine fantasy in terms of a projecting bay window, and her simultaneous identification with her mother and with the child in utero is unusually clear. Furthermore, in the same analytic hour the patient remembered, for the first time, that when she was about three and a half years old, her mother had had a miscarriage. It was in this period of her childhood that she had been deeply attached to her mother and had reacted with such extraordinary aggression to the pregnancy.

The other fragment of the dream: 'I am walking with my youngest sister', likewise expresses the situation before she fell asleep and means: 'I have my beloved one beside me'. This dream situation betrays the analytically established fact that the sexual relationship with her friend also includes a fulfilment of the Oedipal wish, since the new little daughter belongs to her and not to her mother. The dream situation—to reach the mother and bear the child, or, on the contrary, not to reach the mother and to lose the child—portrays with unusual clarity the identity mother-child; that is, 'to bear' equals 'to be born', and relates to the pre-Oedipal situation at the time of the mother's miscarriage. The fusing of this situation with Oedipal wishes and its screening by the wishes of the Oedipus attitude also seem to be clear in this case. I shall report only a fragment of a second dream:

> The patient lies dreaming on a couch, a figure approaches her and tries to expose her. She tries to shriek and wakes up with the exclamation, 'My God, doctor!'

She notices on awakening that she had her hands between her legs.

A series of associations to the dream led to a theme with which her analysis was dealing at this particular time—namely, masturbation. For quite a long time during the analysis the patient had refrained from masturbation because of the embarrassment she might feel in telling me of it. Shortly before, however, she had begun to allow herself to do it—with inhibitions—under the impression that I had nothing against it. Her exclamation, 'My God!' referred to me and meant that I should save her from the danger of punishment—that is, protect her or give her my sanction. This interpretation was clear from the associations, some of which led to the memory of a childhood experience. She had once touched an electric switch with a wet hand, so that the current had run through her, and she could not take her hand away. In response to her outcry ('My God') her mother had hurried to her, and also became a part of the circuit; with this, the current was weakened and the patient was able to release her hand. She had been rescued by her mother's interference. Like her mother, then, in the dream, I was to save her from 'touching'—from the consequences of trespassing and doing a forbidden thing, by coming into the circuit of her excitement myself, by embracing her and gratifying her.

This excerpt from the dream serves to illustrate the other important feature of her homosexuality; her conflict over masturbation is brought to this apparently favourable solution by maternal intervention—that is, by the mother's expressed sanction. In another dream:

> A tall, heavy-set woman whom she takes to be her mother, although she is taller and heavier than the latter, is in deep mourning because Erna (her next younger sister) has died. The father is standing nearby. She herself is in a cheerful mood because she is about to go away with her father on a spree. A glance at her mother warns her that this will not do, and that she must stay with her grieving mother.

This dream interprets itself. The patient is unable to satisfy her Oedipal wishes and cannot be gay and happy with a man, because her feelings of guilt, which refer to the mother whose child she has killed, bind her to her mother and force her into homosexuality. From another long and informative dream, I cite here only a fragment.

> She sees herself in analysis with Miss Anna Freud who is wearing men's clothes. This was explained in the dream by the fact that it was necessary for her to change analysts. With me it had been a question of producing free associations, with Miss Anna Freud it was a question of experiences.

On the evening before this dream, the patient was taken by her friends to a lecture held in the rooms of the Vienna Psychoanalytic Society, at which both Miss Freud and I were present. She told me in connection with this dream, that originally Miss Freud and I had been recommended to her as analysts. From the descriptions of us which she had heard, she had made up her mind what we were like; in her imagination Miss Freud represented a maternal ideal, a person who was motherly to all children, and ready to give them succour whenever they turned to her for help; my motherliness, she imagined, was directed especially toward my own children (that is to say, sexualized). Furthermore, it occurred to her at this point that before making her final decision, she had intended to write to us both, but, as a matter of fact, and as she now remembered for the first time, she had asked only for my address.

The evening before the dream, she had had a chance to compare us. She thought to herself, how true her idea about us had been, and how happy she was to be in analysis with me. This protestation seemed somewhat dubious to me, and I called her attention to the fact that the dream appeared to contradict it. It had struck me that the patient, who had gone to the lecture to see a certain analyst there, had not said a word about him, although he was sitting next to Miss Freud. Furthermore, she had not explained why, in the dream, Miss Freud appeared in men's clothing. A few days later she dreamed:

> I am sitting facing her instead of behind her (as I always do) and am holding a cigar in my hand. She thinks, 'The ashes are so long on the cigar that they will drop off any second.'

She says, as her first association to the cigar, 'Only men smoke cigars.' The masculinity, attributed to me, reminded me of the corresponding detail in regard to Miss Freud in the preceding dream. I then remembered that as the patient sat facing Miss Freud at the lecture, she must at the same time have seen on the wall the picture of Professor Freud, in which he holds a cigar in his hand. A similar picture is on my office desk. I showed this to her, and she agreed that the position of the hand holding the cigar was the same as mine in the dream.

Further analysis showed that she had dearly wished to be analyzed by Professor Freud, but that this wish, springing as it did from her deep longing for the great man—the father—had been repressed, and that along with it, Miss Freud had been included in the repression. In addition, as already stated, she repressed the fact that she had met the analyst referred to above, and her impression of Professor Freud's picture. The repressed then asserted itself in the masculinity attributed to Miss Freud and me.

The way the father reappears in the dreams testifies to the fact that the patient's turning to the woman corresponds also to a flight from the man. The analysis revealed the source from which this tendency to flight originated: feelings of guilt toward the mother, fear of disappointment and of rejection.

To survey the case again briefly, we see that the first period of the patient's life was passed under somewhat unusual conditions. For a while she was nursed together with a younger sister, and when, finally, she had in her sister's interest to give up suckling, she developed (somewhat justifiably) a marked oral envy. When she was three years old, her mother became pregnant again, and she reacted to the anticipation of the child with great hostility and jealousy. The dream of the miscarriage illustrated the psychic condition of the little girl at the time, and her intense wish that she herself should be the child in the mother's womb.

This dream however was screened by reminiscences from a later period of her life (her twelfth year), and in the identification with her mother she betrayed her wish to have the child herself. This wish already is part of the Oedipal attitude, which developed apparently late and slowly, but none the less *powerfully*, as we could see in the analysis.

It is hard to say whether her infantile and never relinquished longing to possess her mother for herself alone and be fed and cared for by her, tended to have an inhibitory effect on normal libidinal development, or whether the difficulties of the Oedipus complex, as we known them in other cases, were the decisive factors in determining the later fate of the little girl's sexuality. I tried to show, above, in interpreting the dreams, that her return to her mother had not made her relinquish her longing for her father, but that she was constantly and anxiously fleeing from him, and consequently repressing her feminine attitude to men.

From the reported material, I should now like to deduce certain theoretical conclusions, which seem to me to represent important additions to our understanding of female sexuality in general, and of female homosexuality in particular.

It is repeatedly stated that our knowledge of *female* sexuality reaches no further than its correspondence with *male* sexuality in *childhood*. Only in *puberty*, when women really become feminine in the biological sense, are the conditions clearer and more comprehensible. Some of the important processes of the early stages of development were clarified by Freud's paper, 'Some Psychical Consequences of the Anatomical Distinction between the Sexes'.[2] In this paper he demonstrates the fact that the Oedipus complex is not established in girls until after the phallic phase. I had already discussed[3] the stage in a girl's development which follows the phallic phase, and in which there is a thrust into passivity (*Passivitätsschub*). The central feature of this phase is the wish to be given an anal child by the father. I pointed out, in this discussion, that the thrust into passivity is really a regressive process, and represents a regression to a phase preceding the phallic organization which is identical in boys and girls. We are too readily fascinated, I think, by the events which take place in the phallic phase and by its manifestations and latent potentialities, so that we have emphasized the phallic phase to the neglect of the succeeding stage of passivity, which has been treated more like a stepchild. We rest content with the fact that the wish to have a penis has been yielded in *exchange* for the wish to have a child, and that then it is up to the normal psychical powers inherent in the child to cope wit the next frustration and to solve the new problem without harming itself. There is, I believe, no clinical observation to confute the idea that the intensity with which a child is desired is entirely dependent on the intensity of the preceding wish for a penis; therefore, one may say that the stronger the wish to have a penis, the stronger will be the subsequent wish to have a child; and the more difficult it is to bear being denied a penis, the more aggression will there be in the reaction to the thwarting of the wish for a child. Thus arises a vicious circle which often obscures the state of affairs for analysts; we find repeatedly that the very women whose violent psychic conflict was occasioned by the castration complex (i.e., by penis envy) are the ones who also have an ardent feminine wish for a child.

A girl may have had a fairly normal sexual development up to the beginning of the Oedipus complex and given up all hope of having a penis, so that she is ready for the transition from phallic activity into passivity—that is to say, she is ready to conceive the anal child by her father. This, however, is not sufficient to enable her to withstand the next bitter disappointment, which appears when she is denied a child. Keeping in mind the scheme of libidinal development we must not forget that along with this thrust into passivity a number of active forces are revived and raise their heads again because of the renewed cathexis of pregenital tendencies. They find their place without difficulty in the normal mental economy. For the role of the mother with the child, as the little girl playing with her dolls well illustrates, is an active one.

But what happens when the girl recoils in fright from the masochistic danger of the thrust into passivity? And when she cannot bear the actual disappointment of being denied a child, yet is convinced of the futility of her wish to have a penis? Let us get the situation clearly in mind: the child is no longer narcissistically stimulated by the wish for a penis which she recognizes cannot be fulfilled; she feels rejected by her father, because of denial, disappointment or anxiety; she is left with libido which has little opportunity for sublimation. What will she do? She will do what all living creatures do in situations of danger. She will flee for refuge to the shelter where she once enjoyed protection and peace, to her mother. To be sure she had been disappointed by her mother too, but preceding all her denials there had been a time of satisfaction, for the refusing, hated mother had been at one time the source of all gratifications.

There is no doubt that even in the phallic phase the sexual instincts derive some satisfaction from the mother's routine care of the child. But apparently the claims at this time are more intense and they cannot, because of their dependence on the functions which are helping to build the ego, be satisfied to the same far-reaching extent as they were in preceding phases. Let us consider also that the phallic sexual aims were undisguised, that they were voiced easily, and that the mother's horror on her discovery of the wishes betrayed by the child was evident. We know from the analyses of mothers that their horror at the masturbatory actions of the child is the greater, the more their own unconscious memories of their own childhood masturbation are mobilized by direct observation of their children's behaviour. The restrictions to which the child is now subjected will cause a stronger reaction the more the mother herself has excited the child, in her unconscious role of seducer. Subsequent *direct* prohibition of masturbation and forcible interference with masturbatory activity rouses the hostility against the disciplinary mother to a high pitch. Moreover, with phallic masturbation comes the *affective* discovery of the anatomical 'defect'.

We already know that the girl blames her mother for depriving her of a penis. The sadistic impulses of the phallic phase are, accordingly, directed against the mother, and they are probably the impetus for the change of object. The change to a sadistic attitude toward the mother facilitates the passive masochistic attitude toward the father; all of this results from the phase that I have called the 'thrust into passivity'. It is certain, however, that the aggression is not entirely conducted into the masochistic passive attitude. Much of the aggressive impulse is turned against the disappointing father, and much remains attached to the mother who is now regarded as a rival. The intensity in any case is dependent upon the strength of the phallic activity. Furthermore, the change to masochism will occur with greater intensity, the more it is nurtured from the sources of aggression. Analysis of patients who have a very strong castration complex shows unequivocally how full of danger the passive attitude is as regards the development of masochism, and how blood-thirsty and murderous are the ideas of revenge on the mother, especially on the mother who in fact or fantasy is pregnant, or who already has another child. This attitude supplies the masochism with its moral component in addition, and the strength of the moral component is directly proportionate to the strength of the aggression.

We are thus aware of the dangers with which the little girl is beset in this phase:

1   Libidinal masochistic danger because of the expectation that her father may fulfil her wishes.
2   The danger of losing the newly chosen object as a result of refusal on her father's part.
3   Dangers of narcissistic injury of the ego libido, incident to the realization of the permanent lack of a penis.

In the midst of these great dangers, the libido, as we have said, turns to the earlier object again, and obviously more easily and more ardently the stronger the earlier attachments had been. It is a reversion to previously enjoyed experiences, as it were. I mean by this, that the aggression due to rivalry arising from the Oedipus complex, and the more highly organized sense of guilt, are now combined with the early infantile ambivalence conflicts.

The economic advantage of this new turning to the mother lies in the release from a feeling of guilt. But it seems to me that its most important accomplishment lies in the protection from the threatened loss of object: 'If my father won't have me, and my self-respect is so undermined, who will love me, if not my mother?'

Analytic experience offers abundant evidence of this bisexual oscillation between father and mother, which may eventuate in neurosis, heterosexuality or inversion. We see the libido swinging between the poles of two magnets, attracted and repelled. Prospects of wish-fulfilment represent the *attraction* by one pole, frustration, fear, and mobilization of guilt feelings the *repulsion* from the other; and we see the same thing happening in the case of other magnets; and as one of the most serious results of this oscillation, an obstinate narcissistic standstill appears somewhere in between. There are cases of blocking of affect, and especially clinical pictures of narcissistic disorders, which do not fit into any of the recognized forms of neurosis, but which do correspond to a standstill in the pendulum swing of libido as just described. If the oscillation is set in motion again in the analytic transference, the obsessional neurosis, whose oscillating ambivalence had been concealed by the emotional block, becomes apparent.

There was in these cases of female homosexuality a longer or shorter phase of indecision, which offers proof that it was not a question of a simple fixation on the mother as the first love object, but rather a complicated process of returning. The decision in favour of the mother as the attracting magnet lies naturally in the old powers of attraction, but also in the repelling forces from other magnets—denial, anxiety, and guilt reactions.

The return to the mother, when once started, needs the completion of still another process before it attains the character of a genuine inversion. First of all, the motives which once really induced the little girl to respond to the biological urge toward the father must be made retroactive. Accordingly, the sexual satisfaction of masturbation, which has been forbidden by the mother, must not only no longer be prohibited, but must be consented to by the mother by an active participation. The denial of the past must be made good by subsequent permissions, and indeed quite as much in reference to the original passive experience as to the subsequent active experience. One might say that the interruption of the phallic activity is made up for by this consent to activity which had been impossible in the past. The form which this active behaviour of the girl toward the maternal object takes depends on the developmental stage at which the homosexual object relationship is taking place; that is, to speak more correctly, it depends on which is the most predominant stage, for, on closer observation, we see in the reactivation *all* phases in which the mother played a role, which is equivalent to saying, all the stages of the preceding infantile development. Usually the most urgent tendencies are the phallic ones, and they cause the relationship of one female to another to assume a male character, whereby the absence of a penis is denied. These tendencies can indeed dominate the general picture of homosexuality, and may give rise to a definite, and as a matter of fact, the most outstanding, homosexual type.[4] This type denies the absence of a penis, expects that her feminine object will grant her her masculinity, and accepts phallic masturbation as a confirmation in the above-mentioned sense. It is then not very important whether the femininity of the object is to be emphasized, or whether both the subject and object are simultaneously affirming possession of a penis, so that the object may also take her turn in playing the masculine role. These are two sub-types of the same species. The extent of the old competitive attitude, especially in cases where an early displacement from the mother on to a sister took place, the quantum of masochistic or sadistic component, that is to say, the preponderance of aggressive tendencies or of reactions of guilt, a more passive or a more active casting of the role—these are all merely details in the total problem of female homosexuality.

I said that the phallic masculine form of homosexuality was the most outstanding one. But there are always many deeper currents hiding behind it. It is my impression, indeed, that this masculine form is sometimes brought into evidence for the very purpose of hiding the more infantile, but none the less predominating tendencies. The majority of the cases which I have analyzed were forced to an honest and extensive relinquishment of their masculine behaviour by the strength of their pregenital urges. The mother-child relationship at pregenital levels, in the deeply entrenched fixation of the pre-phallic phases (whether consciously or unconsciously), dominated the perversion. The wish for activity belonging to the phallic phase is carried along in the regression, and reaches its most satisfactory fulfilment in the homosexual relationship. The frequent expression of the small child, 'when you are little and I am big', finds its realization here in this double role which is always played in this relationship, in which the child does everything with her mother that the mother had at one time done with her. Such freedom of activity, and the giving of free rein to masturbation are motives held in common by all forms of homosexuality. If in the phallic situation the mother compensates for the child's hurt by some sort of assent to the child's belief in the presence of a penis, then, in this new edition of the mother-child relationship, the pregenital frustrations and denials must also be compensated, and this indeed happens often enough in the satisfaction which homosexual persons derive from their activities. Freud laid special emphasis on the marked preference of the oral mucous membrane in the activities of female inverts in the 'Three Essays on the Theory of Sexuality'[5] and Jones[6] has found the disposition to female homosexuality in the oral sadistic phase. I feel that all my cases offer thorough confirmation of this dispositional element. I can state, furthermore, with complete security that not one of my cases failed to have a very strong reaction to the castration complex; a complete Oedipus complex with exceedingly powerful aggressive reactions could be demonstrated in every case.

The return to the mother-child attitude was always introduced by the wish for the child which had been expected long since in place of a penis, but which had continued to be withheld. One of the sources from which the inversion is nourished is the reaction to the fact: 'It is my mother who gets the child, not I.' Not until later when the child herself has become a mother does the disposition for cruelty indicated in this reaction find adjustment, and then in a complicated manner in her own mother-child relationship. The above mentioned patient produced unequivocal evidence for this in her dreams.

Considering the great complexity of the mother-child relationship, it is not surprising that the longing for the mother assumes the character of womb fantasies. We were able to observe this tremendous combination of longing for the mother with a wish to die in our first patient, as a contribution to the subject of mother attachment and fear of death.

I cannot leave this subject without a few remarks on a question which has a bearing in this connection. Is it really necessary to explain the little girl's attachment to a maternal object in such a roundabout way? Would it not be much simpler, for instance, to speak of an original fixation and to look for the causes in constitutional factors? I have considered the material without prejudice, and yet in every one of my cases of analyzed homosexual women, the light or the shadow cast on the original relationship by the father's presence has played an important and necessary part.

As a matter of fact, in recent years, I think I have occasionally observed a state of affairs in certain cases in which the Oedipus complex had apparently played no role at all, or almost none, and in which the libido had never known but *one* object—the mother. But these were very special cases, whose whole neurosis had the character of general psychic infantilism with diffuse anxieties and perversions, and whose transference could not be released from an obstinate incorrigible, anxious attachment.

Under the stimulus of Freud's latest paper,[7] it would be an undertaking well worth while to collect some of the obscure clinical cases, since they might possibly find their explanation in the primary mother attachment. In this group, in addition to the above-mentioned cases of infantilism, there would surely belong certain forms of hysteria whose 'secondary gain' proves so incorrigible because it is a clear repetition of the early infantile situation, when the child was taken care of by the mother.

Returning to my theme, there still remains the question as to when the girl's final decision in favour of homosexuality occurs. It is known that the girl's infantile period of sexual development does not come to such a sudden and radical conclusion as the boy's. The change of object takes place gradually and it would seem that only with puberty comes the final decision both as to the choice of object and the readiness for the passive attitude.

Girls show a much stronger dependence on the mother during the latency period than boys. This may be related to the girl's fear of losing her object, as I have tried to explain above, and also to the type of sublimation, which in girls tends rather to establish affectionate object relationships, and in boys is expressed in an active response to the outer world.

On the other hand, it appears that during puberty the girl shows a more definite sublimation in the direction of the outer world in the 'thrust of activity' (*Aktivitätsschub*), which I have described.[8] This would indicate that the feminine passive attitude is not completely formed during the infantile phase. The tomboyish period during the girl's puberty is widespread and normal. The girl derives from it the best energies for sublimations and for the formation of her personality, and I think I make no mistake in allowing myself this variation of a statement by Richard Wagner: 'The girl who had nothing of the boy in her during her youth will turn out to be a *vacca domestica* in later life.' Of course, we are aware of the great dangers which this period of activity conceals with respect to the 'masculinity complex' and its neurotic consequences. If it is true that the final change of object takes place in puberty, then this shift to activity must add dangers for the heterosexual attitude, and the masculine tendencies of puberty will also contribute their share to homosexuality.

In conclusion, we have still to mention the final struggles in *overcoming* the Oedipus complex during puberty. We have a classical example of this in a case of female homosexuality (to which we were introduced in the above-mentioned publication of Freud), which developed in puberty as a result of difficulties with the Oedipus complex. However, I must repeat that in all of the cases under my observation the corner stone for later inversion had already been laid in the first infantile period.

Notes

[1] Melanie Klein's observations show very clearly how bloodthirsty and aggressive a child's relations to its mother are, especially when an actual event (e.g., the birth of a younger child) mobilizes the aggression. The great value of these observations lies in the fact that they were made directly on children.

[2] Sigmund Freud (1925j), SE 19:243-58.

[3] Helene Deutsch, *Zur Psychoanalyse der weiblichen Sexualfunktionen* (Vienna: Internationaler psychoanalytischer Verlag, 1925).

[4] The case of female homosexuality published by Freud would also be classified under this 'masculine' type, even though the original attitude of the patient was thoroughly feminine,

and the masculine wish corresponded only to a subsequent identification with the once loved father. (Sigmund Freud [1920a], 'The Psychogenesis of a Case of Homosexuality in a Woman', SE 18:147-72.)

The two cases of female homosexuality described by Otto Fenichel in *Perversionen, Psychosen, Charakterstörungen* (Vienna: Internationaler Psychoanalytischer Verlag, 1932) (English translation, by Lewin and Zilboorg, 'Outline of Clinical Psychoanalysis', *Psychoanalytic Quarterly*, vols. 1-3), illustrate the same mental mechanisms as Freud's case. These cases also represent a 'masculine' identification with the father as a reaction to being disappointed by him.

[5] Sigmund Freud (1905d), SE 7:125-243.

[6] Ernest Jones (1927), 'The Early Development of Female Sexuality', above.

[7] Sigmund Freud (1931b), 'Female Sexuality', SE 21:223-43.

[8] Helene Deutsch, *Zur Psychoanalyse der weiblichen Sexualfunktionen* (Vienna: Internationaler psychoanalytischer Verlag, 1925).

16

The Dread of Woman: Observations on a Specific Difference in the Dread Felt by Men and Women Respectively for the Opposite Sex

Karen Horney (1932)

International Journal of Psycho-Analysis 13(1932):348-60

Karen Horney's paper starts with a meditation on poetry to foreground the ideas of woman as other and as primal element (water) that swallows up the man who is seduced. Horney suggests that man strives to free himself from the dread of woman by seeking objective grounds for it and she warns against the cultural consequences of this state of affairs. Thus Horney really asks two questions here: Why this dread of woman, which is kept secret as a strategy in support of male self-respect? And why this abhorrence, or fear, of the vagina that is so blatant in male homosexuality, fetishism and in the dreams of all male analysands, and yet so often concealed behind the dread of the father?

Her reply is that the masculine dread of woman as mother or of the female genital is more deep-seated and more strongly repressed than the dread of the father. Moreover, the father is more tangible and fearing him leaves male self-esteem intact.

Further questions follow from here: What is the origin of this anxiety? And what are its characteristics?

Horney disputes Freud's idea that the vagina remains 'undiscovered' for the child and notes, along with Carl Müller-Braunschweig, that the phallic impulse as such is a desire to penetrate. She infers that the little boy imagines a complementary female organ. The 'undiscovered' vagina is therefore a denied vagina. The little boy's anxiety is linked to the prohibition of instinctual activities enforced by the mother, to his experience of sadistic impulses towards the mother's body and to the specific fate of the genital impulses. The masculine dread of woman is thus a narcissistic anxiety.

Finally, note too that Horney also disputes the equations male=sadistic and female=masochistic.

* * *

In his ballad of *The Diver* Schiller tells how a squire leaps into a dangerous whirlpool in order to win a woman—at first symbolized by a goblet. Horror-struck, he describes the perils of the deep by which he is doomed to be engulfed:

Yet at length comes a lull o'er the mighty commotion,
As the whirlpool sucks into black smoothness the swell
Of the white-foaming breakers—and cleaves through the ocean
A path that seems winding in darkness to hell.
Round and round whirled the waves—deeper and deeper still driven,
Like a gorge through the mountainous main thunder-riven!
Happy they whom the rose-hues of daylight rejoice,
The air and the sky that to mortals are given!
May the horror below never more find a voice—
Nor man stretch too far the wide mercy of Heaven!
Never more—never more may he lift from the sight
The veil which is woven with Terror and Night!
Below at the foot of the precipice drear,
Spread the glowing, and purple, and pathless Obscure!
A silence of Horror that slept on the ear,
That the eye more appalled might the Horror endure!
Salamander—snake—dragon—vast reptiles that dwell
In the deep, coil'd about the grim jaws of their hell.
          (Translation by Bulwer Lytton.)

The same idea is expressed, though far more pleasantly, in the Song of
the Fisherboy in *Wilhelm Tell*:

The clear smiling lake woo'd to bathe in its deep,
A boy on its green shore had laid him to sleep;
Then heard he a melody
Flowing and soft,
And sweet as when angels are singing aloft.
And as thrilling with pleasure he wakes from his rest,
The waters are murmuring over his breast;
And a voice from the deep cries, 'With me thou must go, I charm the
     young shepherd, I lure him below'.
          (Translation by Theodore Martin.)

Men have never tired of fashioning expressions for this experience: the
violent force by which the man feels himself drawn to the woman, and,
side by side with his longing, the dread lest through her he might die and
be undone. I will mention particularly the moving expression of this dread
in Heine's poem of the legendary Lorelei, who sits high on the bank of the
Rhine and ensnares the boatman with her beauty.

Here once more it is water (representing, like the other 'elements', the
primal element 'woman') that swallows up the man who succumbs to a

woman's enchantment. Ulysses had to bid his seamen bind him to the mast in order to escape the allurement and the danger of the sirens. The riddle of the Sphinx can be solved by few, and most of those who attempt it forfeit their lives. The royal palace in fairy-tales is adorned with the heads of the suitors who have had the hardihood to try to solve the riddles of the king's beautiful daughter. The goddess Kali[1] dances on the corpses of slain men. Samson, whom no man could conquer, is robbed of his strength by Delilah. Judith beheads Holofernes after giving herself to him. Salome carries the head of John the Baptist on a charger. Witches are burnt because male priests fear the work of the devil in them. Wedekind's 'Earth Spirit' destroys every man who succumbs to her charm, not because she is particularly evil, but simply because it is her nature to do so. The series of such instances is infinite: always, everywhere the man strives to rid himself of his dread of women by objectifying it: 'It is not', he says, 'that I dread her; it is that she herself is malignant, capable of any crime, a beast of prey, a vampire, a witch, insatiable in her desires. She is the very personification of what is sinister'. May not this be one of the principal roots of the whole masculine impulse to creative work—the never-ending conflict between the man's longing for the woman and his dread of her?[2]

To primitive sensibilities the woman becomes doubly sinister in the presence of the bloody manifestations of her womanhood. Contact with her during menstruation is fatal:[3] men lose their strength, the pastures wither away, the fisherman and the huntsman take nothing. Defloration involves the utmost danger to the man. As Freud shows in 'The Taboo of Virginity',[4] it is the husband in particular who dreads this act. In this work Freud too objectifies this anxiety, contenting himself with a reference to the castration-impulses which do actually occur in women. There are two reasons why this is not an adequate explanation of the phenomenon of the taboo itself. In the first place, women do not so universally react to defloration with castration-impulses recognizable as such: these impulses are probably confined to women with a strongly developed masculine attitude. And, secondly, even if defloration invariably aroused destructive impulses in the woman, we should still have to lay bare (as we should do in every individual analysis) the urgent impulses within the man himself which make him view the first—forcible—penetration of the vagina as so perilous an undertaking; so perilous, indeed, that it can be performed with impunity only by a man of might or by a stranger who chooses to risk his life or his manhood for a recompense.

Is it not really remarkable (we ask ourselves in amazement), when one considers the overwhelming mass of this transparent material, that so little recognition and attention are paid to the fact of men's secret dread of women? It is almost more remarkable that women themselves have so long been able to overlook it; I will discuss in detail elsewhere the reasons for their attitude in this connection (i.e. their own anxiety and the impairment of their self-respect). The man on his side has in the first place very obvious strategic reasons for keeping his dread quiet. But he also tries by every means to deny it even to himself. This is the purpose of the efforts to which we have alluded, to 'objectify' it in artistic and scientific creative work. We may conjecture that even his glorification of women has its source not only in the cravings of love, but also in his desire to give the lie to his dread. A similar relief is, however, also sought and found in the disparagement of women which men often display ostentatiously in all their attitude. The attitude of love and adoration signifies: 'There is no need for me to dread a being so wonderful, so beautiful, nay, so saintly'; that of disparagement implies: 'It would be too ridiculous to dread a creature who, if you take her all round, is such a poor thing'.[5] This last way of allaying his anxiety has a special advantage for the man: it helps to support his masculine self-respect. The latter seems to feel itself far worse threatened—far more threatened at its very core—by the admission of a dread of women than by the admission of dread of a man (the father). The reason why the self-feeling of men is so peculiarly sensitive just in relation to women can only be understood by reference to their early development, to which I shall return later.

In analysis this dread of women is revealed quite clearly. Male homosexuality has for its basis, in common indeed with all the other perversions, the desire to escape from the female genital, or to deny its very existence. Freud has shown that this is a fundamental trait in fetishism,[6] in particular; he believes it, however, to be based not on anxiety, but on a feeling of abhorrence due to the absence of the penis in women. I think, however, that even from his account we are absolutely forced to the conclusion that there is anxiety at work as well. What we actually see is dread of the vagina, thinly disguised under the abhorrence. Only *anxiety* is a strong enough motive to hold back from his goal a man whose libido is assuredly urging him on to union with the woman. But Freud's account fails to explain this anxiety. A boy's castration-anxiety in relation to his father is not an adequate reason for his dread of a being whom this punishment has already overtaken. Besides the dread of the father there must be a further dread, the object of which is the woman or the female genital. Now this dread of the vagina itself appears unmistakably not only in homosexuals and perverts, but also in the dreams of every male analysand. All analysts are familiar with dreams of this sort and I need only give the merest outline of them: e.g. a motor-car is rushing along and suddenly falls into a pit and is dashed to pieces; or a boat is sailing in a narrow channel and is suddenly sucked into a whirlpool; there is a cellar with uncanny, blood-stained plants and animals, or one is climbing a chimney and is in danger of falling and being killed.

Dr. Baumeyer, of Dresden,[7] allows me to cite a series of experiments which arose out of a chance observation and which illustrate this dread of the vagina. The physician was playing ball with the children at a treat-ment-centre and, after a time, showed them that the ball had a slit in it. She pulled the edges of the slit apart and put her finger in, so that it was held fast by the ball. Of 28 boys whom she asked to do the same, only 6 did it without fear and 8 could not be induced to do it at all. Of 19 girls 9 put their fingers in without a trace of fear; the rest showed a slight uneasiness but none of them serious anxiety.

No doubt the dread of the vagina often conceals itself behind the dread of the father, which is also present; or, in the language of the uncon-scious, behind the dread of the penis in the woman's vagina.[8]

There are two reasons for this: in the first place, as I have already said, masculine self-regard suffers less in this way, and, secondly, the dread of the father is more actual and tangible, less uncanny in quality. We might compare the difference to that between the fear of a real enemy and of a ghost. The prominence given to the anxiety relating to the castrating father is therefore tendentious, as Groddeck has shown, for example, in his analysis of the thumb-sucker in *Struwwelpeter*: it is a man who cuts off the thumb, but it is the mother who utters the threat, and the instrument with which it is carried out—the scissors—is a female symbol.

From all this I think it probable that the masculine dread of the woman (the mother) or of the female genital is more deep-seated, weighs more heavily and is usually more energetically repressed than the dread of the man (father), and that the endeavour to find the penis in women repre-sents first and foremost a convulsive attempt to deny the existence of the sinister female genital.

Is there any ontogenetic explanation of this anxiety? Or is it not rather (in human beings) an integral part of masculine existence and behaviour? Is any light shed upon it by the state of lethargy—even the death—after mating which occurs frequently in male animals?[9] Are love and death more closely bound up with one another for the male than for the female, in whom sexual union potentially produces a new life? Does the man feel, side by side with his desire to conquer, a secret longing for extinction in the act of reunion with the woman (mother)? Is it perhaps this longing which underlies the 'death-instinct'? And is it his will to live which reacts to it with anxiety?

If we endeavour to understand this anxiety in psychological and onto-genetic terms, we find ourselves rather at a loss if we take our stand on Freud's notion that what distinguishes infantile from adult sexuality is precisely that the vagina remains 'undiscovered' for the child. According to that view, we cannot properly speak of a genital primacy: we must rather term it a primacy of the phallus. Hence it would be better to describe the period of infantile genital organization as the 'phallic phase'.[10] The many recorded remarks of boys at that period of life leave no doubt of the correctness of the observations on which Freud's theory is based. But if we look more closely at the essential characteristics of this phase, we cannot help asking whether his description really sums up infantile genitality as such, in its specific manifestation, or applies only to a relatively later phase of it. Freud states that it is characteristic that the boy's interest is concentrated in a markedly narcissistic manner on his own penis: 'The driving force which this male portion of his body will generate later at puberty expresses itself in childhood essentially as an impulsion to inquire into things—as sexual curiosity'. A very important part is played by questions as to the existence and size of the phallus in other living beings.

But surely the essence of the phallic impulses proper, starting as they do from organ sensations, is a desire to *penetrate*. That these impulses do exist can hardly be doubted: they manifest themselves too plainly in children's games and in the analysis of little children. Again, it would be difficult to say what the boy's sexual wishes in relation to his mother really consisted in if not in these very impulses; or why the object of his masturbation-anxiety should be the father as the castrator, were it not that masturbation was largely the autoerotic expression of heterosexual phallic impulses.

In the 'phallic phase' the boy's psychic orientation is predominantly narcissistic: hence the period in which his genital impulses are directed towards an object must be an earlier one. The possibility that they are not directed towards a female genital, of which he instinctively divines the existence, must certainly be considered. In dreams, both of earlier and later life, as well as in symptoms and particular modes of behaviour, we find, it is true, representations of coitus which are oral, anal, or sadistic without specific localization. But we cannot take this as a proof of the primacy of corresponding impulses, for we are uncertain whether, or how far, these phenomena already express a displacement from the genital goal proper. At bottom all that they amount to is to show that a given individual is influenced by specific oral, anal or sadistic trends. Their evidential value is the less because these representations are always associated with certain affects directed against women, so that we cannot tell whether they may not be essentially the product or the expression of these affects. For instance, the tendency to debase women may express itself in anal representations of the female genital, while oral representations may express anxiety.

But, besides all this, there are various reasons why it seems to me improbable that the existence of a specific female opening should remain 'undiscovered'. On the one hand, of course, a boy will automatically conclude that everyone else is made like himself; but on the other hand his phallic impulses surely bid him instinctively to search for the appropriate opening in the female body—an opening, moreover, which he himself lacks, for the one sex always seeks in the other that which is complementary to it or of a nature different from its own. If we seriously accept Freud's dictum that the sexual theories formed by children are modelled on their own sexual constitution, it must surely mean in the present connection that the boy, urged on by his impulses to penetrate, pictures in phantasy a complementary female organ. And this is just what we should infer from all the material I quoted at the outset in connection with the masculine dread of the female genital.

It is not at all probable that this anxiety dates only from puberty. At the beginning of that period the anxiety manifests itself quite clearly, if we look behind the often very exiguous facade of boyish pride which conceals it. At puberty a boy's task is obviously not merely to free himself from his incestuous attachment to his mother, but, more generally, to master his dread of the whole female sex. His success is as a rule only gradual: first of all he turns his back on girls altogether, and only when his masculinity is fully awakened does it drive him over the threshold of anxiety. But we know that as a rule the conflicts of puberty do but revive, *mutatis mutandis*, conflicts belonging to the early ripening of infantile sexuality and that the course they take is often essentially a faithful copy of a series of earlier experiences. Moreover, the grotesque character of the anxiety, as we meet with it in the symbolism of dreams and literary productions, points unmistakably to the period of early infantile phantasy.

At puberty a normal boy has already acquired a conscious knowledge of the vagina, but what he fears in women is something uncanny, unfamiliar and mysterious. If the grown man continues to regard woman as the great mystery, in whom is a secret he cannot divine, this feeling of his can only relate ultimately to one thing in her: the mystery of motherhood. Everything else is merely the residue of his dread of this.

What is the origin of this anxiety? What are its characteristics? And what are the factors which cloud the boy's early relations with his mother?

In an article on female sexuality[11] Freud has pointed out the most obvious of these factors: it is the mother who first forbids instinctual activities, because it is she who tends the child in its babyhood. Secondly, the child evidently experiences sadistic impulses against its mother's body,[12] presumably connected with the rage evoked by her prohibitions, and according to the talion principle this anger has left behind a residue of anxiety. Finally—and this is perhaps the principal point—the specific fate of the genital impulses itself constitutes another such factor. The anatomical differences between the sexes lead to a totally different situation in girls and in boys, and really to understand both their anxiety and the diversity of their anxiety we must take into account first of all *the children's real situation* in the period of their early sexuality. The girl's nature as biologically conditioned gives her the desire to receive, to take into herself;[13] she feels or knows that her genital is too small for her father's penis and this makes her react to her own genital wishes with direct anxiety: she dreads that if her wishes were fulfilled, she herself or her genital would be destroyed.[14]

The boy, on the other hand, feels or instinctively judges that his penis is much too small for his mother's genital and reacts with the dread of his own inadequacy, of being rejected and derided. Thus he experiences anxiety which is located in quite a different quarter from the girl's: his original dread of women is not castration-anxiety at all, but a reaction to the menace to his self-respect.[15]

In order that there may be no misunderstanding let me emphasize that I believe these processes to take place purely instinctively on a basis of organ sensations and the tensions of organic needs; in other words, I hold that these reactions would occur even if the girl had never seen her father's penis or the boy his mother's genital, and neither had any sort of intellectual knowledge of the existence of these genitalia.

Because of this reaction on the part of the boy, he is affected in another way and more severely by his frustration at the hands of his mother than is the girl by her experience with her father. A blow is struck at the libidinal impulses in either case. But the girl has a certain consolation in her frustration: she preserves her physical integrity; whereas the boy is hit in a second sensitive spot—his sense of genital inadequacy, which has presumably accompanied his libidinal desires from the beginning. If we assume that the most general reason for violent anger is the foiling of impulses which at the moment are of vital importance, it follows that the boy's frustration by his mother must arouse a twofold fury in him: first through the thrusting back of his libido upon itself and, secondly, through the wounding of his masculine self-regard. At the same time old resentment springing from pregenital frustrations is probably also made to flare up again. The result is that his phallic impulses to penetrate merge with his anger at frustration, and the impulses take on a sadistic tinge.

Here let me emphasize a point which is often insufficiently brought out in psycho-analytical literature, namely, that we have no reason to assume that these phallic impulses are naturally sadistic and that therefore it is inadmissible, in the absence of specific evidence in each case, to equate 'male' with 'sadistic', and on similar lines 'female' with 'masochistic'. If the admixture of destructive impulses is really considerable, the mother's genital must, according to the talion principle, become an object of direct anxiety. Thus, if it is first made distasteful to him by its association with wounded self-regard, it will by a secondary process (by way of frustration-anger) become an object of castration-anxiety. And probably this is very generally reinforced when the boy observes traces of menstruation.

Very often this latter anxiety in its turn leaves a lasting mark on the man's attitude to women, as we learn from the examples already given at random from very different periods and races. But I do not think that it occurs regularly in all men in any considerable degree, and certainly it is not a *distinctive* characteristic of the man's relation to the other sex. Anxiety of this sort strongly resembles, *mutatis mutandis*, anxiety which we meet with in women. When in analysis we find it occurring in any noteworthy intensity, the subject is invariably a man whose whole attitude towards women has a markedly neurotic twist.

On the other hand I think that the anxiety connected with his self-respect leaves more or less distinct traces in every man and gives to his general attitude to women a particular stamp which either does not exist in women's attitude to men or, if it does, is acquired secondarily. In other words, it is no integral part of their feminine nature.

We can only grasp the general significance of this male attitude if we study more closely the development of the boy's infantile anxiety, his efforts to overcome it and the ways in which it manifests itself.

According to my experience the dread of being rejected and derided is a typical ingredient in the analysis of every man, no matter what his mentality or the structure of his neurosis. The analytic situation and the constant reserve of the woman analyst bring out this anxiety and sensitiveness more clearly than they appear in ordinary life, which gives men plenty of opportunity to escape from these feelings either by avoiding situations calculated to evoke them or by a process of overcompensation. The specific basis of this attitude is hard to detect because in analysis it is generally concealed by a feminine orientation, for the most part unconscious.[16]

To judge by my own experience, this latter orientation is no less common, though (for reasons which I will give) less blatant, than the masculine attitude in women. I do not propose to discuss its various sources here; I will only say that I conjecture that the early wound to his self-regard is probably one of the factors liable to disgust the boy with his male role.

His typical reaction to that wound and to the dread of his mother which follows from it is obviously to withdraw his libido from her and to concentrate it on himself and his genital. From the economic point of view this process is doubly advantageous: it enables him to escape from the distressing or anxiety-fraught situation which has developed between himself and his mother, and it restores his masculine self-respect by reactively strengthening his phallic narcissism. The female genital no longer exists for him: the 'undiscovered' vagina is a denied vagina. This stage of his development is fully identical with Freud's 'phallic phase'.

Accordingly we must understand the enquiring attitude which dominates this phase and the specific nature of the boy's enquiries as expressing a retreat from the object and a narcissistically tinged anxiety which follows upon this.

His first reaction, then, is in the direction of a heightened phallic narcissism. The result is that to the *wish to be a woman*, which younger boys utter without embarrassment, he now reacts partly with renewed anxiety lest he should not be taken seriously and partly with castration-anxiety. Once we realize that masculine castration-anxiety is very largely the ego's response to the wish to be a woman, we shall not altogether share Freud's conviction that bisexuality manifests itself more clearly in the female than in the male.[17] We shall prefer to leave it an open question.

A feature of the phallic phase which Freud emphasizes shows up with special clearness the narcissistic scar left by the little boy's relation with his mother: 'He behaves as if he had a dim idea that this member might be and should be larger'.[18] We must amplify the observation by saying that this behaviour begins, indeed, in the 'phallic phase', but does not cease with it; on the contrary, it is displayed naively throughout boyhood and persists later as a deeply hidden anxiety about the size of the subject's penis or his potency, or else as a less concealed pride about them.

Now one of the exigencies of the biological differences between the sexes is this: that the man is actually obliged to go on proving his manhood to the woman. There is no analogous necessity for her: even if she is frigid, she can engage in sexual intercourse and conceive and bear a child. She performs her part by merely *being*, without any *doing*—a fact which has always filled men with admiration and resentment. The man on the other hand has to *do* something in order to fulfil himself. The ideal of 'efficiency' is a typical masculine ideal.

This is probably the fundamental reason why, when we analyse women who dread their masculine tendencies, we always find that they unconsciously regard ambition and achievement as attributes of the male, in spite of the great enlargement of women's sphere of activity in real life.

In sexual life itself we see how the simple craving of love which drives men to women is very often overshadowed by their overwhelming inner compulsion to prove their manhood again and again to themselves and others. A man of this type in its more extreme form has therefore one interest only: to conquer. His aim is to have 'possessed' many women, and the most beautiful and most sought-after women. We find a remarkable mixture of this narcissistic overcompensation and of surviving anxiety in those men who, while wanting to make conquests, are very indignant with a woman who takes their intentions too seriously, or who cherish a lifelong gratitude to her if she spares them any further proof of their manhood.

Another way of averting the soreness of the narcissistic scar is by adopting the attitude described by Freud as the propensity to debase the love-object.[19] If a man does not desire any woman who is his equal or even his superior—may it not be that he is protecting his threatened self-regard in accordance with that most useful principle of 'sour grapes'? From the prostitute or the woman of easy virtue one need fear no rejection, and no demands in the sexual, ethical or intellectual sphere: one can feel oneself the superior.[20]

This brings us to a third way, the most important and the most ominous in its cultural consequences: that of diminishing the self-respect of the woman. I think that I have shown that men's disparagement of women is based upon a definite psychic trend towards disparaging them—a tendency rooted in the man's psychic reactions to certain given biological facts, as might be expected of a mental attitude so widespread and so obstinately maintained. The view that women are infantile and emotional creatures and, as such, incapable of responsibility and independence is the work of the masculine tendency to lower their self-respect. When men justify such an attitude by pointing out that a very large number of women really do correspond to this description, we must consider whether this type of woman has not been cultivated by a systematic selection on the part of men. The important point is not that individual minds of greater or lesser calibre, from Aristotle to Moebius, have expended an astonishing amount of energy and intellectual capacity in proving the superiority of the masculine principle. What really counts is the fact that the ever-precarious self-respect of the 'average man' causes him over and over again to choose a feminine type which is infantile, non-maternal and hysterical, and by so doing to expose each new generation to the influence of such women.

Notes

[1] See Claude Daly's account in his article, 'Hindumythologie und Kastrationskomplex', *Imago* (1927)13:145-98.

[2] Hans Sachs explains the impulse to artistic creation as the search for companions in guilt. In this, I think, he is right, but he does not seem to me to go deeply enough into the question, since his explanation is one-sided and takes into account only part of the whole personality, namely, the super-ego. (*Gemeinsame Tagträume* [Vienna: Internationaler Psychoanalytischer Verlag, 1924])

[3] Cf. Claude Daly, 'Der Menstruationscomplex', *Imago* (1928)14 and Winterstein: 'Die Pubertätsriten der Mädchen und ihre Spuren im Märchen', *Imago* (1928)14.

[4] Sigmund Freud (1918a), 'The Taboo of Virginity', SE 11:193-208.

[5] I well remember how surprised I was myself the first time I heard the above ideas asserted—by a man—in the shape of a universal proposition. The speaker was Groddeck, who obviously felt that he was stating something quite self-evident when he remarked in conversation: 'Of course men are afraid of women.' In his writings Groddeck has repeatedly emphasized this fear.

[6] Sigmund Freud (1927e), 'Fetishism', SE 21:149-57.

[7] The experiments were conducted by Frl. Dr. Hartung at a children's clinic in Dresden.

[8] Felix Boehm, 'Beiträge zur Psychologie der Homosexualität', *Internationale Zeitschrift für Psychoanalyse*, 11 (1925); Melanie Klein, 'Early Stages of the Oedipus Conflict', above, 'The Importance of Symbol-Formation in the Development of the Ego', in her *Love, Guilt and Reparation and Other Works* (New York: Macmillan, 1975), 219-32, and 'Infantile Anxiety Situations Reflected in a Work of Art and in the Creative Impulse', *Love, Guilt and Reparation*, 210-8.

[9] Bergmann, *Muttergeist und Erkenntnisgeist*.

[10] Sigmund Freud (1923e), 'The Infantile Genital Organization', SE 19:141-5.

[11] Sigmund Freud (1931b), 'Female Sexuality', SE 21:281.

[12] Cf. the work of Melanie Klein, quoted above, to which I think insufficient attention has been paid.

[13] This is not to be equated with passivity.

[14] In another paper I will discuss the girl's situation more fully.

[15] I would refer here also to the points I raised in a paper entitled 'The Distrust between the Sexes' (1930). See Karen Horney, *Feminine Sexuality* (London: Routledge, 1967), 107-18.

[16] Cf. Felix Boehm, 'The Femininity-Complex in Men', *International Journal of Psycho-Analysis*, 11(1930):444-69.

[17] Sigmund Freud (1931b), 'Female Sexuality', SE 21:223-43.

[18] Sigmund Freud (1923e) 'The Infantile Genital Organization: an Interpolation into the Theory of Sexuality', SE 19:141-5.

[19] Sigmund Freud (1912d) 'On the Universal Tendency to Debasement in the Sphere of Love', SE 11:179-90.

[20] This does not detract from the importance of the other forces which drive men to prostitutes and which have been described by Sigmund Freud in his 'Contributions to the Psychology of Love', SE 11, and by Felix Boehm in his 'Beiträge zur Psychologie der Homosexualität', *Internationale Zeitschrift für Psychoanalyse*, 6(1920) and 8(1922).

17

The Denial of the Vagina: a Contribution to the Problem of the Genital Anxieties Specific to Women

Karen Horney (1933)

International Journal of Psycho-Analysis 14(1933):57-70

In the present article, which first appeared in 1933, Karen Horney begins by summing up Freud's early views on the sexual development of the little girl, leading to the thesis of penis envy and heterosexual object choice, in order to question the primacy of a phallic sexuality and its consequences for an understanding of female psychology.

If Freud's views relating to the phallic phase and penis envy were right, Horney argues, the following would also be true: overcoming 'masculine impulses' would be imperative to an affirmation of femininity at each critical point in the development of female sexuality; homosexuality would be more common among women; the wish to have a child would have to be secondary and substitutive; and a woman's relation to life would have to spring from resentment.

Horney opposes the theory of penis envy on the basis of observations of little girls aged from 3 to 5 (expressions of a desire for breasts and wish for a child are common in boys of the same age, yet this has no influence on the child's behaviour as a whole) and posits the existence of a bisexual disposition in all human beings that would disappear with the choice of a love object. She then questions Freud's views regarding erotogenic zones and lists a series of situations in which spontaneous vaginal sensations occur as a result of general sexual stimulation. She argues that clitoral masturbation is artificially induced and thus does not reflect 'normality'. She also refers to sexual fantasies which support her hypothesis of the existence of a vaginal sexuality and which explain anomalies such as frigidity and vaginal anxiety.

* * *

The fundamental conclusions to which Freud's investigations of the specific character of feminine development have led him are as follows: first, that in little girls the early development of instinct takes the same course as in boys, both in respect of the erotogenic zones (in the two sexes only one genital organ, the penis, plays a part, the vagina remaining undiscovered) and also in respect of the first choice of object (for both the mother is the first love-object). Secondly, that the great differences which nevertheless exist between the two sexes arise from the fact that this similarity of libidinal trend does not go with similar anatomical and biological foundations. From this premise it follows logically and inevitably that girls feel themselves inadequately equipped for this phallic orientation of their libido and cannot but envy boys their superior endowment in that respect. Over and above the conflicts with the mother which the girl shares with the boy, she adds a crucial one of her own; she lays at her mother's door the blame for her lack of a penis. This conflict is crucial because it is just this reproach which is essential for her detachment from her mother and her turning to her father.

Hence Freud has chosen a happy phrase to designate the period of blossoming of childish sexuality, the period of infantile genital primacy in girls as well as boys, which he calls the '*phallic phase*'.

I can imagine that a man of science who was not familiar with analysis would in reading this account pass over it as merely one of the many strange and peculiar notions which analysis expects the world to believe. Only those who accept the point of view of Freud's theories can gauge the importance of this particular thesis for the understanding of feminine psychology as a whole. Its full bearings emerge in the light of one of the most momentous discoveries of Freud's, one of those achievements which, we may suppose, will prove lasting. I refer to the realization of the crucial importance for the whole subsequent life of the individual of the impressions, experiences and conflicts of early childhood. If we accept this proposition in its entirety, i.e. if we recognize the formative influence of early experience on the subject's capacity for dealing with his later experience and the way in which he does so, there ensue at least potentially the following consequences as regards the specific psychic life of women:

1   With the onset of each fresh phase in the functioning of the female organs—menstruation, coitus, pregnancy, parturition, suckling and the menopause—even a normal woman (as Helene Deutsch[1] has in fact assumed) would have to overcome impulses of a masculine trend before she could adopt an attitude of whole-hearted affirmation towards the processes taking place within her body.

2   Again, even in normal women, irrespective of race and of social and individual conditions, it would happen altogether more readily than in men that the libido adhered, or came to be turned, to persons of her own sex. In a word: *homosexuality* would be incomparably and unmistakably more common amongst women than amongst men. Confronted with difficulties in relation to the opposite sex, a woman would plainly fall back more readily than a man into a homosexual

attitude. For, according to Freud, not only are the most important years of her childhood dominated by such an attachment to one of her own sex but, when she first turns to a man (the father), it is in the main only by way of the narrow bridge of resentment. 'Since I cannot have a penis I want a child instead and "for this purpose" I turn to my father. Since I have a grudge against my mother because of the anatomical inferiority for which I hold her responsible, I give her up and turn to my father.' Just because we are convinced of the formative influence of the first years of life we should feel it a contradiction if the relation of woman to man did not retain throughout life some tinge of this enforced choice of a substitute for that which was really desired.[2]

3   The same character of something remote from instinct, secondary and substitutive, would, even in normal women, adhere to the *wish for motherhood*, or at least would very easily manifest itself.

Freud by no means fails to realize the strength of the desire for children: in his view it represents on the one hand the principal legacy of the little girl's strongest instinctual object-relation, i.e. to the mother, in the shape of a reversal of the original child-mother relationship. On the other hand, it is also the principal legacy of the early, elementary wish for the penis. The special point about Freud's conception is rather that it views the wish for motherhood not as an innate formation, but as something that can be reduced psychologically to its ontogenetic elements and draws its energy originally from homosexual or phallic instinctual desires.

4   If we accept a second axiom of psychoanalysis, namely, that the individual's attitude in sexual matters is the prototype of his attitude towards the rest of life, it would follow, finally, that woman's whole reaction to life would be based on a strong, subterranean resentment. For, according to Freud, the little girl's penis envy corresponds to a sense of being at a radical disadvantage in respect of the most vital and most elementary instinctual desires. Here we have the typical basis upon which a general resentment is wont to be built up. It is true that such an attitude would not follow inevitably; Freud says expressly that, *where development proceeds favourably*, the girl finds her own way to the man and to motherhood. But here, again, it would contradict all our analytical theory and experience if an attitude of resentment so early and so deeply rooted did not manifest itself extremely easily—by comparison much more easily than in men under similar conditions—or at any rate were not readily set going as an undercurrent detrimental to the vital feeling-tone of women.

These are the very weighty conclusions with regard to the whole psychology of women which follow from Freud's account of early feminine sexuality. When we consider them, we may well feel that it behoves us to apply again and again the tests of observation and theoretical reflection to the facts on which they are based and to their proper appraisal.

It seems to me that analytic experience alone does not sufficiently enable us to judge the soundness of some of the fundamental ideas which Freud has made the basis of his theory. I think that a final verdict about them must be postponed until we have at our disposal systematic observations of *normal* children, carried out on a large scale by persons trained in analysis. Amongst the views in question I include Freud's statement that 'it is well known that a clearly-defined differentiation between the male and the female character is first established after puberty'. The few observations which I have made myself do not go to confirm this statement. On the contrary I have always been struck by the marked way in which little girls between their second and fifth years exhibit specifically feminine traits. For instance, they often behave with a certain spontaneous feminine coquetry towards men, or display characteristic traits of maternal solicitude. From the beginning I have found it difficult to reconcile these impressions with Freud's view of the initial masculine trend of the little girl's sexuality.

We might suppose that Freud intended his thesis of the original similarity of the libidinal trend in the two sexes to be confined to the sphere of sex. But then we should come into conflict with the maxim that the individual's sexuality sets the pattern for the rest of his behaviour. To clear up this point we should require a large number of exact observations of the differences between the behaviour of normal boys and that of normal girls during their first five or six years.

Now it is true that, in these first years, little girls who have not been intimidated very often express themselves in ways which admit of interpretation as early penis envy; they ask questions, they make comparisons to their own disadvantage, they say they want one too, they express admiration of the penis or comfort themselves with the idea that they will have one later on. Supposing for the moment that such manifestations occurred very frequently or even regularly, it would still be an open question what weight and place in our theoretical structure we should give them. Consistently with his total view, Freud utilizes them to show how much even the little girl's instinctual life is dominated already by the wish to possess a penis herself.

Against this view I would urge the following three considerations:

1   In boys of the same age, too, we meet with parallel expressions in the form of wishes to possess breasts or to have a child.

2   In neither sex have these manifestations *any influence on the child's behaviour as a whole*. A boy who wishes vehemently to have a breast like his mother's may at the same time behave in general with thorough-going boyish aggressiveness. A little girl who casts glances of admiration and envy at her brother's genital may simultaneously behave as a true little woman. Thus it seems to me still an open question whether such manifestations at this early age are to be deemed expressions of elementary instinctual demands or whether we should not perhaps place them in a different category.

3   Another possible category suggests itself if we accept the assumption that there is in every human being a bisexual disposition. The importance of this for our understanding of the mind has, indeed, always been stressed by Freud himself. We may suppose that though at birth the definitive sex of each individual is already fixed physically, the result of the bisexual disposition which is always present and merely inhibited in its development is that *psychologically* the attitude of children to their own sexual role is at first uncertain and tentative. They have no consciousness of it and therefore naturally give naive expression to bisexual wishes. We might go further and conjecture that this uncertainty only disappears in proportion as stronger feelings of love, directed to objects, arise.

To elucidate what I have just said, I may point to the marked difference which exists between these diffuse bisexual manifestations of earliest childhood, with their playful, volatile character, and those of the so-called latency-period. If, at *this* age, a girl wishes to be a boy—but here again the frequency with which these wishes occur and the social factors by which they are conditioned should be investigated—the manner in which this determines her whole behaviour (preference for boyish games and ways, repudiation of feminine traits) reveals that such wishes emanate from quite another depth of the mind. This picture, so different from the earlier one, represents, however, already the outcome of mental conflicts[3] that she has been through and cannot therefore, without special theoretical assumptions, be claimed as a manifestation of masculinity wishes which had been laid down biologically.

Another of the premises on which Freud builds up his view relates to the erotogenic zones. He assumes that the girl's early genital sensations and activities function essentially in the clitoris. He regards it as very doubtful whether any early vaginal masturbation takes place and even holds that the vagina remains altogether 'undiscovered'.

To decide this very important question we should once more require extensive and exact observation of normal children. Josine Müller[4] and I myself, as long ago as 1925, expressed doubts on the subject. Moreover, most of the information we occasionally get from gynaecologists and children's physicians interested in psychology suggests that, just in the early years of childhood, vaginal masturbation is at least as common as clitoral. The various data which give rise to this impression are: the frequent observation of signs of vaginal irritation, such as reddening and discharge, the relatively frequent occurrence of the introduction of foreign bodies into the vagina and, finally, the fairly common complaints by mothers that their children put their fingers into the vagina. The well-known gynaecologist, Wilhelm Liepmann, has stated[5] that his experience as a whole has led him to believe that, in early childhood and even in the first years of infancy, vaginal masturbation is much more common than clitoral, and that only in the later years of childhood are the relations reversed in favour of clitoral masturbation.

These general impressions cannot take the place of systematic observations, nor therefore can they lead to a final conclusion. But they do show that the exceptions which Freud himself admits seem to be of frequent occurrence.

Our most natural course would be to try to throw light upon this question from our analyses, but this is difficult. At the very best the material of the patient's conscious recollections or the memories which emerge in analysis cannot be treated as unequivocal evidence, because, here as everywhere else, we must also take into account the work of repression. In other words: the patient may have good reason for not remembering vaginal sensations or masturbation, just as conversely we must feel sceptical about her ignorance of clitoral sensations.[6]

A further difficulty is that the women who come for analysis are just those from whom one cannot expect even an average naturalness about vaginal processes. For they are always women whose sexual development has departed somehow from the normal and whose vaginal sensibility is disturbed in a greater or lesser degree. At the same time it does seem as if even accidental differences in the material play their part. In approximately two-thirds of my cases I have found the following state of affairs:

1   Marked vaginal orgasm produced by manual vaginal masturbation prior to any coitus. Frigidity in the form of vaginismus and defective secretion in coitus. I have seen only two cases of this sort which were quite unmistakable. I think that, in general, preference is shown for the clitoris or the labia in manual genital masturbation.

2   Spontaneous vaginal sensations, for the most part with noticeable secretion, aroused by unconsciously stimulating situations, such as

that of listening to music, motoring, swinging, having the hair combed, and certain transference-situations. No manual vaginal masturbation; frigidity in coitus.

3   Spontaneous vaginal sensations produced by extra-genital masturbation, e.g. by certain motions of the body, by tight-lacing, or by particular sadistic-masochistic phantasies. No coitus, because of the overpowering anxiety aroused whenever the vagina is about to be touched, whether by a man in coitus, by a physician in a gynaecological examination, or by the subject herself in manual masturbation, or in any douching prescribed medically.

For the time being, then, my impressions may be summed up as follows: in manual genital masturbation the clitoris is more commonly selected than the vagina, *but spontaneous genital sensations resulting from general sexual excitations are more frequently located in the vagina.*

From a theoretical standpoint I think that great importance should be attached to this relatively frequent occurrence of spontaneous vaginal excitations even in patients who were ignorant, or had only a very vague knowledge, of the existence of the vagina, and whose subsequent analysis did not bring to light memories or other evidence of any sort of vaginal seduction, nor any recollection of vaginal masturbation. For this phenomenon suggests the question *whether from the very beginning sexual excitations may not have expressed themselves perceptibly in vaginal sensations.*

In order to answer this question we should have to wait for very much more extensive material than any single analyst can obtain from his own observations. Meanwhile there are a number of considerations which seem to me to favour my view.

In the first place there are the phantasies of rape which occur before coitus has taken place at all, and indeed long before puberty, and are frequent enough to merit wider interest. I can see no possible way of accounting for the origin and content of these phantasies if we are to assume the non-existence of vaginal sexuality. For these phantasies do not in fact stop short at quite indefinite ideas of an act of violence, through which one gets a child. On the contrary, phantasies, dreams, and anxiety of this type usually betray quite unmistakably an instinctive 'knowledge' of the actual sexual processes. The guises they assume are so numerous that I need only indicate a few of them: criminals who break in through windows or doors; men with guns who threaten to shoot; animals which creep, fly or run inside some place (e.g. snakes, mice, moths); animals or women stabbed with knives; or trains running into a station or tunnel.

I speak of an 'instinctive' knowledge of the sexual processes because we meet typically with ideas of this sort, e.g. in the anxieties and dreams of early childhood, at a period when as yet there is no intellectual knowledge derived from observation or from explanations by others. It may be asked whether such instinctive knowledge of the processes of penetration into the female body necessarily presupposes an instinctive knowledge of the existence of the vagina as the organ of reception. I think that the answer is in the affirmative if we accept Freud's view that 'the child's sexual theories are modelled on the child's own sexual constitution'. For this can only mean that the path traversed by the sexual theories of children is marked out and determined by spontaneously experienced impulses and sensations in its organs. If we accept this origin for the sexual theories, which already embody an attempt at rational elaboration, we must all the more admit it in the case of that instinctive knowledge which finds symbolic expression in play, dreams, and various forms of anxiety, and which obviously has not reached the sphere of reasoning and the elaboration which takes place there. In other words, we must assume that both the dread of rape, characteristic of puberty, and the infantile anxieties of little girls are based on vaginal organ sensations (or the instinctual impulses issuing from these), which imply that something ought to penetrate into that part of the body.

I think we have here the answer to an objection which may be raised, namely, that many dreams indicate the idea that an opening was only created when first the penis brutally penetrated the body. For such phantasies would not arise at all but for the previous existence of instincts—and the organ sensations underlying them—having the passive aim of reception. Sometimes the connection in which dreams of this type occur indicates quite clearly the origin of this particular idea. For it occasionally happens that, when a general anxiety about the injurious consequences of masturbation makes its appearance, the patient has dreams with the following typical content: she is doing a piece of needlework and all at once a hole appears, of which she feels ashamed; or she is crossing a bridge which suddenly breaks off in the middle, above a river or a chasm; or she is walking along a slippery incline and all at once begins to slide and is in danger of falling over a precipice. From such dreams we may conjecture that when these patients were children and indulged in onanistic play, they were led by vaginal sensations to the discovery of the vagina itself, and that their anxiety took the very form of the dread that they had made a hole where no hole ought to be. I would here emphasize that I have never been wholly convinced by Freud's explanation why girls suppress direct genital masturbation more easily and frequently than boys. As we know, Freud supposes[7] that (clitoral) masturbation becomes odious to little girls because comparison with the penis strikes a blow at their narcissism. When we consider the strength of the drive behind the onanistic impulses, a narcissistic mortification does not seem altogether adequate in weight to produce suppression. On the other hand, the dread that she has done herself an irreparable injury in that region might well be powerful enough to prevent vaginal masturbation, and either to compel the girl to restrict the practice to the clitoris, or else permanently to set her against all manual genital masturbation. I believe that we have further evidence of this early dread of vaginal injury in the envious comparison with the man which we frequently hear from patients of this type, who say that men are 'so nicely closed up' underneath. Similarly, that deepest anxiety which springs out of masturbation for a woman, the dread that it has made her unable to have children, seems to relate to the inside of the body rather than to the clitoris.

This is another point in favour of the existence and the significance of early vaginal excitations. We know that observation of sexual acts has a tremendously exciting effect upon children. If we accept Freud's view we must assume that such excitation produces in little girls in the main the same phallic impulses to penetrate as are evoked in little boys. But then we must ask: whence comes the anxiety met with almost universally in the analyses of female patients—the dread of the gigantic penis which might pierce her? The origin of the idea of an excessively large penis can surely not be sought anywhere but in childhood, when the father's penis must actually have appeared menacingly large and terrifying. Or again, whence comes that understanding of the female sexual role, evinced in the symbolism of sexual anxiety, in which those early excitations once more vibrate? And how can we account at all for the unbounded jealous fury with the mother, which commonly manifests itself in the analyses of women when memories of the 'primal scene' are affectively revived? How does this come about if at that time the subject could only share in the excitations of the father?

Let me bring together the sum-total of the above data. We have: reports of powerful vaginal orgasm going with frigidity in subsequent coitus; spontaneous vaginal excitation without local stimulus, but frigidity in intercourse; reflections and questions arising out of the need to understand the whole content of early sexual games, dreams, and anxieties, and later phantasies of rape, as well as reactions to early sexual observations; and finally certain contents and consequences of the anxiety produced in women by masturbation. If I take all the foregoing data together, I can see only one hypothesis which gives a satisfactory answer to all the questions which present themselves, the hypothesis, namely, that *from the very beginning the vagina plays its own proper sexual part.*

Closely connected with this train of thought is the problem of frigidity, which to my mind lies *not* in the question how the quality of libidinal sensibility becomes transmitted to the vagina,[8] but rather, how it comes about that the vagina, in spite of the sensibility which it already possesses, either fails altogether to react or reacts in a disproportionately small degree to the very strong libidinal excitations furnished by all the emotional and local stimuli in coitus? Surely there could be only *one* factor stronger than the will for pleasure, and that factor is anxiety.

We are now immediately confronted by the problem of what is meant by this vaginal anxiety or rather by its infantile conditioning factors. Analysis reveals, first of all, castration-impulses against the man and, associated with these, an anxiety whose source is twofold: on the one hand, the subject dreads her own hostile impulses and, on the other, the retribution which she anticipates in accordance with the law of talion, namely, that the contents of her body will be destroyed, stolen or sucked out. Now these impulses in themselves are, as we know, for the most part not of recent origin, but can be traced to old, infantile feelings of rage and impulses of revenge against the father, feelings called forth by the disappointments and frustrations which the little girl has suffered.

Very similar in content to these forms of anxiety is that described by Melanie Klein, which can be traced back to early destructive impulses directed against the body of the mother. Once more it is a question of the dread of retribution, which may take various forms, but the essence of which is broadly that everything which penetrates the body or is already there (food, faeces, children) may become dangerous.

Although, at bottom, these forms of anxiety are so far analogous to the genital anxiety of boys, they take on a specific character from that proneness to anxiety which is part of the biological make-up of girls. In this and earlier papers I have already indicated what are these sources of anxiety and here I need only complete and sum up what has been said before:

1   They proceed first of all from the tremendous difference in size between the father and the little girl, between the genitals of father and child. We need not trouble to decide whether the disparity between penis and vagina is inferred from observation or whether it is instinctively apprehended. The quite comprehensible and indeed inevitable result is that any phantasy of gratifying the tension produced by vaginal sensations (i.e. the craving to take into oneself, to receive) gives rise to anxiety on the part of the ego. As I showed in my paper 'The Dread of Woman', I believe that in this biologically determined form of feminine anxiety we have something specifically different from the boy's original genital anxiety in relation to his mother. When he phantasies the fulfilment of genital impulses he is confronted with a fact very wounding to his self-esteem ('my penis is too small

or my mother'); the little girl, on the other hand, is faced with destruction of part of her body. Hence, carried back to its ultimate biological foundations, the man's dread of the woman is genital-narcissistic, while the woman's dread of the man is physical.

2   A second specific source of anxiety, the universality and significance of which is emphasized by Daly[9], is the little girl's observation of menstruation in adult relatives. Beyond all (secondary!) interpretations of castration she sees demonstrated for the first time the vulnerability of the female body. Similarly, her anxiety is appreciably increased by observations of a miscarriage or parturition by her mother. Since, in the minds of children and (when repression has been at work) in the unconscious of adults also, there is a close connection between coitus and parturition, this anxiety may take the form of a dread not only of parturition but also of coitus itself.

3   Finally, we have a third specific source of anxiety in the little girl's reactions (again due to the anatomical structure of her body) to her early attempts at vaginal masturbation. I think that the consequences of these reactions may be more lasting in girls than in boys, and this for the following reasons: In the first place she cannot actually ascertain the effect of masturbation. A boy, when experiencing anxiety about his genital, can always convince himself anew that it does exist and is intact:[10] a little girl has no means of proving to herself that her anxiety has no foundation in reality. On the contrary, her early attempts at vaginal masturbation bring home to her once more the fact of her greater physical vulnerability,[11] for I have found in analysis that it is by no means uncommon for little girls, when attempting masturbation or engaging in sexual play with other children, to incur pain or little injuries, obviously caused by infinitesimal ruptures of the hymen.[12]

Where the general development is favourable, i.e. above all where the object-relations of childhood have not become a fruitful source of conflict, this anxiety is satisfactorily mastered and the way is then open for the subject to assent to her feminine role. That in unfavourable cases the effect of the anxiety is more persistent with girls than with boys is, I think, indicated by the fact that, with the former, it is relatively more frequent for direct genital masturbation to be given up altogether, or at least it is confined to the more easily accessible clitoris with its lesser cathexis of anxiety. Not seldom everything connected with the vagina—the knowledge of its existence, vaginal sensations and instinctual impulses—succumbs to a relentless repression: in short, the fiction is conceived and long maintained that the vagina does not exist, a fiction which at the same time determines the little girl's preference for the masculine sexual role.

All these considerations seem to me to be greatly in favour of the hypothesis that *behind the 'failure to discover' the vagina is a denial of its existence.*

It remains to consider the question of what importance the existence of early vaginal sensations or the 'discovery' of the vagina has for our whole conception of early feminine sexuality. Though Freud does not expressly state it, it is none the less clear that, if the vagina remains originally 'undiscovered', this is one of the strongest arguments in favour of the assumption of a biologically determined, primary penis envy in little girls or of their original phallic organization. For, if no vaginal sensations or cravings existed, but the whole libido were concentrated on the clitoris, phallically conceived of, then and then only could we understand how little girls, for want of any specific source of pleasure of their own or of any specific feminine wishes, must be driven to concentrate their whole attention on the clitoris, to compare it with the boy's penis and then, since they are in fact at a disadvantage in this comparison, to feel themselves definitely slighted.[13] If on the other hand, as I conjecture, a little girl experiences from the very beginning vaginal sensations and the corresponding impulses, she must from the outset have a lively sense of this specific character of her own sexual role, and a primary penis envy of the strength postulated by Freud would be hard to account for.

In this paper I have showed that the hypothesis of a primary phallic sexuality carries with it momentous consequences for our whole conception of feminine sexuality. If we assume that there is a specifically feminine, primary, vaginal sexuality the former hypothesis, if not altogether excluded, is at least so drastically restricted that those consequences become quite problematical.

Notes

[1] Helene Deutsch, *Zur Psychoanalyse der weiblichen Sexualfunktionen* (Vienna: Internationaler psychoanalytischer Verlag, 1925).

[2] In a later work I hope to discuss the question of early object-relations regarded as the basis of the phallic attitude in little girls.

[3] Karen Horney, 'On the Genesis of the Castration Complex in Women', *The International Journal of Psycho-Analysis*, 5(1924):50-65.

[4] Josine Müller, 'A Contribution to the Problem of Libidinal Development of the Genital Phase in Girls', above.

[5] In a private conversation.

[6] In a discussion following the reading of my paper on the phallic phase, before the German Psycho-Analytical Society, in 1931, Boehm cited several cases in which only vaginal sensa-

tions and vaginal masturbation were recollected and the clitoris had apparently remained 'undiscovered'.

[7] Sigmund Freud (1925j), 'Some Psychical Consequences of the Anatomical Distinction Between the Sexes', SE 19:243-58.

[8] In reply to Freud's assumption that the libido may adhere so closely to the clitoral zone that it becomes difficult or impossible for sensibility to be transferred to the vagina, may I venture to enlist Freud against Freud? For it was he who showed convincingly how ready we are to snatch at fresh possibilities of pleasure and how even processes which have no sexual quality, e.g. movements of the body, speech or thought, may be eroticized and that the same is actually true of tormenting or distressing experiences such as pain or anxiety. Are we then to suppose that in coitus, which furnishes the very fullest opportunities for pleasure, the woman recoils from availing herself of them! Since to my thinking this is a problem which really does not arise, I cannot, moreover, follow Helene Deutsch and Melanie Klein in their conjectures about the transference of the libido from the oral to the genital zone. There can be no doubt that in many cases there is a close connection between the two. The only question is whether we are to regard the libido as being 'transferred' or whether it is simply inevitable that when an oral attitude has been early established and persists, it should manifest itself in the genital sphere also.

[9] Claude Daly, 'Der Menstruationskomplex', *Imago* , 14(1928):11-75.

[10] These real circumstances must most certainly be taken into account as well as the strength of unconscious sources of anxiety. For instance, a man's castration anxiety may be intensified as the result of phimosis.

[11] It is perhaps not without interest to recall that the gynaecologist Wilhelm Liepmann (whose standpoint is not that of analysis) in his book, *Psychologie der Frau*, says that the 'vulnerability' of women is one of the specific characteristics of their sex.

[12] Such experiences often come to light in analysis, firstly, in the form of screen-memories of injuries to the genital region, sustained in later life, possibly through a fall. To these recollections patients react with a terror and shame out of all proportion to the cause. Secondly, there may be an overwhelming dread lest such an injury should possibly occur.

[13] Helene Deutsch arrives at this basis for penis envy by a process of logical argument. Cf. Deutsch, 'The Significance of Masochism in the Mental Life of Women', above.

18

Passivity, Masochism and Femininity

Marie Bonaparte (1934)

International Journal of Psycho-Analysis. 16(1935):325-33

Marie Bonaparte's important piece on 'Passivity, Masochism and Femininity' was first read at the Thirteenth International Psycho-Analytical Congress in Lucerne (1934). The present version was published in 1935.

Bonaparte teases out here the distinction between masochism and passivity as they relate to the psychosexual development in girls. She starts with the observation that in the sphere of reproduction, and through experiences such as defloration, women experience much more suffering than men. This implies that from a biological and causal perspective women are predisposed towards masochism. She notes Freud's characterization of masochism as having a feminine form and Deutsch's claim that masochism is necessary to woman's psychosexual development.

On the basis of observations of children, with their sadistic conception of coitus, Bonaparte takes her distance from both Freud and Deutsch by ascertaining that women can experience erotic pleasure unpredicated on masochism. The problem, though, is not only that the woman has two erogenous zones for sexual enjoyment, but also that the maternal function seems to highlight pain, fear, and suffering. Thus, Bonaparte's question is, how does the woman negotiate the dualism of erotic pleasure from the maternal function? or, how does woman obtain passive erotic pleasure without sliding into a defensive masochism that shuns penetration and eroticizes the clitoris over the vagina?

In Marie Bonaparte's view, there are two main outcomes in female psychosexual development: a woman will either accept coitus masochistically, or she will replace her infantile fantasies with reality, thereby dissociating coitus from other reproductive functions and accepting it passively as a pleasurable act.

* * *

I-*The pain inherent in the female reproductive functions.*
II-*Erotic pleasure in women.*
III-*The infantile sadistic conception of coitus.*
IV-*The necessary fundamental distinction between masochism and passivity.*
V-*The female cloaca and the male phallus in women.*

I *The pain inherent in the female reproductive functions*

The most superficial observer cannot help noting that in the sphere of reproduction the lot of men and of women, in respect of pain suffered, is an unequal one. The man's share in the reproductive functions is confined to a single act—that of coitus—which he necessarily experiences as pleasurable, since, for him, the function of reproduction coincides with the erotic function. The woman, on the other hand, periodically undergoes the suffering of menstruation, the severity of which varies with the individual; for her, sexual intercourse itself is initiated by a process which involves in some degree the shedding of her blood, namely, the act of defloration; finally, gestation is accompanied by discomfort and parturition by pain, while even lactation is frequently subject to painful disturbances.

Already in the Bible woman is marked out for the pain of child bearing, the punishment for original sin.[1] Michelet describes her as *'l'éternelle blessée'* ('the everlastingly wounded one').[2] And, in psychoanalytical literature, Freud, discussing the problem of masochism, that bewildering product of human psychosexuality, characterizes it, in its erotogenic form, as 'feminine',[3] while Helene Deutsch regards it as a constant factor in female development and as an indispensable constituent in woman's acceptance of the whole of her sexuality, intermingled, as it is, with so much pain.[4]

II *Erotic pleasure in women*

There is, however, another fact no less striking even to a superficial observer. In sexual relations women are often capable of a high degree of erotic pleasure; they crave for caresses, it may be of the whole body or of some particular zone, and in these caresses the element of suffering, of masochism, is entirely and essentially absent. Moreover, in actual copulation the woman can experience pleasurable orgasm analogous to that of the man.

Of course, in this connection we must bear in mind the biological fact of which, for the matter of that, many biologists appear to be ignorant, though Freud has accurately appraised its importance: in women, as contrasted with men, there are two adjacent erotogenic zones—the clitoris and the vagina—and these reflect and confirm the bisexuality inherent in every woman. In some instances there is an open outbreak of antagonism between the two zones, with the result that the woman's genital erotism becomes centred exclusively either in the vagina or in the clitoris, with, in the latter case, vaginal anaesthesia. In other instances, and I think these are the more common, the two zones settle into harmonious collaboration, enabling her to perform her erotic function in the normal act of copulation.

Nevertheless, woman's share in sexual pleasure seems to be derived from whatever virility the female organism contains. The great biologist, Marañon, was in the right when he compared woman to a male organism arrested in its development, half-way between the child and the man—arrested, that is to say, precisely by the inhibitory influence exercised by the apparatus of maternity, which is subjoined to and exists in a kind of symbiosis side by side with the rest of her delicate organism.[5]

The residue of virility in the woman's organism is utilized by nature in order to eroticize her, otherwise the functioning of the maternal apparatus would wholly submerge her in the painful tasks of reproduction and motherhood.

On the one hand, then, in the reproductive functions proper—menstruation, defloration, pregnancy and parturition—woman is biologically doomed to suffer. Nature seems to have no hesitation in administering to her strong doses of pain, and she can do nothing but submit passively to the regimen prescribed. On the other hand, as regards sexual attraction, which is necessary for the act of impregnation, and as regards the erotic pleasure experienced during the act itself, the woman may be on an equal footing with the man. It must be added, however, that the feminine erotic function is often imperfectly and tardily established and that, owing to the woman's passive role in copulation, it always depends—and this is a point which we must not forget—upon the potency of her partner and especially upon the time which he allows for her gratification, which is usually achieved more slowly than his own.

III *The infantile sadistic conception of coitus*

Let us now go back to the childhood situation.

Psychoanalytical observations have proved beyond any doubt that when, as often happens, a child observes the coitus of adults, he invariably perceives the sexual act as an act of sadistic aggression perpetrated by the male upon the female—an act not merely of an oral character, though little children do so conceive of it, because the only relations between one human being and another of which they have at first any knowledge are of an oral nature. But, seeing how early the cannibalistic phase occurs, it seems certain that this oral relation is itself conceived of as aggressive. Nevertheless, it so frequently happens that the child is in the anal-sadistic phase when he makes these observations that his predominating impression is that of an attack made by the male upon the female, in which she is wounded and her body penetrated. Having regard to the primitive fusion of instincts we may perhaps say that the earlier these observations occur the more marked is the sadistic tinge which they assume in the child's

mind. In his perception of the acts of adults the degree of his own aggressiveness, which varies with the individual child, must also play a decisive
part, being projected on to what he sees.

In the mind of a child who has witnessed the sexual act the impressions received form, as it were, a stereotyped picture which persists in the
infantile unconscious. As he develops and his ego becomes more firmly
established, this picture is modified and worked over, and doubtless there
are added to it all the sado-masochistic phantasies which analysis has
brought to light in children of both sexes.[6]

The very early observations of coitus, made when the child was still in
the midst of the sadistic-cloacal and sadistic-phallic phases (which,
indeed, often overlap), were effected in the first instance with partial
object-cathexes relating to the organs which children covet to gratify their
libidinal and sadistic impulses. Little by little, however, the whole being of
the man and of the woman becomes more clearly defined as male or
female, and the difference between the sexes is at last recognized.

Thereafter, the destiny and influence of the infantile sadistic phantasies will differ with the sex of the child. The sadistic conception of coitus
in boys, the actual possessors of the penetrating penis, will evade the cen-
tripetal, cloacal danger and tend to take a form which is centrifugal and
vital and which involves no immediate danger to their own organism. Of
course it will subsequently come into collision with the moral barriers
erected by civilization against human aggressiveness, with the castration
complex especially; but the Oedipal defusion of instincts through which
the boy's aggression is diverted to his father, while the greater part of his
love goes to his mother, is of considerable assistance to him in distin-
guishing sadism from activity and subsequently orientating his penis—
active but no longer sadistic—in the direction of women.

In girls, the sadistic conception of coitus, when strongly emphasized,
is much more likely to disturb ideal erotic development. The time comes
when the little girl compares her own genitals with the large penis of the
adult male, and inevitably she draws the conclusion that she has been castrated. The consequence is that not only is her narcissism mortified by her
castration but also, in her sexual relations with men, the possessors of the
penis which henceforth her eroticism covets, she is haunted by the dread
that her body will undergo some fearful penetration.

Now every living organism dreads invasion from without, and this is
a dread bound up with life itself and governed by the biological law of
self-preservation.

Moreover, not only do little girls hear talk or whispers about the suf-
ferings of childbirth and catch sight, somehow or other, of menstrual
blood; they also bear imprinted on their minds from earliest childhood the

terrifying vision of a sexual attack by a man upon a woman, which they believe to be the cause of the bleeding. It follows therefore that, in spite of the instinct which urges them forward, they draw back from the feminine erotic function itself, although of all the reproductive functions of woman this is the only one which should really be free from suffering and purely pleasurable.[7]

IV *The necessary fundamental distinction between masochism and passivity*

As the little girl grows up, her reactions to the primal scene become more pronounced in one direction or another, according to the individual case, the determining factors being, on the one hand, her childhood experiences and, on the other, her constitutional disposition.

In the first place, there is bound to be a distinct difference between the reactions of a little girl who has actually witnessed the coitus of adults and those of a little girl who has fallen back upon phylogenetic phantasies, based on her inevitable observations of the copulation of animals. It seems that the severity of the traumatic shock is in proportion to the earliness of the period in which the child observes human coitus and to the actuality of what she observes.

Above all, however, the violence of the little girl's recoil from the sexual aggression of the male will depend on the degree of her constitutional bisexuality and the extent of the biological bases of her masculinity complex. Where both these factors are marked, she will react in very much the same way as a little boy, whose reaction, since he also is bisexual, will be likewise of the cloacal type, though very soon his vital phallic rejection of the passive, cloacal attitude will turn his libido into the convex, centrifugal track of masculinity.

For there are only two main modes of reaction to the sadistic conception of coitus harboured by the little girl's unconscious mind throughout childhood and right up to adult life. Either she must accept it and, in this case, in order to bind masochistically her passive aggression there must be an admixture of eros equivalent to the danger which, she feels, threatens her very existence. Or else, as the years pass and her knowledge of reality increases, she must recognize that the penetrating penis is neither a whip nor an awl nor a knife nor a cartridge (as in her sadistic, infantile phantasies) and must dissociate passive coitus from the other feminine reproductive functions (menstruation, pregnancy, parturition); she must accept it as the only act which is really purely pleasurable, in sharp contrast to the dark background of feminine suffering, an act in which libido—that biological force of masculine extraction—is deflected to feminine aims, always passive but here not normally masochistic.

It is true that in woman's acceptance of her role there may be a slight tincture—a homeopathic dose, so to speak—of masochism, and this, combining with her passivity in coitus, impels her to welcome and to value some measure of brutality on the man's part. Martine declared that she wished 'to be beaten'. But a real distinction between masochism and passivity must be established in the feminine psyche if her passive erotic function is to be normally accepted upon a firm basis. Actually, normal vaginal coitus does not hurt a woman: quite the contrary.

If, however, in childhood, when she is brought up against the sadistic conception of coitus, she has, if I may so put it, voted for the first solution, namely, a masochism which includes within its scope passivity in copulation, it by no means follows that she will accept the masochistic erotization of the vagina in coitus. Often the dose of masochism is in that case too strong for the vital ego, and it is a fact that even those women in whom the masochistic perversion is very pronounced often shun penetration and content themselves with being beaten on the buttocks, regarding this as a more harmless mode of aggression since only the outer surface of the body is concerned.

The vital, biological ego protests against and takes flight from masochism in general and may establish very powerful hypercathexes of the libido's defensive positions.

V *The cloaca and the phallus in women*

At this point we must remind ourselves that in females there are two erotogenic zones and that woman is bisexual in a far higher degree than man.

Earlier in this paper I quoted the views of the Spanish biologist, Marañon, who holds that a woman is a man whose development has been arrested, a sort of adolescent to whose organism is subjoined, in a kind of symbiosis, the apparatus of maternity, which is responsible for the check in development.

In woman the external sexual organs, or, more correctly, the erotogenic organs, appear to reflect her twofold nature. A woman, in fact, possesses a cloaca, divided by the recto-vaginal septum into the anus and the specifically feminine vagina, the gateway to the additional structure of the maternal apparatus, and a phallus, atrophied in comparison with the male penis—the little clitoris.

How do these two zones react, on the one hand to the little girl's constitution and, on the other, to the experiences which exercise a formative influence upon her psychosexuality?

There are various stages and phases in libidinal development.[8] The oral phase is succeeded by the sadistic-anal phase which, in view of the anatomical fact of the existence of the vagina in little girls, I should prefer to call the sadistic-cloacal phase.

There is, therefore, a cavity (as yet, no doubt, imperfectly differentiated in the child's mind) which in the little girl's sadistic conception of coitus is penetrated in a manner highly dangerous. (The little boy, for his part, arguing from his own physical structure, often recognizes the existence of the anus only.) Consequently, when coitus is observed at this early age, the result is the mobilization, firstly, of the erotic wish for the penis, coveted by the oral and cloacal libidinal components, and, secondly, of the dread of penetration which wounds and is to be feared.

Before long, however, the phallic phase, which is a regular stage in the biological development of both sexes, is reached by little girls, as by little boys, being accompanied in the former by clitoridal masturbation. Doubtless, at this period, masturbation is not confined exclusively to the clitoris but is extended in a greater or lesser degree to the vulva and the entrance to the adjacent vagina. How far this is so depends on the individual and on the amount of her constitutional femininity (her pre-feminine, erotogenic cloacality).

At this point, however, through a confusion of passivity with masochism, the little girl may take fright and reject her passive role. The dread of male aggression may be too strong, the admixture of masochism already present too great, or too potent a dose of it may be required to bind and accept the dread. When this is the case, her ego draws back and her eroticism will cling, so to speak, to the clitoris. The process is something like that of fixing a lightning-conductor to a house in order to prevent its being struck; the electricity (in this case, the child's eroticism) is diverted into a channel in which it does not endanger life.

Thus a sort of *convex erotic engram*, upon which her erotic function as a woman will be modelled, is set up in opposition to the *concave erotic engram* which is properly that of the female in coitus.

Now the convex orientation of libido is the very direction taken by the eroticism of the male, as he develops anatomically, and, further, the erotogenic, centrifugal orientation of the penis. Consequently, such an orientation of libido in a woman is highly suggestive of a considerable degree of constitutional masculinity. Here, passivity being more or less inextricably confused with erotogenic masochism, its *vital* (self-preservative) rejection and its *masculine* rejection coincide. *Moral* repression, on the other hand, which has its source in educational influences and is maintained by the super-ego, tends to attack feminine sexuality as a whole, without discrimination of its specifically vaginal or clitoridal character, and, when carried to its extreme, tends to result in total frigidity.

Nevertheless the phallus itself, an organ essentially male even when it goes by the name of the clitoris, can be used for ends which are, at bottom, feminine.

It is true that the clitoris, the rudimentary phallus, is never destined to achieve, even in its owner's imagination, the degree of activity to which the penis can lay claim, for in this respect the male organ is far better endowed by nature. The clitoris, like the little boy's penis, is first aroused when the mother is attending to the child's toilet, the experience being a passive one. Normally the clitoris, after passing through an active phase, should have a stronger tendency than the penis to revert to passivity; the little girl's biological castration complex paves the way for her regression. Next, when her positive Oedipus complex is established, with its orientation to the father, the clitoris readily becomes the instrument of those libidinal desires whose aim is passive. And this prepares the way for the clitoridal-vaginal erotic function by means of which, in so many women, the two zones fulfil harmoniously their passive role in coitus and which is opposed to the functional maladjustment of women of the clitoridal type, in whom the phallus is too highly charged with active impulses.

From the biological standpoint, nevertheless, the ideal adaptation of woman to her erotic function involves the functional suppression of the active, and even of the passive, clitoris in favour of the vagina, whose role is that of purely passive reception. But in order that the vital ego may accept this erotic passivity, which is specifically and essentially feminine, a woman, when she reaches full maturity, must as far as possible have rid herself of the infantile fear which has its origin in the sadistic conception of coitus and from the defensive reactions against the possibility of masochism which are to be traced to the same source.

Notes

[1] Genesis iii, 16.

[2] Jules Michelet (1859), *L'Amour* (Paris: Calmann Lévy, 1910), 57.

[3] Sigmund Freud (1924c), 'The Economic Problem of Masochism', SE 19:157-70.

[4] Helene Deutsch, *Zur Psychoanalyse der weiblichen Sexualfunktionen* (Vienna: Internationaler psychoanalytischer Verlag, 1925); 'The Significance of Masochism in the Mental Life of Women', above.

[5] Gregorio Marañon, *La Evolucion de la Sexualidad y los Estados Intersexuales* [The Evolution of Sexuality and Intersexual States] (Madrid: Morata, 1930).

[6] Cf. especially Melanie Klein (1932), *The Psycho-Analysis of Children* (New York: Macmillan, 1975).

[7] In my opinion this primitive drawing back is a motion of the *vital ego* and not primarily, as Melanie Klein holds, that of a precocious *moral super-ego*. In this connection my view agrees more nearly with that of Karen Horney, though I differ from her on another point, namely, the constitutional phallic element—what I should term the bisexuality—in the nature of women. Cf. Melanie Klein, *The Psycho-Analysis of Children*, quoted earlier in this paper, and

Karen Horney (1926), 'The Flight from Womanhood', above, and (1933), 'The Denial of the Vagina', above. The outbreak of rage to be observed in so many children, when an attempt is made to give them an enema, is, I believe, to be explained as the defence set up by this same instinct of self-preservation against penetration of their bodies. This seems to me much more probable than that it is the expression of a kind of orgasm, as Freud holds (no doubt with some justice in certain cases), following Ruth Mack Brunswick. (Freud [1931b], 'Female Sexuality', SE 21:223-43.)

8 Sigmund Freud (1905d), *Three Essays on the Theory of Sexuality*, SE 7; Karl Abraham (1924), 'A Short Study of the Development of the Libido', *Selected Papers of Karl Abraham* (London: Hogarth Press, 1927), 418-501. See Part 2, 'Origins and Growth of Object Love', reprinted above.

19

Early Female Sexuality

Ernest Jones (1935)

International Journal of Psycho-Analysis 16(1935):263-73

Ernest Jones's lecture 'Early Female Sexuality' was read before the Vienna Psycho-Analytical Society on 24th April 1935 and published in English shortly afterwards. It was intended to inaugurate a dialogue between Vienna and London at a time when the divergences between the two psychoanalytic societies were prompting talk about two distinct schools. Somewhat ironically, this lecture also closes the debate on femininity.

Jones starts his lecture with a list of points upon which Vienna and London disagree: the early development of sexuality, particularly female sexuality, the genesis of the super-ego and its relation to the Oedipus complex, the technique of child analysis, and the conception of a death instinct. He then sums up his position vis-à-vis Melanie Klein and the early Horney and proceeds to review the topics of main interest, noting the points of agreement and disagreement. The point of this is to ask two questions about early female development: Is the pre-oedipal stage a concentration on a single object, the mother? If so, is this a particularly masculine attitude? He answers these questions by opposing Freud, particularly with regard to the phallic phase.

Like Klein, Jones posits a primary feminine phase which is incorporative and receptive. This phase is manifest in the early wish for a penis induced by oral frustration that is predicated upon the child's oral conception of coitus. Jones notes that at this pre-oedipal stage the little girl is only concerned with the part object; she then turns towards her father near the end of her first year of life; and by the second year the Oedipus complex is established. The little girl's sadistic attitude in regard to the contents of her mother's body is explained in biologistic and object-relations terms.

According to Jones, although all agree on the importance of the oral stage as the prototype of later femininity, two points remain obscure: the question of early vaginal sensations and what he terms the 'clitoris-penis question'.

He has three theories for the obscurity of the vagina in childhood, mostly inspired by Horney: fantasies relating to it are in sharp conflict with the rival mother; the vagina is the seat of the deepest anxieties; and the vagina has no physical function before puberty.

For Jones the real problem is the motivation behind penis envy. Though he agrees with Horney that it arises from the auto-erotic wish for urethral pleasure,

he argues for a theory of secondary motivation grounded in the little girl's endeav-
our to cope with her sadism towards her parents. Jones enumerates ways in which
the fantasy of possessing a penis attempts to allay this sadism and accompanying
anxiety, developing as he does in Kleinian fashion the concept of a good and bad
penis. Behind penis envy, Jones argues, against Freud, is a complex network of
fantasies whose aim is essentially defensive. This is in keeping with the view of an
innate femininity which presupposes the existence of a primary penis envy con-
sisting in an innate desire to have a child, a desire expressed by the wish to incor-
porate the penis into the leading erogenous zone.

* * *

This lecture is intended to be the first of a series of exchange lectures
between Vienna and London which your Vice-President, Dr. Federn, has
proposed for a special purpose. For some years now it has been apparent
that many analysts in London do not see eye to eye with their colleagues
in Vienna on a number of important topics: among these I might instance
the early development of sexuality, especially in the female, the genesis of
the super-ego and its relation to the Oedipus complex, the technique of
child analysis and the conception of a death instinct. I use the phrase
'many analysts' without attempting to enumerate these, but it is evident
that there is some danger of local views becoming unified to such an
extent as to enable people to speak of a Vienna school or London school as
if they represented different tendencies of a possibly divergent order. This,
I am convinced, is in no wise true. The differences are of just that kind that
go with imperfect contact, which in the present case are strongly contributed to by geographical and linguistic factors. The political and economic disturbances of the past few years have not brought London and
Vienna nearer to each other. Many English analysts do not read the
Zeitschrift, and still fewer Vienna analysts read the *Journal*. And I have not
as yet succeeded in making the interchange of translations between the
two as free as I could wish. It is true that German work has much freer
access to the *Journal* than English work has to the *Zeitschrift*, but this one-
way avenue, far from perfect as it is, is not at all a satisfactory solution. The
fact is that new work and ideas in London have not yet, in our opinion,
been adequately considered in Vienna.

Dr. Federn has had the happy thought of remedying the present difficulty by arranging a direct personal contact and discussion. In my opinion
also, this is the most promising way to proceed. In the first place, I have
the impression that nowadays far more psycho-analysis is learnt through
the spoken than through the written word. The habit of reading has certainly declined among analysts in the past twenty years and correspond-

ingly the habit of writing has taken on a more narcissistic bent. In the second place, this method enables speakers to be chosen who have prominently identified themselves with one or another point of view or method of investigation.

That I should have selected the present theme to discuss with you is natural. Already at the Innsbruck Congress eight years ago I supported a view of female sexual development that did not altogether coincide with the one generally accepted, and at the Wiesbaden Congress three years ago I amplified my conclusions and also extended them to the problems of male development. Put colloquially, my essential point was that there was more femininity in the young girl than analysts generally admit, and that the masculine phase through which she may pass is more complex in its motivation than is commonly thought; this phase seemed to me a reaction to her dread of femininity as well as something primary. Many women analysts have supported this view. It was Karen Horney who first, in her vigorous fashion, protested that the development of the young girl had been observed too exclusively through male eyes and, although her later views seem to me to be more than questionable, I would pay a tribute to the fresh stimulus she gave to the investigation of these problems. Since then child analysts, particularly Melanie Klein, have been able to get to closer quarters with them and to report direct observations of inestimable value.

Let me now review the themes of chief interest and note separately the points of agreement and of difference. To begin at the beginning. The assumption of inborn bisexuality seems to me a very probable one, in favour of which many biological facts can be quoted. But it is an assumption that is very hard to prove, so I do not think we should take it absolutely for granted and fall back on it whenever we encounter clinical difficulties.

Coming to the beginnings of individual life we shall agree that at least in the first year, and probably later, the mother plays a much greater part in the child's life than does the father. Of this phase Freud says, 'Everything in the sphere of this first attachment to the mother seemed to me so difficult to grasp in analysis—so grey with age and shadowy and almost impossible to revivify—that it was as if it had succumbed to an especially inexorable repression.'[1] What we evidently need, therefore, is a finer analysis of the girl's earliest period of attachment to the mother, and that, in my opinion, is what the 'early analyses' of young children are giving us. It is highly probable that the differences of opinion in respect of the later stage of development are mainly, and perhaps altogether, due to different assumptions concerning the earlier stage.

We begin, therefore, with the most difficult point, the crux of all the problems. Is this first stage a concentration on a single object, the mother?

And is it a masculine attitude, as clitoritic masturbation would seem to indicate? Roughly speaking, this would appear to be Freud's view. In that case the girl has in her development to change both her sexual attitude and the sex of her love-object, and the well-known difficulties she experiences in her development would be explained by the complexity of these tasks.

In London, on the contrary, as the result especially of the experience of Melanie Klein's early analyses, but also confirmed by our findings in adults, we hold quite a different view of this early stage. We consider that the girl's attitude is already more feminine than masculine, being typically receptive and acquisitive. She is concerned more with the inside of her body than the outside. Her mother she regards not as a man regards a woman, as a creature whose wishes to receive it is a pleasure to fulfil. She regards her rather as a person who has been successful in filling herself with just the things the child wants so badly, pleasant material of both a solid and liquid kind. Her endeavour is to get this out of the mother, and the various obstacles interposed by the delays and numerous other imperfections of feeding stimulate the aggressive components of her desires. The dissatisfaction with the nipple and the wish for a more adequate penis-like object to suck arises early and is repeated at a later period in the familiar clitoris dissatisfaction and penis envy. The first wish for a kind of penis is thus induced by oral frustration. At this suckling stage we are still concerned with interest in a part-object, much less with father-love. The part-object is still felt to belong to the mother's body. But the father comes into account as the source whence she obtained it by the oral form of coitus which Freud has shown to be the child's initial conception of this act; indeed, in so far as the girl holds as well the converse of this theory, a mammalingus as well as a fellatio theory of coitus, the father is regarded as a rival for the mother's milk. In the second half of the first year, and regularly by the end of it, the personality of the father plays an increasingly important part. True feminine love for him, together with the desire for access to his sexual organ, begins to conflict with his evident relationship to the mother. In the second year we can definitely speak of an Oedipus complex. It differs from the later more familiar form in being more deeply repressed and unconscious; also the 'combined parent imago' plays a greater part in it.

The girl's sadistic attitude towards the contents of the mother's body is recorded in innumerable phantasies of cutting, robbing and burning that body. The oral sadism soon extends to urethral and anal sadism, and it would seem that the destructive idea of excrement is even more pronounced with girls than with boys. There are two definite reasons why the girl's task of coping with this sadism, and the anxiety it gives rise to, is a good deal harder than the boy's. In the first place her anxiety essentially relates to the inside of the body and has no external organ on which to concentrate as the boy's has. There is only the clitoris, which is inferior as a source of reassurance in the respects first emphasized by Karen Horney when she contrasted the boy's freedom in seeing, touching and urinating with his external organ. In later years the girl displaces much of her anxiety to the whole exterior of the body, including her clothes, and obtains reassurance from its integrity and general satisfactoriness, but this plays a much smaller part with the young child. In the second place, the boy has another personal lightning-conductor for his sadism and hate, namely his sexual rival, the father. The girl, on the contrary, has as her sexual rival and the object of her sadism the same person, the mother, on whom the infant is completely dependent for both libidinal and all other needs of life. To destroy this object would be fatal, so the sadism, with its accompanying anxiety, is pent up and turned inwards far more than with the boy. In a word, the girl has for two reasons less opportunity to exteriorize her sadism. This explains the remarkable attachment to the mother, and dependence on her, to which Freud has called special attention in a recent paper. We think that these considerations also yield an explanation of what he termed the obscurity and 'inexorable repression' so characteristic of this stage of development.

What I have just been relating of the earliest stage, say the first year of life, seems to be very differently conceived of in Vienna and London, and I am convinced that practically all the differences of opinion in respect of later stages of development go back to these fundamental ones. Let me next try to show how this is so.

Fortunately we all agree about the importance of the oral stage, and that the oral stage is the prototype of the later femininity is also a widely accepted tenet, though perhaps less so. Helene Deutsch in this connection has pointed to the sucking nature of the vaginal function. The question of early vaginal sensibility is admittedly obscure, but several women analysts, the latest being Dr. Payne and Dr. Brierley, have produced, if not absolutely conclusive, at least highly significant evidence of its occurrence together with breast feeding. It is, however, hard to discriminate between it and vulval sensations on the one hand, and on the other hand the general retentive sensations and phantasies relating to the anus, womb and the inside of the body generally. One can at all events hardly sustain any longer the view that the vaginal attitude does not develop before puberty. The impressive facts of adult vaginal anaesthesia or even dyspareunia, with the suggestion of what they are the negative of, seem to me definitely to refute the idea of the vagina being an indifferent or merely undeveloped organ. They prove rather the erotic cathexis of the vagina and the deep fear of this. The obscurity of the organ in childhood I should attribute to three causes: (1) Phantasies relating to it, those concerning the wish for a penis and baby, are the ones most directly in conflict with the rival mother, and for obvious reasons the girl cannot display her hostility against her mother even as much as the boy can against his father. (2) The vagina is the seat of the deepest anxieties, so an extensive displacement outwards takes place, both of its erotogenicity and the accompanying anxieties. It is felt, like the mouth, to be an evil and dangerous organ which must therefore be kept hidden. (3) It has no physical function before menstruation and is relatively inaccessible, facts which prevent it being used as a reality and libidinal reassurance in the way that a penis or even a clitoris can be.

We now come to the clitoris-penis question, and here the sharpest differences of opinion obtain. This is shown most clearly by considering the connection between the question and the relation to the parents. If for brevity you will allow me purposely to exaggerate the differences of opinion one might say that according to one view the girl hates her mother because she has disappointed her wish that her clitoris were a penis, whereas according to the other view the reason that the girl wishes that her clitoris were a penis is that she feels hatred for her mother which she cannot express. Similarly according to one view the girl comes to love her father because she is disappointed in her clitoris, whereas according to the other view she wishes to change her clitoris for a penis because of the obstacles in the way of loving her father. You will agree that we have here very decided differences of opinion, even allowing for my over-sharp way of presenting them.

I have elsewhere pointed to the confusion arising from the three senses in which the phrase 'penis-wish' is used in this connection, and will try to avoid it by defining the sense I mean. At the moment we are talking of the wish that the clitoris were a penis, and I trust that this is unambiguous. We are all familiar with the dissatisfaction and resentment connected with this wish and the part it plays in the girl's psychology. But the fact that so many girls envy boys need not blind us to her feminine attributes, her coquetry, etc., and the important fact of the existence of dolls.

Now the problem here is the motivation of this wish. We agree that a part of it arises from the simple auto-erotic envy most fully described by Karen Horney: the freedom the boy enjoys in seeing and touching and his use of the organ in micturition. According to one view, however, this is the main motive for the wish, whereas for other authors it accounts for only the smaller part. Far more important, in my opinion, are what may be called the secondary motives for the penis-wish. These, in a word, are concerned with the girl child's various endeavours to cope with her sadism directed against the parents, especially the mother. At the risk of repetition I would again mention and lay stress on what we regard as the fundamental expression of this sadism, the wish to tear a way into the mother's body and devour the father's penis she believes to be incorporated there. What Melanie Klein happily terms the 'combined parent concept' here corresponds approximately to what in Vienna is often called the pre-oedipal stage, but we would extend the term 'Oedipus complex' to include this stage also. The sadism so characteristic of this stage gives rise to the girl's corresponding anxiety lest the inside of her own body be similarly robbed and destroyed.

Let me now enumerate the ways in which the phantasy of possessing a penis attempts to allay this terrible sadism and its accompanying anxiety. I should start by saying that the value the idea of the penis has for the girl is essentially bound up with its capacity to excrete and direct the flow of urine. Helene Deutsch and Karen Horney have called special attention to this association between penis envy and urethral sadism, while Melanie Klein and, lately, Marjorie Brierley have dealt extensively with the intimate connection between oral sadism and urethral sadism. According to the 'homeopathic principle' which I expounded before the Oxford Congress the most successful way of dealing with this repressed urethral sadism would be by finding a way in which it can be expressed in reality and thus provide the reassurance of its not being deadly. This is what the boy can do with his urinary games, thanks to the reassurance afforded by the visibly intact penis.

The girl's idea of the penis is, of course, an ambivalent one. On the one hand, it is good, friendly, nourishing and the fluid emanating from it is equated to milk. On the other hand, it is evil and destructive, its fluid having a corroding power. The use to which the girl puts her imaginary penis in her phantasies is therefore a double one. In so far as it is evil, sadistic and destructive it is a weapon that can be used to attack the mother in the way she fancies her father does, and thus obtain what she wants from her mother's body. In so far as it is good and beneficent it can be used to restore to the mother the penis the girl thinks she has robbed her of; this is especially so when the girl thinks her father whom she has castrated is impotent to satisfy the mother, an attitude very common in homosexuality. It can also be used to neutralize and thus make good again the bad internalized penis, the one the girl has swallowed and by her sadism turned into a harmful and self-destructive organ inside her own body; a visible and intact penis would be the best reassurance against the inaccessible internal anxieties. Thirdly it can be used to effect restitution to the castrated father by first identifying herself with him and then developing an intact penis by way of compensation.

Behind the girl's wish that her clitoris were a penis, therefore, is the most complex network of phantasies. The aim of them is partly libidinal, but for the most part defensive—consisting of various disparate attempts to get her sadism under control and to allay the desperate anxiety it has engendered. Freud asks in connection with this phallic phase why there should be any flight from femininity unless it were due to primary natural masculine strivings. In answer I should agree with Melanie Klein's conclusion that the girl's repression of femininity springs more from her hatred and fear of her mother than from her own masculine attitude. It goes hand in hand with an excessive fixation on the mother, one which often seriously hampers the girl's development. There is, in our opinion, such a thing as a primary natural wish for a penis on the girl's part, but this we regard not as a masculine striving in clitoris terms, but the normal feminine desire to incorporate a man's penis inside her body—first of all by an oral route, later by a vaginal one.

This wish seems to us to lead on directly to the wish for a baby, the normal wish to take in a penis and convert it into a child. This again is in contradiction to Freud's view that the girl's wish for the child is mainly compensatory for her disappointment in not having a penis of her own. I could agree with Freud's description if it referred not to what we may call the clitoris-penis of the phallic phase, but to the original orally incorporated penis. I think there is no doubt that the disappointment at not being able to receive this penis (not the clitoris one) is largely compensated for by concentration on babies, usually in the form of dolls. We are familiar with the same phenomenon in the excessive maternalism of some women who, for either internal or external reasons, are deprived of sexual enjoyment. But this is not what Freud means.

I should like to say a word about the girl's attitude towards the father. She transfers to him the guilt and fear she developed towards the mother when sadistically robbing her of the penis. After all it is the father's penis as well as the mother's that she devoured, so he also is injured. There is much more envy and jealousy of the mother than of the father, and much of the latter that we observe clinically is really displaced from the former. But once there is great anxiety about the evil internalized penis, harmful because of the sadistic way by which it was obtained, the homeopathic principle again comes into play. Then the girl, as we so commonly find with homosexuals, is impelled to bite the man's penis off so as to obtain reassurance for the anxiety of the original phantasies. If, on the other hand, the relation to the mother is predominantly a good and affectionate one, that to the father will develop on less sadistic lines and will become satisfactory.

We come now to the passing of the phallic phase and the development of a manifest femininity. Here also we must expect divided opinions, since it is easy to see that the view taken of this stage in development must be profoundly influenced by that of the earlier ones. In the first place, just as I am more sceptical about the existence of the phallic phase as a stage in development, so am I more sceptical than the Viennese seem to be about the idea of its passing. It would seem to be more accurate to use the expression 'phallic position'[2] to describe the phenomena in question. We are concerned with an emotional attitude[3] rather than a stage in libidinal development. This attitude is maintained by certain forces or needs, diminishes whenever these are weaker, but persists just so long as they persist—often throughout life. The 'phallic position' is not seldom quite as pronounced at the age of six, ten or thirty as at the age of two or three. What Viennese analysts describe as the passing of the phallic phase is rather the period in which they recognize the femininity of the girl which London analysts think they can recognize earlier in its more repressed state. There remains, it is true, the question why the femininity is often less repressed, and therefore more visible, as the girl grows, and this question I propose to deal with next.

You will remember the distinction I drew in my Wiesbaden paper between the proto-phallic and the deutero-phallic phases, the separation between them being marked by the conscious discovery of the sex difference. This discovery often results in envy and imitation, which are the main characteristics of the deutero-phallic phase. One very important observation about which there is general agreement is that the passing of this phase—or rather the plainer evidence of femininity—is apt to be accompanied by unmistakable hostility and resentment against the mother. Freud in his explanation has coupled these two events together not only chronologically but intrinsically. The reasons he gives for the girl's emerging from the phallic phase can be summarized in one word-disappointment. The girl comes to realize that her wish to have a penis of her own is doomed to disappointment, and so she wisely resigns herself to seeking other sources of pleasure that will console her. In doing so she exchanges both her own sex, from male to female, and that of her love-object from mother to father. The passing of the deutero-phallic phase, therefore, ushers in the Oedipus complex with its rivalry with the mother. This accords with the undoubted observation that the normal Oedipus situation is more visible after the phallic phase has weakened. As Jeanne Lampl de Groot concisely puts it, the girl has to traverse an inverted Oedipus situation before arriving at the normal one.

In London, on the other hand, we regard the deutero-phallic phase as essentially a defence against the *already existing* Oedipus complex. To us, therefore, the problem of why the defensive phallic phase comes to an end puts itself quite differently, being not altogether unlike the problem of why an infantile phobia ever disappears.

The answer I should give resembles Freud's in so far as both could be given in terms of 'adaptation to reality'. But the way in which the impressions of reality work does not seem to me at all the same as they do to Freud. Fundamentally they strengthen ego development at the expense of phantasy. The phantasy of the penis as a defence is given up because (1) it is recognized as a phantasy and therefore not an adequate protection, (2) there is less anxiety and therefore less need for defence, and (3) other defences are available.

Let me now consider these reasons in order. We know that there are definite limits to the power of hallucinatory wish-fulfilments, at least in the normal person, a fact which Freud has often illustrated by the case of hunger. This is true whether the wish is for the satisfaction of a body need, e.g. a libidinal one, or for a protection against anxiety. In this case the phantasied protection is found not to work well just because it does not give the reassurance of external reality, which is what the girl needs and is what she is beginning to find elsewhere.

In the second place, her anxiety has diminished as her ego has got stronger. She is better able to see her mother as a real and usually affectionate person rather than as the imaginary ogre of her phantasy. She is also no longer so dependent on her mother as she was in the first two or three years of life. She can therefore afford to display more sadism against her and other persons of the environment instead of locking it up and developing internal anxiety. This is the well-recognized stage when the environment finds the growing girl 'difficult' and hard to manage.

Thirdly, the girl is now learning to exteriorize both her libido and her anxiety. She has passed the stage of part-object love and is more interested in her father or brother as a whole. This replaces the early part-object incorporated in the mother. Her anxiety is much less internal and is taking the form of the characteristic dread of desertion, one that often lasts through life.

The young girl is now much bolder in her claims, and dares for the first time to be the open rival of her mother. The resentment she displays against her has not only the meaning Freud attaches to it, of reproach that her clitoris is not a penis, but is also the bursting through of the older animosity long pent up. It is not merely the reproach that her mother gave her only a clitoris, it is the reproach that her mother had always kept the breast and father's penis in her possession and not allowed the girl to incorporate them into her body to her heart's desire. The sight of a boy's penis is not the sole traumatic event that changes her life; it is only the last link in a long chain. Nor do I think that if a girl never experienced this trauma she would be masculine, which would seem to follow from the view that this is what drives her into femininity.

I may now sum up my contentions in a few sentences. The main facts to be explained are the young girl's desire for a penis and her resentment against her mother. The central difference between the two points of view, which for present purposes I have exaggeratedly called the London and Vienna ones, seems to me to turn on the question of the early Oedipus complex, ushered in by oral dissatisfaction. Being unable to cope with the anxiety this engenders she more or less temporarily takes flight in the 'phallic phase' and then later resumes her normal development. This view seems to me more in accord with the ascertainable facts, and also intrinsically more probable, than one which would regard her femininity to be the result of an external experience (viewing a penis). To my mind, on the contrary, her femininity develops progressively from the promptings of an instinctual constitution. In short, I do not see a woman—in the way feminists do—as *un homme manqué*, as a permanently disappointed creature struggling to console herself with secondary substitutes alien to her true nature. The ultimate question is whether a woman is born or made.

Put more generally, I think the Viennese would reproach us with estimating the early phantasy life too highly at the expense of external reality. And we should answer that there is no danger of any analysts neglecting external reality, whereas it is always possible for them to underestimate Freud's doctrine of the importance of psychical reality.

Notes

1 Sigmund Freud (1931*b*), 'Female Sexuality', SE 21:223-43.
2 Cf. 'libido position' and the psychotic 'positions' in Melanie Klein's Lucerne paper.
3 Not so much definite ideas.

Bibliography

Abraham, Karl. 1910. 'Remarks on the Psycho-Analysis of a Case of Foot and Corset Fetishism'. *Selected Papers of Karl Abraham*, 125-36.

—.1914. 'Restrictions and Transformations of Scoptophilia in Psycho-Neurotics: with Remarks on Analogous Phenomena in Folk Psychology'. *Selected Papers of Karl Abraham*, 169-234.

—.1916. 'The First Pregenital Stage of the Libido'. *Selected Papers of Karl Abraham*, 248-79.

—.1917. 'Ejaculatio Praecox'. *Selected Papers of Karl Abraham*, 280-98.

—.1921a. 'Contributions to a Discussion on Tic'. *Selected Papers of Karl Abraham*, 323-5.

—.1921b. 'Contributions to the Theory of the Anal Character'. *Selected Papers of Karl Abraham*, 370-92.

—.1922. 'Manifestations of the Female Castration Complex'. *International Journal of Psycho-Analysis* 3:1-29.

—.1924. 'A Short Study of the Development of the Libido, Viewed in the Light of Mental Disorders'. Part 1 'Manic-Depressive States and the Pre-Genital Levels of the Libido'. Part 2 'Origins and Growth of Object-Love'. *Selected Papers of Karl Abraham*, 418-501.

—.1927. *Selected Papers of Karl Abraham*. Translated by Douglas Bryan and Alix Strachey. Reprint. London: Maresfield Library, 1988.

Alexander, Franz. 1922. 'The Castration Complex in the Formation of Character'. *International Journal Of Psycho-Analysis* 4:11-42.

—.ed. 1966. *Psychoanalytic Pioneers*. New York: Basic Books.

Anzieu, Didier. 1981. *Le Corps de l'oeuvre*. Paris: Gallimard.

Appignanesi, Lisa, and John Forrester. 1992. *Freud's Women*. London: Weidenfeld and Nicolson.

Bergmann. *Muttergeist und Erkenntnisgeist*. No publication details.

Boehm, Felix. 1925. 'Beiträge zur Psychologie der Homosexualität'. *Internationale Zeitschrift für Psychoanalyse* 11.

—.1930. 'The Femininity-Complex in Men'. *International Journal of Psycho-Analysis* 11:444-69.

Bonaparte, Marie. 1935. 'Passivity, Masochism and Femininity'. *International Journal of Psycho-Analysis* 16:325-33.

—.1953. *Female Sexuality*. London: Imago.

Brierley, Marjorie 1936. 'Specific Determinants in Feminine Development'. *International Journal of Psycho-Analysis* 17:163-80.

Brunswick, Ruth Mack. 1928. 'A Supplement to Freud's History of an Infantile Neurosis'. *International Journal of Psycho-Analysis* 9:439-76.

—.1940. 'The Pre-Oedipal Phase of the Libido Development'. *Psychoanalytic Quarterly* 9:293-319.

Chadwick, Mary. 1925. 'Notes on Curiosity'. *Internationale Zeitschrift für Psychoanalyse* 11.

Daly, Claude. 1927. 'Hindumythologie und Kastrationskomplex'. *Imago* 13:145-98.

—.1928. 'Der Menstruationscomplex'. *Imago* 14:11-75.

Deutsch, Helene. 1925. 'The Psychology of Women in Relation to the Functions of Reproduction'. *International Journal of Psycho-Analysis* 6:405-418.

—.1925. *Zur Psychoanalyse der weiblichen Sexualfunktionen*. Vienna: Internationaler Psychoanalytischer Verlag.

—.1930. 'The Significance of Masochism in the Mental Life of Women'. *International Journal of Psycho-Analysis* 11:48-60.

—.1932. 'On Female Homosexuality'. *Psychoanalytic Quarterly* 1:484-510.

—.1944-1945. *The Psychology of Women : A Psychoanalytic Interpretation*. 2 vols. New York: Grune & Stratton.

Fenichel, Otto. 1925. 'Introjection and the Castration Complex'. *Collected Papers of Otto Fenichel*, 1:39-70.

—.1927. 'Examples of Dream Analysis'. *Collected Papers of Otto Fenichel*, 1:123-7.

—.1928. 'The Long Nose'. *Collected Papers of Otto Fenichel*, 1:155-7.

—.1931. 'The Pregenital Antecedents of the Oedipus Complex'. *International Journal of Psycho-Analysis* 12:141-66.

—.1932-1934. 'Outline of Clinical Psychoanalysis'. Parts 1-3 and 5-10. *Psychoanalytic Quarterly* 1:121-65, 292-342 and 545-652; 2:94-122, 260-308 and 562-91; 3:42-127, 223-302.

—.1946. *The Psychoanalytic Theory of Neurosis*. London: Routledge & Kegan Paul.

—.1949. 'The Symbolic Equation: Girl = Phallus'. *Psychoanalytic Quarterly* 18:303-24.

—.1953. *Collected Papers of Otto Fenichel*. Vol. 1. New York: Norton.

Ferenczi, Sándor. 1909. 'Introjection and Transference'. *First Contributions to Psycho-Analysis*, 35-93. London: Hogarth Press, 1952.

—.1912. 'On the Definition of Introjection'. *Final Contributions to the Problems and Methods of Psycho-Analysis*, 316-18. London: Hogarth Press, 1955.

Ferenczi, Sándor. 1916. 'The Nosology of Male Homosexuality (Homoeroticism)'. *First Contributions to Psycho-Analysis*, 296-318.

—.1924. *Thalassa, a Theory of Genitality*. Albany, New York: Psychoanalytic Quarterly Inc., 1938.

Flugel, John Carl. 1925. 'A Note on the Phallic Significance of the Tongue'. *International Journal of Psycho-Analysis* 6:209-15.

Freud, Anna. 1923. 'The Relation of Beating Phantasies to a Day Dream'. *International Journal of Psycho-Analysis* 4:89-102.

Freud, Sigmund. 1900a. *The Interpretation of Dreams*. SE vols. 4-5.

—.1905d. *Three Essays on the Theory of Sexuality*. SE 7:123-245.

—.1908c. 'On the Sexual Theories of Children'. SE 9:205-26.

—.1909b. 'Analysis of a Phobia in a Five-Year-Old Boy'. SE 10:1-149.

—.1910h. 'A Special Type of Choice of Object made by Men' (Contributions to the Psychology of Love, I). SE 11:163-75.

—.1912d. 'On the Universal Tendency to Debasement in the Sphere of Love'(Contributions to the Psychology of Love, II). SE 11:177-90.

—.1914c. 'On Narcissism: An Introduction'. SE 14:67-102.

—.1916d. 'Some Character-Types Met with in Psycho-Analytic Work'. SE 14:311-33.

—.1917c. 'On Transformations of Instinct as Exemplified in Anal Erotism'. SE 17:127-33.

—.1918a. 'The Taboo of Virginity' (Contributions to the Psychology of Love, III). SE 11:193-208.

—.1918b. 'From the History of an Infantile Neurosis'. SE 17:3-123.

—.1919e. 'A Child Is Being Beaten: A Contribution to the Study of the Origin of Sexual Perversions'. SE 17:175-204.

—.1920a. 'The Psychogenesis of a Case of Homosexuality in a Woman'. SE 18:145-72.

—.1921c. *Group Psychology and the Analysis of the Ego*. SE 18:67-143.

—.1923b. *The Ego and the Id*. SE 19:3-66.

—.1923d. 'A Seventeenth-Century Demonological Neurosis'. SE 19:69-105.

—.1923e. 'The Infantile Genital Organization: An Interpolation into the Theory of Sexuality'. SE 19:141-5.

—.1924d. 'The Dissolution of the Oedipus Complex'. SE 19:173-9.

—.1925j. 'Some Psychical Consequences of the Anatomical Distinction Between the Sexes'. SE 19:243-58.

—.1926d. 'Inhibitions, Symptoms and Anxiety'. SE 20:77-175.

—.1927e. 'Fetishism'. SE 21:149-57.

—.1931*b*. 'Female Sexuality'. SE 21:223-43.

—.1933*a*. 'Femininity'. Lecture 23. *New Introductory Lectures*. SE 22:112-35.

—.1937*c*. 'Analysis Terminable and Interminable'. SE 23:209-53.

—.1940*e*. 'Splitting of the Ego in the Process of Defence'. SE 23:273-8.

—.1953-1974. *Standard Edition of the Complete Psychological Works of Sigmund Freud*. 24 Vols. Translated and edited by James Strachey in collaboration with Anna Freud, assisted by Alix Strachey and Alan Tyson. London: The Hogarth Press and the Institute of Psycho-Analysis; New York: Norton.

—.1971. 'Letter to Carl Müller-Braunschweig'. Published as 'Freud and Female Sexuality: A Previously Unpublished Letter'. *Psychiatry* 34:328-9.

—.1985. *The Complete Letters of Sigmund Freud to Wilhelm Fliess 1887 - 1904*. Translated and edited by Jeffrey Moussaieff Masson. Cambridge, Mass. & London: Harvard University Press.

—.*The Diary of Sigmund Freud 1929-1939: A Record of the Final Decade*. Translated, annotated and with an intro by Michael Molnar. London: The Hogarth Press,1992.

Gillespie, William. 1979. 'Ernest Jones: The Bonny Fighter'. *International Journal of Psycho-Analysis* 60:273-79.

—.1987. 'Melanie Klein: Her World and Her Work'. *International Journal of Psycho-Analysis* 68:138-42.

Glover, Edward. 1925. 'Notes on the Oral Character Formation'. *International Journal of Psycho-Analysis* 6:131-54.

Groddeck, Georg. 1923. *The Book of the It*. New York: International Universities Press, 1976.

Grossman, William I. 1976. 'Discussion of "Freud and Female Sexuality"', *International Journal of Psycho-Analysis* 57:301.

Hamon, Marie-Christine. 1992. *Pourquoi les femmes aiment- elles les hommes?* Paris: Seuil.

Hárnik, J. 1928. 'The Economic Relations between the Sense of Guilt and Feminine Narcissism'. *Psychoanalytic Review* 15:94-95.

Heine, Heinrich. 1916. *The Complete Poems of Heine*. Translated by Edgar Alfred Bowring. G. Bell and Sons.

Horney, Karen. 1924. 'On the Genesis of the Castration Complex in Women'. *International Journal of Psycho-Analysis* 5:50-65.

—.1926. 'The Flight from Womanhood: The Masculinity-Complex in Women, as Viewed by Men and Women'. *International Journal of Psycho-Analysis* 7:324-39.

—.1930. 'The Distrust between the Sexes'. *Feminine Sexuality*. London: Routledge, 1967.

Horney, Karen. 1932. 'The Dread of Woman: Observations on a Specific Difference in the Dread Felt by Men and Women Respectively for the Opposite Sex'. *International Journal of Psycho-Analysis* 13:348-60.

—.1933. 'The Denial of the Vagina: A Contribution to the Problem of the Genital Anxieties Specific to Women'. *International Journal of Psycho-Analysis* 14:57-70.

—.1950. *Neurosis and Human Growth; The Struggle toward Selfrealization.* New York: Norton.

—.1937. *The Neurotic Personality of Our Time.* New York: Norton.

Jones, Ernest. 1922. 'Notes on Dr Abraham's Article on the Female Castration Complex'. *International Journal of Psycho-Analysis* 3:327-28.

—.1927. 'The Early Development of Female Sexuality'. *International Journal of Psycho-Analysis* 8:459-72.

—.1933. 'The Phallic Phase'. *International Journal of Psycho-Analysis* 14:1-33.

—.1935. 'Early Female Sexuality'. *International Journal of Psycho-Analysis* 16:263-73.

—.1951. *Essays in Applied Psycho-Analysis.* 2 vols. London: Hogarth Press.

—.1967. *Papers on Psycho-Analysis.* 5th edition. Boston: Beacon Press.

Klein, Emanuel. 1951. 'Johan H. W. van Ophuijsen'. *International Journal of Psycho-Analysis* 32:134-35.

Klein, Melanie. 1926. 'The Psychological Principles of Early Analysis'. *Love, Guilt and Reparation and Other Works 1921-1945,* 128-38.

—.1927. 'Symposium on Child-Analysis'. *Love, Guilt and Reparation and Other Works 1921-1945,* 139-69.

—.1928. 'Early Stages of the Oedipus Complex'. *International Journal of Psycho-Analysis* 9:167-80.

—.1929. Infantile Anxiety Situations Reflected in a Work of Art and in the Creative Impulse'. *Love, Guilt and Reparation and Other Works 1921-1945,* 210-18.

—.1930. 'The Importance of Symbol-Formation in the Development of the Ego'. in *Love, Guilt and Reparation and Other Works 1921-1945,* 219-32.

—.1932. *The Psycho-Analysis of Children.* New York: Macmillan, 1975.

—.1975. *Love, Guilt and Reparation and Other Works 1921-1945.* New York: Macmillan.

Lampl de Groot, Jeanne. 1928. 'The Evolution of the Oedipus Complex in Women'. *International Journal of Psycho-Analysis* 9:332-45.

—.1933. 'Problems of Femininity'. *Psychoanalytic Quarterly* 2:489-518.

—.1962. 'Ego Ideal and Superego'. *Psychoanalytic Study of the Child* 17:94-106.

Liepmann, Wilhelm. *Psychologie der Frau*. No publication details.

Loewenstein, Rudolf. 1963. 'Marie Bonaparte:1882-1962'. *Bulletin of the American Psychoanalytic Association* 19:861.

Marañon, Gregorio. 1930. *La Evolucion de la Sexualidad y los Estados Intersexuales*. Madrid: Morata.

Mitchell, Juliet. 1983. Introduction I to *Feminine Sexuality: Jacques Lacan and the Ecole Freudienne*, edited by Juliet Mitchell and Jacqueline Rose, 1-26. London: Macmillan.

Michelet, Jules. 1859. *L'Amour*. Paris: Calmann Lévy, 1910.

Müller, Josine. 1932. 'A Contribution to the Problem of Libidinal Development of the Genital Phase in Girls'. *International Journal of Psycho-Analysis* 13:361-68.

Müller-Braunschweig, Carl. 1926. 'The Genesis of the Feminine Super-Ego'. *International Journal of Psycho-Analysis* 7:359-62.

Oberndorf, C. P. 1953. 'Dr. Karen Horney'. *International Journal of Psycho-Analysis* 34:154.

Ophuijsen, Johan. H. W. van. 1920. 'On the Origin of the Feeling of Persecution'. *International Journal of Psycho-Analysis* 1:235-9.

—.1924. 'Contributions to the Masculinity Complex in Women'. *International Journal of Psycho-Analysis* 5:39-49.

Rank, Otto. 1924. *The Trauma of Birth*, London: Paul, Trench, Trubner, 1929.

—.1926. 'The Genesis of Genitality'. *Psychoanalytic Review* 13:129-44.

Reich, Wilhelm. 1925. *Der triebhafter Charakter*. Vienna: Internationaler Psychoanalytischer Verlag.

—.1927. *Die Funktion des Orgasmus; zur Psychopathologie und zur Soziologie des Geschlechtslebens*. Vienna: Internationaler Psychoanalytischer Verlag.

Riviere, Joan. 1927. 'Symposium on Child-Analysis'. In *The Inner World and Joan Riviere*, edited by Athol Hughes, 80-7. London: Karnac Books, 1991.

—.1929. 'Womanliness as a Masquerade'. *International Journal of Psycho-Analysis* 10:303-13.

Roazen, Paul. 1985. *Helene Deutsch, a Psychoanalyst's Life*. New York: Anchor Press/Doubleday.

Roudinesco, Elisabeth. 1990. *Jacques Lacan & Co. A History of Psychoanalysis in France, 1925-1985*. Translated by Jeffrey Mehlman. Chicago: University of Chicago Press.

Sachs, Hans. 1923. 'On the Genesis of Perversions'. *Psychoanalytic Quarterly* 55(1986):477-88.

—.1924. *Gemeinsame Tagträume*, Vienna: Internationaler Psycho-analytischer Verlag.

Searl, Nina. 1929. 'Danger Situations of the Immature Ego'. *International Journal of Psycho-Analysis* 10:423-35.

Simmel, Georg. 1919. *Philosophische Kultur*. Leipzig: Alfred Kröner Verlag.

Stärcke, August. 1920. 'The Reversal of the Libido-Sign in Delusions of Persecution'. *International Journal of Psycho-Analysis* 1:231-34.

—.1921. 'The Castration Complex'. *International Journal of Psycho-Analysis* 2:179-201.

Strachey, James. 1963. 'Joan Riviere (1883-1962)'. *International Journal of Psycho-Analysis* 44:228.

Strümpell. 1907. *Lehrbuch der speziellen Pathologie und Therapie der inneren Krankheiten*, vol.1.

Uexküll, J. von. 1909. *Umwelt und Innenwelt der Tiere*. Berlin.

—.1913. *Biologische Weltanschauung*. Munich.

Vaerting, Mathilde, and Mathias Vaerting. 1923. *The Dominant Sex: A Study in the Sociology of Sex Differentiation*. London: Allen and Unwin.

Weiss, Edoardo. 1926. 'The Delusion of being Poisoned in the Light of Introjective and Projective Procedures'. *Archives of Psychoanalysis* 1:226-28.

Winterstein, A. 1928. 'Die Pubertätsriten der Mädchen und ihre Spuren im Märchen'. *Imago* 14.

Index